Don't Let's Be Beastly to the Germans

Daniel Cowling is a historian at the National Army Museum, London, where he specializes in modern British and European history. Originally from Manchester, he completed his PhD at the University of Cambridge, where he wrote a thesis on the British occupation of Germany. *Don't Let's Be Beastly to the Germans* is his first book.

Don't Let's Be Beastly to the Germans

The British Occupation of Germany, 1945–49

DANIEL COWLING

HEAD
ᵹZEUS

An Apollo Book

First published in the UK in 2023 by Head of Zeus,
part of Bloomsbury Publishing Plc

9 7 5 3 1 2 4 6 8

A catalogue record for this book is available from the British Library.

ISBN (HB): 9781800243507
ISBN (E): 9781800243521

Extract on page 75 from *Germany 1945–1949 A Sourcebook*, Manfred Malzahn © 2014,
Routledge. Reproduced by permission of Taylor & Francis Group.

Title reference from © N.C. Aventales AG successor in title to The Noel Coward
Estate c/o Alan Brodie Representation Ltd abr@alanbrodie.com
By arrangement with Alan Brodie Representation
and the Noel Coward Archive Trust www.noelcoward.com

Maps by Jeff Edwards
Typeset by Ed Pickford

Printed and bound in Great Britain by
CPI Group (UK) Ltd, Croydon CR0 4YY

Head of Zeus Ltd
5–8 Hardwick Street
London EC1R 4RG

WWW.HEADOFZEUS.COM

For Alexandra

Contents

Part Four: Get Out Now!

Part Five: Changing Enemies

Allied Advance Into Germany, 1945

→ Western Allied advance

--→ Soviet advance

0 — 100 miles

0 — 100 km

N

SWEDEN

DENMARK

Baltic Sea

North Sea

Kiel

Danzig

EAST PRUSSIA

Bremerhaven

Wilhelmshaven

Hamburg

Lübeck

NETHERLANDS

Bremen

Osnabrück

Hannover

Berlin

Warsaw

RUHR

Dortmund

Paderborn

Magdeburg

POLAND

Düsseldorf

Cologne

GERMANY

LUXEMBOURG

Prague

CZECHOSLOVAKIA

FRANCE

Munich

Vienna

Bern

AUSTRIA

SWITZERLAND

HUNGARY

Part One

THE GERMAN PROBLEM

1

A Strange Enemy Country

In September 1946, a group of women huddled together on one of the several long platforms inside Hamburg's vast *Hauptbahnhof* (central train station). They each wore a dark-blue beret and matching military tunic, the latter sporting a distinctive red shield emblem on each sleeve embossed with 'CCG' in gold lettering. It identified them as members of the Control Commission for Germany, a force of British civilians tasked with building a democracy out of the ruins of Hitler's Third Reich. But for these women, surrounded by an assortment of suitcases and bags, the first piece of business was to find their accommodation before dark.[1]

Even though it was late, the Hamburg *Hauptbahnhof* was a hive of activity as frantic passengers zigzagged between platforms. Above them, the grand glass and steel roof which had stood since 1906 was a shadow of its former glory: broken girders and smashed windowpanes were a reminder of several Allied bombing raids on the city that had destroyed the station's ticket office, baggage counter and one of two brick clock towers.[2]

As a station porter hurriedly approached, the group pleaded with one of their number, thirty-six-year-old Katharine Morris, to talk to him: 'you know how to speak German! Tell him which bags are ours and where we want to go!' This was something of an exaggeration – yes, she had read the English–German textbook during their train trip from Hanover, but she'd never actually spoken the language. Yet Morris was undaunted and plucked up the courage to practise her rudimentary German for the first time. 'It was', she later recalled, 'a revelation, like crossing a bridge into another life.'

Before the war Katharine Morris had written several novels chronicling life in the Nottinghamshire villages of her youth. But with the outbreak of the fighting she had joined the Women's Auxiliary Air Force, while her brother Robert tragically lost his life serving with the Sherwood Foresters Regiment in Italy.[3] Now, more than a year after VE Day, she was beginning a new posting in the British Zone of occupied Germany.

Her linguistic efforts worked well enough and soon the group were on their way to requisitioned flats and houses across the city. In a few short, hesitant sentences, Morris had immersed herself into an 'other world' of 'those people who had been the enemy for six long years'.[4] It was the beginning of an adventure that would not only make its mark on her own life, but also help to reshape Germany and Europe for decades to come.

*

The following morning Katharine Morris awoke in the middle of Hamburg, a devastated city that she would call home for the next year. Her new apartment was well furnished, with twin mahogany beds, chests of drawers, a dressing table and two wardrobes. British soldiers had requisitioned the premises, as well as these items of furniture, from its existing German tenants. It was not uncommon for military government officers to give local residents just a few days' notice to gather together their personal belongings and leave.[5] This was a city where intact buildings – not to mention beds – were in short supply.

That morning, gazing out from her ninth-floor window across the cityscape, she saw that hardly a standing wall was to be seen among acres and acres of endless rubble. It was a landscape that to many observers was reminiscent of some long-lost civilization – a Pompeii for the modern age.[6] But evidence that this apocalyptic scene was the result of more recent events was inescapable: when

German civilians in Elmshorn, Schleswig-Holstein, evacuate their
requisitioned houses in order to make way for British soldiers.

you ventured out into the streets, the noxious stench of rotting
bodies filled the air.

In anticipation of her arrival, Morris was warned about the
dangers of contracting 'Hamburg throat' and told she should be
careful not to drink tap water without first boiling it. Little had
prepared her for a scene of such utter devastation. The British
army pamphlet – simply entitled *Germany* – that she had been
handed on her outward journey was primarily concerned with
the mission ahead: it emphasized Britain's endeavour to 'win the
peace' through an uncompromising military occupation and told
British occupiers that they were 'about to meet a strange people in
a strange, enemy country'.

There was, however, little time for reflection: it was her first day
of work and after a breakfast of beans on toast in the ground floor
canteen, Katharine Morris set out for her orientation interview in
the centre of this shattered metropolis. To get there, she jumped

into one of the numerous Volkswagen Beetles lined up outside her block of flats, a sort of 'occupiers only' taxi rank. While mass ownership of Hitler's famous 'people's car' had never become a reality for the German people, in June 1945 the British authorities had taken over the Volkswagen factory in Wolfsburg and were soon turning out hundreds per week for use as staff cars. She noticed her German driver, along with all his colleagues, was unshaven – hardly the gravest concern amid the devastation of post-war Hamburg, but surprising nonetheless. This, it turned out, wasn't a fashion choice or a uniform requirement, but rather the result of an ongoing shortage of soap and razor blades.

Morris arrived at the British Control Commission headquarters, located in an imposing grey building overlooking the Bleichenfleet canal that had served as the Gestapo's centre of operations in Hamburg. She was taken to her office, which was evidently a former interrogation cell complete with thick steel bars and a self-locking door. Morris had been assigned a role in the Welfare Department, a bureaucratic arm of the Control Commission that concerned itself with the well-being of British personnel – something akin to a modern HR department, albeit one based in a former Gestapo torture chamber. In the coming days she would seek out the assistance of a nearby florist to help brighten up this starkly unwelcoming workplace.

Katharine Morris was one of many thousands of British civilians and soldiers who lived and worked in the towns and cities of north-west Germany between 1945 and 1949, each playing their own small part in what was nothing less than an attempt to rebuild a country from top to bottom. Some were tasked with 'denazification', whether that be hunting Nazi fugitives or removing swastikas from public buildings. Some were employed in re-education, writing new school textbooks or removing fascist literature from public libraries. Legal experts set out to reform the judiciary, economists attempted to rebuild a war economy shattered by years of bombing raids, and crack squads of soldiers tried to locate secret technologies. Britain's attempt to 'win the peace' in Germany was an undertaking unprecedented in both its scale and complexity.

*

The post-war years were a time of extreme uncertainty, hardship and distress for people across Europe. From Berlin to Bratislava, material deprivation was the order of the day, while recriminations swirled among defeated and exhausted populations. For the people of Germany, life seemed to have suddenly and traumatically ground to a halt at the end of the war; 1945 became known to some as *Stunde Null* ('zero hour'), signifying a total break with the past.

In comparison, Morris and her Control Commission colleagues were the lucky ones, provided with ample rations of food and alcohol, as well as a generous selection of British-only clubs and dance halls to enjoy them in. On the shores of the Außenalster, the large artificial lake contained within Hamburg's city limits, lay one of the most ostentatious: the Atlantic Club. The grand white façade of the world-famous Atlantic Hotel had miraculously remained more or less intact during the war. In May 1945 British army officers hastily requisitioned the building for their own purposes.

Over the next four years, hundreds of British men and women traipsed arm in arm through the tall pillars at the Atlantic's entrance. Here they were sure to find a good meal cooked by the hotel's chefs – regular menu items included turtle soup, roast chicken, and ice cream with raspberries. In the hotel's numerous bars, they were amply supplied with beer, brandy and champagne. But in their eagerness to enjoy the fruits of occupation life, most British officers likely strode through the elevator lobby of the Atlantic Club without paying much mind to the extravagant red-and-grey carpet below their feet. If they had, they would have noticed an unusual omission from the map which had stood at its centre since 1909: Britain. The homeland of Hamburg's new rulers had been, quite literally, wiped off the face of the earth. It was a subtle reminder that British–German relations had a complex history, stretching far back before the Second World War.

British tanks of the 21st Army Group in occupied Hamburg
shortly before VE Day.

For much of the nineteenth century, British relations with
Germany – or, to be precise, with the forerunners of the modern
German state prior to 1871 – had been relatively cordial. The
two nations found themselves bound closely together through
trading networks, a shared royal lineage and mutual interests on
the continent. Hamburg and other medieval cities in north-west
Germany had long-standing mercantile links with the British
Isles. In 1815 British *and* German troops defeated Napoleon
at Waterloo. And by the 1850s, Germans made up the largest
immigrant group in the United Kingdom, bringing with them all
manner of culinary, religious and cultural traditions – not least

the Christmas tree.[7] Alongside sugar-bakers, butchers, clerks and traders, these British-Germans included Queen Victoria's consort, Prince Albert, and the political theorist Karl Marx. Even after 1871, when the medley of German kingdoms, duchies and principalities had unified into a single nation state, Anglo-German political relations remained friendly.

In the first decade of the twentieth century, however, growing economic and military rivalry saw relations between these two great European powers sour dramatically – a state of affairs exemplified by the omission of the British Isles from the Atlantic Hotel's map of the world. In 1914 mutual hostility reached fever pitch as Britain and Germany went to war. The following months saw the rise of intense anti-German feeling across Britain, fuelled by 'spy-fever' and stories of German atrocities and savagery in occupied Belgium.[8] In the course of the First World War, there were anti-German boycotts and even riots in several British cities.[9] In response, the British government interned German civilians in camps dotted across the country.[10] Many British-Germans decided to flee, while others, from all walks of life, opted to change their names: many a 'Schmidt' became 'Smith', while in 1917 the dynastic name of the British royal family was transformed from the Germanic 'Saxe-Coburg and Gotha' to the reassuringly English 'Windsor'. In Germany, too, a wave of antipathy was directed towards 'Perfidious Albion', albeit more often coming in the form of hostile rhetoric and anti-British poems than smashed shopfronts.[11] The words '*Gott strafe England*' ('May God punish England') were found on commemorative mugs, handkerchiefs and badges and were even engraved on wedding rings.[12]

In the aftermath of victory in the First World War, British politicians, egged on by a vengeful public keen to 'Hang the Kaiser' and 'Make Germany Pay', had sought to reduce Germany's weight of influence within the European balance of power.[13] In 1919, the British were a powerful part of the Allied delegation which enforced the Treaty of Versailles, a punitive agreement requiring Germany to take full responsibility for the war, pay substantial sums in reparations and accept significant territorial changes.

The same year, John Maynard Keynes, a British delegate at the peace conference, denounced it as a 'Carthaginian Peace' that was unnecessarily – and dangerously – hard on the defeated Germans.[14]

As part of this exacting settlement, British, French, Belgian and American troops were permitted to occupy the demilitarized Rhineland until 1934. These Allied troops were there to protect against any German counterattack and to ensure the timely supply of reparations. The first British Army of the Rhine, a 10,000-strong occupation force, was stationed in the area around Cologne and soon established its own shops, bakeries and even an English-language newspaper, the *Cologne Post*.[15]

Yet for Britain's political leaders, fixated on domestic and imperial concerns, the first occupation of Germany was an unwelcome continental commitment.[16] During the 1920s, British diplomats consistently favoured a more lenient approach towards Germany – championing the country's revival as a European power. This, they hoped, would lessen their own obligations while also limiting French ambitions in Europe and holding off what they perceived to be a new and perhaps even graver threat: Russian Bolshevism. The British public, increasingly sympathetic or at the very least ambivalent towards the Germans, offered little in the way of opposition. From 1924 onwards a series of revisions to the Versailles Treaty saw Britain's role on the continent steadily reduced and in 1929 British troops were withdrawn from the Rhineland. This retreat from Europe set the stage for Britain's policy of appeasement during the next decade, as the country's leaders stood aside while Adolf Hitler's troops marched into the Rhineland itself, Austria and, finally, Czechoslovakia.

In 1939, Germany's invasion of Poland signalled the destruction of the fragile interwar peace and with it any notion that Britain could remain aloof from European affairs. As Nazi forces conquered most of Western Europe, the British empire was left to fight on alone. After the summer of 1940, when the Royal Air Force (RAF) permanently forestalled a German invasion of Britain, the tide began to turn. The following year saw Hitler's forces begin their ill-fated invasion of the Soviet Union, while the Japanese attack on

Pearl Harbor led the United States to enter the conflict, assembling the 'Big Three' alliance that would ultimately ensure the defeat of the Axis powers.

In 1941, the British and their allies could begin to envisage the prospect of eventual victory – even if this was still far from guaranteed. Over the next four years, they were compelled to consider the shape of the post-war world: what could be done to safeguard peace and prosperity in Europe once and for all? It was, of course, the second time in a generation that such questions had been raised and, once again, the future of Germany stood at the forefront of deliberations. This time there could be no mistake.

2

Black Record

The story of how a full-scale military occupation of Germany became British policy by the end of the Second World War begins – at least in the authorized account of events – in early August 1941, with Winston Churchill sailing across the Atlantic in the middle of a storm. HMS *Prince of Wales* was on its own, having earlier dismissed its escort of slower destroyers; timeliness was, on this occasion, pivotal. The prime minister, who had uncommonly good sea legs, walked around the lower decks, played the occasional game of backgammon and continued to track U-boat sightings in his impromptu map room.[1] But all the while he remained consumed by the task at hand: his first face-to-face meeting with US President Franklin Delano Roosevelt since the outbreak of war.

It was three months before the attack on Pearl Harbor, and the United States, though sympathetic towards Britain's fight, remained neutral. The forthcoming conference was a vital opportunity for Churchill to press Roosevelt into further support for the British war effort and nothing could be left to chance. As the weather gradually improved, the prime minister ordered repeated dress rehearsals on the quarterdeck: Sir Alexander Cadogan, permanent under-secretary of the Foreign Office, was cast as FDR, while the Royal Marine band practised their rendition of 'The Star-Spangled Banner'. Churchill, in the guise of director *and* lead actor, worked to perfect this moment of political theatre until he was completely satisfied.

On Saturday, 9 August, the *Prince of Wales* approached its destination: the US Naval Station Argentia, in Newfoundland, Canada.* Churchill wasted no time in boarding the USS *Augusta*, greeting his American counterpart with characteristic swagger: 'at long last, Mr President'. The British prime minister was immediately asked to brief onlooking US officials on the state of the war, itself more of a performance piece than a practical necessity – FDR was playing to Churchill's vanity. Then the real work began, as both statesmen and their advisors set to work discussing plans for the future of the Anglo-American relationship.

A few days later, on 14 August, they jointly issued the Atlantic Charter. This agreement tied the British and Americans to the following pledges: the peace would result in no territorial gains for the victors; territorial adjustments would be made according to 'the wishes of the people concerned'; there would be a right to self-determination, lower trade barriers, global economic cooperation and the advancement of social welfare and disarmament for all peoples; and both nations would support efforts towards securing freedom of the seas and a world free of want and fear.

The Atlantic Charter was an illustration of Anglo-American unity and the firmest indication yet that the US might eventually enter the war. But in terms of the post-war peace, the communiqué remained more of a statement of principles than a political programme. It was hamstrung, in part, by the lack of Soviet involvement, despite coming a month after the signing of the Anglo-Soviet Agreement.† In addition, a great deal of prevailing uncertainty over the eventual outcome of the conflict remained, making detailed planning almost impossible.

---

* The US Naval Station Argentia was a legacy of the Anglo-American Destroyers-for-bases deal of 1940, when fifty US Navy ships were transferred to the Royal Navy in exchange for rent-free leases on British land in various locations across the world including Canada.

† The Anglo-Soviet Agreement formalized a military alliance between Great Britain and the Soviet Union, ensuring mutual assistance and ruling out any separate peace deals with Germany.

Back in Britain, a government memorandum on the uncertain future of Europe reminded ministers to be 'guarded in public statements and not give undertakings which may be impossible to fulfil or lead to charges of bad faith'.[2] It was a warning steadfastly observed for much of the war: while Churchill's ministry periodically considered the question of 'what to do with Germany', definitive answers were seldom forthcoming. The war cabinet held no formal discussions on post-war questions until 1942, while the Foreign Office remained largely reticent on such issues until the very end of the conflict.[3] When these matters were finally broached, Britain's wartime coalition government found itself bitterly divided: the Churchillians, convinced that the roots of the issue lay in Germany's militaristic culture, faced off against Attleeian socialists, who demanded expansive reform of German social and economic structures. Their disagreements regarding the post-war peace went hand in hand with opposing interpretations of Britain's war aims: broadly, whether this conflict should usher in a reinstatement of the status quo or progressive change.

Yet beyond this political infighting, the British public were understandably eager for some sense of what they were fighting for, and many would find their answer from an unexpected source. In the autumn of 1940, just as London was facing the most intense weeks of the Luftwaffe's bombing, Robert Vansittart had escaped to his grand Buckinghamshire mansion in the quiet village of Denham. There, in his customary double-breasted grey suit and black spectacles, he customarily liked to sit and work in his wood-panelled library. At his feet lay an Airedale terrier, Sam, and a German shepherd, Peter – although the latter was known to Vansittart and most of his compatriots as an Alsatian wolf dog. This linguistic shift was a legacy of the British repudiation of anything and everything Germanic at the height of the First World War. Now, with the country at war with Germany once again, there was seemingly little appetite for reversing the change.*

---

* The British Kennel Club formalized this terminological shift and only reverted to the original in 1977.

Vansittart had been born in 1881 to a well-to-do military family in Farnham, Surrey, and lived what he described as a 'jolly and humdrum' existence before being shipped off to St Neot's preparatory school in Hampshire and, subsequently, Eton College.[4] There Van, as he was known to his friends, distinguished himself as a linguist and orator. In 1900 he led the college's annual 4 June celebrations with a reading of Rudyard Kipling's 'The White Man's Burden', a display of his fervent support for Britain's colonial war against Boer farmers in South Africa.

As a young man Vansittart harboured literary ambitions and he would eventually publish a number of plays, poems and novels.[5] But upon finishing his education, a keen interest in foreign languages inspired him to embark on a formative two-year tour of Europe and led him on an entirely different career path. In Germany Vansittart encountered fierce anti-British feeling – in part due to the unsavoury legacy of the Boer War – and was even challenged to a duel, which he evaded only thanks to his silver-tongued skills as a budding diplomat. Indeed, upon his return to England Vansittart sat for the Foreign Service examination.

In the following years he worked in Paris, Tehran and Cairo before returning to London to take up a position at the Foreign Office.[6] There he rose through the ranks, becoming private secretary to two prime ministers – Stanley Baldwin and Ramsay MacDonald – and in 1930 was appointed permanent under-secretary at the Foreign Office, the highest position a British diplomat could hope to attain. During his tenure, he maintained a characteristically steadfast opposition to the policy of appeasement and often warned of Germany's aggressive intentions. At the time this was a contentious stance and one that would ultimately lead to his de facto demotion: in 1938 he was reassigned to the ambiguously defined role of inaugural chief diplomatic advisor to the British government. The outbreak of war only a year later imbued him with a sense of righteousness and helped to craft his reputation as a prescient anti-conformist.[7]

In the autumn of 1940, and in a pique of frustration with the limitations of his new role, Vansittart sat down to write what would turn out to be one of the most divisive and inflammatory texts to emerge in Britain during the Second World War. *Black Record: Germans Past and Present* took aim at the German people and their supposed 'black record' of misdeeds. Germany's history was, Vansittart alleged, a foul succession of aggression and wrongdoing that stretched as far back as the first century AD. The German 'butcher-bird' was accused of embracing war and militarism with a unique zeal and of being responsible for a series of preplanned wars – five in the last seventy-five years alone.[8]

Lord Vansittart, author of *Black Record: Germans Past and Present* and the leading British campaigner for a 'hard peace' in Germany.

Vansittart's essay introduced a new term into the British lexicon: the 'German Problem'. It became a shorthand for Britain's troubled relationship with Germany as the apparent root cause of two world wars and would remain in common usage for much of the 1940s. In his reading, the entire German people were at the heart of the so-called 'German Problem', not just their fanatical leaders:

> The battle still rages round the question: are we fighting the Germans or the Nazis? One day historians will rub their eyes, and wonder how such silly questions could be discussed... No one was fool enough to pretend that we were fighting anything but the Germans in 1914. Indeed, all these fallacies about 'Hitlerite Germany' calmly overlook the last war altogether.[9]

In the coming months, Robert Vansittart would quickly establish himself as *the* pre-eminent theoretician of the 'German Problem' and in the process became an unlikely *éminence grise* ('one exercising unofficial power') of wartime Britain. His meteoric rise as a public figure, and the growing popularity of his virulently anti-German philosophy, would lay the intellectual foundations for Britain's post-war occupation of Germany.

*

In December 1940, British Minister of Information Duff Cooper gave official approval for Vansittart to broadcast his polemic on the BBC Overseas Service, deeming it a potentially powerful form of 'political warfare'. This decision was, in hindsight, a brazen expression of Cooper's own anti-appeasement and anti-German sympathies. His endorsement of Vansittart's opinion ran contrary to the official government position on Germany at the start of the war, which was that the Nazi state had been imposed upon the German people.[10] In September 1939, as Wehrmacht forces invaded Poland, the then Prime Minister Neville Chamberlain spoke in the House of Commons of how 'we have no quarrel with the German people, except that they allow themselves to be governed by a Nazi government'.[11]

Vansittart's radio broadcasts marked the beginning of a gradual evolution of the British government's wartime propaganda, as Germanophobic rhetoric began to be employed as a means of unifying the British people behind an ever intensifying war effort. It was a significant change of course and one that did not escape the attention of the British press: extensive extracts from Vansittart's radio broadcasts soon appeared in the *Sunday Times*, the *Daily Mail* and the *Daily Telegraph*.[12] In January, Vansittart seized the moment and published his full text as a short sixpenny pamphlet.[13] His anti-German rhetoric took the country by storm: a first print run of 25,000 sold out within just two days and in August 1941, as Churchill was sailing across the Atlantic, it went into a thirteenth edition, with an estimated 324,910 copies having been sold.[14] By the end of the year, sales of *Black Record* surpassed an astonishing 500,000.[15] The publisher Victor Gollancz, an outspoken opponent of Vansittart, estimated that 'at least three million people have read the pamphlet... a very high percentage of the adult reading public of this country'.[16]

For much of 1941, Britain was awash with discussion of Germany's supposed 'black record'.[17] Vansittart found a great many influential supporters from within the British establishment and across the political spectrum. William Temple, soon to be installed as the archbishop of Canterbury, offered his gratitude for Vansittart's efforts to reveal the 'tradition of Prussia and of Prussianized Germany'.[18] In the media, while the *Sunday Times* was particularly sympathetic, support for Vansittart's ideas could be found right across the press.[19] A review in the *Manchester Guardian* suggested that 'at this time there are few who will deny the large measure of unhappy truth in [*Black Record*]'.[20] In the *Daily Mail*, H. G. Wells thanked Vansittart for his 'great service' in 'reminding us of the power and persistence' of the 'German tradition' that had made Germany a country of 'invincible uniforms'.[21] The *Daily Mirror*'s editorial went even further and pronounced *Black Record* a 'true history' which recognized the German instinct for cruelty and destruction and reminded readers 'that Germany is Hitler, and Hitler is Germany'.[22] Vansittart's populist diatribe was also becoming popular among some rank-and-file members of the Labour Party, even though it explicitly went against any Marxist interpretation of fascism as a product of the class struggle.[23]

At the same time, *Black Record* was by no means without its critics. By far the most common objection was that Vansittart's ideas about the German people were racist and his analysis was said to be little more than a crude inversion of Nazi theories about race.[24] In the *Daily Express*, the journalist Tom Driberg labelled *Black Record* as 'uncharitable, unhistorical, ungentlemanly' and claimed it echoed 'the Nazi habit of racial generalization'.[25] In *Picture Post*, left-wing Labour MP Aneurin Bevan described Vansittart's thesis as the 'blood stream theory of history'.[26] Likewise, the bishop of Bradford denounced the 'idea of racial qualities and racial defects' as 'untrue to history', 'pernicious to human morality' and an exact parallel of Nazi racism.[27] For historian G. P. Gooch, Vansittart wrote 'as if he had never studied the history of other countries'.[28]

Another criticism ran that it was simply unacceptable for a leading member of the British government – and a diplomat no less – to be expressing such forthright views in public. Francis W. Hirst, journalist and former editor of *The Economist*, wrote to the editor of the *Manchester Guardian* to signal his disgust at Vansittart's 'false pictures of the past' that were reminiscent of 'the mendacity of Dr Goebbels'.[29] Others went even further, suggesting that *Black Record* was a 'gift to Goebbels' that would help bind the German people ever more closely to the Nazi war effort.[30] In retrospect, this was not without foundation: the Reich Minister of Propaganda wrote glowingly of Vansittart in his personal diary, describing him as 'the Englishman who rendered the greatest service to the German cause during the war'.[31]

The ultimate result of this controversy was open disagreement among members of Churchill's war cabinet over the value of *Black Record* as an instrument of propaganda.[32] In the late spring of 1941, it came as no surprise when Vansittart announced his retirement from public service. Now, freed from the constraints of life as a civil servant, he could enthusiastically embrace his newfound status as an eminent public intellectual. Later that year, he was raised to the peerage as Baron Vansittart of Denham in recognition of his long diplomatic career. For the remainder of the war, Lord Vansittart would preach his anti-German gospel from the red benches of the upper chamber. He would also go on to write numerous books and pamphlets that reaffirmed the historical diagnosis of Germany he had first outlined in *Black Record*.[33]

Black Record catalysed a shift in British thinking about Germany and encouraged a retreat into the Germanophobic imagery of the 'savage Hun' that had prevailed during the First World War. Vansittart's vivid prose, reflective of his talents as a published poet and playwright, gave his historical thesis a lively and memorable quality. His pamphlet, if sensationalist and intentionally provocative, nevertheless succinctly and emphatically reinvigorated a familiar image of Germany as Britain's arch-enemy and the root of Europe's troubles. It elevated Vansittart to a singular position. His ideas would, from this point on, be used as a yardstick in British public *and* political discussions about the 'German Problem'.

3

Wishful Thinkers

In February 1941, Victor Gollancz sat glumly in his office on Henrietta Street in London's Covent Garden, thumbing through a copy of *Black Record*. He cut a short, stout figure, sporting a moustache and round black spectacles partially obscured behind wild tufts of grey hair on each side of his head. The bare white walls and simple furnishings of his workplace were suggestive of a devotion to ideas rather than worldly possessions.[1] This was the headquarters of Gollancz's eponymous publishing house, which since its founding in 1927 had counted George Orwell, Daphne du Maurier and Ford Madox Ford among its authors. The austerity of Gollancz's office was, however, something of a pretence: away from his professional life he enjoyed the finer things, from expensive cigars to luxury wines, and in peacetime he made a daily trip to the nearby Waldorf Hotel for lunch. But Gollancz's commitment to promoting socialist, liberal and humanitarian ideas was unquestionable. Through his publishing venture, and especially the 'Left Book Club', he brought left-wing ideas to mass audiences. In the 1930s this included staging a principled opposition to the policy of appeasement and spearheading efforts to draw the world's attention to the Third Reich's anti-Semitic terror.[2]

During the war Gollancz would campaign for Allied action to help Europe's beleaguered Jews and did his utmost to support the budding British socialist movement. But in the spring of 1941,

Gollancz's thoughts were consumed with the so-called 'German Problem' and the pamphlet that had recently taken the country by storm. As he saw it, *Black Record* had unleashed a mood of hatred among the British people which ran contrary to everything that Britain ought to be fighting for. Gollancz resolved to combat what he regarded as the scourge of Vansittartism: he would write a text as eye-catching as *Black Record*, but in support of magnanimity rather than revenge, love rather than hate. There was, however, one problem – Gollancz's knowledge of German history was rudimentary at best. He set to work assembling a small personal library of key historical texts and consulting with German exiles now resident in London.[3]

It was not until the following spring that Gollancz's response emerged: the emphatically titled *Shall Our Children Live or Die? A reply to Lord Vansittart on the German problem*.[4] He attempted to reframe the issue, rejecting *Black Record*'s divisive Germanophobia in favour of a more internationalist explanation of Europe's troubled twentieth century. Nazism, he insisted, was not the result of some peculiar German trait but rather a symptom of the capitalist system's inherent frailties: namely, the tendency of people in the midst of despair to 'vote for anyone who will promise them bread, hope and a job'. In short, the decisive factor in international relations was, Gollancz argued, capitalism rather than 'German-ism'.

In his reading, German history was not an unbroken line of authoritarian militarism but a more complex tale that included democrats, virtuoso composers and brilliant scientists as well as despots.[5] From this foundation, Gollancz outlined a radical vision for the post-war world: if, as he fervently believed, Nazism had emerged from a particular set of social and economic conditions, then the only solution was revolution. In *Shall Our Children Live or Die?*, Gollancz argued that the Third Reich must be defeated from within by a popular uprising.[6] In fact, he assured readers that an 'Other Germany', including the nation's oppressed working classes, would lead the way in fighting for an end to Hitler's dictatorial rule. But Gollancz also insisted that Allied plans for the post-war peace needed to look beyond Germany to consider the ills of the entire capitalist system. The argument ran that the world could only be freed from the threat of war if monopoly capitalism was replaced in favour of international democratic socialism.[7]

Gollancz produced an impressive work of scholarship, drawing heavily from Marxist analyses of the European class struggle prominent among the exiled veterans of the German socialist movement. But despite Gollancz's express intention to write a 'popular and introductory essay', his initial 25,000-word manuscript had swollen into a rather academic 70,000-word book.[8] If not quite reaching the masses, Gollancz's radical humanitarianism still found an audience among liberals, socialists and church leaders. It eventually sold over 50,000 copies: an impressive figure, though less than one-tenth of the sales of *Black Record*.

Victor Gollancz, author of *Shall Our Children Live or Die? A reply to Lord Vansittart on the German problem*. In 1945 he founded the pressure group Save Europe Now.

Shall Our Children Live or Die? also established Gollancz as the de facto head of an anti-Vansittart movement that sought to draw a distinction between 'Nazism' and 'Germany' and fought against the growing tide of wartime nationalistic fervour.[9] Gollancz's study soon inspired like-minded academics, writers and journalists to write their own critiques of *Black Record*.[10] Douglas Brown argued in his pamphlet *Commonsense versus Vansittartism*, published under the auspices of the Labour Party, that Nazism was the inevitable result of Western imperialism and the wrongs of the capitalist system.[11] The assistant editor of *The Times*, E. H. Carr, characterized *Black Record*'s thesis of inherent German wickedness as an unreasoned 'emotional reaction' advocated by a defunct scholar of history. The bishop of Chichester, George Bell, faced off against Vansittart in the House of Lords and demanded official recognition of a distinction between the 'Hitlerite State' and the German people.[12]

*

By the time Gollancz's *Shall Our Children Live or Die?* was published, Lord Vansittart had himself emerged as the figurehead of an ever expanding faction of anti-German commentators, a miscellaneous group of politicians, activists, writers and academics whose ideas maintained an intellectual orbit around the basic precepts set out in *Black Record*.[13] Rolf Tell's brashly titled *The Eternal Ger-Maniac: Hitler and His Spiritual Ancestors* is just one example of the many publications echoing Vansittart's understanding of the 'German Problem'.[14] From leading historians such as A. J. P. Taylor and Rohan Butler to anti-German fanatics such as Eleonora Tennant,* almost anyone associated with hostile views towards Germany came to be

---

* The Australian-born Eleonora Tennant was a far-right nationalist who stood unsuccessfully as a Conservative parliamentary candidate in the 1930s. She had explicit Nazi sympathies, joining the notorious Anglo-German Fellowship and even attending a Nuremberg rally. The outbreak of war saw a rather abrupt conversion to an extreme anti-German, anti-Semitic nationalism and later Tennant even accused Vansittart of succumbing to the influence of the Germans.

regarded as an advocate of 'Vansittartism'.[15] Their ideas became a well-known part of Britain's wartime discourse and reverberated across much of the political establishment and the media.[16]

Vansittart, the Eton-educated baron with decidedly Edwardian sensibilities, could hardly be described as a man of the people. Yet for all his vanity and grandiloquence, he was an able and willing communicator who regularly made speaking tours of the country. Since the unexpected success of *Black Record*, Vansittart had become a tireless devotee of his own cause, never shy of an opportunity for self-promotion; he had, his biographer Norman Rose notes, 'learned the stock-in-trade tricks of every politician'.[17] There were few major publications to which Vansittart didn't at some point contribute an article, column or letter, and he also took up invitations to appear on newsreel films and BBC radio shows.[18] His message remained consistent: the soul of the German people was militaristic and, as such, it was only right to blame *all* Germans for the crimes of Nazism.[19]

In 1943 he decided to take his message to the British people even more directly in the form of his own political lobby group: the Win the Peace Movement.[20] He installed himself as president and travelled round the country to host luncheons and meetings with all manner of audiences.[21] Vansittart gave rousing speeches, on one occasion even inspiring a Cardiff audience to chant 'For He's a Jolly Good Fellow'.[22] These were popular events: *The Scotsman* estimated 3,000 people attended a talk in Edinburgh, the *Birmingham Post* spoke of a 'largely attended meeting' and there were claims that the Bristol branch of the association mustered over 10,000 supporters.[23] In his 1945 book *Bones of Contention*, Vansittart asserted, with some justification, that the Win the Peace Movement had 'recruited and enlightened many scores of thousands of the men and women of this country in support of the aims, ideals and practical policies I have advanced'.[24]

Vansittart also developed close affiliations with two more lobby groups: the British Prisoner of War Relatives Association, an organization that shared his Germanophobic views and to whom he gave speeches, and the Never Again Association.[25] This latter group, which had the stated aim of ensuring that 'never again must we allow Germany to make war', began life in the summer of 1942 and became a wellspring of anti-German rhetoric with branches across Britain.[26] Vansittart, although never formally a member, gave numerous talks at association meetings, including one recorded on vinyl, while his wife, Sarita Enriqueta, took up a place on the executive committee.[27]

An inherently complex political discussion about German history was soon abbreviated into a dichotomized culture war. This was, at its core, a clash between two radically different outlooks: Gollancz was actively involved with left-wing and liberal politics, ecumenical Christianity, socialist internationalism and notions of 'Europeanness'. In contrast, Vansittart was emphatically jingoistic and hawkish, and loosely if not exclusively associated with the right wing of British politics. Likewise, their means of interrogating the 'German Problem' were wholly opposed: for Vansittart this was a cultural phenomenon, whereas Gollancz viewed it in socio-economic terms. In time, vitriol and mutual contempt took centre stage.

There was scarcely a newspaper in the entire country that didn't, at some point, play host to a feud over conflicting ideas about Germany and the Third Reich. *Black Record* had ushered in a bellicose tone from the very start, its polemical style inspiring supporters and opponents with equal ferocity. Soon, Vansittart's rhetorical axe fell fiercely upon those who challenged him or his ideas. In subsequent editions of *Black Record*, the forewords of other publications, and in the letter pages of the national and regional press, he countered perceived slights with characteristic callousness. His opponents were branded the 'Suckers Chorus', 'illusionists', 'Innocents at Home', 'Wishful Thinkers', 'intellectual dove-cotes', 'confident amateurs' and the 'invincibly ignorant'.[28] Vansittart suggested that his adversaries were advocating another form of appeasement and it was his task, once more, to stand firm.[29] 'This country has been, and still is, full of this rubbish', he exclaimed, denouncing the 'Germanophiles at Westminster' who had 'believed blindly in Germany' since before the First

World War.[30] These excoriating remarks were matched by some of his allies, including Conservative MP Beverley Baxter who proclaimed that he 'would not mind if the people who urged us not to hate the Germans were dropped into Germany from a Lancaster'.[31] In December 1941, *The Economist* lamented 'the rise of brutality' which had begun to accompany discussions of the post-war peace.[32] It was a trend set to continue for some years yet.

*

While the more intellectually rigorous publications of the anti-Vansittart movement were critically well received, they never threatened to match the popular sensation that now greeted every proclamation from the self-styled 'diplomat with his coat off'.[33] Vansittart's ideas had quickly gained ground among the British public, as shown by a Mass-Observation survey of December 1942 which stated that a 'high percentage' of the population believed Germany to be a warlike nation that would always cause trouble.[34] In early 1943, 43 per cent of respondents to a Mass-Observation poll claimed they 'hated or had no sympathy for the German people'.[35]

That spring, an expectant crowd, most of them in the blue and green hues of the British armed forces, gathered outside Foyles Bookshop in London's Charing Cross Road.[36] Things had changed a great deal since the summer of 1940, when London had each night fallen victim to the Blitz. It is said that the shop's eccentric owner William Foyle had taken it upon himself to cover the rooftop with copies of Hitler's *Mein Kampf* to ward off enemy bombers.[37] This wasn't his only attempt at using up dead stock: the piles of sandbags that had surrounded most buildings in central London were quite different at Foyles, where they were filled not with sand but old books. Now, almost three years later, the shopfront of Foyles was concealed instead by cigarette-smoking men in trench coats and young Royal Navy sailors eagerly glancing through Lord Vansittart's latest non-fiction sensation, his political memoir *Lessons of My Life*. Vansittart was now a great cause célèbre of wartime Britain and copies of his new book were piled high, together with a large photograph of their author. Alongside them were stacks of his first political polemic, *Black Record*, its bright-red cover illustrated with a black-and-white swastika – an arresting image for any unsuspecting passer-by.

As part of his promotional activities, and with the government still reluctant to outline any plans for the future peace, Vansittart now advanced his own vision of the post-war world. In the *Daily Mail* he argued that the treatment of Germany's 'black record' had to be 'the most drastic cure in history' or else 'the world will die of the German disease'.[38] Later in 1943 he wrote a comprehensive twelve-point peace plan, publicized with much aplomb by his Win the Peace Movement.[39] Vansittart's 'hard peace' proposal comprised an extensive list of demands including unconditional surrender; a 'prolonged' military occupation, lasting for 'at least a generation'; punishment for those guilty of war crimes; complete and permanent disarmament; decentralization and demilitarization of the German police; abolition of all forms of military training; reparation for damages; the destruction of Germany's military industrial potential; a ban on financial aid to Germany without Allied agreement; re-education; and supervision of all forms of media.[40] Vansittart openly admitted that his diagnosis was 'extremely harsh' but assured readers that it was civilization's last chance to resolve the 'German Problem'.[41]

Meanwhile, his opponents described the proposal as vindictive and vengeful, with one commentator describing it as 'eyeless in hate'.[42] But with Victor Gollancz's predicted anti-Hitler revolution yet to materialize, those who placed their faith in an 'Other Germany' were on the defensive. As the Nazi state intensified the terror against its own people, there seemed little prospect that any such revolutionary change would come to pass, at least not until the war's end. In June 1943, overworked and burdened with guilt over the plight of Europe's Jews, Gollancz himself suffered what his biographer describes as a 'very serious nervous breakdown'.[43] Without its principal figurehead, the anti-Vansittart campaign soon ground to a halt. In the final two years of the war, few, if any, noteworthy attempts were made to revisit the increasingly improbable proposals for a revolutionary resolution to the 'German Problem'. In the same period Vansittart's proposal for an exacting 'hard peace', comprising a military occupation of indefinite length that would oversee the complete revision of German society, gradually established itself as mainstream political opinion.

4

Theatrics

At the heart of London's West End stands the Theatre Royal Haymarket, its six Corinthian columns projecting grandly over the front pavement. Inside, golden balconies and ornate decorations hint at some of the illustrious patrons of this famous playhouse, a favourite of Queen Victoria. In June 1943 the Haymarket played host to a private party to mark the end of an eight-week run of works by the playwright Noël Coward. It proved to be quite a gathering – attended not merely by the great and good of London society, but also by controversy.[1] On stage, Coward and his band performed songs from their back catalogue of musical hits, as well as a rather provocative new number: 'Don't Let's Be Beastly to the Germans'.

Incorporating references to the Anglo-German Naval Agreement of 1935, the German occupation of the Rhineland the following year and the Nazi invasions of Czechoslovakia, Poland and the Netherlands as well as, perhaps most strikingly, outlining proposals for the possible mass sterilization of the German people, this was no ordinary pop song. It was a satirical attack directed, Coward would later recall, against 'a small minority of excessive humanitarians, who, in my opinion, were taking a rather too tolerant view of our enemies' – in other words, Victor Gollancz and the anti-Vansittartists.[2] The song's chorus speaks for itself:

Don't let's be beastly to the Germans,
When our victory is ultimately won,
It was just those nasty Nazis who persuaded them to fight,
And their Beethoven and Bach are really far worse than
   their bite,
Let's be meek to them
And turn the other cheek to them,
And try to bring out their latent sense of fun.
Let's give them full air parity
And treat the rats with charity,
But don't let's be beastly to the Hun.[3]

'Don't Let's Be Beastly to the Germans' stood up for the ideas outlined in *Black Record* and took issue with the notion that it was 'just those nasty Nazis' who had brought about the war. It was only right, Coward insisted, to lay the blame upon the German people as a whole.[4] That evening at the Haymarket, it was made clear that the British prime minister wholeheartedly agreed: Winston Churchill sat in raptures among the crowd of assembled VIPs before demanding that Coward perform the song a second and then a third time.

Not everyone was quite so enthusiastic. The sarcastic observations of 'Don't Let's Be Beastly to the Germans' were regarded by some as an affront to decency and mistakenly interpreted by others as a sincere plea for clemency.[5]

It wasn't long before the song was removed from the BBC's playlists after a number of listener complaints. Some complainants considered the song to be xenophobic, while others condemned Coward as a pro-German apologist – although many were simply appalled at its novel use of the word 'bloody'! Indeed, it may well have been this use of language which BBC censors deemed to be profane that ultimately did for the song's chances of further airplay. Nevertheless, 'Don't Let's Be Beastly to the Germans' found many fierce advocates, not only the prime minister but also his new chancellor of the Duchy of Lancaster, Duff Cooper. The man who had permitted the broadcast of *Black Record* personally wrote to

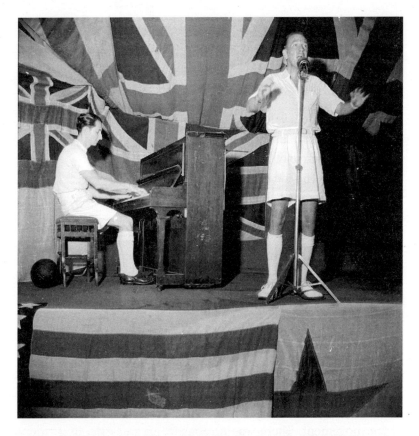

The entertainer Noël Coward (right), who wrote and first performed
the song 'Don't Let's Be Beastly to the Germans' in 1943.

Coward to tell him that if he were still minister of information he
would insist it be broadcast nightly as a message to 'all the silly,
sloppy sentimental shits' who wanted to be 'kind to the Germans'.[6]

That one of the nation's most revered entertainers chose to pen a
song lampooning the intricacies of British foreign policy illustrates
just how close to the surface anxieties over the prospective peace
were in wartime Britain. But Coward's song also shows the extent
to which the starkly anti-German message of *Black Record* had
permeated all sections of British society, politics, media, military
and civil service, even finding a champion in Downing Street.[7] In
the final two years of the war, as Allied leaders finally began to

draw up plans for the post-war world, it was widely accepted that an uncompromising peace settlement would be required in order to resolve the 'German Problem' once and for all.

*

While British policy for Germany emerged from this fractious domestic context, plans for the future of the world could only take shape in the course of negotiations with the Soviet Union and the United States. The ideas of Vansittart and Gollancz were just two of the many strands of opinion in the wide-ranging discussions of the Allied powers.[8] In January 1942, Britain, the USA, the Soviet Union and China issued the Declaration by United Nations, in which they pledged their allegiance to the edicts outlined in the Atlantic Charter. Even more significantly, the signatories agreed to repudiate any potential peace deals with Germany, binding themselves together in the fight against Nazism to the bitter end. This marked a vital precursor to the policy of unconditional surrender that would be formally announced – at the bequest of President Roosevelt – during the Casablanca Conference of January 1943.[9] It was a momentous decision which precluded any possibility of embracing the overtures of a prospective German peace movement. There was no longer any question of publicly encouraging the overthrow of the Nazi regime from within and, as a result, the governance of defeated Germany would, at least for an interim period, fall to the victorious armies of the 'Big Three' (Britain, the USA and the Soviet Union).

As the tide turned against Hitler's forces in both the Soviet Union and North Africa, the precise programme of reforms to be implemented at the end of the conflict remained far from clear. The establishment of two committees with long-winded titles, the Post-Hostilities Planning Sub-Committee and the Ministerial Committee on Armistice Terms – the latter of which Labour leader Clement Attlee chaired – signalled a brief acceleration of Britain's preparations for the peace.[10] They were, in part, a response to Roosevelt's Advisory Committee on Post-war Foreign Policy. Yet over the coming months, with conditions at the end of the war still hard to predict, officials on both sides of the Atlantic remained reluctant to make firm decisions.[11]

It was not until October 1943 that inter-Allied deliberations on the future shape of Germany began in earnest.[12] At the Moscow Conference of foreign ministers both the British and American delegations pushed for only the 'minimum necessary' safeguard, namely comprehensive disarmament, in order to allow a reformed Germany to play a full part in Europe's recovery.[13] While no concrete decisions were made in Moscow, the aftermath of the conference saw the establishment of the European Advisory Commission, an inter-Allied body based in London that was intended to formalize plans for post-war Germany.

A month later, at the Tehran Conference (28 November – 1 December 1943), the leaders of the 'Big Three' convened for the first time in the war to consider inter-Allied military strategy and plan for a future peace settlement. At the end of their discussions, the three leaders sat genially for publicity photographs beside the grand white columns of the Soviet embassy in the Iranian capital. To Stalin's relief, Roosevelt and Churchill had finally agreed to open up a second front in Europe, setting in motion preparations for the invasion of France in May 1944 and thereby ensuring the three-power alliance was strengthened yet further. But the preceding four days of talks had been fraught with tension.

Things got off to a bad start when Churchill presented the Soviet leader with the Sword of Stalingrad, a ceremonial longsword forged on behalf of King George VI in homage to the city's heroic defenders. Stalin passed the sword to Marshal Kliment Voroshilov, who grasped it by the scabbard rather than its eighteen-carat gold handle and sent the blade crashing to the floor. This was a portent of the strained discussions that followed.

During the conference, the British prime minister was relentlessly mocked by his Soviet and American counterparts. It was emblematic of relations between the three men: the prime minister was the odd man out, an arch-conservative who stood at the head of an empire in terminal decline. Roosevelt and Stalin presided over more radical ideological projects, the New

Deal and Soviet communism respectively, which afforded them much greater power on the world stage – and they knew it. At Tehran, Roosevelt hoped to build a personal rapport with Stalin by eviscerating Churchill for his British demeanour and ridiculing him as a grumpy imperialist who chain-smoked cigars. The Soviet leader, meanwhile, joked with even less delicacy about the possible execution of 50,000 to 100,000 German officers. Roosevelt facetiously retorted that 'maybe 49,000 would be enough', while an exasperated Churchill hurriedly left the room.[14]

Churchill began to feel increasingly isolated, a sense only exacerbated when he was excluded from private meetings between Roosevelt and Stalin. It fed into the British delegation's broader concerns about the wartime alliance: they felt progressively uneasy about the long-term commitment of the US to Europe and divided over the potential threat posed by the Soviet Union. While representatives of the Foreign Office were anxious to maintain the 'Big Three' coalition at all costs, the British chiefs of staff warned that Soviet Russia would present the biggest threat to the European balance of power.[15] As a result of these anxieties, the British were unwilling to commit to any precise programme for the future of Germany. When the staff cars left Tehran, there was still no plan for the post-war peace.

Almost a year went by before the 'Big Three' ratified the European Advisory Commission's top secret 'Attlee plan' in September 1944 – otherwise known as the London Protocol.[16] This scheme proposed a military occupation of Germany and the partition of Berlin. It was a hard-line approach to the peace that would result in the victorious Allies taking direct control of the entire nation, a radically different prospect from the Allied occupation of the Rhineland in 1919, during which the Germans themselves had governed the occupied territory. The London Protocol was a significant step forwards, even if many key details, including the length and administrative machinery of the occupation, the means of enforcing disarmament, the mechanics of Germany's surrender and the value and/or practicality of territorial alterations or decentralization, remained undecided.

Later the same month Roosevelt and Churchill met in Quebec to discuss the Anglo-American approach to the forthcoming occupation. They gave their joint approval to the Morgenthau Plan, a memorandum written by FDR's treasury secretary, Henry Morgenthau Jr. It advocated the almost total de-industrialization of Germany, an extreme notion that would have reduced a great industrial powerhouse to a pastoral economy. Churchill, who had arrived in Quebec with an eye to securing badly needed American aid, accepted this 'swords into ploughshares' scheme at least partly as an act of diplomacy. Yet the prime minister was also undoubtedly drawn to the possibility of Britain emerging from the war as the unchallenged economic power in Europe.[17] The deal also came with another carrot: the Americans agreed to occupy the southern part of Germany, leaving the north-west – with most of the country's industrial capacity – to the British.[18]

By the time Churchill returned to London, however, the Morgenthau Plan had already begun to provoke sharp criticism from within the US State Department, from some of the military top brass, as well as among senior British civil servants. For Morgenthau's opponents this 'Carthaginian' peace went against the fundamental foundations of the Atlantic Charter and could only lead to disaster: 70 million Germans would either starve or become a charge on other nations.[19] The British also feared that prisoners of war stuck in German camps might face immediate retribution from their captors. In early October details of the plan were leaked to the American press, with *Time* magazine describing it as a 'Policy of Hate'.[20] The Morgenthau Plan was abruptly abandoned, though not before the US joint chiefs of staff had agreed to JCS 1067, a military government handbook which echoed Morgenthau's thinking and would remain in place in the American Zone of occupation until 1947.[21] Britain's brief flirtation with the Morgenthau Plan illustrated the extent to which thinking about post-war Germany had evolved: there now seemed to be an acceptance across the political spectrum that far-reaching economic and social reforms were required, even among those like Churchill who perceived the 'German Problem' in primarily cultural terms. There was one other long-term ramification too: in November, the London Protocol was updated to reflect the newly agreed allocation of the north-western part of Germany to Britain.

*

In February 1945, just weeks before the first Allied troops entered German territory, all three Allied leaders came together once more at the Livadia Palace in the Crimean city of Yalta. The palace, which had only nine functioning toilets, was hardly suited to the demands of a major international conference. Over the eight days of the meeting, delegates made endless complaints not only about long queues for the bathroom, but also infestations of bedbugs and swarms of mosquitoes. 'If we had spent ten years on research we could not have found a worse place in the world', Churchill exclaimed to American policy advisor Harry Hopkins.[22]

Nevertheless, the atmosphere among the three leaders was markedly more convivial than it had been at Tehran, no doubt helped by liberal supplies of 'Caucasian champagne' and Russian vodka. The 'Big Three' resolved some of the outstanding territorial disputes relating to Germany, while Churchill successfully lobbied for the inclusion of the French as an occupying power.[23] Agreement on the issue of Germany's future borders followed on from the notorious 'Percentages Agreement' of October 1944, a secret and informal pact – initially written on the back of a napkin – between Churchill and Stalin.[24] It established a consensus for Soviet influence in Eastern Europe: Greece was, for instance, to be 90 per cent within the Western sphere, while Bulgaria was to be 75–80 per cent under the control of the Soviet Union, and Hungary and Romania also firmly in the Soviet camp. Poland's borders would be radically altered: the Soviet Union would be allowed to retain eastern areas annexed in 1939 and the Polish state was to be compensated with German land to its west. In an instant, the fortunes of millions were divvied up between East and West.

Crucially, it was also at Yalta that detailed plans for post-war Germany finally began to take shape: discussions outlined the basic machinery of a military occupation and the overarching policy aims of the occupiers. In the first place, Germany was to be totally demilitarized: the country's armed forces were to be disbanded, removing its ability to wage war. There would also be a large-scale programme of reparations, with the removal of raw materials and industrial equipment and the use of forced labour designed to compensate the victors.[25] It was also proposed that 'denazification', ridding Germany, its people, institutions and culture of Nazism, should be implemented. What it would look like in practice remained a mystery and it was decided that the final details would be dealt with in another conference at the end of the war.

If this proposal wasn't quite so vindictive as Morgenthau's, it was certainly a punitive settlement that would impose drastic changes and penalties upon Germany. In this respect, it offered a distinctly Vansittartist solution to the 'German Problem'. It was also a vision of the peace that chimed with British public opinion in the spring of 1945, with a Mass-Observation poll at the time reporting that 54 per cent of the general public 'hated or had no sympathy for the German people'.[26]

The Allies had at long last agreed a plan for post-war Europe – and not a moment too soon. British soldiers were busy preparing for the final offensive of the war against Hitler: the invasion of Germany itself. Just a few months later, tens of thousands of their civilian compatriots would be setting out by boat and train to join them in the British Zone of occupied Germany. Together, they were to take on near-total responsibility for a vast area of territory and for the more than 20 million Germans who lived there. As one British official would later state, this was 'an enterprise of great magnitude and difficulty' for which there was 'no precedent in human history'.[27]

5

Over the Rhine

In the spring of 1945, Norman Cole's troop transport trundled along through fields, eventually passing a large roadside sign that read: 'YOU ARE NOW ENTERING GERMANY'. Cole had been part of the Allied advance through Europe since his unit, the 9th Survey Regiment of the Royal Artillery, landed at Sword Beach on D-Day. He had fought his way through France, Belgium and the Netherlands – and befriended the locals along the way. But Germany was different. Along the same stretch of road, his convoy of British army trucks passed an elderly couple busily tilling a parcel of land. These were the first German civilians that Cole had seen and he was immediately incensed: 'Work, you bastards, work!' he shouted in his thick Devonshire accent.[1] A few decades later he would reflect with some embarrassment on his conduct: 'That's not me. [But] we'd got to the point where we hated Germany and everything to do with it'.

The previous December, German forces had attempted their final major offensive of the war, breaking through a weak spot in the Allied lines in the Ardennes Forest. The Wehrmacht hoped to push through to the Belgian port of Antwerp, cutting off this vital supply route and in the process splitting the British and Americans forces. The 'Battle of the Bulge' was Hitler's final gamble, a last-ditch attempt to force the Western Allies into a negotiated peace. But a strong American defence and counter-offensive saw the

Wehrmacht forced back. By the end of January, Soviet troops had overrun most of Poland, and the outcome of the war in Europe was all but sealed.[2]

In March 1945, when the Red Army was massed on the Oder–Neisse line,* less than 50 miles (80 kilometres) east of Berlin, Allied forces in the West pushed the Wehrmacht back over the Rhine. As units of Montgomery's 21st Army Group, including Norman Cole's regiment, moved up towards the river they came across large amounts of abandoned equipment of all shapes and sizes. To Cole's astonishment, he even found a large cooking pot filled with still-warm soup: the Germans had retreated as fast as they could.[3] At Remagen, south of Cologne, the 9th Armored Division of the American First Army advanced so rapidly that they managed to capture something even more valuable: the last remaining intact bridge over the Rhine. It was an unexpected bonus, but General Dwight Eisenhower, as supreme commander of the Allied Expeditionary Force, still felt that an amphibious assault in the northern Rhineland – codenamed Operation Plunder – was necessary. If successful, it would allow for a broader and swifter advance into Germany, even if the ambition of beating the Soviets to Berlin looked increasingly unattainable.

Field Marshal Montgomery began meticulous planning, comparable in scope to the preparations for the Normandy invasion: thirty full-strength divisions, numbering more than 1.25 million men, prepared to cross the Rhine at Rees, Xanten and Rheinberg. Alongside this huge amphibious assault, a simultaneous operation, codenamed Varsity, saw two divisions of paratroopers land behind enemy lines. Weeks of sustained bombing raids – more than 11,000 sorties – and artillery bombardments cleared the way on the east side of the river, including flattening the nearby city of Wesel. Forty-five years later, British troops would contend that their hearing had never quite recovered from the ceaseless pounding of the heavy guns.[4]

---

* A demarcation line running along the Oder and Lusatian Neisse rivers that was soon to be recognized as the German–Polish border.

On the evening of 23 March, British troops began the river crossing and met with little resistance. The previous night, General Patton had overseen an American attack across the Rhine at Oppenheim and Nierstein, where seven startled German defenders promptly paddled themselves across the river unescorted in order to surrender.[5] By the following day, as Montgomery's million-strong formation were making their Rhine crossings under the cover of an intense barrage of artillery and smoke, Patton triumphantly announced that American troops could cross the Rhine anywhere, anytime and without the assistance of artillery or airborne troops.

In the days that followed a mass of men and equipment made its way into Germany, crossing the river on a series of hastily constructed bridges. At first light on 28 March, Private Skinner of the 7th Armoured Division took a hurried breakfast before driving his transport out onto a mud track. There he joined the seemingly endless convoy of vehicles heading up a steep incline: truck after truck of troops, supplies and war machinery inching towards a gap that Royal Engineers had forged in the steep bank on the horizon. As Skinner reached the top, it was the first time he set eyes upon the Rhine, a body of water so broad and fast-flowing that it scarcely seemed passable. A line of vehicles was making its way across a Bailey bridge which stretched more than 320 yards (300 metres) across the river.[6] The structure was scarcely wider than a single truck, with a criss-cross of metal girders skirted by a narrow walkway on either side. Skinner watched as vehicles passed over each bridging section, the flat-bottomed pontoons below sinking slightly into the water before rising once more. When his truck finally reached the bank, he could hear the bridge creaking under the dual strain of a fast current and its heavy load. It seemed impossible that it could hold, but moments later he found himself and his cargo safely on the opposite bank. 'The last big obstacle had now been passed,' he wrote in his memoir, 'nothing at all could now stop the Allied Forces from sweeping ahead into the heart of Germany.'

*

During the next fortnight British and American forces established a bridgehead east of the Rhine, advancing rapidly across the North German Plain towards the Elbe.[7] It was then that Robert Souper, a troop commander in the 7th Survey Regiment of the Royal Artillery, encountered German civilians for the first time.[8] Most, it seemed, were relatively friendly, some even leaving their houses to shake hands with bewildered British troops. But outside one country cottage a stern-looking elderly resident stood waving her fists and shrieking abuse at the troop transports. Souper quickly turned to his radio: 'Wilco, calling rear transports. 100-yards, on your left. Angry woman. Worth seeing. Wilco, out.' Private Skinner recalled that 'the young girls looked at us with such hatred in their eyes. I am sure they would have killed us if they could have done'.[9] Yet, passing through towns with white sheets hanging from windows, he also recognized a defeated people: 'I never thought I would live to see the day that the Germans would be showing the white flag of surrender. This really made us feel that the end of the war was in sight.'

The Allied advance met with sporadic resistance from fleeing army units, ad hoc squads of SS soldiers and members of the newly formed *Volkssturm* ('people's storm'), a national civilian militia. The latter comprised teenagers and elderly men without training, adequate equipment or even uniform; most simply wore civilian clothes and a red-and-black armband with the inscription 'Deutscher Volkssturm Wehrmacht'. Goebbels had envisaged an army of 6 million men that would defeat the Allies through force of will; the reality was quite different.[10] Charles Chester, a machine gunner with the Northumberland Fusiliers, came across one silver-haired *Volkssturm* fighter fast asleep in a bush beside an important crossroads. Realizing the absurdity of the situation, he confiscated the man's rifle and simply offered him a pack of cigarettes before telling him to 'go home and be a good boy'.[11] Many others were not so lucky, either killed in battles with the enemy or executed by their own side for supposed cowardice.[12] As the war drew to an end, the Nazi regime further intensified its terror, assembling roving death squads to summarily execute any apparent deserters.[13]

Over the course of just a few weeks, Allied forces successfully encircled more than 300,000 soldiers of Army Group B in the 'Ruhr Pocket', the last effective force of German resistance in the west. Their surrender on 18 April preceded the final advance of British and American forces, with Montgomery's 21st Army Group holding the northern flank towards Lübeck and conquering much of the area that was set to become the British Zone of occupation.[14] Along the way, they faced only limited resistance from the depleted and poorly organized defenders of so-called 'fortress cities'.[15] It was increasingly clear that the German war machine had collapsed and, for most soldiers, the prime concern now became one of avoiding trouble until a ceasefire was officially declared. After fighting through North Africa, Italy, France, the Netherlands and now Germany, Private Skinner stood on guard in a wooded area in late April, nervously listening to the sound of gunfire in the field ahead and silently counting down the minutes until he could return to the relative safety of his camp bed.[16] In the spring of 1945, this restlessness was felt on both sides – for most people, getting out alive was now all that mattered.

There were other ways in which the Allied sweep into Germany was markedly different from previous advances through France, Belgium and the Netherlands. Here there was no underground resistance movement or government in exile that could be expected to take over the reins of power once the frontline armies had moved on. Rather, every inch of German territory captured by Allied forces became their direct responsibility. As official plans for the post-war military occupation, codenamed Operation Eclipse, made clear, the Germans were to be conquered and not liberated.[17]

In the first instance, it was the Civil Affairs Division of the 21st Army Group that was charged with taking responsibility for the area now under British control. It was ultimately expected to establish a military government that could replace the defunct German state while ensuring civil obedience.[18] But in the short term, with the war ongoing, the overriding priority of Allied commanders was 'to control the civilian population so as to facilitate and promote the success of military operations'.[19] This was not an exercise in long-term state-building, but rather an attempt to establish authority and maintain order. In other words, Civil Affairs would piece things together and fight only the most urgent fires, all in preparation for the civilian-led Control Commission for Germany to take over and 'win the peace'.[20]

As a result, the bulk of the work carried out by Allied forces in these first weeks and months was of a practical nature, ranging from the everyday to the extraordinary. Civil Affairs detachments did their best to maintain a basic level of public health, ensuring – with mixed results – that adequate supplies of food and other basic necessities of life were available to the local population.[21] Public Safety officers, many recruited from the ranks of the British police, attempted to maintain law and order in German towns and cities.[22] To protect against much-feared vigilante attacks, all German civilians had their guns, ammunition, radios, binoculars and cameras confiscated. The British also instigated strict local curfews: in Gladbeck, in the northern part of the Ruhr, for instance, civilians were banned from venturing outside between 6 p.m. and 7 a.m.[23] In the rolling fields near the river Weser, interpreter Peter Wayne witnessed a British medical officer hastily milking cows, their owners having seemingly fled to avoid the fighting.[24] Around the same time, some 3,000 British and American investigators of the clandestine T-Force were scouring the area, attempting to locate and secure scientific and industrial technology and expertise.[25]

These were hectic, violent days as the war approached its endgame. All across the country millions of German women were the victims of violence, rape and sexual assault committed by soldiers of all Allied nations, although the vast majority of these attacks occurred in areas under Soviet control.[26] As many as 100,000 rapes were reported in Berlin alone, while some historians estimate that during the Red Army's offensive in Germany, Soviet soldiers committed more than 2 million rapes against German women.[27]

In the course of the occupation, Allied soldiers of all four occupying powers, including British troops, perpetrated numerous rapes and vicious sexual assaults against German women.[28] The British Zone's military courts saw a steady stream of cases, including the premeditated rape of two young women at gunpoint in Oyle, south of Bremen.[29] Those found guilty were usually handed sentences in military prisons, although there were undoubtedly some instances where senior officers protected British servicemen from prosecution. One harrowing case came to trial in 1949, and William Claude Hodson Jones was found guilty at Bow Magistrates Court of murdering Waltraut Lehman near Rotenburg.[30] In June 1945, Jones had, according to his own testimony, stopped at a cottage for a drink of water before coming across Lehman, who was picking flowers to place on a shrine dedicated to her deceased fiancé. Jones alleged that the pair had then walked into a nearby wood where they were 'intimate'. The defendant went on to claim that Waltraut Lehman had asked for chocolate and cursed him in German when he could only provide cigarettes. 'I was furious,' he said. 'Sometimes I have a temper which is very hasty and I stop at nothing.' Jones proceeded to shoot the defenceless Lehman in the back, before dragging the corpse through the wood, removing her engagement ring and concealing the body under bracken. He then attempted to clear the blood trail and cover his tracks, before returning to the cottage. Jones evaded capture by returning to England and waited for several years before deciding that he wanted 'a fresh start in life' and ought to 'get it off [his] chest' by providing a statement to the police.[31] He was sentenced to death and executed by hanging at Pentonville Prison on 28 September 1949.[32]

The final weeks of the war also saw huge and chaotic mass movements of people across the country. Bands of newly liberated forced labourers, many of whom had been relocated from Eastern Europe by the Nazis, roamed Germany in search of food, shelter, retribution or simply a route home. Over 6 million of these so-called 'Displaced Persons', or DPs, and refugees inhabited the Western zones of occupation alone.[33] In the first instance, the British placed many into 'assembly centres' in an attempt to keep them away from the front line, but their future remained uncertain.[34] Non-German DPs also received assistance in the form of food, medicine or other material help from the recently established United Nations Relief and Rehabilitation Administration. Meanwhile, hundreds of thousands of German civilians fled devastated towns and cities in panic or desperation: on 2 March, Cologne experienced its 262nd and final bombing raid of the war, prompting as many as 80,000 of the city's inhabitants to leave.[35] When Allied troops entered the city four days later, surveys of the central districts showed only 8 per cent of the pre-war population remained.[36] In the coming months, as many as 6,000 people would return to Cologne each week, a challenge for the city's new British administrators, who were already struggling to maintain adequate supplies of housing and food.

For those that remained in urban areas life was extremely difficult. In Hanover 75 per cent of the city's buildings had been destroyed and the electricity, water and sewage networks had all broken down. In the words of the British war correspondent Leonard O. Mosley, an estimated 500,000 people were inhabiting 'the ruins of this once prosperous city, and no Wild West town of the last century could compare with the lawlessness of the life they lived. It was a town of drunkenness and murder.'[37] It was not long before looting broke out with reports of masses of people fighting over the contents of a doorknob emporium; hardly a prized asset in other contexts, perhaps, but most likely some of the only consumer goods remaining in the city.[38] In the midst of this chaotic scene, the temporary American Military Governor Major G. H. Lamb strode out into the middle of the thoroughfare and fired his revolver in the air, employing his rudimentary German to disperse the crowd: '*RAUS! RAUS! RAUS!*' ('OUT! OUT! OUT!').[39] The following days saw Lamb, with the help of a rag-tag force of British prisoners of war and Dutch policemen, restore order. Yet Mosley reported that Hanover, even ten days after its capture, was 'hardly a city to which you would have taken your maiden aunt', describing it as 'a dark, fearsome, dangerous place, where you faced death or attack at every corner; a place of menace, of mysterious bangs and explosions, of furtive figures among the bomb ruins. Life, if not so lawless as before, was still rough and lusty.'[40]

In the main, however, German civilians responded to the collapse of the Third Reich with a passivity that reflected both a widespread desire for the fighting to be over and fear of what was yet to come.[41] In larger towns and cities, British military commanders sought out reliably non-Nazi former councillors or politicians to oversee the work of basic reconstruction.[42] It was obvious that establishing any semblance of order would require clearing streets of rubble and bringing back essential utilities as soon as possible. While much has been made of the *Trümmerfrauen* ('rubble women') who helped clear the streets of Germany's bombed cities, this phenomenon has recently been exposed as something of a post-war myth – more often than not it was prisoners of war who were put to work.[43]

Meanwhile, smaller towns which had escaped bomb damage, including Minden, Herford, Bünde and Lübbecke, were earmarked as potential divisional headquarters for the future Control Commission. Here, British officers began the process of requisitioning property for use as accommodation and offices. In Bad Oeynhausen, where British forces would eventually establish their main HQ, over 70 per cent of the town's population – somewhere between 6,500 and 9,000 people – were told on 4 May that they had a week to leave their homes, with all furniture to be left behind for the use of the occupiers.[44]

For British soldiers themselves, a number of technical guides and handbooks were issued including *Instructions for British Servicemen in Germany*, published by the Foreign Office.[45] Somewhat akin to a travel guide, the book includes a section of basic German phrases, a handy map, an explanation of German money and a brief assessment of the national culture: readers were told that 'beer is best', that cheap schnapps would 'take the skin off one's throat' and that German football was played 'less vigorously than in Britain', with 'charging' regarded as rough play. But behind this veneer of a holidaymaker's guide, the handbook betrayed the tough, unsentimental and distrustful outlook expected of British troops. Its foreword reminds readers to be mindful of the supposed deceitfulness and aggression of the German people, who had 'much to unlearn' and 'much to atone for'. Soldiers were warned to 'be on your guard against "propaganda" in the form of hard-luck stories' and to maintain 'constant vigilance, alertness and self-confidence'.

A short table of 'dos and don'ts' provides a useful snapshot of how the British army's top brass conceived of the Germans – and the nature of the forthcoming occupation – as the war came to a close:

Dos	Don'ts
REMEMBER you are a representative of the British Commonwealth.	DON'T sell or give away dress or equipment.
KEEP your eyes and ears open.	DON'T be sentimental. If things are tough for the Germans they have only themselves to blame. They made things much worse for the innocent people of the countries they occupied.
BE SMART and soldierly in dress and bearing.	DON'T believe German accounts of the war or the events that led up to it. The Germans got their ideas on these subjects from lying propaganda.
AVOID loose talk and loose conduct.	DON'T fall for political hard-luck stories.
BE FIRM AND FAIR in any dealings with Germans.	DON'T believe tales against our Allies or the Dominions. They are aimed at sowing ill will between us.
KEEP GERMANS AT A DISTANCE, even those with whom you have official dealings.	DON'T be taken in by surface resemblances between the Germans and ourselves.
STEER CLEAR of all disputes between German political parties.	DON'T go looking for trouble.
GO EASY on Schnaps. [sic]	
REMEMBER that in Germany 'venereal diseases strike every fourth person between the ages of 15 and 41.'	

British troops' wariness towards the German people was further intensified by the prospect of so-called *Werwolf* attacks by die-hard Nazis. In October 1944 Heinrich Himmler had called for the creation of a resistance network of Nazi fighters to engage the Allies from behind enemy lines.[46] In hindsight, it is clear that the threat posed by these 'werewolves' was inconsequential, but the very idea was enough to trigger feelings of deep unease among the Western media and Allied commanders alike. In Frank Capra's uncompromisingly Germanophobic orientation film *Your Job in Germany*, American and British troops were warned that 'just one mistake may cost you your life. Trust none of them.'[47]

As a result, 'fraternization' between Allied troops and Germans was to be 'strongly discouraged'.[48] It was the duty of the occupiers to convey to the German people that their country had been 'well and truly beaten'. Germany was to be treated 'as a defeated nation' and the occupiers were to be 'just but firm and aloof'. As British troops entered Germany, Field Marshal Montgomery sent an even more unequivocal message to the men of the 21st Army Group:

> You must keep clear of Germans – man, woman and child – unless you meet them in the course of duty. You must not walk with them or shake hands or visit their homes. You must not play games with them or share any social event with them. In short, you must not fraternize with the Germans at all.[49]

This non-fraternization rule was an embodiment of the 'hard peace' ethos that Lord Vansittart had promoted in Britain throughout the war.[50] It codified the notion that the German people were not to be trusted and should *all* be treated with suspicion.[51] In the spring of 1945, shocking revelations from the heart of Germany would only serve to strengthen this attitude.

*

On 12 April 1945, forward troops of the British 11th Armoured Division were met with an unexpected sight: a black Mercedes staff car containing two Wehrmacht colonels was driving towards them with a white flag attached to its bonnet.[52] While German resistance was ongoing in the area, these emissaries approached British lines in the hope of arranging a truce. There was, they explained, an outbreak of typhus among inmates of a nearby prison camp, located in a forest not far from Celle. The British agreed to designate some 19 square miles (49 square kilometres) around the village of Belsen as neutral territory and, three days later, took control of the exclusion zone. While Special Air Service patrols had confirmed the existence of a camp, the British knew very little else about the area now placed under their control.

In the preceding months, Soviet troops in Poland had uncovered harrowing evidence of the Third Reich's most heinous crimes when liberating numerous concentration and extermination camps including Majdanek (July 1944) and Auschwitz-Birkenau (January 1945). In early April 1945 American troops came across large numbers of emaciated inmates and piles of unburied corpses at Buchenwald concentration camp, near Weimar. But for the British public it was not until troops liberated Bergen-Belsen concentration camp that the horrors of the Holocaust were brought home to them. Bergen-Belsen, and its three satellite camps, had held tens of thousands of Jews, political prisoners, gay men, Roma, Jehovah's Witnesses and so-called 'asocials'. While it was not an extermination camp like Auschwitz, it is still estimated that over 50,000 inmates died in Bergen-Belsen from starvation and disease, among them the teenage diarist Anne Frank. When British troops first arrived on 15 April, around 60,000 emaciated men, women and children, many of whom had survived 'death marches' from camps in the east, were crowded in huts. Beside them piles of skeletal bodies lay unburied. Among the survivors, disease, including typhus, was rife and in the next few weeks around a quarter of them would die.

Dick Williams, a major in the Royal Army Service Corps, was part of the reconnaissance party that first entered Bergen-Belsen. Williams and his small team drove down a narrow lane through a forested area before reaching a German pillbox with its customary red, black and white stripes.[53] A Hungarian guard let them pass and before them they could see a large barbed-wire fence with a group of SS and Wehrmacht troops outside. Williams was greeted by the camp commandant, Josef Kramer, and assigned an SS guard to accompany him on a tour of the compound. Immediately the stench of rotting flesh filled his nostrils. Entering the main gate, he witnessed things he would never forget. In the smoky haze of burning huts bundles of what looked like rags turned out on closer inspection to be corpses. More bodies had been left hanging on the barbed wire, while others lay collapsed beside it. The dead were indistinguishable from the living, most of whom were sitting around motionlessly; others crawled or stumbled over the dusty ground. In later life, Williams could not escape memories of that tragic scene: 'I have never seen such horror in my life'.[54]

British troops stand guard at the Bergen-Belsen concentration camp as captured members of the SS are forced to transport dead bodies to a mass grave in April 1945.

In the camp that day was Agnes Lichtschein, a young Jewish girl who had grown up in Bratislava before moving to Hungary.[55] In October 1944 she was deported to Dachau concentration camp in Upper Bavaria before being forcibly marched to Bergen-Belsen the following spring. Before the British arrived, the twelve-year-old had collapsed, weak from lack of basic sustenance and with a serious leg wound after a Nazi guard had shot her. It was only when she was moved onto a heap of corpses that Agnes regained consciousness and managed to attract the attention of a passing British soldier. At some point later she woke up confused and scared on a hospital bed surrounded by German nurses and British doctors. In the following weeks she would follow a strict diet: given her physical deterioration any sudden return to normal rations was potentially fatal. Her British doctors, who she remembers as kindly and affectionate towards her, would not allow her a mirror, fearful that the sight of her own corpse-like body would be too distressing. Mercifully, Agnes survived.

There was a sense of urgency among those who witnessed these events first-hand to prove their authenticity, especially after many of the tales of wartime atrocities that had emerged during the First World War were later discredited.[56] Jean McFarlane, who had recently arrived at Bergen-Belsen as a member of the British Red Cross, wrote to her mother back in Tunbridge Wells: 'I hope you'll believe me there's no exaggeration in what I have to say, nor is there any tall story or faked photographs in any of your papers. German Concentration Camps are hell.'[57] In the search for the truth, a growing public appetite called for more and more details of the 'horror camps'. Throughout April and May countless newspaper reports, radio broadcasts, newsreels and photographs flooded back to Britain. These first public confrontations with Nazi genocide were a hugely significant moment: the greatest mass murder in history was also a media event.[58] On 17 April, the BBC's Richard Dimbleby broadcast a report from the camp that would shape many British attitudes towards Germany and the forthcoming occupation:

I find it hard to describe adequately the horrible things that I've seen and heard but here unadorned are the facts... I wish with all my heart that everyone fighting in this war – and above all those whose duty it is to direct the war from Britain and America – could have come with me through the barbed-wire fence that leads to the inner compound of the camp. Outside it had been the lucky prisoners – the men and women who had only just arrived at Belsen before we captured it. But beyond the barrier was a whirling cloud of dust, the dust of thousands of slowly moving people, laden in itself with the deadly typhus germ. And with the dust was a smell, sickly and thick, the smell of death and decay of corruption and filth. I passed through the barrier and found myself in the world of a nightmare.[59]

In May the *Daily Express* opened a free public exhibition entitled 'The Horror Camps' on London's Regent Street, attracting long queues of those who wanted to see evidence of the Nazi crimes for themselves.[60] The Ministry of Information even commissioned a documentary film about the camps in order to explain the evils of Nazism to German, British and American viewers.[61] A distinguished team of expert filmmakers including Alfred Hitchcock and Sidney Bernstein was assembled, before delays meant the film was eventually shelved.[62]

While much of this media reportage did a good job documenting the horrors of the camps, it often obscured the victims. At the time there was little comprehension of the genocidal anti-Semitism that had underpinned what we now know as the Holocaust and almost no recognition that many of those killed – whether Jews, political prisoners or otherwise – were themselves German. Rather, the revelations of the camps, above all Bergen-Belsen, only amplified popular anti-German sentiment in Britain, building support for a 'hard peace'.[63] It was news that reinforced a now well-established *Feindbild* ('image of the enemy'), a black-and-white, 'us versus them' portrayal whereby the entire German population, as the savage perpetrators of these atrocities, stood in contrast to the virtuous British liberators.[64] This interpretation was actively encouraged by the British government's Psychological Warfare Executive, who recommended emphasizing cases of terror, persecution and tyranny as being 'committed in the name of the whole German people'.[65]

In the House of Lords, Vansittart was quick to assert that the German people, though now allegedly feigning ignorance, were willing executioners.[66] The revelations seemed to many to vindicate *Black Record*'s thesis and Vansittart quickly incorporated these crimes into his narrative of Germany's long history of barbarity.[67] There was, he declared, only one conclusion to be drawn: 'every single German throughout Germany is responsible'.[68] In April these views were broadcast in a *British Movietone News* newsreel, in which Vansittart told his interviewer, Leslie Mitchell, that he was not surprised at the revelations because of the 'deep underlying streak of cruelty' in a 'perfectly horrifying number of Germans'.[69]

*

The events of spring 1945 would have a momentous impact upon the eventual shape of the post-war peace. It was in these disorderly days that the occupation of Germany began in earnest, even if the formalities of the inter-Allied administration were yet to be agreed. As the lid lifted on the ruins of the Third Reich, the complexities of the task at hand became apparent. The horrendous evidence of the Holocaust brought into stark focus questions of recrimination, complicity and guilt that the occupiers would now be required to consider. But first, British military administrators were compelled to confront the seemingly incomprehensible jumble of practical challenges – from milking cows to mending drainpipes. In this, the Civil Affairs Division proved their worth, but there would be sterner tests to come. As BBC reporter Patrick Gordon Walker noted, 'military government is tackling its immediate problems with vigour and considerable success. But soon problems must arise that are bigger than the scale of a town or a group of villages.'[70]

The end of the war was drawing close: in the east, the Red Army was preparing for the final attack on Berlin and, on 25 April, Soviet and American soldiers greeted one another near Torgau on the river Elbe.[71] American forces were racing to capture Hitler's Eagle's Nest near the town of Berchtesgaden in Bavaria. Meanwhile, the British 7th Armoured Division advanced into the outskirts of Hamburg, the last site of Nazi resistance in northern Germany. There, the 1st Parachute Army – a motley collection of SS men, paratroopers, Volkssturm, Wehrmacht, sailors, policemen, firemen and Hitler Youth – attempted to mount a hopeless final stand under the command of Generalmajor Alwin Wolz.

On 30 April, shortly after midnight, Adolf Hitler committed suicide in Berlin and his successor as president of the German Reich, Grand Admiral Karl Dönitz, soon instructed Wolz to

Field Marshal Bernard Montgomery (left) receives a delegation of surrendering German officers at Lüneburg Heath, south of Hamburg, in May 1945.

surrender Hamburg to the British forces massed at the edge of the city. For Ilya Suster, an interpreter with the 131st Armoured Brigade of the 'Desert Rats', it was a particularly fitting way for the war to come to a close. The son of a Latvian businessman, Suster had lived in Hamburg in the 1930s before leaving for Britain. Now, on 2 May 1945, he returned in a British army uniform and was quickly ushered to Brigadier John Spurling's caravan. Inside, the moustachioed Spurling, seated at a table opposite a nervous-looking Alwin Wolz, beckoned Suster to an empty chair.[72] Thus it was that he helped to negotiate the British takeover of a city he had once called home. Spurling turned to his small cocktail cabinet, pulled out a bottle of whisky and poured all three men a glass. Two days later, at Lüneburg Heath, Field Marshal Montgomery would accept the unconditional military surrender of all remaining German forces in the area. Finally, on 8 May, the war in Europe was over.

6

Victors and Vanquished

Victory in Europe Day is remembered, in the popular imagination, as a moment of rhapsodic unity across Britain, when huge crowds were flocking to Buckingham Palace and Trafalgar Square to dance the conga, sing patriotic songs and wave Union Jacks. There, people from all walks of life – bus drivers, councillors, housewives, poets, seamstresses, the nineteen-year-old Princess Elizabeth – came together to celebrate the end of a long and devastating war, even if the conflict against Japan was not yet over. But our memory of that day is dominated by events in London's West End; in a starkly divided country, the reality was much more complicated.

It was certainly no ordinary Tuesday. It had been designated a national holiday: that morning, crowds assembled in most large cities and towns, even if wet weather put a hold on proceedings across much of northern England and Scotland.[1] Elsewhere, in smaller towns and villages, impromptu street parties were held, with celebratory red, white and blue bunting made available for purchase without the need for precious ration coupons. In Cambridge the residents of Gwydir Street changed into their Sunday best and arranged rows of tables and chairs in the middle of the road.[2] At the side of a now defunct air raid shelter, men and women of all ages sat together to eat and drink whatever they could lay their hands on – sandwiches, jelly, bottles of beer from the nearby Dewdrop Inn. It was a scene repeated across the country.

But for others, 8 May 1945 was relatively uneventful. In West London Cecil Beaton commented that Kensington was 'as quiet as Sunday' with 'no general feeling of rejoicing'.[3] Many made the BBC's Home Service the focal point of their day. It carried Winston Churchill's short speech outside 10 Downing Street at 3 p.m., declaring that 'the evil-doers now lie prostrate before us' and offering a rallying call of 'Advance Britannia!' to the many millions who listened over the radio and loudspeakers.[4] Then at 3:20 p.m. almost a third of the population listened to Bells and Victory Celebrations, a vivid medley of church bells, songs and cheering crowds recorded at numerous locations across the country. Later, a Tribute to the King was followed by George VI's longest ever broadcast.[5] In a Chelsea pub, patrons who had been 'waiting all this time for something symbolic' rose for the national anthem following the king's speech – all except for twin brothers, both committed Marxists, who refused.[6] Here, as in many pubs across the country, people enjoyed a drink or three; by the evening, with beer stocks depleted, the only tipple left was gin.

That night all over the country small crowds assembled in local recreation grounds and parks as bonfires were lit, although these gatherings often lacked the exuberant atmosphere of the street parties taking place in central London. In the Cheshire town of Wilmslow, Raymond Streat attended a Boy Scouts' bonfire and remarked upon the unusual sombreness of proceedings: 'what curious people are we English? There was no cheering or rowdying. About two thousand folk stood there silently watching flames lighting up the dark skies… one or two attempts to launch a song died away.'[7] In fact, numerous contemporary reports note the relatively low-key atmosphere of VE Day: after years of fighting, and with a great deal of uncertainty about the future, people were perhaps wary of overdoing things.[8] As the writer Denton Welch noted, 'there were awful thoughts and anxieties in the air – the breaking of something – the splitting apart of an atmosphere that had surrounded us for six years'.[9]

Where more ebullient celebrations had broken out, they often had belligerent undertones. That morning, the *Daily Express* was one of several national and local newspapers to proclaim in some way or another the collective guilt of the entire German people for the war.[10] In thousands of towns and villages effigies of Hitler, Goebbels and other Nazi leaders were ceremonially burnt atop bonfires.[11] In the Hampshire town of Andover, a swastika flag was pinned outside a shop on the High Street to be kicked and spat at by passers-by before being torn to shreds. Meanwhile in a Coventry suburb two men appointed themselves 'mayor' and 'mayoress', the latter described as the 'fattest' and 'jolliest' man on the street, and conducted an elaborate mock funeral for Hitler to the cheers of onlookers.[12] For a substantial proportion of the British population, the end of the war in Europe had not dampened the desire for vengeance.

Such feelings certainly weren't unanimous: a VE Day controversy that played out within the Church of England encapsulates the extent to which the country remained divided on the issue of the so-called 'German Problem'. At this time, a significant proportion of the British public were regular churchgoers and thanksgiving services were an important part of the day's festivities. In preparation, the new archbishop of Canterbury, Geoffrey Fisher, had circulated forms of service for the day which emphasized a spirit of forgiveness and called for reconciliation with Germany.[13] At Westminster Abbey, where 'thanksgiving for victory' services were conducted every hour from 9 a.m. to 10 p.m., more than 25,000 worshippers attended.[14] When members of the congregation were invited to pray, they heard words adapted from President Abraham Lincoln's second inaugural address of 1865, in which he had offered a path towards Reconstruction in the aftermath of the US Civil War:

> Grant, O merciful God, that with malice toward none, with charity to all, with firmness in the right as thou givest us to see the right, we may strive to finish the task which thou hast appointed us; to bind up the nation's wounds; to care for him who shall have borne the battle, and for his widow and his orphan; to do all which may achieve and cherish a just and lasting peace among ourselves and with all nations; through Jesus Christ our Lord. Amen.[15]

But the conciliatory proclamations of the archbishop of Canterbury were not well received in every parish: the vicar of Mapledurham in Oxfordshire, Dr Ernest L. Macassey, told the press 'there is nothing manly or British about them. They are in the tone of the whining mendicant, the general trend is "let us be kind to the Germans".'[16] Instead, the people of Mapledurham – alongside many others who attended Anglican services across Britain that day – were greeted with impassioned orations on the glorious defeat of their ungodly enemy.

The notion that Britain was either united or magnanimous in victory is a convenient myth: across the country, people had radically different experiences of 8 May, ranging from ambivalence to high-spirited joy to righteous anger. It was symptomatic of an even greater question that now lay at the heart of British society: what exactly had the war been fought for?

*

In Germany itself on the morning of VE Day, Field Marshal Montgomery stepped out of his mobile headquarters in Lower Saxony to address the throng of British troops who had massed outside. Now the fighting was finally over, celebrations were breaking out spontaneously among the crowd. Yet among this atmosphere of revelry Monty did not dwell upon the glory of having overcome Hitler's war machine. Rather, his short sombre speech warned of the challenges yet to come: 'we have won the German war. Let us now win the peace'.[17]

A ceasefire on the western front had been in place since 5 May, when Karl Dönitz, as the newly installed head of state, had made agreements with British and American commanders at Lüneburg Heath and Haar respectively. The following day, representatives of the German High Command met with British, American, French and Soviet officials at Reims in France. Inside a redbrick schoolhouse, formerly the Collège Moderne et Technique de Reims but now functioning as Supreme Headquarters Allied Expeditionary Force (SHAEF), the unconditional surrender of German armed forces was signed at 2:41 a.m. and would take effect at 11 p.m. on 8 May.

There was a slight problem, however. While General Eisenhower, as the Supreme Allied Commander, had consulted with chief of the Soviet general staff Aleksei Antonov on the final surrender terms, at the time of the signing there had been no final confirmation from Moscow. Six hours later the Soviet leadership communicated their rejection of the Reims surrender, suggesting it had been altered from earlier texts. It was a pretext for the organization of another, more grandiose surrender in Germany itself – one where the Soviets would take centre stage.[18] On the evening of 8 May the leading commanders of the Allied armies assembled once more, this time inside a former Wehrmacht officer's mess in the Karlshorst district of Berlin, to finally, officially, accept the German surrender. But even this wasn't without hiccups: while all parties agreed with the few minor Soviet amendments to the Reims document, there was some dissension over exactly who should sign the agreement. After numerous redrafts, all of which had to be translated and retyped, the unconditional surrender of Germany's armed forces was actually signed in the early hours of 9 May.[19]

By then, celebrations among the British forces in Europe were in full swing. Daphne Smith was in Belgium, serving with the Auxiliary Territorial Service (the ATS, the women's branch of the British army). A native of Upper Norwood in London, she had required the consent of her parents when she enlisted at the age of nineteen to serve as a secretary for the 21st Army Group, including in Normandy shortly after D-Day. In the following months Smith had been part of the British advance across France and the Low Countries and now, based in Brussels, she had heard rumours all week that the surrender was imminent. But it was only on 7 May that flags began to be flown outside houses.[20] Later that day, at around 10:45 p.m., she wrote excitedly to her family back in Britain: 'the last all clear has just sounded. The lights are going up all over town – all over Europe – buildings are floodlit, flares are being let off, everybody seems a bit dazed.'[21]

Those on the front lines found their own ways to celebrate. Norman Skinner was enjoying a glorious sunny day on Lüneburg Heath when the news came through. 'I do not think any of us could really believe that the war was really over,' he remembered. 'None of us in our camp could settle, we were on cloud nine, we had come through all these years of war and were alive to see this wonderful day. No words can really express just how we felt.'[22] That evening, most of Skinner's unit celebrated on a small farm near their camp, enjoying a seemingly inexhaustible supply of alcohol while dancing and singing around a bonfire alongside a group of Polish displaced persons.

Charles Chester, a member of the 3rd Independent Machine Gun Company, was just north of Hamburg when the surrender was announced and he proceeded, with the help of his men, on a final strategic manoeuvre: taking over the local pub. As soon as they had successfully tapped the beer barrels, the celebrations began, giving them their first – and certainly not their last – taste of German beer.[23] Chester, a veteran of the North African campaign, D-Day and the Allied advance across the Low Countries, took himself outside, glass of beer in hand, and shot his pistol into the air. Above him, the night sky was illuminated with trails of bright lights, as nearby units fired tracer bullets in celebration.

But, as in Britain, not everyone in Europe was feeling quite so euphoric. Peter William Johnson, born Wolfgang Josephs, was a German Jew who had fled to Britain in the 1930s before being classified as an enemy alien, interned, and later transported to an internment camp in Australia.[24] In 1941 he had volunteered to join the Pioneer Corps and, in 1944, set sail for Europe. On VE Day, Johnson was sitting the final examination of his interpreters' course in Brussels, prior to joining the British army of occupation.[25] He took the rest of the day off but did little in the way of celebrating. Johnson recalled that he and his fellow trainee interpreters 'were not big boozers, we were not English'.

Likewise, Jean McFarlane was in no mood to rejoice: she was still working with the British Red Cross in the hospital of Bergen-Belsen, helping to nurse desperately weak survivors from the camp. There could be no break in her routine, even if there was a slight pause at 6 p.m. on 9 May as a victory parade went by. McFarlane complained in her journal that the ceremonial gun salute was wholly inappropriate, considering the seriously ill and traumatized people who were in attendance.[26] That evening, she attended a small gathering in the mess alongside other British Red Cross personnel and the hundred or so medical students who had recently arrived from London. McFarlane noticed that these young volunteers, tasked with incredibly harrowing work of overseeing the 'human laundry' – namely, a set of tables where surviving inmates were individually washed, shaved and sprayed with pesticide – were very keen to drink 'all they could lay their hands on' but had very little desire 'to make whoopee'.

Peter Wayne was in Minden on VE Day acting as an interpreter for hastily established military government courts. It was his birthday: twenty-five years earlier he had been born in Berlin to a Jewish German family as Hans Dieter Wolff, before emigrating to Britain in the 1930s and changing his name in honour of his favourite film star, John Wayne.[27] While patrolling the area with a Scottish corporal that morning, he saw notices explaining that any German found with a weapon would be sentenced to death.[28] Only a few hours later, driving in a jeep, he heard a bullet whizz past his ear. Wayne and his driver jumped out, ran into a nearby ditch and opened fire on the cherry tree where the shot had emanated from. Within seconds, a young woman holding a rifle with its barrel sawn off jumped down and promptly surrendered. She was taken to Wayne's colonel and broke down when threatened with execution; in the end they let her go. Later the same day, in Barkhausen, he was sitting inside the Hotel Kaiserhof, now functioning as a British HQ, when he heard the distinctive sound of tank tracks moving along cobbled streets. A few minutes later he was called outside and before him stood eight pristine Tiger tanks. A tall major in his grey leather coat jumped out and offered his dagger and pistol as a token of their surrender. Realizing it was impractical to accommodate these prisoners of war – not to mention their tanks – Wayne sent them on their way: 'I'm sorry, the hotel has no vacancies.'

*

The end of the fighting did little to alleviate the most pressing concern of most British service personnel in the summer of 1945: soldiers' thoughts inevitably turned to home, as they wondered exactly how long it would be until they could get back to 'civvy street'. Twenty-year-old Daphne Smith was worried that the government would repeat the mistakes of the last war, and feared it would be eighteen months or more before her demobilization from the forces.[29] At least, she consoled herself, her time in Germany was likely to help her understand first-hand the problems that would confront her generation during the next decade.[30] For many, however, this was a time of boredom: veterans of the fighting felt constrained living in impromptu bases and faced an interminable wait to see loved ones. John William Booth, who had been with the 'Desert Rats' since 1940, was distraught when a Battalion Order stated that he was unlikely to be demobilized before March 1946. 'I ask you, how can one cope with such carryings on?', he wrote in a letter to his parents back home in Sheffield.[31] Likewise, Captain Henry Hughes of the Royal Regiment of Artillery was left 'very depressed' at the news that all officers in his unit would have their release deferred – not least because he had very little to do.[32]

As soldiers counted down the days until their discharge from the forces, they busied themselves with whatever entertainment could be found: cinema trips, football games, sports days and dances. But the combination of monotony, the psychological scars of war and the availability of drink resulted in an inevitable decline of army discipline. For many of the thousands of British soldiers awaiting a ticket home, Germany quickly became a playground of excess.

As for the country itself, the peace only intensified the difficulties facing the German people, as well as the Allied armies in their new role as occupiers. In particular, the vast scale of the destruction meted out to towns and cities had now become clear. It wasn't much of an exaggeration when Field Marshal Montgomery reported that Germany was 'a country that has been completely destroyed'.[33] In the area under British control, which contained some of the most heavily industrialized and thickly populated areas of the entire country, the level of damage was unparalleled. In the words of the poet and essayist Stephen Spender, it had created 'corpse-towns', a 'shape created by our century as the Gothic cathedral is the shape created by the Middle Ages'.[34] In Cologne, where over 60 per cent of the city had been wrecked, British army interpreter William Peters noticed how 'people talk in low voices as if they are afraid to wake the dead below the debris. This is a cemetery and one does not make any noise in a cemetery!'[35]

Back in Britain the next year saw the release of films, photographs and newsreels instilling the notion that Germany had been thoroughly and perhaps irretrievably beaten during the course of the war. The *British Movietone News* film *Berlin – Carcass City* is a prime example, describing Germany's capital as 'more or less dead', a 'corpse' which stood as a 'crestfallen memorial of the Hohenzollerns'.[36] The government's Crown Film Unit released their first cinematic portrayal of Germany under occupation, *A Defeated People*. This eighteen-minute-long documentary film was originally commissioned in late summer of 1945 and directed by Humphrey Jennings. He was the outstanding auteur of the Documentary Film Movement, a successful and pioneering group of British filmmakers active since the 1930s. He had a reputation as an expert filmmaker, and his cinematic articulations of a heroic but reserved patriotism had widespread appeal.[37] Jennings's oeuvre includes iconic films such as *London Can Take It* and *Fires Were Started*, now recognized as some of the key works in creating the mythic image of the London Blitz.[38] With images demonstrating the country's overwhelming physical destruction, *A Defeated People* left viewers in no doubt about the unconditional defeat of Germany.

But the ruined towns and cities of Germany were merely the most obvious feature of a nation in almost complete disarray. The war had devastated much of the continent's agricultural production and trade infrastructure, which led to a worldwide food shortage.[39] The provision of food became, as one member of the British occupation staff remarked, 'almost as international a means of understanding between the nations as music and the

British soldiers march past the Siegessäule in Berlin's Tiergarten.

arts'.[40] For the people of Europe, victors and vanquished, victims and perpetrators, hunger of varying degrees was a fact of life.

The area under British control was particularly vulnerable. It was almost impossible to run an arbitrarily delimited geographic area historically dependent on food imports, dominated by the heavy industry of the Ruhr and now severely impaired by months of British and American bombing raids, as a viable economy.

Communication lines, infrastructure and above all housing, of which as much as 45 per cent had been destroyed, were in a sorry state.[41] For the German people, finding just the basic necessities – shelter, food and fuel for fires – soon defined the rhythm of everyday life. In November 1945 the writer Hans-Erich Nossack wrote to a friend to describe his daily routine:

> Our day begins at 5:30 a.m., when we are woken up by our neighbours who do not need to get up at this hour but do it anyway just for the heck of it. From 8 a.m. to 3 p.m. I suffer the office – all transport stops until 3 – but then I am so frozen that I can hardly walk, the more so because I can only take two slices of dry bread in to work. And then a hard battle for the tube [U-Bahn underground railway] begins. In the meantime, my wife has been giving lessons in the morning, then it takes her an hour rushing off at noon to get our food from the soup kitchen which we depend on because of the lack of gas, electricity and cooking facilities, although the most important food coupons are used up this way; and then the most urgent errands are done. Around 3 p.m. she heats up our food on the little stove, so the room becomes slightly warmer. After the meal, I always have some DIY job to do, or logs to split etc. Between 5 p.m. and 6 p.m. I try to sleep, to draw a curtain on the day so far and to compensate for the missing calories at the same time. Later we take something reminiscent of tea and a little snack, and then, if there isn't one of the occasional visits arranged, we sit facing each other working over a 15-Watt lightbulb. At ten, the sirens scream three times, at a quarter past twice and at half past ten once; then, as they say here, there is a 'curfew', i.e. it is forbidden to go out. Most often I myself will sit up until one, wrapped in blankets, then I crawl into bed frozen. For a man who has the habit of walking up and down when doing creative work, these blankets are an irksome problem. There you have an average life. Different lives are possible.[42]

These arduous conditions were further exacerbated by the arrival of some 3 million newly released German prisoners of war – all of whom required food and accommodation. Those who were discharged from captivity faced no easy task in returning to their own loved ones across Germany: the railway network had been heavily bombed, causing a huge backlog in passenger transports, while the telephone and postal services had also collapsed.[43] Many families faced weeks, months or even years of anxiety, hoping against hope that a son, husband, brother or father would return alive. A report in the *Marburger Presse* from September 1945 gives a sense of the mass dislocation experienced across the country:

On the roads and in the refugee camps, every single day, one encounters thousands of refugees and released soldiers, who have been wandering from town to town for weeks and months to look for their relatives. Even the fact that many towns have taken action against the population influx from outside, and no longer give any food coupons to non-entitled incomers, is not enough to deter the searchers who, in their distress, often act without deliberation in order to achieve their goal in one way or another.[44]

While the job of reuniting families in Germany was entrusted to the Red Cross, in many instances worried families spent their last money on private tracing services or simply took it upon themselves to search for their missing relatives. Noticeboards sprung up in towns and cities across Germany where pictures and identifying details of missing persons were pinned up in desperation. In some cases, returning POWs came back to discover their own family had been killed during the war or that their wife or girlfriend had found a new partner.[45] By 1948 it was estimated that as many as 2 million *Heimkehrer* ('homecomers') across the three Western zones actually had no home to return to.

Furthermore, large numbers of refugees from eastern Germany migrated to the towns and cities now under British control in the hope of evading the much-feared Soviet troops.[46] At the same time, more and more 'Displaced Persons' – concentration camp survivors, slave labourers and others – scoured the countryside, seizing foodstuffs and valuables from farmhouses or taking vengeance against their former oppressors, whether they be suspected Nazis, factory owners, farmers or simply anyone German.[47]

It was a dangerous and unstable situation. The end of the Third Reich had seen the bureaucratic structures and institutions of the German state collapse. British Civil Affairs detachments, only ever envisaged as stopgaps, were now confronting problems that even the most pessimistic of planners had not foreseen and which went far beyond their capabilities as administrators. It was increasingly clear to those on the ground in Germany that things needed to change – and fast. As the writer and historian A. G. Dickens, then serving with the military government in Lübeck,* wrote, the British could 'scarcely accept as a permanent basis of life this State of Nature, where the life of man remains, in Hobbes's famous phrase, "solitary, poor, nasty, brutish and short"'.[48]

At the beginning of April 1945 advance units of the Control Commission for Germany (British Element) had been put on standby to move at a week's notice.[49] The Control Commission was the civilian-led administration that would spearhead the British occupation, intended to take over from the Civil Affairs Division when the fighting was over as part of a transition to civilian oversight of affairs in Germany.[50] This body would be under the overall command of the Allied Control Council, in which British, American, Soviet and French commanders-in-chief would work towards the common goals of the post-war occupation. But by mid-May the Control Council was yet to be established and there remained little clarity as regards the precise character of Allied rule, the day-to-day work of the occupiers and the eventual path to German democracy. There were also problems with the practical challenges of the transition

---

* Dickens's account of his experiences in post-war Germany, *Lübeck Diary*, was published in 1947. He would later establish himself as a distinguished expert on the history of the Reformation in England and Germany.

from military government to Control Commission – not least the difficulties of finding four-way agreement on issues such as access to Berlin.[51]

On 16 May an exasperated General Eisenhower, Supreme Commander of the Allied Expeditionary Force, felt compelled to lobby his political superiors, and called on Churchill's war cabinet to hasten the transition from temporary military authority to full-scale occupation administration.[52] The prime minister appreciated the gravity of the situation, fearing that Europe 'might well be faced with Buchenwald conditions on a vast scale'.[53] At the same time, he seemingly lacked any detailed understanding of the most up-to-date plans for post-war Europe, and proclaimed that the control of Germany should remain the responsibility of the army until 'some other body' was in a position to take over. It was not until 5 June 1945, with the signing of the Berlin Declaration, that the British, American, Soviet and French governments officially declared their supreme authority over German territory and paved the way for the occupation to begin in earnest.

In the following weeks, the Allied armies retreated from the lines of contact established at the end of the fighting and occupied their separate zones: the British in the north-west, the Americans in the south, the French in the south-west and the Soviets in the east.* At the same time, scores of British personnel began to enter Germany in preparation for the transition from military to civil control. Daphne Smith was one of the many thousands of British personnel waiting to move into the Zone. In early June, she was finally told that her unit would imminently be swapping the 'gay city' of Brussels for a 'barbed wire encampment in enemy country'.[54] 'I think we are going to be glad of that barbed wire', Smith wrote to her parents, 'to keep *all* the wolves – were or otherwise – out'.

---

* Smaller contingents from other Allied nations also took part in the occupation. From November 1945, Luxembourgish troops took over part of the French Zone, while in April 1946 the Belgian Occupation Army were handed responsibility for an area around Cologne in the south of the British Zone. The Independent Norwegian Brigade Group in Germany and the Polish 1st Armoured Division also served in the British Zone between 1945 and 1949.

Part Two

WINNING
THE PEACE

7

Potsdam

On the final day of June 1945 Joan Bright arrived in Berlin, one of the first Britons to see the German capital since the end of the war.[1] In the coming years, most Anglophone visitors would rush to view the city's famous monuments: the Tiergarten, the burnt-out shell of the Reichstag, or the Brandenburg Gate, newly adorned on its westward side with a literal sign of the times: 'You Are Now Leaving The British Sector'. But Joan Bright, tasked with an important if unusual mission, had little time for sightseeing. As a trusted assistant of Prime Minister Winston Churchill, she was sent on ahead at all the major conferences of the war to make sure everything was shipshape. It was the perfect job for an organized, highly professional and charismatic person: at one time she had dated Ian Fleming, and the affable Miss Bright is said to have been his inspiration for Miss Moneypenny.[2] There was perhaps no greater stage for her many skills than July 1945: the 'Big Three' were set to meet for the first time since VE Day and iron out the precise principles, aims and aspirations of Allied rule in Germany. Nothing could be left to chance.

On this occasion, the Soviets had chosen a former seat of the German royal family, the Cecilienhof Palace in Potsdam, as the venue. It was a grandiose setting which, remarkably enough, had survived the war largely intact, although most of the interior decoration had been put into storage and subsequently lost to fire. To mitigate this shortcoming, local detachments of Soviet soldiers had been busy scouring nearby residences for suitable furnishings. The palace gradually filled up with an assortment of ornate antique armchairs and an incongruous collection of humdrum paintings ranging from seascapes to village street scenes. It made for an unusual palatial interior design scheme, but the Cecilienhof itself was a lesson in mismatched styles: completed in 1917 for Crown Prince Wilhelm, it had been modelled on an English Tudor manor house, featuring exposed beams but also, puzzlingly enough, neo-Gothic spires. According to one British official who attended the conference, it looked like 'a stockbroker's idea of paradise'.[3] A final touch of Soviet flair was added to this peculiar spectacle: a star of red begonias now took pride of place in the palace's courtyard.

Upon her arrival at Cecilienhof, Joan Bright quickly got to work among the swarms of mosquitoes that plagued the area. Over the next few days, she accomplished all manner of things, from designating access to the laundry facilities to fitting out the British rooms. A partial list of the odd requests sent back to London tells its own story: bell transformers, 230 volts; bells; bell wire; wood screws, 1 × 6 inches; 2,000 conference passes; 100 Union Jack flags for cars; 60 dustpans, brushes and brooms; 200 house flannels; and 200 cotton sheets.[4] It was hard graft but also provided a chance for Joan to catch up with friends and colleagues from the British and American delegations: 'absolutely *everyone* was there', she recalled; it was 'the last great beano of the war'.

When, at long last, everything was ready for the dignitaries, Joan and her friend Betty Gibbs were taken out for a celebratory tea by the Soviet General Karanadze and his team of assistants. The 'usual vodka marathon' ensued before the two women absconded in a British army staff car: 'We told the driver to drive anywhere, while we sat by open windows and tried to get the fumes of drink and cigarette smoke out of our system'.[5] As they well knew, in just a few hours the leaders of the 'Grand Alliance' would be arriving in Berlin to finalize plans for the post-war world – it was no time to be feeling the effects of their unplanned revelry.

*

In the lead-up to the Potsdam Conference the 'Big Three' underwent one substantial change, as President Harry S. Truman took the place of Franklin D. Roosevelt, who had died on 12 April after several years of failing health. Moreover, with the war against Japan ongoing, the Americans announced during the meeting that they had successfully tested a new atomic superweapon. It was a disclosure that ratcheted up already heightened inter-Allied tensions. A week after the conference at Potsdam, atomic bombs would be dropped on the cities of Hiroshima and Nagasaki, killing as many as 200,000 civilians and prompting the Japanese surrender.*

Truman, still in the first 100 days of his presidency, stayed in a lakeside villa at 2 Kaiserstraße, dubbed the 'Berlin White House', which, according to an official report, 'was nicely furnished during our stay but, like most European homes, the bathroom and bathing facilities were wholly inadequate'.[6] The president, it turned out, had to share a bathroom with his chief of staff, Admiral Leahy.[7] In the run-up to discussions, Truman met Churchill for the first time, reflecting in his diary upon 'a most charming and very clever person – meaning clever in the English not the Kentucky sense... I am sure we can get along if he doesn't give me too much soft soap.' Britain's prime minister was, however, in a less sanguine mood. He had spent the previous week on a painting holiday in the south of France, refusing to look at briefings or even respond to telegrams from London.[8] The British public – along with their wartime leader – were impatiently awaiting the result of the general election of 5 July; the complex task of counting the ballots of British soldiers across the world led to a nervous three-week wait. 'I'm very depressed', Churchill told his doctor. 'I don't want to do anything. I have no energy. I wonder if it will come back.'[9]

---

* In the aftermath of the war, the Allies also instigated a military occupation in Japan. While this was led by US forces, it also included the British Commonwealth Occupation Force, a 40,000-strong contingent of British, Australian, Indian and New Zealand troops.

The conference at Potsdam did little to lift his spirits: the attendees could not help but recognize the grand significance of their task, imbued with a sense that this was a second and perhaps final chance to secure a sustainable peace in Europe. The memory of the failures at Versailles in 1919 hung heavy.[10] Then, as negotiations got underway, the new American president and his Soviet counterpart once again dominated proceedings.[11] It was abundantly clear that Britain, which had turned from the world's greatest creditor into its greatest debtor during the war, could not contest the authority of the two superpowers.[12] Things went from bad to worse when, on 22 July, a storm swept through the district of Babelsberg where the palace was located; outside Churchill's lakeside villa an uprooted lime tree damaged a water pipe. According to Alexander Cadogan, who had replaced Vansittart as permanent under-secretary at the Foreign Office, the prime minister was 'very annoyed at not being able to have a bath'.[13] Four days later, during a mid-conference break, Churchill returned home to learn of his unexpected and overwhelming electoral defeat at the hands of Clement Attlee's Labour Party.

Britain's new prime minister was not the revolutionary figure many assume: when the *Daily Mail* insisted on drawing comparisons between Attlee and Lenin, it was well wide of the mark.[14] Winston Churchill also got it fundamentally wrong when he reputedly once described Attlee as 'a modest man with much to be modest about'. There's no doubting that Attlee was rather unassuming in appearance, and in his rhetoric he often came across as shy, taciturn and even cautious – unlike his predecessor, Attlee was certainly no great orator. But it was this reserve that led many of his political opponents, including Churchill, to underestimate Attlee time and time again. Here was a man of great intellectual and political ability, widely regarded as trustworthy and respected across the political fault lines – even among those who did not share his socialist convictions. Britain's most radical prime minister to date was, according to the historian R. J. Cruikshank, 'a revolutionary buttoned up inside a cricket blazer'.[15]

Attlee's foreign secretary Ernest Bevin was a very different man from Britain's new prime minister. As Attlee himself once said of his great political ally: 'if you've got a good dog, you don't bark yourself'.[16] While Attlee had received a traditional establishment education at Haileybury College and University College, Oxford, before starting work as a barrister, Bevin was a man of the working class through and through. As a labourer in his native Somerset the physically imposing Bevin had emerged as a leading figure in the trade union movement and, subsequently, the Labour Party. He never lost his thick West Country accent nor his distaste for the Germans: in 1947 he famously said to Brian Robertson, then military governor of the British Zone, 'I tries hard Brian, but I hates them'.[17] Bevin could be obstinate, he was a fierce opponent at the negotiating table and, most crucially, he had a sharp-eyed sense of Britain's place in the post-war world.[18]

The shock election result that brought these two men to power would have major repercussions in both Britain and Germany. 'It's such a lovely smack in the eye for so many smug capitalists of all classes,' wrote an ecstatic Daphne Smith to her mother back in England.[19] It was the first time she had voted in an election and, like so many of her compatriots, Smith had demanded radical progressive change after all the sacrifices of wartime. Labour's victory signalled the beginning of the 'post-war consensus' in domestic politics, ushering in the creation of the National Health Service, the nationalization of key industries and a major expansion of the welfare state. The new administration's foreign policy was less radical, however, and the Labour victory did little to alter official thinking about the future of Germany in the summer of 1945. Attlee was a long-standing advocate of a hard-line peace settlement: he had, after all, been at the forefront of British planning for post-war Europe, and the first firm commitment of the Allied powers to a military occupation was generally known as the 'Attlee plan'. Over the next few years, the new prime minister and his forthright foreign secretary would inevitably play a significant role in shaping the post-war peace.

The general election result had one immediate consequence: the British delegation at Potsdam had to accommodate a change of leadership in the middle of this all-important conference. Bevin and Attlee had been in attendance at Potsdam prior to the election results, waiting in the background on the off-chance that they might end up winning.

Now, on Saturday, 28 July, they returned to Berlin as Britain's leading representatives. At their first plenary session Bevin instructed his Russian interpreter to explain that 'in the Labour Party we call a spade a spade'.[20] It was fighting talk, but in reality Britain's new leaders had little room for manoeuvre. For a start, the pair's arrival was hardly greeted with universal acclaim. In the view of certain members of the British delegation, Labour's victory

Prime Minister Clement Attlee (centre) and Foreign Secretary Ernest Bevin (right) return to the Potsdam Conference as heads of the British delegation after their triumphant election victory.

was a betrayal of the country's great war leader. Oddly enough, this was a view shared by Joseph Stalin. In purely ideological terms the Soviet delegation remained deeply sceptical of two men whom they regarded as betrayers of true socialism – a distrust that was very much mutual.* Meanwhile, in his personal correspondence, President Truman scolded Attlee and Bevin as 'a couple of sourpusses'; it would take some time for the new American administration to warm to them.[21] For the Soviets, Attlee and Bevin weren't radical enough, while for the Americans they were firebrand leftists.

Beyond personal animosities, the Labour Party's electoral success left Joseph Stalin as the sole survivor of the wartime 'Big Three'. It was a change that only exacerbated Britain's perceived weakness at the negotiating table, as the American and Soviet delegations continued to dominate discussions – and now without the rhetorical spark of the outgoing prime minister's interventions.[22] Attlee's watchword over the course of the remaining negotiations was simple: 'cake for none until all have bread'. Yet it was increasingly clear that the British had little power to force their hand.

*

Over the two weeks at Potsdam, the Allies formally established the four-power military government of Germany. In Berlin, an Allied Control Council (ACC) was to act as a kind of proxy government, responsible for matters affecting Germany as a whole and where decisions required unanimous assent. It would be supported by the bureaucracy expected of a modern nation state: a co-ordinating committee, an Allied secretariat and numerous directorates, each dealing with a specific area of policy from transportation to finance. The ACC would work in conjunction with the newly

---

* In the Marxist–Leninist theory of historical change, social democratic parties were castigated as sell-outs and bourgeois revisionists all too willing to compromise with the forces of capitalism in the international class struggle. As far as the British Labour Party was concerned, many of those on the right of the party (including Bevin) regarded communists as ideological purists whose espousal of totalitarianism impeded attempts to enact radical change through the ballot box.

created Council of Foreign Ministers, an international body tasked with drawing up final peace treaties and resolving any outstanding territorial disputes. But the victorious Allies - including the French, despite their exclusion from the conference itself – were to govern independently in their own occupation zones, with total control over all areas of state and society in the pursuit of the shared aims set out at Potsdam. Likewise, Berlin, though located deep inside the Soviet Zone, would be split between the four occupiers, resulting in each sector being ruled independently.

These shared aims were as follows: the occupiers were to implement a course of far-reaching reforms, in order to radically alter Germany's social, economic, political and cultural structure from the top down. In the first instance, a process of denazification would abolish the National Socialist German Workers' Party (NSDAP) and its laws, remove Nazis from positions of authority, and pursue war crimes prosecutions against those deemed responsible for the Third Reich's transgressions of international law and crimes against humanity. It was believed, however, that the extirpation of Nazism from Germany also demanded a more radical programme of re-education: the Allies would supervise all aspects of the judiciary, schools and universities, government administration, media and wider society. It was hoped that, in time, these efforts would allow the occupiers to create a more democratic and decentralized German state – although these long-term plans remained vague.

The Allies also agreed that Germany should undergo root-and-branch economic reform: the country's entire economy would be subject to stringent regulation, entirely eradicating the means of making war, breaking apart industrial cartels and decentralizing control over Germany's industry. German living standards were not to exceed the average across Europe.* The Allies would instigate a series of reviews to monitor the state of the post-war economy and set an appropriate level of production across the four zones.

---

* Crucially this average was to exclude British and Soviet living standards, the expectation being that the war's victors were entitled to live much more prosperously than their defeated foe.

Any industrial output which exceeded these limits would be liable for confiscation by the occupiers.

This economic strategy fed into one of the most contentious and complicated aspects of Allied policy towards Germany: reparations. It was widely acknowledged that the Versailles Treaty's imposition of crippling monetary reparations in the aftermath of the First World War had been a disaster, spawning the hyperinflation which hit Germany in the 1920s and greatly contributing to the instability of the Weimar Republic. In the hope of avoiding a repeat, the Allies concluded that this time around reparations should come in kind rather than as hard currency. At Potsdam the 'Big Three' agreed that large quantities of industrial machinery, trains, merchant ships, military hardware, foreign stocks, intellectual property and much more besides would be removed from Germany as compensation for the cost of the war. Allied reparations would have a significant impact upon the German economy: with much fewer exports, Germany's capacity to import foodstuffs would be greatly reduced. Ultimately, therefore, the level of reparations demanded by the occupying powers would dictate whether the defeated Germans had the financial capacity to feed themselves or were to go hungry.

The Soviets, whose wartime losses were unparalleled among the victors, and who were keen to exploit German industry to the fullest extent, persuaded the British and Americans to accept their claim to 50 per cent of all Allied reparations. But the Allies struggled to find common ground on the precise scale of total reparations and could agree only an uneasy compromise. Even as removals of materials and assets in the east continued over the late summer and autumn of 1945, the overall figure was yet to be agreed.[23] It was not until March 1946, when the first Level of Industry plan was published, that the Allies finalized a figure. This reparations plan distinguished among three types of industry: sectors that were now entirely prohibited, such as arms manufacturing; those which could continue within the limits of available resources, such as construction; and others, including pharmaceuticals and steel production, which were to be restricted by the Allies.[24] In aggregate, Germany's heavy industry was limited to half of its 1938 levels of output and, to achieve this, more than 1,600 manufacturing plants were to be physically dismantled. If this wasn't already convoluted enough, at Potsdam the Soviets had insisted that only 42 per cent of retrievable German wealth could be found in their Zone of occupation; the shortfall would have to be found within the Western zones.[25] After a series of tense negotiations this accommodation was accepted by the Western Allies, but only on the condition that the Soviets would deliver food, ceramics and other goods from eastern Germany in exchange for industrial goods delivered from the British, French, and American zones.

Finally, the Potsdam Agreement set in motion significant territorial changes to the German state. Large areas of land were to be ceded to Poland in anticipation of a final peace treaty, with East Prussia partitioned between Poland and the Soviet Union. Germany's eastern border would henceforth be located on the Oder–Neisse line. This radical alteration to the country's territory found most of its support from the Soviets, who were now free to extend their sphere of influence westwards.

*

At 12:30 a.m. on 2 August 1945 the Potsdam Conference came to a close after a final plenary session which had lasted almost two hours.[26] On their way back to London, Prime Minister Attlee and Foreign Secretary Bevin took the opportunity to drive through central Berlin. Alongside the battered remnants of the Reich Chancellery, which, as *The Times* reported, had become the 'showpiece of Berlin's ruins', they saw street after street of shattered buildings, piles of rubble and burnt-out vehicles.[27] It was a scene that left them with little doubt as to the gargantuan scale of the task that lay ahead.

Back in Britain, there had been a dearth of information from the conference itself while it was in progress; the Allies had imposed a news blackout purportedly in fear of Japanese spoiling tactics.[28] But at the end of the meeting, the British press was allowed to report on the details of the agreement in full, leaving the country in little doubt about the proposed direction of the peace settlement.[29] The single communiqué issued by the three signatories proclaimed that ties between the 'Big Three' had been strengthened yet further.[30] The Potsdam Agreement, as the historian Alan Bullock notes, perpetuated a popular expectation that the wartime Allies would continue to work together after the war was over.[31]

There was an unusual degree of uniformity in the response of the British newspapers, which struck an optimistic note more or less across the board.[32] Given the popular appetite for a stringent peace settlement, this consensus was hardly surprising. As the senior Foreign Office official Gladwyn Jebb noted, 'any settlement which we may impose on Germany is likely to win popular approval here provided it can be represented as "hard".[33] The Potsdam Agreement was conspicuously branded in these terms, and pronounced an unprecedented attempt to pacify a conquered foe, eradicate Nazism and safeguard the European peace. That said, it certainly wasn't to everyone's liking: Victor Gollancz and the Labour MP Richard Crossman were among those who questioned the technical aspects of the agreement, the extent to which it could be effectively enforced, and the administrative capacity of the British authorities to implement such a far-reaching programme.[34] But the decisions made at Potsdam were generally welcomed as a practical means of tackling the 'German Problem'. The effectiveness of their implementation became the essential yardstick for measuring Allied success or failure.

In hindsight, however, it is clear that the Potsdam Agreement was a flawed settlement, as some British and American officials acknowledged in private even as its terms were being finalized.[35] In the first place, the war-ravaged condition of Germany would prove a substantial impediment and called into question the forecasts for reconstruction. Moreover, the French, included in the system of zonal administration but excluded from the discussions at Potsdam, refused to be bound by the agreement. Even more problematically, these proposals had established no clear hierarchy of priority between economic recovery and military security. Finally, while the Potsdam Agreement was wide-ranging in its potential scope, it remained ambiguous in terms of application. As was perhaps inevitable, each occupying power had a distinctive, often ideological perspective on key concepts like democratization, re-education and denazification. Potsdam was an imperfect compromise between wartime Allies whose differences had become more marked in recent months. In the first year of the peace, these disagreements, coupled with escalating practical problems in Germany itself, would render the Potsdam Agreement largely unworkable.[36]

Yet in the summer of 1945, all these shortcomings were far from clear. Rather, there was finally some cause for optimism: the Potsdam Agreement had set in motion the Allied occupation. Germany, under the rule of the Allies, was to be rebuilt in the image of its conquerors. On 25 August 1945 Montgomery's British Liberation Army was re-designated the British Army of the Rhine (BAOR). Five days later, the Allied Control Council constituted itself in Berlin and issued its first proclamation, informing the German people of its existence and supreme authority.[37] In the four zones of occupation, as well as the four sectors of Berlin, the British, French, Soviet and American occupiers set to work.[38] It was, according to the first military governor of the British Zone, Field Marshal Montgomery, 'one of history's boldest experiments'.[39] John William Booth, an office clerk with the 5th Royal Tank Regiment, realized it was his time to shine. 'Well, the transition from war to peace has been completed – from a conquering army we have become forces of occupation', he wrote to his parents, '... and up to the forefront of things have come the non-combatants keen to grapple with the new problems which now confront us!'[40]

8

The British Zone

Before the Second World War, Barkhausen, a village on the left bank of the river Weser near Minden, was best known as a tourist destination. Visitors from across Germany flocked to see a grand memorial to Kaiser Wilhelm I on a wooded hillside overlooking this small municipality. Below the monument sat the Hotel Kaiserhof, a favourite among sightseers and notable for its distinctively Germanic appearance: exposed timber beams in the Fachwerkhaus* style, complementing a steep Gothic roof tower, creating a vertical triptych of grey, white and black. In 1944, however, this upscale hotel was commandeered by SS officers and used as a satellite camp of the Neuengamme concentration camp.[1] As many as 1,300 slave labourers were crammed into four-level bunkbeds in the grand ballroom and tasked with digging a series of tunnels under the adjacent hillside. Industrial machinery, including an oil refinery, was relocated to these tunnels in order to escape the threat of bombing raids. Then, in the dying days of the Third Reich, this impromptu camp was evacuated and its prisoners forced on brutal, and in many cases fatal, marches across Germany to escape the advancing Allied armies. Finally, in the summer of 1945, the British arrived in Barkhausen and repurposed the building once again, this time as a local headquarters for an

---

* Half-timbered house.

occupying army. For the next four years, BAOR soldiers marched out from the front entrance of the Kaiserhof to a nearby flagpole every morning and evening, raising and lowering the Union Jack to mark the beginning and end of the military day.

Peter Wayne had been stationed in Barkhausen since the end of the fighting and, as an acting sergeant major, he would on occasion find himself the ranking officer, tasked with calling the regular commands during the flag ceremony. One evening during the first weeks of the occupation, Wayne bellowed 'Attennnntion!' at a line of British army soldiers, standing with their rifles at slope, as a bugler began to play a traditional retreat.[2] Before them, as had become customary, a small group of German onlookers had gathered: young boys in cloth caps, middle-aged women in thick woollen sweaters and men in tired grey business suits. For most Germans, entertainment of any kind was at a premium. Among the crowd were two of Wayne's interpreter colleagues – Sergeant Welden and Sergeant Talbot. Both undoubtedly had their minds on other things: the three men were planning an excursion to a local bar. But, as the flag reached its resting point and the bugler finished his tune, the three sergeants couldn't help overhearing the remarks of a young German standing beside them. Like them he was in his early twenties, but he was propped up on crutches and had only one leg. The young man turned to a friend and commented loudly that in *his* panzer regiment they had performed a much more *zackig* ceremony – loosely translated, 'snappy' or 'zippy'. He soon found himself confronted by an irate Sergeant Wayne: if the Wehrmacht was quite so glorious then 'warum sind sie dann nicht hier? Warum sind *wir* hier?'[*]

'Here' was the British Zone, an area of around 39,000 square miles (100,000 square kilometres) in the north-west of Germany that was home to more than 22 million people – in both geographical extent and population size, almost half the size of the United Kingdom in 1945. In the north of the Zone were the major cities of Hamburg and Hanover, and in the south-west,

---

[*] 'Why aren't they here, then? Why are *we* here?'

the Ruhr district, the centre of the nation's war production and industrial output, incorporating the cities of Dortmund, Duisburg, Bochum, Essen and Gelsenkirchen. Two more significant urban centres, the cities of Düsseldorf and Cologne, lay not far south of the Ruhr.

During the war, the area had come under by far the heaviest bombardment of any of the four Allied zones of occupation.[3] In July 1943 the RAF had bombed the city of Hamburg repeatedly over ten nights, creating a firestorm so great that it starved the city of oxygen: at least 37,000 people were killed, including many of those who had taken shelter, while almost two-thirds of available housing stock was destroyed and much of the city's infrastructure devastated.[4] It was just one of numerous heavy raids on the Ruhr region in which almost every urban area suffered huge loss of life and physical destruction at the hands of Allied bombers.

Across the Zone, the resulting levels of destruction were extraordinary. One intelligence officer reported soon after the end of the war that he was yet to come across a city where all three of the main utilities – water, gas, electricity – were working.[5] People were crammed into every available shelter, including cellars buried beneath piles of rubble, odd rooms in half-destroyed tenement blocks or spaces inside the imposing concrete air raid shelters dotted across the region. There were shortages of even the most basic of goods, from cooking equipment, cups and knives to needles, medicines and soap. The grand bridges over the Elbe were now heaps of twisted metal. Most of the railway lines were buckled and broken. In every key city the overall damage was estimated to be over 75 per cent.

In the summer of 1945, the British took responsibility for the shattered remnants of what had once been the thriving economic heart of central Europe. As General Gerald Templer, deputy chief of staff in the Control Commission, wrote:

Military government was met by chaos. A team of four officers and six other ranks would be confronted by an area of many square miles. There was no local authority whatever with whom to deal. Devastation was often on a prodigious scale. There were no communications, no power. Fields were deserted... Everything was at a standstill.[6]

*

All three branches of the armed forces were to take an active part in the British occupation: British Naval Forces Germany, British Air Forces of Occupation and, most importantly, the British Army of the Rhine. These military formations were primarily based in Germany on security grounds: to stop the revival of militarism, to protect and safeguard the British civilian occupiers and to maintain law and order. Yet throughout the course of the occupation, they would each play integral supportive roles as part of the British administration in the Zone.

In August 1945 the BAOR was formed from the 21st Army Group and consisted of 77,000 troops* in four divisions, although including support staff – from doctors and dentists to shopkeepers – there could be more than 200,000 men and women working across the British Zone at any one time.[7] In 1945 almost all the soldiers were veterans of the fighting, but by the end of the decade a growing proportion of the British forces in Germany would be conscripts following the introduction of National Service† in January 1949.[8]

The Rhine Army was housed in barracks across the Zone, from Aachen to Wuppertal, while Bad Oeynhausen, a town of no more than 40,000 people, was chosen as the overall HQ of the British army in Germany. This choice of location was officially due to its centrality in the Zone, the intact transport routes within its vicinity and a surviving supply of suitable buildings for an army of occupation; it also happened to be where the 21st Army Group was

---

* At the end of the fighting in May 1945, by contrast, several hundred thousand British soldiers on German soil were awaiting redeployment or demobilization.

† National Service had originally been introduced in 1939, allowing full conscription of all able-bodied men between eighteen and forty-one years of age for the 'duration of the emergency'. This legislation continued into peacetime, before the National Service Act (which came into force in January 1949) compelled all able-bodied men between seventeen and twenty-one to serve for eighteen months.

at the cessation of the fighting.[9] In May 1945 around two-thirds of the town, including the renowned spa and bathhouse, had been requisitioned and – as in many other locations – was quickly transformed into a British compound complete with barbed-wire fences, sentry posts and English-language signage.

The Control Commission for Germany (British Element), usually known as the Control Commission or simply CCG, was an entirely different story. In the face of such challenging circumstances, there was initially a great deal of uncertainty over exactly how direct British rule should be. Many officials in Whitehall originally favoured some form of indirect control, whereby a department of state back in London coupled with a small number of British officials in Germany would oversee the work of trusted Germans – not unlike the apparatus of the Colonial Office.[10] But as the near total collapse of Germany's state and political machinery became ever more apparent, and without specific guidance on the matter from the Foreign Office or Downing Street, the British authorities eventually chose to govern their Zone by bringing in a large number of British staff to administer the occupation in Germany itself.[11] It helped that the bulk of the costs for maintaining a force of occupation was to be charged against the German economy.†

The decision to implement direct rule also reflected the prevailing British belief that the Germans could not be trusted, even outspoken opponents of the Nazi regime. As a case in point, in 1945 the British writer Christabel Bielenberg returned from Germany, where she had lived with her German husband Peter since the 1930s. The pair had associated with anti-Nazi resistance networks and Peter Bielenberg had been arrested in the aftermath of the 20 July Plot against Hitler. Now, upon her return to Britain, Christabel offered

---

* There were still some exceptions, as the Allies agreed that they should use existing local German administrations for matters of police, law, finance, tax, public health and a small number of other local concerns.

† The bill eventually reached several thousand million Marks; see Official Report, Fifth Series, Parliamentary Debates, House of Commons, Vol. 485 (1951), 14 March 1951, Col. 174W. In 1953 the London Debt Agreement instigated a long-term repayment plan for Germany's many outstanding international debts. The final payment was made in October 2010.

her services to the Control Commission, suggesting that she could help put them in touch with reliable, trustworthy Germans – only for her overtures to be roundly rejected.[12]

The CCG was created specifically to run the British Zone and functioned in the mould of a civil service. It had fifteen separate divisions, each covering a particular area of policy: Internal Affairs and Communications; Manpower; Political; Prisoners of War and Displaced Persons; Public Relations and Information Services; Trade and Industries; Food, Agriculture and Forestry; Reparations, Deliveries and Restitutions; Transport; Army; Navy; Air; Finance; Legal; and Intelligence. There were several branches too, including Education and Religious Affairs (which later split into two) and Public Health. At every level of this structure the British established a substantial bureaucracy of administrators, advisors and consultants: from deforestation specialists to public relations experts, there was no shortage of know-how – or officialdom – among the British staff. To the casual observer, however, the overall character of the British occupation remained markedly military in nature throughout its existence; fitted out in military tunics and often accompanied by BAOR escorts, members of the Control Commission did not look like your average bureaucrats.[13]

The American Zone's counterpart to the CCG, the Office of Military Government, United States (OMGUS), was, in comparison, a smaller organization with more responsibility invested in the American Army.[14] In most other respects, however, the British and American zones were to be governed along similar lines. The Sovietskaya Voyennaya Administracia v Germanii (SVAG, or Soviet Military Administration in Germany, SMAG) broadly imitated the approach of the British and American zones, at least in the early days of the occupation,* albeit with

---

* There remains some debate over the extent to which the Soviet Zone was explicitly modelled on the Soviet system and when exactly 'Sovietization' began, although there is little evidence that it started much before 1947; see Naimark, Norman M., *The Russians in Germany*. This debate mirrors, in some respects, the vast body of literature on the 'Americanization' of West German society after 1945.

more responsibility handed to exiled German communists and a particularly strong emphasis on security considerations and reparations.[15] In the French case, the Gouvernement Militaire de la Zone Française d'Occupation (GMZFO) was not long in the planning and also borrowed much from the Anglo-American model. The French Zone must be considered in the context of France's own occupation by the Nazis and was thus laden with historical baggage. With that said, the notion that the French Zone was 'a colony of exploitation' has now been discarded in favour of a more nuanced picture.[16] It is also worth noting France's demands for significant territorial changes on Germany's western border: French occupiers took control over the Saar in the south-west and established the Saar Protectorate, a territory that France now deemed to be separate from Germany and, as such, not under four-power control of the Allies.* The French authorities deported hundreds of residents and ultimately hoped to annexe this economically important region, but in 1955 a referendum saw Saarland become a state of West Germany.

By the end of 1946, the British Control Commission could call upon 26,280 men and women from a wide range of professional backgrounds: large numbers of demobilized veterans of the forces who, as one official memorandum noted, were 'being gradually fitted out with bowler hats', career civil servants and young, inexperienced recruits desperate to 'do their bit'.[17] Among the latter was Edna Wearmouth, who was aged just twenty-one when she joined the CCG in 1946 and found herself plucked from her home in the north-east of England to Bletchley Park in Buckinghamshire for a crash course in all things German. Wearmouth came from relatively modest origins – her father had worked at Montagu View Colliery in Northumberland – and she had no experience

---

* It was a decision strongly opposed by the Soviet Union. It also caused considerable tension among the Western powers, as the British and Americans remained wary of French intentions despite tacit acceptance of the Saar Protectorate after 1947. These anxieties were augmented with further French demands for a similar arrangement in the Ruhr, something the British firmly rejected.

of foreign travel. This was to change in the spring of 1947 when, after taking a temporary posting with the Forestry Commission in London, Wearmouth finally achieved what she described as her 'life's ambition' of seeing Germany first-hand.[18]

Another source of manpower for the CCG was Britain's global empire. Colonial administrators were transferred directly to Germany from all four corners of the earth, bringing with them methods and approaches that bore the imprint of an imperialist mindset. In one instance, a British administrator came from Nigeria and demanded a list of staff under headings 'European' and 'non-European'.[19] In 1947 Kurt Schumacher, the leader of the German Social Democratic Party, remarked that the only thing he regretted about India getting its independence was that the Indian Civil Service would now turn up in Germany – a fear that was by no means baseless.[20] In this the British were not alone: many of the French occupiers had experience leading colonial troops during the war or as part of imperial projects in Africa and Asia.

Jobs with the Control Commission were not greatly sought after; in the early days vacancies far outnumbered applicants.[21] This was undoubtedly partly a result of war-weariness, but it also stemmed from a certain scepticism at the prospect of moving to Germany and ambivalence over the conditions of employment offered there. A job with the CCG was not a long-term civil service appointment but was rather a temporary short-term contract with few guarantees over future prospects. The uncertain value of a posting to Germany was only amplified by the fact that it was still far from clear exactly how long the Allies intended to remain there – an ambiguity that was never properly resolved. In contemporary accounts estimates ranged from five to twenty-five years.[22] Lord Vansittart publicly demanded that an 'occupation lasts in some form for at least the generation', while more liberal voices were still contemplating a fifteen-year stay for British forces in Germany.[23] In official circles, there was a degree of 'strategic ambiguity', albeit with an underlying assumption that the British would remain in Germany for several years at the very least.[24]

In terms of administrative units, the Control Commission split up the British Zone largely in line with recent conventions in Germany, but with new internal boundaries. At the provincial level there were *Gemeinde* (equivalent to an English parish) and then the larger *Kreis* (a town- or district-sized region comparable to a county council), which might include anywhere between 20,000 and 200,000 civilians. A collection of *Kreise* formed a *Regierungsbezirk* ('regional administration'), while above that came the four *Länder* – North Rhine, Westphalia, Hanover and Schleswig-Holstein – each under the command of a regional commissioner.* It was believed that the division of the Zone into separate *Länder* would impede any one area from ever becoming too dominant over the country as a whole. Even so, within a year, the first of these two *Länder* were merged to become North Rhine-Westphalia, while the city of Hamburg was also run under a separate command. The State of Hanover would exist only for ninety-two days before becoming part of the new state of Lower Saxony in November 1946. All these regions were formerly part of Prussia, a state regarded by many as the root of the 'German Problem' and which would be officially abolished by the Allies in 1947.

Within this organization, the CCG sought to ensure that each *Kreis* had a British presence – namely, a Kreis resident officer (KRO) who was the face of the occupation as far as the local population were concerned. Each KRO commanded his own staff, sometimes just a handful of men and women based in small towns dotted throughout the Zone. As it happened, a substantial proportion of the British civilians in Germany ended up living in quaint spa towns and rural retreats which had escaped the worst

---

* British civilian regional commissioners – William Asbury in the North Rhine Region; Henry Vaughan Berry in Westphalia; Air Vice-Marshal Hugh Champion de Crespigny in Schleswig-Holstein; and Lt.-Gen. Sir Gordon Macready in the Hanover Region – were not handed power until May 1946, with BAOR corps commanders taking responsibility until that date. The first three men were all Labour Party activists, while Macready was chosen to appease the British army contingent in Germany.

of the bombing. Likewise, the Zonal Executive Offices, essentially
CCG headquarters, were split between the medium-sized towns of
Minden, Herford, Lübeck and Bad Oeynhausen.

All British personnel in Germany, civilian and military, worked
under the authority of the resident military governor,* first Field
Marshal Bernard Montgomery (1945–6), then Marshal of the
Royal Air Force Sholto Douglas (1946–7) and finally General Brian
Robertson (1947–9).[25] Back in London, the chancellor of the Duchy
of Lancaster, essentially a minister without portfolio, was gifted
responsibility for the British Zone: John Hynd (1945–7), Frank
Pakenham (1947–8) and Hugh Dalton (1948–9) oversaw events
from Whitehall as head of the London-based Control Office for
Germany and Austria (COGA).†

The quirks of British cabinet government helped muddy the
waters even further: COGA – which by March 1946 had more
than 3,000 staff – was more of a bureaucratic clearing house
than a government ministry; consequently, policy decisions
remained firmly under the control of the Foreign Office and
more senior government ministers.[26] The chancellor of the
Duchy of Lancaster couldn't even claim a permanent seat in
the cabinet and John Hynd, a former railway clerk and trade
unionist, found he was all too often excluded from the most
important discussions about Germany. As the toothlessness
of his position became clear, Hynd lobbied for permission to

---

* The military governor stood as commander-in-chief of British forces in
Germany as well as head of the Control Commission for Germany (British
Element) and usually split his time between Berlin and the British Zone.
† The occupation of Germany took place in conjunction with a similar
undertaking in Austria, as agreed at Potsdam. However, the two were distinct
experiences, in large part due to the Allies' decision to regard Austria as the
first victim of Nazism. As a result, the *Anschluß* ('union') of 1938 was declared
null and void and the occupation took on a radically different character. In
November 1945 the Austrians held their first post-war general election and the
Second Control Agreement of June 1946 set the path towards independence.
While the four-power occupation of Austria remained in place, it could only
overturn decisions of the Austrian parliament through unanimous veto,
which, in the context of the emerging Cold War, proved unlikely. In 1955
Austria gained full independence on the condition of neutrality.

establish a permanent office in the British Zone itself. But with Bevin unwilling to compromise, COGA would quickly acquire an unfortunate nickname: the Hyndquarters.

*

The complex and unwieldy British occupation administration now set to work 'winning the peace' in Germany. In the first instance it was, of course, essential that the practical work begun by Civil Affairs detachments be continued: there could be no prospect of any real progress without clearing the streets of rubble, repairing buildings, mending the broken transportation and communication infrastructure and, ultimately, bringing back the basic means of existence for the local population. But now, in the aftermath of the Potsdam Agreement, the British could begin to implement the most important elements of the peace settlement. It was up to the men and women of the Control Commission and the British Army of the Rhine to end the military threat posed by Germany once and for all, to bring Nazi war criminals to justice, and, eventually, build democracy in the place of dictatorship.

It is fair to say that not everyone was filled with confidence. In September 1945 Gerald Lenanton moved to the Zone to begin his stint as the head of North German Timber Control, making him one of the more senior officials in the organization. Lenanton had been highly commended for his efforts to increase domestic timber production during the war and was sent to Germany in the hope of securing Britain's allocation of timber reparations.[27] A few days after his arrival, Lenanton took a tour of Hanover, where he found the level of devastation to be almost incomprehensible and witnessed German civilians milling around listlessly, seemingly resigned to their fate. It was all part of Lenanton's initiation, designed to help him understand the task facing the CCG as it embarked on its ambitious mission. 'I can't really say that I have great hopes of concrete results', he wrote to his wife, 'and if not, I can see some real trouble next spring.'

9

The Four D's

In the two months after the fighting ended, no British, American or French troops had been permitted entry into the German capital, which lay deep inside the Soviet Zone. It was only in late June, when each occupying power withdrew to its allocated zone, that the Soviets finally allowed the three Western allies to occupy their own sectors of the city. On 3 July British journalist Edwin Tetlow accompanied troops from the 7th Armoured Division and the Grenadier Guards as they entered Berlin for the first time. 'Cossack horsemen, cavorting in the early morning drizzle and shouting their traditional war cries, gave us a rousing welcome', he reported.[1] 'We entered Berlin with warm hearts after a journey which began at dawn. In a few hours now the full occupation of the silent capital by the victorious Powers will have begun'. On 6 July the Union Jack was ceremonially raised at the base of the Siegessäule, a victory column in the Tiergarten built to commemorate Prussia's victory in the wars of German unification (1866–71). In a symbolic display of their own triumph, pipers of the Argyll and Sutherland Highlanders of Canada performed a march past along the Siegesallee.

A couple of days earlier, twenty-two-year-old John Rhys had commandeered a jeep and set off for Berlin as soon as he heard that the Soviets were lifting visitor restrictions.[2] He was a member of the Ministerial Collecting Centre, an inter-Allied organization tasked with tracking down the surviving traces of the German government, from experienced personnel to official records.[3] This task was seen as imperative to the success of the forthcoming occupation, as it would provide Germany's new rulers with the administrative framework and institutional know-how necessary to govern with some degree of competence. In the German capital, Rhys's first stop was the burnt-out remains of the British embassy where he had worked as a junior clerk in the late 1930s. He was the son of a British accountant who had worked in Berlin, the family escaping to Britain only five days before the outbreak of war. As a teenager, Rhys had witnessed the emergence of the Nazi Party first-hand, and now he found himself one of the first Western witnesses to the site of its ultimate downfall. He proceeded to Hitler's Chancellery complex where, under the watchful eyes of Soviet sentries, he hoped to find up-to-date records of the German civil service. Inside was a shambles of broken furniture, rubble and shattered glass, as well as a huge repository of papers and miscellaneous ephemera from the desk of the Führer. As Rhys began rummaging through filing cabinets, he discovered boxes of Hitler's unused stationery, including invitations to state galas and signed commendation certificates. He stashed them inside his tunic and made his way past the guards – a memento for the ages.

A few weeks later, Rhys's unit moved into Berlin on a permanent basis as part of the Control Commission's entry into the city. It provided him with another unmissable opportunity: a tour of the *Führerbunker*. With the help of an American intelligence unit who had permission to visit this subterranean structure, Rhys toured the complex of underground rooms which included offices, conference areas, medical facilities, kitchens and even wine cellars. It wasn't long before they came across a velvet sofa and carpet bearing the bloodstained evidence of Hitler's and Eva Braun's suicides. In the weeks since their deaths the bunker had been starved of all ventilation and now had a stagnant, pungent odour. Whether it was the smell or simply the eeriness of their surroundings, Rhys and the rest of his tour party soon found themselves looking for the exit.

A group of British soldiers from the Royal Army Service Corps are
shown the gravesite of Adolf Hitler and Eva Braun in the garden
of the Reich Chancellery.

John Rhys, who had seen the rise *and* fall of the Third Reich
from up close, was determined to do his bit to help rebuild this
shattered country. Over the next two years he would remain
in Berlin, working as part of the British administration in the
Planning and Intelligence Section and, latterly, the Berlin Labour
Control Office. He was just one cog in the elaborate machinery of
the British occupation administration that was attempting to run
a whole country – or at least a substantial part of one – from top
to bottom. Inevitably, the day-to-day reality of this undertaking
was almost incomprehensibly complicated, as the Control
Commission and British Army of the Rhine took on responsibility
for everything from sewage to the restitution of stolen art. But
their efforts focused on four overarching objectives outlined
by the Potsdam Agreement: the 'Four D's' of demilitarization,
denazification, de-industrialization and democratization.

*

In May 1945 Lord Vansittart had authored a series of characteristically cantankerous letters on the aims of the occupation and made the point that there was agreement across the political fault lines on at least one objective: the total demilitarization and disarmament of Germany.[4] In the aftermath of the First World War the Allies had attempted unsuccessfully to restrict the size of Germany's armed forces and for many commentators that historic failure was the most urgent lesson for the post-1945 peace.[5] It was in this context that the British media eagerly reported on the efforts of the occupiers to destroy Germany's surviving naval and air power, demobilize the Wehrmacht, disband all military organizations and enforce 'industrial disarmament' – essentially, the eradication of war production. The newspapers and newsreels hailed the images of irreparable damage inflicted upon the remnants of the once powerful German military. The front page of the *Daily Mirror* featured the work of the RAF's Air Disarmament Wings, who were busy 'blowing up Nazi bombs' once 'familiar during the Blitz'.[6] In *Picture Post* the obliteration of Germany's once much-feared naval fleet at the hands of British engineers was applauded, with 'the graveyard of the German navy' at Kiel held up as an enduring symbol of Britain's ultimate victory.[7] At long last, the British were 'drawing Germany's teeth'.

Additionally, there came the less eye-catching but nevertheless vital work of clearing the Zone of tank carcasses, unspent munitions, weapons and much more besides. George James, a former Royal Navy seaman, had joined the Control Commission as part of the nearly 30,000-strong German Mine Sweeping Administration. This organization was created by the Allies in June 1945 from crews and vessels of the now-disbanded Kriegsmarine and tasked with the dangerous work of removing mines from the North and Baltic seas between 1945 and 1948.[8] James worked aboard an R boat,* one of the small minesweeping vessels originally built for the

---

* *Räumboote*, literally 'clearing boats', were primarily used as minesweepers by the Kriegsmarine.

Wrecked German U-Boats sit in a dry dock at Kiel,
as featured in *Picture Post*.

the Kriegsmarine.[9] Out to sea in his British uniform, it was clear to James that the revolver holstered at his waist was 'a rather daft' protection against a crew of battle-hardened German sailors, who could quite easily 'chuck you over the side' if they so desired. He quickly discarded it and in time found his new shipmates to be amiable colleagues who worked tirelessly to clear the seas of both British and German mines. It was a far cry from the summer of 1943, when James had patrolled the same waters on the hunt for German ships during the Battle of the Atlantic.

Alongside the practical business of neutralizing Germany's military power, the equally important – but less readily quantifiable – task of denazification was underway, as the Allies attempted to extirpate Nazism from German society and root out those implicated in the crimes of the Third Reich. This process included an expansive programme of war crimes trials, the destruction of physical artefacts of Nazism, the disbandment of organizations and institutions associated with the Nazi Party and, most importantly, the removal and disbarment of those deemed to be Nazis from positions of power and influence. Without a clear definition of exactly what it meant to be 'guilty', this was no easy task: if it was generally accepted that the leading members of the Nazi Party, Gestapo and SS were responsible for atrocities and war crimes and should be punished, what about civil servants, political underlings, Wehrmacht commanders, soldiers or lawyers? The morally and legally complex matter of having to judge the varying levels of complicity – ranging from passive or pragmatic acceptance of Nazism through to active identification with and participation in its values and policies – among thousands of implicated individuals was a challenging but unavoidable reality for the occupying powers.

One of those confronting this gargantuan task was thirty-eight-year-old Mary Bouman, who arrived in Germany in January 1946 to begin work as a translator in the Legal Division of the Zonal Executive Offices in the Westphalian town of Herford, a position she would retain until the end of 1949. Bouman was the daughter of an *Associated Press* correspondent and had briefly lived in both Paris and Berlin before the war. Now, as a fluent German speaker, she returned to Germany as part of the Control Commission and was part of the team tasked with the tricky work of bringing war criminals to justice.[10]

Bouman and her colleagues approached the task with an ambitious zeal and all Germans were to be treated with suspicion. The *Fragebogen*, a questionnaire comprising 131 separate questions, was circulated in the four zones of occupation as a means of classifying an individual's allegiance to Nazism. The form asked respondents for their name, date of birth, hair colour and other such particulars, as well as an array of more detailed queries: 'Welcher Kirche gehören Sie an?' ('Which church do you belong to?'), 'Welchen deutschen Universitäts-Studentenburschenschaften haben Sie je angehört?' ('Which German university student leagues have you been a member of?'), 'Waren Sie Generalstäbler?' ('Have you ever been a member of the General Staff Corps?'). Then there was the requirement to list in detail any affiliations with the vast array of Nazi organizations that existed between 1933 and 1945, regardless of whether it was the SS or the Reichsmusikkammer.*

Those whose answers demonstrated a sufficiently 'clean' record received a certificate, dubbed the *Persilschein* ('Persil ticket', after the popular detergent). Each of the occupying powers took a different approach to the implementation of the *Fragebogen*: while the Americans printed more than 13 million forms in the hope of examining everyone under their control, the British used it more selectively as a prerequisite for taking up work in a large variety of professions in the Zone, from the civil service to university teaching. All in all, more than 20 million Germans filled in a *Fragebogen* between 1945 and 1949.[11] The completed questionnaires were assessed by denazification panels and review boards, and those suspected of complicity with the Nazi regime classified and penalized accordingly.

---

* The Reich Chamber of Music was a corporation through which the Nazi state controlled German music and musicians, extolling 'good German music' while censoring what was considered degenerate.

By early 1947 around 200,000 Germans had been removed or excluded from jobs in the British Zone owing to their previous Nazi affiliations.[12] The application of penalties was inconsistent: in the first year of occupation, 41 per cent of those involved in food production and 31 per cent of postal workers in the British-run province of Oldenburg were dismissed, compared to only 9 per cent of teachers and 8 per cent of police officials.[13] This disparity seems curious in light of the fact that the latter professions are now known to have been heavily populated with active members of the Nazi Party. In many instances, decisions were clearly influenced by pragmatic considerations, such as the need to educate children or maintain industrial and agricultural production. But this was not always the case. The British sometimes pursued denazification measures despite their having a negative impact upon productivity or safety – including cases involving leading Ruhr industrialists and senior officials in the mining industry. It is unlikely to be entirely coincidental that the coal mines in the British Zone were rocked by a series of deadly accidents in the aftermath of sweeps of denazification in the early months of the occupation. On 20 February 1946 an underground explosion at Monopol Grimberg III/IV near Dortmund claimed over 400 lives. The incident remains the country's worst mining disaster.[14]

In the course of lengthy investigations into their past, many thousands of Germans were subject to mass confinement in civilian internment camps (CICs). CICs were sometimes located in former concentration camps, where conditions were grim: severe overcrowding and undernourishment were common, while prisoners were often treated harshly by their British guards.[15] By November 1945 the British had arrested more than 50,000 suspects, although in the vast majority of cases individuals were not held under any specific charge.[16] Internees were categorized as 'automatic arrests' because of their membership of a proscribed organization or apparent threat to the security of the occupiers, with only a small proportion held in relation to specific war crimes. Back in Britain, the news was widely applauded as just deserts. In the

British Movietone News film *Hun Prisoners: How the Mighty Have Fallen*, narrator Leslie Mitchell explains how the Wehrmacht had 'butchered thousands' and now faced the iniquities of captivity.[17]

Inevitably, this programme of extrajudicial detention caused friction within communities and between occupiers and occupied. For one, it was a system ripe for abuse: in a context where facts were hard to ascertain, dishonest accusations were levelled between feuding neighbours or old enemies.[18] The Germans also grew increasingly incensed at bureaucratic inefficiencies and perceived injustices. A common joke during these years was that Hitler's Thousand-Year Reich consisted of 12 years of Nazism and 988 years of denazification.[19] But, above all, it was felt in many quarters to be cruel and undemocratic. In March 1946 the bishops of Cologne and Paderborn wrote a pastoral letter which criticized the arrest of 'thousands of people without judicial verdict, their deprivation of liberty without the possibility of defence'.[20] They concluded with a warning to the British occupiers: 'If an internal recovery of the people is to be initiated, then everything that reminds us of the Gestapo, concentration camps and similar things must be punished from public life.'

In Britain, a parliamentary select committee of 1946 noted that around 40,000 Germans were being held in internment camps in the British Zone, some of them having waited over a year without trial.[21] Deputy Military Governor Brian Robertson noted in private correspondence that there were 'undoubtedly many thousands who would be discharged immediately if their screening were complete. This is a most unsatisfactory state of affairs and one liable to excite sharp and justified criticism.'[22] Indeed, it wasn't long before questions were being raised in both the House of Commons and the British press. By the end of the occupation in 1949, at least 91,000 Germans, most of whom never faced any kind of formal prosecution, had experienced life inside a British CIC.[23] This figure doesn't stand out in comparison with the other zones, with the Soviet Zonal authorities estimated to have interned around 189,000 (of whom 130,000 were German), the French 21,500 and the American 170,000 (a figure inflated in part owing to those who fled from the east in 1945).[24] However, the British were alone among the Western occupiers in their policy of preventative detention, whereby suspects were deemed to be dangerous due to membership of specific organs of the Nazi state rather than individual charges.[25]

＊

Eradicating Germany's military power and tracking down fugitive Nazis were regarded as two of the most urgent tasks in 1945, but the occupiers also set in motion long-term plans for the reconstruction of a shattered country. In the British Zone of occupation, the staff of the Control Commission set out with their own prejudices, aspirations, expectations and methodologies as they sought to build a nation in their own image.

These efforts included major economic reforms, regarded not only as a vital component of nullifying Germany's means of making war, but also as a means of strengthening Britain's hand on the continent in the years to come. In London the influential Labour politician Herbert Morrison privately advised Prime Minister Attlee that Britain ought to 'start shaping the German economy in the way that will best assist our own economic plans' and stop it from once again becoming 'an unnecessarily awkward competitor'.[26]

This attitude was embodied in the creation of T-Force, a joint Anglo-American programme which sought to secure valuable scientific and industrial technologies. In the course of the occupation, T-Force, working with investigators from the British Intelligence Objectives Sub-Committee, was associated with a number of controversial actions. These included defying the ceasefire in May 1945 to capture Kiel before the Soviets arrived and kidnapping German scientists in the dead of night. The latter was euphemistically termed 'enforced evacuation' but, according to one British official, it was a procedure that 'savours very much of the Gestapo methods'.[27]

Alongside these secretive methods of limiting Germany's future economic competitiveness, the British also pursued more conventional strategies designed to impose lasting changes on the German economy. This included a process of 'decentralization', in which large-scale firms like Krupp and Thyssen, regarded as the economic backbone of the German military, were to be taken under Allied control and broken up.

This policy was primarily carried out in heavy industry and in the chemical and banking sectors. In the case of the banks, the Reichsbank (the country's central bank since 1876) and the 'Big Six' national banks, which included Deutsche Bank and Commerzbank, were split into thirty smaller regional institutions.* The Rhineland's coal mines were taken over by North German Coal Control (NGCC), an agency staffed by British officers, including many brought over from the British coal industry. The NGCC sought to oversee coal production, regarded as the jewel in the crown of German war production, and was pointedly housed in the Villa Hügel on the outskirts of Essen. This grand house was the former residence of the Krupp family, a world-renowned industrial dynasty. Lieutenant Colonel Basil Reckitt, an artillery officer during the war who now worked in the Trade and Industry Division, visited this palatial headquarters in the course of his efforts to restart steel production in the area around Dortmund: 'The entrance-hall was an enormous room lined with family portraits from the fine-looking founder of the business to his increasingly less prepossessing descendants. Opposite hung paintings of the successive Kaisers, their masters and accomplices... Everything was there that money could buy from a magnificent library to an organ which could be played pianola fashion, for the delectation of guests'.[28]

Decentralization emerged as part of a broader programme of enforced de-industrialization in which factories and other industrial plants were to be requisitioned, physically dismantled and taken back to Britain piece by piece as reparations.[29] These plans would take years to come to fruition, but there can be no

---

* In the 1950s these smaller regional banks were reconsolidated into larger concerns once again.

doubt that the British often pursued a path that served their own economic interests. The Salzgitter Steelworks is a case in point: the Ministry of Supply quickly identified it as the most efficient and important steel plant in the Zone and earmarked it for seizure.[30] In both Germany and Britain there was some opposition to the plan, considering that Salzgitter was operational, the main source of indigenous ore for the country's steel industry and the primary source of employment for a large region now under British control. Nevertheless, Salzgitter was soon being dismantled and by 1951 three-quarters of the blast furnaces, the entire steel and rolling mill systems and a coking plant had been taken back to Britain or destroyed.[31] By the end of the occupation, Britain would receive more than $100 million worth of German capital equipment and other assets as reparations.[32]

The Control Commission, with the support of the Attlee administration, also seriously considered nationalizing heavy industry in the Ruhr. This, it was felt, would bring the economic powerhouse of Europe more directly under the control of the Allies – at least in the short term.[33] The idea did not, however, sit well with the Americans, who were seeking to promote free market enterprise in the Western zones; in the end, the nationalization question was left for a future German government to decide.[34] Another abortive policy was land reform.[35] The Soviet occupiers expropriated and broke up the large estates under their control, and distributed the confiscated land equally among workers, landless peasants and refugees from the east. Yet no such policy was implemented in any of the Western zones.[36] In the British case, Military Government Ordinance No. 103 was passed in September 1947 – allowing estates over 150 hectares to be confiscated by the *Länder* – but it was seldom enforced, in large part due to a lack of eagerness among German politicians.[37]

A remarkable story of ingenuity that exemplifies the ways in which the British did, in some instances, radically reshape the German economy is the rebirth of Volkswagen.[38] In April 1945 American troops captured the Stadt des KdF-Wagens, literally

'City of the Strength Through Joy Car' in reference to the Nazi leisure organization. At the heart of this planned city, which was soon renamed Wolfsburg, lay Volkswagen's enormous auto works, now very heavily damaged by Allied bombing. In June, responsibility for the region was handed over to the British and, in particular, twenty-nine-year-old Ivan Hirst, a major in the Royal Electrical and Mechanical Engineers. Hirst was no stranger to industry: he had grown up in Saddleworth, on Yorkshire's border with Lancashire, before attending the University of Manchester and founding his own optical instruments company.[39] But management of the Volkswagen factory was on a wholly different scale, and with totally different pressures, than anything he had experienced before. Almost immediately the Soviets demanded surviving machinery as reparations, while the Americans were insistent that the battered remains of the plant should be scrapped entirely.[40] Hirst had other ideas.

Major Ivan Hirst at the wheel of a Volkswagen Beetle in 1946.

Having found a pre-war prototype Volkswagen *Käfer*, or Beetle, Hirst, alongside his commanding officer Colonel Charles Radclyffe, set about restarting production with the aim of providing transportation for the British military government. They successfully persuaded the British authorities in Germany to order 20,000 cars for delivery by 1948 and began to crank up production, with Hirst resisting all calls for the name or the VW badge to be changed.* At the end of 1945, the factory had a workforce of over 6,000 and had assembled almost 2,000 cars for the British army and German Post Office.

As Wolfsburg rose from the ashes, there was growing interest in the future of the VW factory. On one occasion, Hirst deliberately showed visitors from the French car company Renault only the most damaged parts of the factory. Senior executives of the British car industry, on the other hand, needed less trickery to be dissuaded. When Ford was offered the entire company for free, Sir Patrick Hennessy, managing director of Ford of Britain, explained to his boss, Henry Ford II, 'I don't think what we are being offered here is worth a damn'.[41] The influential British car manufacturer Lord Rootes felt that the VW Beetle was technically deficient and warned Hirst that 'if you think you're going to build cars in this place, young man, you're a bloody fool'.[42]

Undeterred, Hirst continued to build up the factory's productive and corporate structures, hiring more experienced staff that included RAF officer Richard Berryman, who had previously worked for General Motors, and Heinz Heinrich Nordhoff,† technical director for Opel before the war. As the Wolfsburg factory grew, Hirst resisted growing pressure from the British car industry, as well as from both the Ministry of Trade and Ministry

---

* Volkswagen was founded in 1937 by the Nazi *Deutsche Arbeitsfront* ('German Labour Front'), although only a handful of civilian cars had been produced when the factory was converted to war production. Nevertheless, the 'People's Car' was inevitably still closely associated with the Nazi regime in the minds of most Germans.

† Nordhoff, who had been awarded for his business acumen by the Nazis, was barred from working in the American Zone. Hirst found him working in a Hamburg garage.

of Supply, to wind down Volkswagen and do away with a potential competitor.[43] Instead, under Nordhoff's stewardship, Volkswagen produced more than 20,000 vehicles in 1949 alone, the year that the company, now reformed as a trust, was handed over to the government of the new Federal Republic. Volkswagen became an international symbol of West Germany's economic revival and growing numbers of cars were produced for export: by 1954 it was the world's fourth-largest car manufacturer, and in 1972 the VW Beetle became the bestselling car of all time.[44]

*

Alongside these practical efforts to reshape the country's economy, the British were also preoccupied with the mind and soul of the Germans. Accordingly, the Control Commission set upon a programme of re-education, aimed at instilling values of democracy and peace.[45] It was a policy infused with Lord Vansittart's conception of the 'German Problem', namely a historicist reading of Germany's society and culture as wholly defunct.[46] In fact, Vansittart's *Black Record* had itself popularized the idea of re-education before it was fully integrated into the inter-Allied planning for the occupation. In July 1944 a Draft Directive on the Re-education of Germany included the long-term objective of fostering 'interest in the ideas of popular democracy, such as freedom of opinion, speech, the press and religion'.[47] There were also other long-term factors behind the British belief in re-education, most obviously the deeply held conviction in the reformative power of education, which had underpinned the liberal politics and imperial rule of the Victorian era. The German people, said to have been conditioned by undemocratic, authoritarian, militaristic and 'Prussian' ideas for centuries, needed new and more positive influences. And, the occupiers concluded, what better model than Britain itself, the home of modern democracy?

In practice, the policy of re-education was founded upon a newfound faith in the 'science' of political messaging. During the course of the war, propaganda or 'political warfare' had earned an outsized reputation as a means of energizing mass action or even changing a nation's beliefs. In Britain, government media management was believed to have effectively engaged the 'home front', while it seemed as if Nazi propaganda had fashioned a mass movement with unprecedented levels of popular devotion.[48] Now it was felt that a course of re-education could effectively undo this satiation in Nazism, instilling democratic virtues in place of the creed of the *Herrenvolk*.[49] This was the most ambitious of propaganda projects, signifying a high-water mark of belief in the power of censorship, state broadcasting and the manipulation of information provision.[50]

The British occupiers sought to control and manipulate the 'media of opinion formation', including culture and news, as well as other 'agencies of attitude formation', most obviously the education system from *Kindergarten* through to *Universität*.[51] At the end of the war the Allies quickly closed down all radio stations and newspapers, with the Control Commission licensing – and censoring – a new era of German media. When it came to schools, in the first two years of the occupation the primary focus would be pragmatic: purging Nazi-era textbooks and politically compromised teaching staff from the education sector while getting classrooms up and running once again. This was one of the most strongly 'Nazified' professions, with 70 per cent of teachers former members of the NSDAP.[52] Likewise, the universities were renowned for their associations with the Nazi Party.[53] It was also a sector severely hamstrung by the level of damage inflicted upon Germany's towns and cities. At the time, the famed German educationalist Adolf Grimme remarked that 'Wir stehen vor dem Nichts' ('We stand before a void').[54]

Captain John (Jack) Boyce had been a schoolteacher before the war and was appointed as a military government staff officer in the Education Branch at Minden. A letter home demonstrates the challenges being confronted in the first months of the peace:

> It means setting up the complete German educational administration all over again, getting rid of the Nazi element from among teachers and officials. I hope to have some of

the Schools ready to start by the end of the month but it is a slow business, and damaged buildings and evacuated children complicate the process. I am told by German officials that they have some children of nine years of age in the area who have never been to school for more than a few months.[55]

At the end of August 1945, after managing to 'spur the German administration on to further efforts', Boyce was able to report back to his wife – with some excitement – at the end of August 1945 that 168 schools had reopened, 'with more coming along every day'.[56]

By September 1946 more than 3 million children were attending 619 secondary schools, 11,500 primary schools and 1,830 vocational schools across the Zone – estimated to be 80 per cent of the number of equivalent institutions functioning in 1940, with 750,000 more pupils. In addition, 24 teacher training colleges had opened, which would result in more than 20,000 new teachers enrolled in emergency one-year programmes by 1949.[57] Moreover, all six universities and eight vocational colleges in the British Zone were back up and running by the end of 1945, with twice as many students as in 1939. It was a remarkable achievement and something that Jack Boyce himself found personally rewarding: 'I've completely lost that awful feeling of frustration I've had for so long in the army, because although I'm still a captain, this job is a far more important one than most.'[58]

In the longer term there were grand plans to abolish the hierarchical tripartite secondary education system that was regarded as a bastion of nationalism.[59] In its place the British intended to establish comprehensive schools across the Zone, with educationalists and civil servants supervising politically suitable textbooks and curriculums. Furthermore, the Education Branch also planned to oversee the creation of numerous adult education programmes.

Alongside work to reform German schooling, the British cooperated with the German churches, believing a resurgence of the Christian faith to be a vital ingredient in the moral rejuvenation of the country. The men and women of the Religious Affairs Branch worked with Protestants and Catholics alike as the church played an increasingly important role as a stabilizing social force.[60]

Another important policy was the establishment of British information posts known as *Die Brücke* ('The bridge'). These offices, which often comprised a reading room filled with military government communications alongside British newspapers and periodicals, were established across the Zone. Around sixty of them were in existence by the middle of 1947.[61] They would become a place for Anglo-German dialogue and engagement, eventually hosting discussion groups between occupiers and occupied.

The work of re-education even extended to the thousands of German POWs residing in Britain at the end of the war, many of whom were sent on programmes of instruction at Wilton Park in Buckinghamshire as part of plans to produce a new generation of German democrats.[62] It was Heinz Koeppler, a German-born British émigré who had worked for the Intelligence Department of the Foreign Office since 1939, who devised the idea of a centre for instruction in democracy, politics, economics and 'the British way of life' for those likely to be involved in the higher echelons of a future democratic Germany.[63] In 1946 specially selected German prisoners still in Britain were invited to the first Wilton Park seminar, which eventually evolve into a regular programme of courses to which numerous celebrated thinkers of the era, including Bertrand Russell and Lord Beveridge, were invited to share their wisdom. By 1948 more than 4,000 Germans had taken part, at which point the centre was re-devised as a forum for Anglo-German discussion and reconciliation.

*

Re-education was an attempt to 'win the peace' through psychological means rather than traditional territorial, financial or military methods.[64] In the first months of the occupation it found widespread support across Britain, with the *Manchester Guardian* highlighting the supposed urgency of the 'gigantic task' of bringing about a democratic revival in a 'desert of political thought'.[65] On VE Day a letter from the educationalist Robert Birley, headmaster of Charterhouse School, appeared in *The Times*, expressing his optimism about the re-education of the German people.[66] This mission was, he suggested, an 'unavoidable duty' for the military administration; he called on the occupiers to instil a sense of responsibility in a people who had allowed Hitler to become their leader, to encourage them to take pride in the noble German traditions of Goethe and liberalism, and to teach them respect for 'the Slavs'. Within two years Birley would himself be appointed to lead the British re-education mission in Germany.[67]

In October 1945 a *Pathé News* film entitled *Young Germany* featured Minister of Education Ellen Wilkinson outlining the work British officials were doing in Germany.[68] In the newsreel Wilkinson narrates her experiences during a recent visit to the British Zone, where the legacy of Hitler's Germany was said to lie heavily upon the children of Europe. There was, she explains, a good deal of assurance to be found in the 'kind of education which we hope will combat the evil effect of Hitler's cradle snatching' whereby 'flag-wagging and military parades' were replaced with 'simple children's games common to all nations'. It wasn't often in history that 'a conqueror made his first job to educate the children of the conquered', but this was the wise path being taken by the British authorities. The colossal task of the 'training of these young minds in the ways of peace and justice' was hailed as vital for the future security of Britain and the world.

Re-education was envisaged as the first stage in an expansive programme of democratization. This would involve wholesale reform of the law courts, the development of trade unions and ultimately the creation of a democratic politic through which the German people could decide their own destiny.[69] When it came to establishing a non-Nazi legal system, the British moved with admirable haste in the first months of the peace. At the beginning of the occupation all German courts were closed and replaced by military government courts modelled on British procedure.[70] Robert Souper was in charge of law and order in the town of Hardegsen, near Göttingen, and regularly appeared as part of three-man judging panels alongside German interpreters.[71] 'You just had to use your loaf,' he recalled. 'I'd never had any kind of training in this sort of thing'. These impromptu courts tried Germans for crimes such as stealing or assault, as well as more serious charges including murder and the possession of firearms (both of which could be punished by death under Allied rule).

The task of reopening German courts was quickly underway, with 266 civil courts functioning by the end of 1945. In August of that year, Basil Reckitt was given the honour of reopening the courthouse in Siegen, North Rhine-Westphalia. [72] He travelled to the ceremony in a large saloon car alongside the local Regierungspräsident ('district president') and an interpreter. On arrival the trio were greeted by a guard of honour from the 103rd Anti-Aircraft Brigade of the Royal Artillery. Inside the courthouse Siegen's chief judge denounced past practices before calling on those judges standing before him to resign if they were not prepared to administer fair and honest justice. They all proceeded to take an oath and then Reckitt declared the court open, before leading the congregation outside in the pouring rain for 'an excellent lunch at a country house'. In 1946, as high courts and appeal courts got back to work, a central German legal authority for the Zone was set up in Hamburg, the *Zentral-Justizamt für die Britische Zone*, with power to legislate and appoint judges subject to British approval.[73]

Yet by no means all areas saw such rapid progress. In 1946 Margarita Ostermann joined the Political Division of the Control Commission. where she worked to build up women's organizations – and in the process met all the most important political figures of the era.[74] During the previous thirty years she had lived a life that exemplified the instability of the Anglo-German relationship. The daughter of an English mother and German father, she had grown up in London. But in 1914, on the outbreak of the First World War, her family was forced to move to a country she barely knew. In Cologne she experienced life under the first British occupation, before returning with her family to her native London and studying history at King's College. Then, in the 1920s, she moved back to Germany and by 1933 was working for MI6, translating Hitler's speeches for the British embassy while also teaching English to the Führer's personal adjutant. Four days before the war broke out, Ostermann returned to England, just as her father was making the reverse journey for the second time in his life. It was not until her return to Germany as a member of the Control Commission, by which time he was in a British POW camp, that the two were reunited. Ostermann and her colleagues envisaged that democratization would take years or even decades to complete, building up from the local level subject to the close oversight of the Allied powers. A military government directive on the topic from February 1946 emphasized the size of the challenge that lay ahead:

> Although the Germans are to some extent of the same stock as the British, democracy as we understand it, government of the people, by the people and for the people, has never really flourished on the plains of Germany as it has in Island Britain. After the last war the Allies left it to the Germans to sow the seeds of democracy afresh themselves; as we know they were early choked in their growth by the foul weed of a new form of German authoritarianism. This time the Allies have determined to do the job more thoroughly... But no one must imagine that this is anything but a hard, slow and uphill task or that there will not be many disappointments.[75]

10

Seeking Justice

In the first months of the British occupation a series of momentous events thrust the sleepy town of Lüneburg – once upon a time described by the nineteenth-century German poet Heinrich Heine as a 'residence of boredom' – onto the world stage. Already, on 4 May 1945, German commanders had formally surrendered to the British army on Timeloberg hill, situated in the heathland overlooking this old Hanseatic stronghold. Later that month a short, ill-looking man in shabby clothing sporting an eye-patch appeared before Captain Selvester, an interrogation officer at a civilian internment camp on the outskirts of the town.[1] The prisoner removed his patch, replacing it with a pair of spectacles, and revealed his identity: former head of the SS, chief of German police and Reich Minister of the Interior Heinrich Himmler.

British officers searched their prisoner and found two metal tins upon his person, one containing a small glass phial, which the subject claimed was stomach medication but was quite evidently a suicide capsule. The other was conspicuously empty, and a more thorough examination led interrogators to believe Himmler was concealing the second capsule in his mouth. In an attempt to force the issue, Selvester presented his prisoner with a tray of cheese sandwiches and a cup of tea. But the former Reichsführer-SS managed to enjoy his meal without removing anything from his mouth. In the following hours Himmler sat in his undershirt with a blanket draped over his shoulders, answering questions, and at times appeared almost jovial. At some time around midnight, the officers, unable to retrieve the hidden object, sent their prisoner to a British army HQ in the town of Lüneburg itself, housed in a large redbrick dwelling on Uelzener Straße overlooking the city's Kurpark. There a British army doctor, Captain Wells, completed a medical and noticed a blue-tipped object in Himmler's half-closed mouth. As he moved to retrieve it, the prisoner jerked his head and bit into the phial of cyanide. He was soon pronounced dead and quietly buried in an unmarked grave close to where the Wehrmacht's surrender had taken place only weeks earlier. It wasn't long before the striking image of the lifeless Himmler, lying flat on the floor, half concealed by a blanket, was splashed across the front pages of newspapers around the globe.[2]

In late September Lüneburg again found itself the focus of the world's attention, the small town playing host to the inaugural war crimes trial of the post-war era as the British and their allies began the knotty task of seeking justice for victims of Nazism. A black sign with 'COURT ROOM' emblazoned in large white letters signalled the repurposing of a former municipal gym on Lindenstraße. In front, the thoroughfare was blocked off with red-and-white striped barriers consisting of a single pole resting horizontally between criss-crossing wooden beams before which stood British army sentries.[3]

Inside, rows of chairs and desks were set out across one half of the main hall, from where journalists and invited guests would be able to watch the courtroom drama unfold. From their seats spectators could see the long wall on the right-hand side was draped with two large Union Jack flags, which hung over a long grey-white desk: a hastily constructed judges' bench for five British army officers and a civilian judge advocate. On the opposite side, another nondescript desk with an identical series of black lamps was provided for defence lawyers, who were also British officers. Behind them was a raised wooden dock where the German defendants seated three rows deep awaited their fate. This was the setting of the 'Belsen trial' in which forty-five SS men and women and kapos ('prisoner functionaries' who worked for the SS) were accused of the ill-treatment and deaths of inmates at both the Bergen-Belsen concentration camp and the Auschwitz-Birkenau extermination camp. They were, according to one newsreel, 'the foulest set of war criminals ever to have blackened the history of mankind'.[4]

Gerald Lenanton was one of those who witnessed the proceedings first-hand. He admitted in a letter to his wife, the writer Carola Oman, that while he had some misgivings, 'I thought I ought not to miss the opportunity of seeing a piece of history'.[5] The accused, he suggested, fell into three distinct classes: 'the brutal beasts… [who] you would recognize at sight as thugs… the semi-idiots, who you would expect to obey an order whatever it was… and, lastly, and most surprisingly, the perfectly ordinary looking simple-minded German men and women' whom you

A view of the court dock at the Belsen trial in September 1945.

would have had 'no hesitation in engaging as servants in your own house.'

For Lenanton, and many other observers, two of the defendants merited particular attention. Josef Kramer had overseen the gas chambers at Auschwitz-Birkenau before becoming overall camp commander at Bergen-Belsen, where his cruelty gained him the moniker 'Beast of Belsen'. After the camp's liberation, Kramer soon came to be portrayed in the British press as the personification of evil and he would feature prominently in coverage of the trial.[6] In reports from the courtroom, his domineering presence ran the risk of overshadowing the appalling facts revealed during the trial – the sufferings of his victims thus obscured by the public's lurid fascination with their oppressor.[7] This dynamic was even more evident in the case of Irma Grese, who had worked as a guard at the Auschwitz-Birkenau extermination camp before accompanying a prisoner transport first to Ravensbrück concentration camp and then to Bergen-Belsen in the final months of the war. Grese was known for administering impromptu beatings and carrying a whip and punishment stick with her at all times. But it was her age – she was only twenty-one at the time of her arrest – and gender that inspired especially intense public interest: Grese was dubbed the 'Bitch of Belsen' and the 'Blonde Beastess'.[8] As question and answer passed between council and witness, Lenanton found his attention unavoidably drawn to prisoner number 9:

> If ever I saw active malevolent evil in a human face it is in Irma Grese's. She is not a bad looking girl, indeed when she smiles, as she did once or twice during the time I was there, she is almost attractive. But she has a straight cruel mouth, a heavy jaw and – I don't know in what words I can describe her eyes. She has a trick of turning her eye balls, when she wants to look to the right or left, and especially upwards, without moving her head... She seemed the very incarnation of violent planned evil.

Irma Grese and Josef Kramer, who were both sentenced to
death at the Belsen trial.

*

As early as October 1941, the British and American governments
had agreed that the punishment of Nazi crimes was among the
primary goals of the war.[9] But as the conflict came to a close,
there was less clarity on exactly what form this might ultimately
take. In April 1945 Churchill's war cabinet declared that a full trial
under judicial procedure for the principal Nazi leaders was 'out
of the question'.[10] Lord Chancellor John Simon was especially
worried that a judicial process would be deemed illegitimate
and might give leading Nazis a public platform. 'Fancy "trying"
Hitler!' he exclaimed to cabinet colleagues.[11] To resolve the
problem, Churchill himself proposed that leading Nazis should
be killed upon capture, with summary executions at six hours'
notice following identification of the prisoner by a senior
military officer.[12] The British found some support for this idea in

Washington – not least from Henry Morgenthau Jr, Roosevelt's influential treasury secretary.

It was the Soviets who pressed instead for a trial of leading Nazis, confident that a public display of justice was a necessary component of victory. In 1945 the inauguration of President Truman on 12 April also shifted American policy conclusively in this direction. But it was only after Hitler's suicide at the end of the month that the British government formally relented.[13] From that point on, a programme of war crimes trials was the accepted position across the Allied nations and even found support from the strongest anti-German voices, including Lord Vansittart.[14]

In June 1945 a royal warrant was issued to regulate trials in the British Zone of Germany.[15] These proceedings would follow the model of a British court martial and were to be overseen by the newly formed British War Crimes Group. Based at Bad Oeynhausen, this organization was authorized to hand out punishments ranging from fines to the death penalty.[16] In August of that year the European Advisory Commission – which since its inauguration had been working on the legal basis for Allied war crimes prosecutions – issued the London Charter. This decree stipulated that crimes against peace, war crimes or crimes against humanity committed by the European Axis powers could be tried before a panel of judges. It was the foundation for the 'Belsen trial' and the extensive judicial programme which followed. The British now vowed to prosecute German atrocities committed against Allied nationals as well as other crimes committed in their Zone of occupation.[17]

Over the course of the investigations, British prosecutors could access a list of suspects held by the Central Registry of War Criminals and Security Suspects, otherwise known as CROWCASS. This organization was originally a British– American venture, with its head office in Paris, before Soviet pressure led to an ill-fated relocation to Berlin.[18] Its task was a mammoth one: in October 1945 one War Office official estimated that there might be as many as 20,000 potential suspects in the British Zone alone.[19] Identification was not helped by the huge number of Germans who changed their names or identities in these years, a sizeable proportion of whom were attempting to evade capture. It has been estimated that as many as 80,000 Germans went underground in 1945.[20]

In selecting potential defendants, the British trials had a specific focus on the 'foot soldiers' of Nazism, revealing an official belief that the crimes of the Third Reich went far beyond its leaders.[21] Prosecuting the guards, soldiers and administrators who had carried out Nazi crimes was not only felt to be morally right, but would constitute an important proof – and symbol – of the denazification and re-education efforts that underpinned the entire occupation.

From the very beginning of British war crimes trials at Lüneburg, Bergen-Belsen guards and other low-ranking camp personnel were tried alongside camp commanders. In November 1945 the panel of British judges found thirty-one of the forty-five defendants guilty. Of these, eleven, including Kramer and Grese, were sentenced to death, while the remainder were sentenced to prison terms ranging from one year to life.[22] In hindsight, the lack of attention given to the particularity of the Nazi persecution of Jews is notable, with all victims instead grouped indistinctly. But the Lüneburg trial did help to establish important facts about the Holocaust, such as the links between Bergen-Belsen and the broader camp network, including extermination camps like Auschwitz. Back in Britain, there were concerns over the number of those acquitted and also over the time that the proceedings had taken, which at two months was double the original expectation.[23] But in the main the trial was celebrated as proof of Britain's contribution to the pursuit of justice, while the crimes it revealed – and punished – were regarded as ample justification for the military occupation of Germany.[24]

*

In November 1945, as the proceedings at Lüneburg were drawing to a close, the most famous of all the war crimes trials to take place in post-war Germany was just beginning. Over the course of the next year, the International Military Tribunal (IMT) at Nuremberg in the US Zone tried the most infamous surviving representatives of Nazism – including Hermann Göring and Rudolf Hess. It was something of a legal experiment: for the first time, leaders of a major state were arraigned by the international community on charges of conspiring to perpetrate, or causing to be perpetrated, a whole series of crimes against peace and humanity.[25] The trial resulted in seven custodial sentences and twelve death sentences, while the SS, the Gestapo, the SD (Nazi intelligence agency), the Reich cabinet and the Nazi Party leadership corps were all declared to be criminal organizations.

When the IMT began it was covered in detail by the world's media. In the British press the tone was generally one of hopefulness in the face of historic crimes. As the *Daily Telegraph* noted, 'no future Germany will have any excuse for saying that justice was not done'.[26] There were certainly dissenting voices, with some in Britain questioning the fairness of these trials and wondering if they might be an instance of victor's justice.[27] In the first instance, this view was expressed by right-wing extremists such as Montgomery Belgion and F. J. P. Veale, but it soon found proponents from within more mainstream political circles, most prominently the former cabinet secretary Lord Hankey.

The trial dragged on over many months; Lord Vansittart later complained that 'the protraction of the Nuremberg trial' gave the 'bloated "martyr"' Göring a chance to 'forge his own aureole'.[28] Nevertheless, most observers regarded this trial as an important step on the road to peace and justice. In the *Daily Express*, the tribunal was described as a 'service to mankind' and the judgment at Nuremberg was expected to hinder 'any attempt that may be made in the days to come to re-erect those scoundrels into heroes, to falsify the evidence of the great Nazi plot, to hush up the frightful story of the concentration camps, the Jewish massacres'.[29] In the years since, the Nuremberg Trial has remained by far the most well known of all the judicial proceedings held in occupied Germany.

After Nuremberg the Allies continued to pursue a wide-ranging judicial programme. As with most things in post-war

Germany, the four occupying powers each pursued their own agenda and instigated trial programmes in their individual zones that conformed more precisely to their particular conceptions of justice. In the British Zone the occupiers brought hundreds of individuals to trial in hundreds of separate court cases.[30] Many dealt directly with the crimes of the Holocaust, including the 1946 trial of staff from the Neuengamme concentration camp held at the Curio-Haus in Hamburg. This was the first of thirty-three trials held over the next two years which dealt with the camp and its many satellites, including the subcamp located in the Hotel Kaiserhof.

It was clear from the very start that a major facet of the Allied push towards justice was didactic: to assist in the processes of denazification and re-education, the German people ought to confront the crimes that had been committed in their name. In the spring of 1945, Allied soldiers had taken local residents on tours of the recently liberated camps to see the horrific conditions first-hand or, alternatively, exhibited posters or screened films detailing the atrocities. Now the courts continued to document and bear witness to the programme of systemized murder operating under Hitler's regime.

British prosecutors also focused on cases where atrocities had been committed against British servicemen.[31] The most notorious of these related to the murder of British airmen from the Stalag Luft III prisoner-of-war camp. Seventy-six British prisoners escaped from the camp in a daring break in March 1944. Most were recaptured and fifty were executed, a story later immortalized in the classic war film *The Great Escape*. When the news reached Britain that summer it created shockwaves among the British public and prompted demands for justice.[32] In June 1944 Foreign Secretary Anthony Eden declared that the government would 'never cease in their efforts to collect the evidence to identify all those responsible... these foul criminals shall be tracked down to the last man wherever they may take refuge'.[33] It was not an idle promise and the subsequent investigation would consume a great deal of the British War Crimes Group's limited resources.[34] On 1 July

1947 the first trial of the Stalag Luft III murders began in Hamburg, with charges brought against eighteen members of the Gestapo and *Kriminalpolizei* ('criminal investigation department').[35] All but one of them were found guilty of murder, and thirteen were sentenced to death.

*

With the war crimes trials now in motion, the Allied authorities had to confront some of the practical issues arising from a wide-ranging trial programme, not least the question of what to do with those condemned to death.[36] The occupiers realized that their conduct in handling the remains of the dead would have major implications for memorialization of the Third Reich in Germany. Fears that conventional burial sites would become shrines were heightened when Hermann Göring remarked from his jail cell at Nuremberg that 'those who are sentenced to life imprisonment never become martyrs'.[37] In addition, the occupying authorities were anxious to be seen as conducting themselves with propriety and sensitivity: there remained a widespread belief that everyone – even Nazis – deserved some sort of dignity in death.

The British, as the first of the occupying powers to hold a war crimes trial, were also the first to encounter this quandary. At the end of the war, the Foreign Office and War Office were resolute in their rejection of firing squads for executions: they were regarded as providing too honourable a death given the nature of the crimes on trial.[38] Instead, it was agreed that Albert Pierrepoint, the nation's official executioner,* would fly out for high-profile cases, such as the 'Belsen trial', and hang the condemned at Hamelin Prison.[39] In early December 1945 Pierrepoint arrived at RAF Northolt where a gaggle of newspapermen and photographers chased him across the tarmac; Field Marshal Montgomery had announced with some fanfare that Pierrepoint would shortly be arriving in the British Zone.[40] After his flight to RAF Bückeburg, Pierrepoint made the

---

* In this role, Pierrepoint was following in the footsteps of both his father and uncle.

German civilians from the town of Burgsteinfurt in the British Zone
are shown evidence of the atrocities committed at Bergen-Belsen
and Buchenwald concentration camps.

forty-minute journey to the town of Hamelin, previously best known for the legend of the Pied Piper, and began his meticulous preparations. On Friday 13 December 1945, the British state executioner hanged thirteen prisoners, including Josef Kramer and Irma Grese. For many people back in Britain, as Pierrepoint himself recalled, he transformed into a 'stand-in avenger, not only for the wrongs of the SS but for all their grief at the deaths in this long war'.[41]

Yet the procedure of judicial hanging was a specialized task and, even though Pierrepoint made repeated trips to the Zone, the occupiers still lacked adequate manpower to carry out the growing number of death sentences. In his absence, British officials were occasionally forced to take on responsibility for executions, with limited success. In one instance, a Foreign Office report lamented that the procedure was carried out in an 'inefficient' manner, which prompted a rethinking of the aversion to firing squads. But on the first and only occasion this method was employed it was terribly botched by inexperienced British soldiers.[42] Meanwhile, the denazification courts of the Control Commission turned to the guillotine for those found guilty of crimes against humanity. Many back in Britain, including the foreign secretary, felt this method was barbaric. The CCG used the pre-existing German infrastructure for capital punishment, which meant the very same guillotines that had been used by the Nazi dictatorship[*] in the very same locations: of the eighty-seven executions by guillotine under British authority, sixty-seven took place in Wolfenbüttel Prison in Lower Saxony, previously the main execution site for the Gestapo.[43] Among those thus despatched was the notorious Willi Herold, a Nazi paratrooper who had impersonated an officer in order to murder 172 Germans he suspected of desertion in the final months of the war.

The Allied occupiers were authorised to implement capital punishment even after the new Federal Republic outlawed the

---

[*] While use of the guillotine had a long-standing history in Germany, it was relatively rare until the Nazis came to power, when it was made the official means of execution.

practice in May 1949, and the final executions took place in 1951 at Landsberg Prison in the US Zone. This legal complexity caused some confusion in November 1949, when Hamburg authorities were said to be 'somewhat perturbed at the prospect of once more having to haul [the guillotine] out of a local museum' to carry out pending death sentences. The following month Labour MP Elwyn Jones received clarification in the House of Commons from Christopher Mayhew, under-secretary of state at the Foreign Office, that the use of the guillotine, specifically, was no longer permissible in Germany.[44]

As regards the disposal of Nazi remains, British officials were still undecided as late as December 1945 and considered options including burial at sea, cremation, and simply following the existing German legal code, which required bodies be handed over to relatives, medical institutions or the local police.[45] It was not until two days before the Belsen death sentences were carried out that Deputy Military Governor Brian Robertson finally made a ruling. He decreed the remains of executed war criminals would be disposed of according to standard British procedure for capital punishment: burial, without ceremony or publicity, in unmarked graves within prison grounds. Over the next five years, 155 executions and burials took place within the grounds of Hamelin Prison, with bodies sent to their final resting place in simple coffins stacked three deep. By the end of 1946, the number of executions had exceeded available space and plain-clothes military police officers began to secretly transport bodies to a nearby public cemetery.

At the root of this decision was a desire for secrecy, which the British hoped would allow the troubling memories of the Nazi era to pass away quietly. But the clandestine burials served only to sour relations with the local population, as concerned relatives sought answers over exactly where their loved ones had been laid to rest.[46] In the early 1950s a series of articles appeared in the German press criticizing the supposedly callous disregard of British prison guards. These revelations threatened to damage the fragile Anglo-German alliance of the early Cold War. In 1954 remains were exhumed from the grounds of Hamelin Prison and reinterred in marked graves at a nearby burial site.[47] Yet in a final twist, and perhaps vindicating the original British preference for concealment, neo-Nazis and SS veterans' associations started to use this location as a meeting spot and soon the bulldozers had to be brought in.

The British approach to death sentences and burials was, however, not imitated across the whole of Germany. At the Nuremberg Tribunal a quadripartite commission agreed to the use of hanging; as a result, executions were carried out in the Nuremberg gymnasium by two Americans, Master Sergeant John C. Woods and his assistant, military policeman Joseph Malta.[48] The bodies of the ten men* sentenced to death were cremated and scattered in secrecy.† Those sentenced to prison sentences were held at Spandau Prison in the British sector of Berlin – albeit under four-power control – until the death of the final inmate, Rudolf Hess, in 1987.

*

While the moral and practical questions of enforcing the death penalty were predictably controversial, the fundamental requisite of the war crimes trials was to deliver justice. To this end, there can be no doubt that the International Military Tribunal, as well as the numerous smaller trials in the four zones of occupation, punished *some* of those guilty of the Third Reich's reign of genocidal terror. In the process, the trials helped to document the systematic mass murder of the Jewish people and the murder of Soviet civilians, Soviet prisoners of war, people with disabilities, Romani, Freemasons, Serbs, Poles, Slovenes, homosexuals, Jehovah's Witnesses and religious minorities, socialists, communists and

---

* While twelve defendants had been sentenced to death, Hermann Göring committed suicide the night before his execution, while Martin Bormann was tried *in absentia*. Bormann's whereabouts remained a mystery until 1972, when his remains were uncovered in Berlin.

† Even though it is often stated as fact that their ashes were spread over the river Isar, there remains no definitive evidence for such claims; see Sharples, Caroline, 'What Do You Do With A Dead Nazi?', p. 101.

political prisoners. It was, for instance, at Nuremberg that the now well-known fact that 6 million Jews had been murdered was first established.[49] The war crimes trials also marked an important moment in the development of modern international justice by establishing the legal precedent for trying crimes against humanity and genocide.[50]

At the same time, there were a number of significant failings in the handling of the war crimes trials. In the years since, historians have pointed out how the IMT and other hearings helped to instil a variety of damaging misapprehensions about the Holocaust, including a failure to distinguish between extermination and concentration camps, as well as an outsized interest in perpetrators over victims.[51] On a more practical level, many suspects went into hiding or evaded capture, and the hunt for Nazi criminals quickly became something of a paperchase.[52] Matters were not helped by the very general descriptions issued to the officials tasked with bringing fugitives to justice, such as 'brown hair, medium height, blue eyes'. It was also apparent that the register of Nazi suspects ran to its own very particular set of rules: in 1946, among the 40,000 names a certain 'Hitler, Adolf' was listed as 'wanted' because CROWCASS had 'not been officially told he's dead'.[53] The War Office estimated that CROWCASS had successfully located as few as eighty suspects when it was wound up in May 1946.[54]

Even those who were identified and arrested often evaded justice. In October 1945 Attorney General Hartley Shawcross suggested to the War Office that there were 'tens of thousands of Germans responsible for millions of murders' and that they must set 'an absolute minimum of prosecuting at least ten per cent of those criminals'.[55] He called for at least 500 cases trying 2,000 individuals to be heard in the British Zone by 30 April 1946. Yet when the message was forwarded to the War Crimes Group in Bad Oeynhausen, the target was downgraded to 500 individuals.[56] Even this turned out to be hugely optimistic: by the deadline only 200 persons had seen the inside of a courtroom.[57]

One major problem was the serious shortage of British solicitors and barristers willing to prosecute cases or represent defendants.

This lack was largely due to the very small fee received for their services when compared to private practice in the UK as well as to the assorted inconveniences of working in the British Zone.[58] In many instances, individuals with no experience of the courtroom or even formal legal training were hired from within the Control Commission to make up the shortfall. They were each provided with a short pamphlet entitled *Hints to New Prosecutors in War Crimes Trials*.[59] There were also complaints in some quarters that trials were taking far too long, which reduced the number of cases that could be heard. Lieutenant Colonel Leicester-Warren suggested that one court president always gave the 'impression that there is absolutely no hurry and spins the case out by a considerable number of short adjournments for tea-drinking'.[60]

But more fundamental than frequent tea breaks was a general unwillingness – both on the part of the British government and the occupation authorities in Germany – to prosecute cases. As early as 1946 the whole trials process was gradually winding down and in November of that year Attlee's cabinet agreed to bring about an end to war crimes proceedings.[61] This was despite the obvious failure of the Western Allies to bring anything like a substantial proportion of those guilty to court.[62] As the war receded into the background and the challenges of military occupation became ever more apparent, the British authorities would pay less and less attention to bringing war criminals to justice.

11

Fratting

While the planning for the post-war occupation mainly concerned plans for denazification and re-education, leading British officials were nevertheless aware that any such enterprise would rely, first and foremost, on its personnel. Members of the occupying forces were urged to follow the general rule that the Germans were not to be trusted. Nevertheless, it was abundantly clear that any serious attempt to bring about change would require an effective working relationship between occupiers and occupied.

An illustration of these complexities comes from the city of Düsseldorf. In 1937 Walther Hensel had been arrested by the Nazis for his association with the anti-Nazi opposition. Following the arrival of the Allies in 1945, Hensel, a trained lawyer and experienced government official, was installed as part of Düsseldorf's municipal government – eventually becoming *Oberstadtdirektor* ('senior town clerk'). In the course of his duties, he was required to engage with British officers who, he recalled, insisted that Hensel and his colleagues always remain three steps away from their desk.[1] On one occasion, he was ten minutes late to a meeting and was warned sharply that if it happened again he would be imprisoned, to which he replied that it could be no worse than his time in a Nazi jail. This was hardly an atmosphere conducive to productive cooperation, although Hensel himself recognized that not everyone was the same: in time, he began to check the nationality of any British officer he was set to meet, assured that if his opposite number was Scottish, Welsh or Irish they were likely to be more agreeable.

In April 1944 the Combined Chiefs of Staff Directive 551 explained that 'the conduct of affairs vis-à-vis the civil population' in Germany would be 'totally different' from that in 'liberated, friendly territories'.[2] It decreed that the military government administration was to be 'firm' and that 'fraternization between Allied troops and German officials and population' was to be 'strongly discouraged'. Rather, it was the duty of the occupiers to 'impose the will of the Supreme Commander upon the German people'. Likewise, the Joint Chiefs of Staff Directive 1067, issued in April 1945, explained that Germany was to be treated 'as a defeated nation' and that occupiers were to be 'firm and aloof'.

As the occupation got underway, the military government began to enforce an exacting array of regulations centred upon this principle of non-fraternization, whereby all non-urgent contact between Britons and Germans was strictly forbidden. In particular, there were unambiguous warnings about engaging in relations with the opposite sex. The Foreign Office booklet *Instructions for British Servicemen in Germany* advised: 'don't be too ready to listen to stories told by attractive women. They may be acting under orders.'[3] For some, the ruling was interpreted as an order to refuse even the most basic standards of politeness; as we've seen, Germans were forced to keep their distance in official meetings, while in many cases handshakes were declined. The German population of the Zone could even be forced to step aside on public pavements.

In the first months of the occupation many of the nation's leading newspapers conveyed their pride and delight that well-behaved British troops were purportedly displaying the reserve and aloofness befitting a victor. In the *Daily Mail*, a full-page spread lauded Montgomery's admonition of the German people to 'feel guilt for the World War' and his resolution to avoid the mistakes of his predecessors in 1919: 'Enemy Told: This Is Why We Ignore You' ran their triumphant headline.[4] Likewise, in May

1945 the *Manchester Guardian* published a report on 'Hamburg's Divided Beaches', detailing how the shores of the Außenalster had been split into areas for British and Germans in accordance with 'the non-fraternization principle'.[5] This way, the German girls could 'splash about happily' in their summer frocks and bathing dresses, while the British soldiers were able to 'bathe without distraction'. A British colonel remarked that the Germans would save themselves a great deal of embarrassment if they stopped trying to fraternize, for 'no Englishman shakes hands with a foul fighter'. A few days later the *Daily Mirror* published a photograph of three British soldiers perched beside the river Elbe in Hamburg conspicuously ignoring two German women.[6] The accompanying caption professed satisfaction that 'our men' hadn't 'forgotten the tricks of the Hun' and when these 'two Nazi girls, however pretty, sidle up to their part of the wall they just turn their disgusted backs'.

Perhaps unsurprisingly, the reality was quite different. The policy of non-fraternization with the defeated enemy proved impractical and unworkable. It wasn't long before British soldiers went rogue. The rules of non-engagement were routinely ignored, precipitating one of the great scandals of Britain's post-war occupation and, in the process, introducing a new expression to the English language: fratting.

*

While non-fraternization ostensibly covered all types of interaction with the local population, it boiled down, in the minds of many, to one thing: sex. It was abundantly clear that sexual relations between occupiers and occupied would be a significant part of life in post-war Germany.

Such sexual intimacy was often born of necessity. In a time of food shortages, where many faced destitution, transactional sex became a means of survival for many German women. The result was a marked increase in sex work, as well as less formal liaisons taking place in what has been described as a 'grey zone' whereby gifts of food or cigarettes – the de facto currency of post-war Germany – were expected in return for sexual favours.[7] In the British Zone, the restructuring of the German police included the recruitment of women, who were specifically tasked with confronting those suspected of working the streets at night.[8] Sophie Alloway, a New Zealand-born police officer, was seconded from the Metropolitan Police to the Control Commission to help reform the ranks of German women in law enforcement.[9] By 1948 more than 500 women police officers had been trained in the British Zone, plus another 100 in the British sector of Berlin, and put to work tackling problems such as youth offending and sex work. However, against a backdrop of crippling deprivation and widespread unemployment, the authorities could do little to reduce the pervasive presence of sex work. It is with good reason that the image of young women befriending Allied troops in clubs and bars in the hope of some material recompense became a common trope in fictional representations of the occupation. There were also a whole range of other relationships between occupiers and occupied, from casual sex to lifelong commitments.[10]

It wasn't long before the newspapers changed their tune.[11] A number of articles began to appear in the British press documenting various amorous interactions between British troops and German civilians. 'Fratting is Rife in the Reich' declared the *Liverpool Daily Post*, suggesting that the 'old army game' of 'boy meets girl' was a growing phenomenon 'regardless of Allied military edicts'.[12] The coming months would see the pages of the national and regional press filled with salacious tales of dangerous liaisons in occupied enemy territory. For domestic audiences, the illicit exploits of British personnel were at once shocking and titillating, as residual anti-German feeling accompanied a lurid interest in the underworld of post-war Europe. To put it more bluntly, sex sells.

British reporters in Germany uncovered a steady stream of official reprimands and charges handed out to British soldiers who had contravened the rules.[13] On 5 July 1945, for instance, the *Daily Telegraph* reported the court martial of a thirty-seven-year-old lieutenant in the Royal Army Ordnance Corps who had pleaded guilty to fraternizing with a German woman he encountered while out walking.[14] The woman, aged twenty-three, allegedly spoke to him

British troops 'fratting' with German women. There was an outcry when these kinds of images began to appear in the British newspapers.

in German and the accused responded 'mainly by signs', resulting in the pair walking to the nearby woods 'where intimacy took place'. The court was asked to show leniency on the grounds that his record was hitherto unblemished, that his offence was the result of 'sudden temptation' and that 'the accused has had his punishment of having to explain affairs to his wife'. As a result, the man in question was only deprived of a forthcoming promotion and severely reprimanded.

As similar cases of fratting appeared more and more frequently in the British papers, cartoonists in popular newspapers were soon lambasting the apparent futility of the non-fraternization policy. The *Daily Express* joked that schoolboys in Britain, determined not to 'let our brave boys in Berlin down', were themselves busily engaging in a spot of fraternization with the opposite sex.[15] Some cartoons had a more distinctly anti-German bent. The *Daily Mail* depicted two passing Tommies mocking a rotund, Himmleresque German woman for causing 'casualties'.[16] Furthermore, the papers published photographs that revealed 'fratting' in action. The majority of these images were relatively modest, such as the *Daily Mail*'s photograph of British soldiers talking with smiling German women with the caption 'So this is fraternisation'[17] Yet there were also more indecent images, like *Picture Post*'s photograph of two scantily clad bodies entwined on a beach, emblematic of the suggestive tone that characterized much of the press coverage.[18] Likewise, the front page of the *Birmingham Daily Gazette* featured a pair of photos exhibiting the ubiquity of fraternization in Germany, including one euphemistic rendering of British soldiers walking arm in arm with German women 'down a shady lane'.[19]

*

The proliferation of stories and photographs in the local and national press raised the ire of many in Britain and inspired public pronouncements of moral outrage that the British occupiers were forgetting their duty and even risking the peace. In one letter to the editor of *The Times*, it was suggested that 'the photographs in the Press of British troops "fraternising" with half-naked smiling German girls' were 'somewhat astonishing'.[20] They stood in stark contrast, the letter writer continued, to the shaven heads of those women adjudged to have been too intimate with Germans in the liberated countries of Europe. The letter concluded that 'fratting' would damage any attempt to 'promote that understanding of and faith in Britain which is so desperately needed if Europe is to rise once more from the abyss'. This was but one example of many reprimanding British troops for 'fratting' with German women. In January 1946 the Marchioness of Huntly remarked in the *Aberdeen Press and Journal* that she had 'never found a word which produced, both with the public at home and with the British army in Germany, so heated a response as the word fraternization'.[21]

Some sought to temper the growing public fury. Rhona Churchill (no relation) wrote at length, and with justification, in the *Daily Mail* that this was a problem shared across all the occupation zones, rather than anything peculiar to British troops – 'boys will be boys' was the message.[22] She went on to argue that it was an almost inevitable outcome of the peculiar situation of post-war Europe: the average Allied soldier, battle-scarred and homesick 'for his mother, his girl and for the children he never found time to raise', was 'the loneliest guy in the world'. To seek female company under such circumstances was 'only human'. In the *Daily Mirror*, George McCarthy took a slightly different line, emphasizing that 'Tommy is curious' and just wants 'to discover what kind of people they are', and 'to find out, if they can, why these apparently sane men and women followed Hitler into doom and disaster'.[23] It was a mistake, he continued, to 'overemphasize the man-woman aspect of the case'. He assured readers that British soldiers were certainly not dealing in the 'kiss-and-make-up sentiment' that the word 'fraternization' might imply. Meanwhile, in *People*, it was brazenly suggested that British women should shoulder much of the blame, as their own fraternization with the 'yanks' and 'wops' currently residing in Britain had damaged the morale of Britain's 'heroes abroad'.[24] In Germany itself, Bishop von Galen of Münster, a noted opponent of the Nazi regime, declared non-fraternization a 'denial of justice and love' based on the assumption that 'every German person participated in the guilt of each criminal act' of the Third Reich.[25]

In the face of the public furore in Britain, members of the occupation army were quick to defend themselves in letters to the popular press. They protested that they were guilty of little beyond good-natured friendliness and that complaints from the public were simply 'narrow-minded'.[26] In the *Daily Mirror*, an anonymous member of the British occupation forces wrote a lengthy article in which he disingenuously suggested that he and his colleagues didn't want 'to mix with German girls' but simply to teach them the ways of democracy:

This is Germany – I've seen it and I want to get out of it. The people seem to be laughing at us and some of them do. Some want to talk to us, children take our hands and talk German to us. People pretend not to notice us and then give us a sly glance. Curtains are pushed back and heads are turned. Police salute us and some spit on the ground (but, of course, not to appear deliberate). My finger itches on the trigger of my rifle as I walk through the streets and, at times, I wish they would be openly hostile so that we could have another showdown. The war is over – but another war has begun between the Army of Occupation – us – and the German civvies. This situation surely cannot keep up. How will these Germans get to know our way of thinking if we do not fraternize?[27]

Other men of the British Army of the Rhine and the Control Commission were quick to lay the blame on German women for allegedly flirtatious behaviour. This response appealed to Germanophobic stereotypes and reflected misogynist attitudes to female sexuality. It was also an excuse that leading British officials were all too happy to endorse, even accepting it as a defence in disciplinary proceedings. In the aforementioned trial of the Royal Army Ordnance Corps lieutenant, for instance, it was noted that the 'intimacy' had been initiated by the woman in question.[28] Commander-in-chief Field Marshal Montgomery went so far as to declare that the female inhabitants of the British Zone were practising a 'new form of German sabotage by wearing fewer and fewer clothes'.[29]

The British media also embraced the notion that German women were to blame. Evadne Price, war correspondent for *People*, wrote a stern defence of the non-fraternization policy with the subheading 'we must hate – or lose the peace'.[30] The article suggested that 'these Boche women' who exuded 'feminine appeal' with their smiles, silk stockings, short skirts and expensive make-up had stood 'a hundred per cent behind Adolf Hitler' and were now attempting to fool the Allied troops into a false sense of security. A few months later Price proclaimed herself to be 'campaigning against the German woman' whose loyalty to the Wehrmacht was said to be unremitting.[31] The notion that the Nazis, and especially Adolf Hitler himself, had emanated a perverse sexual appeal to German women was an increasingly common trope of British reporting, and was encouraged by the British army's public relations officials.

In June 1945 both the *Daily Mirror* and the *Daily Mail* carried articles lambasting the 'women auxiliaries of the Wehrmacht' for being 'red-hot anti-British'.[32] The story claimed that while British troops were 'putting up "a good show" in observing the ban', the 'scantily clothed' German girls were 'carrying out an organized plan to break it'.

But this imbroglio could not be easily sold to the British public as simply the result of entrapment or naïveté. In the first place, many in Britain felt that any close association with the Germans was wholly unacceptable considering the evidence of wartime Nazi atrocities. In the *Daily Mail*, satirist Maurice Lane-Norcott slyly asked whether the silk stockings of your average Fräulein had been 'imported from France, Holland, Belgium, Denmark, Norway, Poland, Czechoslovakia, Yugoslavia or Greece' while these countries had been under Nazi occupation.[33] The *Western Daily Press* quoted a former inmate at Ravensbrück concentration camp who condemned fraternization as 'terrible' and warned that German women could not be trusted.[34]

Moreover, the conduct of some soldiers simply could not be passed off as youthful exuberance. In August 1945, for instance, a forty-three-year-old major in the Royal Tank Regiment, married, and father to three young children, was found guilty of conducting a sexual liaison with a German woman.[35] There were dozens of similar stories, seemingly exposing what many perceived as a culture of immorality and debauchery incompatible with popular expectations of 'winning the peace', and which even appeared to risk undermining Britain's image and prestige on the world stage.

Perhaps most importantly, the revelations about fraternization contrasted with increasingly sacrosanct memories of the war. In July 1945 the *Liverpool Echo* featured a letter from 'Three Bewildered Young Ladies' who felt that fraternization proved 'the original object of this war is being forgotten and many lives have been lost in vain'.[36] Tellingly, there was widespread coverage of the statement provided by Divisional Officer J. M. Kelly, leader of the 500 members of the National Fire Service who had been working temporarily alongside British troops in Germany.[37] The firemen were, he suggested, 'in no humour to fraternize with Germans' since they had all 'done duty during the blitz'. Likewise, Monty assured journalists that his fabled 'Desert Rats', celebrated veterans of the war in North Africa, had 'no interest in fraternising'; while the claim certainly wasn't true, it made for a good story.[38] Montague Calman, himself a member of the occupation forces, wrote to his local newspaper and declared his emphatic rejection of any form of fraternization: 'while London, Coventry, Canterbury and other cities still contain the memorials of Nazi "military" bombing... We [should] refuse to even acknowledge the German as a human being, as is defined in any self-respecting dictionary!!'[39]

The wives and girlfriends of British servicemen had a more personal cause for concern, something they made abundantly clear to their partners in Germany. Members of the 549th company of the Royal Engineers protested at the 'accusing and critical letters from their wives and sweethearts' they had received in the wake of the commotion over fraternization.[40] But British women also made more public appeals. The *Lancashire Evening Post* published a letter from 'an interested and affected party' who wanted to 'draw attention to the feelings of wives here at home on the subject of "fratting"'.[41] 'It is quite the time our men had an opportunity of "fratting" with their own wives', she wrote, before emphatically signing her letter '"WATCHING", Preston'. The righteous indignation of wives and girlfriends, playing upon popular expectations of domesticity and conjugal fidelity, would have a powerful impact upon public opinion.[42] In late July Bristol resident Miss M. Cutts wrote a letter to *People* suggesting that the men found guilty of such misdeeds should be barred from ever returning to England: 'I am not affected personally by the question... [but] it made me see red when I saw those letters you published of English wives whose husbands preferred German sluts!'[43]

*

It was increasingly apparent that the non-fraternization ruling had been made more or less redundant through widespread disobedience, leaving many to conclude that it was only a matter of time before a change in policy was announced.[44] As early as May 1945, Joe Illingworth wrote in the *Liverpool Daily Post* that 'fratting can't be stopped' and would only get worse if things remained as they were.[45] The following month the *Daily Mail* published an editorial on this 'acute international problem', stating that while the rationale to 'kill any possible attempt by the Nazi elements to make use of the Allied Forces in keeping their doctrines alive' was commendable, in the long run the policy was unworkable.[46] A reporter for *The Times* also proclaimed the ban to be unenforceable but accepted there would be serious drawbacks to any alteration as it 'would probably distress a large number of women at home' who were unlikely to 'believe that fraternization means much besides association with German girls, and they will certainly be right'.[47] Yet the article concluded on a pragmatic if slightly coy note: 'it seems clear that the anti-fraternization policy will inevitably be modified under what may be described as biological pressure, if under no other'.

The British authorities in Germany were themselves concerned at increasing levels of insubordination, as well as the negative publicity stemming from the non-fraternization controversy.[48] In response, the rules on contact with the local population were altered and, on 12 June 1945, Montgomery issued a new message to his troops, stating that while 'we cannot let up on this policy... these orders need no longer apply to small children'.[49] A month later a second revision allowed for 'conversation with adult Germans in the streets and in public places'. These changes were covered extensively in the British media, including newsreel reports from *British Pathé*, *British Movietone News* and *Gaumont-British News*.[50]

Neither of these adjustments actually dealt with the sexual fraternization which had caused a public outcry in the first place. As a result, the shift in official policy did little to resolve the controversy, and questions of morality and concerns over damage to national prestige remained. In fact, many warned that the partial relaxation of the ban had already given implicit official sanction to 'fratting' in the form of sexual relations between occupiers and occupied, which was strongly suggested by the jubilant reaction of British personnel in Germany to the rule changes. The *Daily Mirror*, the *Daily Mail* and the *Daily Telegraph* all reported with some disdain that British soldiers 'threw their caps in the air and behaved just as though their favourite football team had won the cup... wasting no time in acting on the announcement'.[51]

The controversy dragged on, with commentators continuing to question whether the relaxation of the policy was indeed a positive development. In July 1945, Lord Vansittart suggested in a broadcast for the American Broadcasting Company that the easing-up of non-fraternization rules was 'Nazi victory number one'. His speech, covered extensively in the British press, cited the Allied climb-down as evidence of weakness and indecision that risked a repeat of the failures of the last peace.[52] These claims were countered in a *Manchester Guardian* editorial which suggested that upon reflection the 'defeat' of this unworkable policy, which had stood 'as an example of how not to go about the occupation of a conquered country', was for the best:

> After years of hard fighting the soldiers should not be asked to turn themselves into celibate missionaries... To say that the Germans have won their first victory of the occupation is short-sighted and untrue. If there has been any victory it is a victory for common sense and for the warm humanity of British and American soldiers.[53]

But others remained sceptical, including enraged wives and girlfriends: in late August Gertrude B. Cook wrote to the *Manchester Guardian* to reiterate her husband's concerns that the new laws tended 'to throw soldiers into the wrong element of the German people', namely the 'lower side' of German girls who go out 'clicking' in streets and cafes.[54]

On 25 September the British authorities, in conjunction with the other occupying powers, agreed that the non-fraternization rules were to be fully relaxed, with continued restrictions on the billeting of British personnel with German households, and marriage between members of the occupying forces and German citizens being the only exceptions. This latter restriction was eventually lifted in July 1946, momentarily reviving the media's interest in the topic of fratting.[55]

To illustrate that it wasn't all light-hearted frolics and short-lived affairs, between 1947 and 1950 an estimated 10,000 British–German marriages took place, in spite of exacting stipulations which included a six-month 'cooling off' period and a mandatory medical examination for German women.[56] These newly-weds often faced a great deal of prejudice. In 1947 Control Commission official Jan Thexton requested permission from his commanding officer to marry a German woman, a supervisor in the Hanover telephone exchange whom he had met in the course of his work. He was told in no uncertain terms that while there was no official regulation prohibiting him, 'I'd much sooner you married a wog, than marry a German.'[57] Yet others were more open-minded: the *Daily Mirror* featured the curious story of Herbert Butterworth, twenty-six, from Bolton, Lancashire, who was making plans to wed a German he had never actually met.[58] During the years of the occupation, his brother had married a woman from Osnabrück – and now Herbert was intending to marry her sister Grete. 'If she is anything like her sister I shall be getting a good wife,' he explained to a reporter.

Another consequence of British–German sexual relations was illegitimate children.[59] Between 1946 and 1955, official records suggest that more than 8,500 *Besatzungskinder*, literally 'occupation children', were born out of wedlock to British fathers and German mothers.* This includes children conceived as a result of rape as well as love affairs, flings and sex work. In all cases the children in question had no family relationship with their father, resulting

---

* This is based on a West German survey conducted in 1956. In the US Zone there were an estimated 37,000 *Besatzungskinder* in the same period. These estimates excluded children whose mothers had followed the fathers as 'war brides', those who had been adopted, had died, had been born within existing marriages or had been declared legitimate as a result of their mother's subsequent marriage. In reality, the number in both cases was most likely substantially higher.

in most being brought up by their maternal family. It could be a challenging situation: there was no legal means of enforcing alimony payments from those fathers who were identified, while in many cases single mothers and their children faced pervasive social stigmas.[60]

There was also, notably, an ongoing concern with the sexual health of the occupation forces. A Public Health Branch report from October 1945 warned:

> It is sheer stupidity and wishful thinking to adopt the attitude that there ought to be no promiscuity amongst the troops and therefore since there ought to be none there is no need to supply condoms. To all clear-sighted people it is axiomatic that amongst any body of troops – young, physically fit, no longer fighting arduous battles and enduring separation from their homes in anything but home-like conditions – there will inevitably be a considerable percentage who will indulge in promiscuous sexual intercourse, and it is purely realistic and practical to provide them with condoms if there is any real desire to reduce the incidence of V.D. amongst the troops.[61]

*

The controversy over fratting marks a significant moment in the history of the occupation. For many of those on the ground it had been apparent from the very beginning that maintaining a strict line of separation between the British and Germans would be counterproductive. In the face of media outrage at the all-too-frequent breaching of the line, the authorities in the British Zone recognized that a policy born of wartime prejudice, rather than rational thinking, was not helping their cause. But fratting was also significant for the impression it made upon public perceptions of the occupation back in Britain. In the following months and years, news reports and fictionalized portrayals of post-war Germany would routinely refer to fraternization and illicit liaisons, thus establishing an enduring association between the British occupation and sex.

The breakdown of non-fraternization rules was mirrored across the US and French zones. However, even as the British and Americans eased restrictions, the French authorities maintained firmer rules on interactions with the Germans.[62] The French Military Governor Marie-Pierre Kœnig, for instance, only allowed French–German sporting competition to begin in 1948.[63] There was also a heated public response in America when news of US servicemen engaging in fratting with Germans *and* Japanese women hit the headlines.[64] This was the subject of Billy Wilder's 1948 black comedy *A Foreign Affair*, starring Marlene Dietrich.[65] The film, released to much acclaim in the UK, follows Congresswoman Phoebe Frost as she investigates, and gets caught up in, the 'moral malaria' of fratting among Allied troops in Berlin. In the French and American cases, the non-fraternization controversy was further inflected with a racial dimension: sexual relations between Germans and African-American GIs or French troops from North Africa caused further controversy, considering the deeply ingrained prejudices of the time. It is also likely that same-sex fratting occurred in all four zones – but unsurprisingly, in light of attitudes towards homosexuality in the late 1940s and the potential consequences of exposure, this history remains largely hidden from view.

Despite being a truly inter-Allied phenomenon, much of the British newspaper coverage of fratting in the summer and autumn of 1945 suggested that this was specifically a problem among the British occupiers. And even though the non-fraternization scandal was itself relatively short-lived, it left an indelible mark on the reputation of the British occupation forces. In the opinion of certain newspapers, fratting exposed a level of ill-discipline that did not bode well for the ultimate success of the mission in Germany. But it was the supposed threat to Britain's national prestige and collective identity as a morally righteous people that continued to trigger the greatest outrage. The image of unruly British men tempted by coquettish foreign women ran contrary to the expected behaviour of members of a well-ordered military government, while also contravening mid-century Britain's sense of decency. The lasting impact of fraternization upon British conceptions of the occupation is particularly clear in some of the letters of complaint that were sent to government officials over the next four years.[66] In May 1948 Mr J. H. Webster wrote to the private secretary of Clement Attlee and implored the prime minister himself to visit the British Zone as soon as possible, where young men 'too often associate with & frequently marry German prostitutes'.[67] Attlee, he felt, ought to 'put right at once things which are doing the British government harm and unfortunately [also] the good name of England'.

12

Save Europe Now

On 22 August 1945 two British journalists travelled to the Stettiner Bahnhof ('Stettin railway station') in the Russian sector of Berlin. It was a station where trains from Eastern Europe arrived. Norman Clark, the experienced foreign correspondent of the *News Chronicle*, was joined by a relative novice, Charlie Bray. Bray, best known as a reliable middle-order batsman for Essex County Cricket Club in the early 1930s, had become a war correspondent for the official newspaper of the Labour Party, the *Daily Herald*. The pair could scarcely believe the scene that greeted them.

This once grand brick structure was a shadow of its former glory – the steep, curved windows that dominated the frontage now just a criss-cross of metal beams that gave the impression of a prison or long-abandoned warehouse. Looking out from the station in almost every direction, they saw the carcasses of bombed-out buildings. But that was all par for the course in post-war Berlin. It was the sight below the cantilevered entryway to the Stettiner Bahnhof that caused alarm: an overflowing of miserable-looking people and their belongings; men, women and children massed along the station walls, accompanied by handcarts and odd assortments of bags. Inside, the spectacle was repeated tenfold, as train after crowded train disgorged an unending stream of passengers, some of them hanging from the sides of carriages or perching on carriage roofs, onto the already inundated concourse.

Bray's poignant report captured the unfolding horror of Germany's refugee crisis:

I saw at the Stettiner Station miserable remnants of humanity, with death already shining out of their eyes – with that awful, wide-eyed stare. Four were dead already, another five or six were lying alongside them, given up as hopeless by the doctor, and just being allowed to die. The rest sat or lay about, whimpering, crying or just waiting, hanging on to the slenderest hope that something, somehow, sometime would be done for them. They are past helping themselves.[1]

In one particularly harrowing passage, the one-time cricketer described a woman 'emaciated, with dark rings under her eyes and sores breaking out all over her face' who was 'trying desperately to force milk from her milkless breasts – a pitiful effort that only left her crying at her failure'. This was 'the aftermath of war, raising problems more difficult to solve than almost any that existed during it'.

Clark's story was no less shocking. 'Here in Berlin we are living under this shadow, not just of hunger and want, but of death, and epidemics on a scale that the world has not seen in recorded history'.[2] It was, he proclaimed, a humanitarian crisis that required immediate action, without which as many as 13 million homeless Germans would die over the winter. Clark, like his colleague, was quick to broach the moral quandary at the heart of the story: 'whether or not all this happened before at the hands of the Germans... these excesses, wreaked only on the women and the children of Germany, on families of the modest means of shopkeepers or small farmers, cannot be allowed to continue'.

The refugee crisis that the two men witnessed was already nearly a year old. Since the autumn of 1944, as Soviet troops advanced towards eastern parts of what was then German territory, large swathes of locals fled west. By the end of the war, several million Germans – among them wartime evacuees, recent settlers and *Volksdeutsche* ('ethnic Germans') – had been displaced from Eastern Europe.[3] Almost immediately, the Soviet authorities and their allies in the newly installed provisional governments of Poland and Czechoslovakia began enforcing mass evictions of the remaining German inhabitants. Removals also took place in Hungary, Romania and Yugoslavia. These 'wild expulsions' were loosely in keeping with wartime agreements between the 'Big Three': as agreed at Potsdam, the Soviet Union's sphere of influence was to stretch to the Oder–Neisse line and territorial boundaries were to be radically altered. The eastern part of Germany was truncated and, almost overnight, cities that had been in Prussia for centuries became part of Poland: the city of Stettin, terminus of the railway line that served the Stettiner Bahnhof, readopted its historic Polish name of Szczecin.

The resulting mass movement of people was an act of state-sponsored ethnic cleansing. Article XII of the Potsdam Agreement had stipulated the 'population transfer' of the Germans remaining in Poland, Czechoslovakia and Hungary was to be effected in 'an orderly and humane manner'.[4] Yet Soviet troops and, in particular, their Czech and Polish allies implemented the evictions in an uncompromising fashion, with those expelled often given only a few hours, and in some cases minutes, to pack their belongings and leave.[5] In the shadow of the brutal Nazi occupations of Eastern Europe, violence and reprisals were commonplace. In East Prussia, thousands of German orphans were left to fend for themselves, escaping to a nearby forest and later acquiring the moniker of *Wolfskinder* ('wolf children').[6] In Přerov, Czechoslovakia, 265 *Sudetendeutsche* ('Sudeten Germans') were removed from their transport train by Slovakian troops and forced to dig their own graves.[7] All of them, including 120 women and 74 children, were then shot. Alongside such episodes of violence, the conditions of transit were potentially deadly: refugees, including the elderly and very young, were often packed into overcrowded cattle cars without food or water. In total, there were an estimated 600,000 deaths – although some put the figure as high as 2 million – along with innumerable sexual and physical assaults.[8]

Whether fleeing in terror or forcibly removed, several million refugees, along with their few remaining possessions, were travelling westwards on overloaded trains or by road. In time, an estimated 14 million ethnic Germans would be relocated, with as many as 8 million making their way to towns and cities in Germany. It was the greatest forced migration in human history.[9]

A huge number of these refugees inevitably found their way from the Soviet Zone of Germany to the neighbouring British Zone. The mass relocation of people on such a scale inevitably touched upon every aspect of military government, intensifying existing shortages of shelter, clothing and, above all, food.[10] Yet the British occupation authorities were slow to react to the unfolding crisis. In early August the Allied governments called for restraint from the Soviets and their allies in the east in their policy of expulsion – but since the Western Allies had no way of forcing the Soviets to conduct a more orderly population transfer, their words were little more than empty rhetoric. That September Adrian Kanaar, a British military doctor who had recently spent time as a medical officer at Bergen-Belsen before transferring to Berlin, felt compelled to

Refugees from the east arrive at a displaced persons camp in the British Zone, November 1945.

break the chain of command by sending an eyewitness report to the Foreign Office demanding action.[11] Kanaar declared his readiness to face a court martial, explaining that he had not 'spent six years in the army to see a tyranny established which is as bad as the Nazis' in reference to the behaviour of the Soviet Union in precipitating the crisis.[12]

*

Back in London the British media had remained quiet on the refugee crisis amid reporting restrictions as well as the distractions of the fratting controversy, the first war crimes trials and the surrender of Japan on 15 August (VJ Day).[13] There was, at this time, a general reluctance to dwell on the sufferings of the German people. The publisher Victor Gollancz, however, now recovered from his nervous breakdown and involved in a number of new campaigns, raised concerns about the plight of ethnic Germans in Soviet-occupied Europe.[14] But in the immediate aftermath of the war, with anti-German feeling at an all-time high, it was an unpopular cause: even progressive allies rebuked him, with *New Statesman and Nation* editor Kingsley Martin criticizing Gollancz's 'useless moral indignation'.[15] It was only after 24 August, following the publication of Clark's and Bray's reports on the harrowing scenes at Stettiner Bahnhof, that the British people – or at least some of them – took notice of the refugee crisis unfolding on the continent. A few days later, the Foreign Office demanded a full investigation into exactly what was going on.[16]

Now, with public interest in the story finally piqued, Gollancz's post-war moral crusade burst into life. In the final months of 1945, he led a national campaign aimed not only at helping those in need, but at challenging the entire ethos of the 'hard peace' agreed at Potsdam. The callousness towards the ethnic Germans was, Gollancz insisted, symbolic of a broader malaise: Europe had stared too long into the abyss of moral depravity and was now itself tainted with traits of Nazism.[17] He felt it was the responsibility of Britain to lead the way on the continent's moral regeneration.[18] A good start would be for Britain to demonstrate its determination to feed the people of Europe that winter, whether friend or foe: French, German or Pole.[19]

On 9 September 1945 Gollancz made a public appeal. He sent a letter to a number of local and national newspapers co-signed by, among others, the philosopher Bertrand Russell, the Bishop of Chichester George Bell and the Oxford classicist Gilbert Murray.[20] They insisted it was 'not in accordance with the traditions of this country to allow children – even the children of ex-enemies – to starve', and they proposed a cut to British rations in order to 'save' Europe. Readers were asked to send a postcard to 'Save Europe Now', indicating their willingness to have their own rations cut to aid their European neighbours. The initial reaction seemed promising: within a week, more than 20,000 people had responded. It prompted Gollancz to compose a new letter, this time calling upon the British government to facilitate a voluntary scheme for those who wished to donate ration coupons, food and clothes to Germany.[21] It was the beginning of a concerted campaign with a new pressure group: Save Europe Now (SEN).[22]

In early October Gollancz organized a public meeting at Conway Hall in central London. He invited all Liberal and Labour MPs, along with a number of leading Anglicans, members of the media and various other dignitaries.[23] The forty or so Labour backbenchers, newspaper editors, bishops and assorted members of the literati – including T. S. Eliot and George Orwell – who filled the venue reiterated demands for a voluntary scheme of ration cuts. The resolutions of the Conway Hall meeting also included an appeal to the British government to negotiate an end to expulsions from Eastern Europe until a four-power policy was agreed, a demand for a common policy across the Western zones for the reception of refugees and, finally, the release of Britain's food reserves.[24] Yet SEN's demands went beyond the refugee crisis, calling for increased production in the Ruhr, the mobilization of all available vehicles to break the transport bottleneck in Germany and the creation of a Supreme Economic

Council to oversee long-term reconstruction across Europe.[25] In short, the overriding aim of Save Europe Now was to push the climate of public and political opinion towards more generous treatment of the Germans.[26]

Over the following weeks further meetings took place across the country, including one at the Royal Albert Hall. The campaign attracted political attention and even led to a Commons debate on the issue in October 1945.[27] Gollancz also secured a meeting with the prime minister to discuss his concerns, but Attlee stood firm in refusing to cede to SEN's demands.[28] The Labour administration, its diplomatic backchannels with the Soviets seemingly exhausted, was focused on remedying the numerous problems confronting them in the British Zone itself.[29]

The wider public response to Save Europe Now was a different matter. There certainly was some degree of public backing for the work of SEN. Its well-attended meetings and successful postcard campaign are proof enough of that. That said, by far the most common public response to the humanitarian crisis, and Gollancz's campaign in particular, was one of ambivalence. While the group's activities were publicized and supported in the pages of *The Times*, elements of the regional press and, most frequently, the liberal-minded *Manchester Guardian*, there was next to no coverage of SEN in the country's most popular newspapers, including the *Daily Mail*, the *Daily Express*, the *Daily Mirror* and *Picture Post*.

When Gollancz's crusade was mentioned, it was often castigated as the moralistic grandstanding of the chattering classes.[30] In February 1946 a letter from one P. G. Rose appeared in *The Times* complaining that Save Europe Now 'tend to miss the point of the average citizen's grievance', namely that 'this little island is very much part of Europe and has its own belt sharply pulled in at the waistline, and could do with a bit of "saving" itself'.[31] Indeed, the popular press most often considered the refugee crisis in the context of British self-interest, rather than as a humanitarian catastrophe.[32] Bernard Buckham's *Daily Mirror* column of October 1945 entitled 'Feed the Brutes?' is a case in point.[33] Buckham told his readers that there should be 'no sympathy for the German people, or for the victims of those mass evacuations which have caused this nightmare of suffering, disease and death'. Yet he also acknowledged the practical necessity of dealing with the crisis, 'to feed and shelter these refugee hordes, and set them to work'. At the forefront of such analyses were concerns over disease that might eventually endanger British lives.

An apparent lack of public interest in the plight of the German people was recognized by a number of contemporary commentators, most skilfully in satirist David Low's cartoon for the *London Evening Standard* published in November 1945.[34] It shows a middle-aged, middle-class couple sitting down at breakfast, the husband reading a newspaper with the headline 'Winter in Central Europe'. Ghostly, stooped figures, representing Europe's wandering millions, surround them at the table. They include a skeletal figure with the face of death and a banner stating that 'Disease Knows No Frontiers'. The couple, however, sit oblivious to the scene around them: 'Why should we fuss about the Germans? They deserve it, don't they?'

*

That winter the expulsions of German populations from Eastern Europe continued – albeit with somewhat less brutality than had been the case. In late November Foreign Secretary Ernest Bevin reported to the House of Commons that British lobbying for a more orderly and humane population transfer had met with a degree of success.[35] The four occupying powers had reached an agreement on the reception of 6.5 million Germans from Poland and Czechoslovakia over the next nine months.[36] In time, temporary transit and internment camps were set up across the continent in schools, barracks and even former concentration camps. The prevailing conditions remained tough; one official report noted how at the Auschwitz I camp 'prisoners do not receive any food and hunger is steadily increasing'.[37] In many camps sexual violence, torture and conditions of degradation were common.[38] A severe housing shortage meant that many thousands of refugees would remain in this improvised accommodation for months or even years to come. During the duration of the occupation, it is estimated that the average intact floor space per person in the British Zone was only 6.2 square metres, compared to 7.6 in the American Zone and 9.4 in the French.[39]

Over the next year, the British Zone received a huge number of refugees, joining the millions of displaced persons – the freed slave labourers, concentration camp survivors, and others from Eastern Europe or the Baltic states now stranded in Germany – who were unable or unwilling to return home. As the number of mouths to feed steadily increased, the food supply now presented the most urgent and challenging issue to the British authorities in Germany.[40]

As an economic area the British Zone was dominated by the heavy industry of the Ruhr and was particularly vulnerable to food shortages. Historically, it had relied on imports from other areas of Germany. At Potsdam the requirement to treat Germany as a single economic unit, whereby industrial output from one Zone could be exchanged for food from another, had been emphasized by British negotiators. Yet there was no clear settled hierarchy of priorities among the various provisions of the agreement, and the Soviets, whose wartime losses were unmatched, took reparations as the principal concern. They demanded an allocation of $10 billion worth of reparations in kind prior to any domestic trade of food from their own, largely agricultural, Zone.[41] Thus, while consumer goods and industrial products went from west to east, there was no reciprocal exchange of foodstuffs as anticipated. The problem was augmented by Soviet attempts to collectivize German farmland, breaking up large estates and in the process hampering that year's harvest.[42]

As a result, with the approach of cold weather in late 1945 there was a very real fear of catastrophe in the British Zone. Pervasive homelessness and hunger, shattered transportation networks and inadequate supplies of clothing threatened to bring famine and disease. '[A] lot of folk out here are taking a very gloomy view of the winter from the German stand point,' remarked Captain

Henry Hughes in a letter to his wife, 'what a horrible mess the whole world seems to be in'.[43] As the crisis deepened, daily rations in the British Zone were cut to just 1,550 calories per person* – and even this meagre allocation was often hard to come by.[44] For most Germans, each day was a struggle for survival. In Anna-Maria Weber's cookbook, *Zeitgemäßes Kochen*, ('Contemporary Cooking'), readers were reminded that 'when spreading on bread, you save butter or margarine if you first stir it until it is frothy'.[45] In the country's newspapers improvised recipes appeared that used the few ingredients that were freely available, including one for 'pine needle tea': 30 grams (1 oz) needles to 1.1 litres (2 pints) water, with a recommended brewing time of three to five minutes.[46] This wasn't the only culinary use of trees: in the *Pathé News* film *Germany's Food – The Truth* a factory near Arnsberg was shown making 'liver sausage' from timber. 'Beechwood is used but the product can also be made from pine,' explained the narrator. 'Ten tons a week is produced here and sold to the Germans in place of fish or meat'.[47]

For British occupiers, the sight of young children waiting expectantly outside messes for scraps of discarded food soon became commonplace. Many opted to give up their own rations to help those so obviously in need. A. G. Dickens recalled a German man pointing to a British soldier and exclaiming to his child 'Look, there goes the Chocolate Uncle!'[48] Mick Morris-Metcalf, serving with the Royal Military Police, was forced to explain to his superiors that he had given away his rations to children in Bad Salzuflen. 'Well, we'll be bloody hungry,' replied his captain. 'We gave ours too.'[49]

But individual acts of generosity were never going to be enough. In November 1945 a cabinet meeting heard that Britain simply could not supply enough food to sustain the 25 million Germans

---

* There were special categories for different groups, including Holocaust survivors, miners and displaced persons, who were entitled to claim higher rations. Finding these extra supplies could prove challenging though, and, in the case of victims of Nazi oppression, it was not always easy to prove one's eligibility.

In September 1945 German school children in the British sector
of Berlin await their daily ration of gruel.

now living under their rule. In the short term, food shortages were
causing increasing levels of absenteeism in key industries such as
coal mining, as workers scavenged the countryside for foodstuffs
and black market trades. This further exacerbated the problem, as
reduced coal output not only worsened domestic fuel scarcities but
also diminished the potential income from coal exports that could
pay for food from abroad.[50] In the longer term, the very real danger
of a famine in central Europe was becoming all too clear.[51] With the
news of other serious food shortages in India and Malaysia, then
still part of the British Empire, there was a need for urgent action.
Attlee's cash-strapped government was forced to redirect grain
imports set for the British Isles to Germany, all while attempting to
persuade the Americans to take on more responsibility for feeding
the German people.* In the late summer of 1945 the British had

* It was a more radical response than had been taken during the war, when a
man-made famine in British-run Bengal had led to millions of deaths.

already set about releasing thousands of German prisoners of war to help bring in the harvest (Operation Barleycorn) and to work in the Ruhr's coalmines (Operation Coalscuttle).

Even with these efforts there remained a critical shortage of food in the British Zone during the first six months of 1946.[52] In January of that year infant mortality was estimated at 136 per 1,000 births, while in January 1938 it had stood at 61.[53] In case of any cessation in the supply of North American wheat, the ration in the British Zone would reduce to 900 calories per person per day – around one-third of the UK's allocation.[54] In that eventuality there would be a serious risk of mass starvation and disease, a flu epidemic being a major fear. In March, even without a total breakdown of supplies, the average ration available in parts of the British Zone hovered around 1,000 calories per day – half of daily requirements.[55] British government officials remained in close contact with their military commanders in the Zone and assessed the potential threat to law and order if food imports to Germany were impeded any further.[56]

*

It was a close-run thing, but Britain's response proved to be just enough to stave off a full-blown famine. That a humanitarian catastrophe was averted during the 'Battle of the Winter' is a minor miracle and one for which British administrators deserve their fair share of credit. Yet, remarkably, the news actually prompted some backlash in the British press. In February 1946 Edwin Tetlow wrote in the *Daily Mail* of how 'one remembers the prophecies of last autumn that thousands, possibly millions of Germans would now be dead from hunger. They aren't. Don't believe any tales of mass misery among the Germans'.[57] It was another illustration of the persistent depths of ill-feeling towards Germany, even as tragedy loomed.

Any relief among the occupiers that disaster had been averted was short-lived. The British found themselves in an unenviable position: they were now entirely dependent on food imports from North America to maintain even a meagre ration in the Zone.[58]

In late 1945 a British medic weighs passing Germans to ascertain the degree of malnutrition among the civilian population.

The cost of these imports would consume Britain's dwindling supply of dollar reserves and represented an unacceptable financial burden. Another solution had to be found, and fast.

The war had been a huge drain on Britain's finances and the problem was exacerbated when American financial aid in the form of lend-lease abruptly ended in September 1945. That decision reignited fears in London that the United States was reverting to its pre-war isolationism. Now, the outlay required to stave off disaster in the British Zone only further deepened the country's financial quagmire. In 1946 the exchequer projected that annual Control Commission expenditure would be an astonishing £80 million, but even this proved an underestimate: the bill reached £119 million for the year, just over 3 per cent of the central government's entire expenditure.[59] It was an imposition that Chancellor of the Exchequer Hugh Dalton openly resented: 'I am quite sure that the British taxpayer cannot, and should not, much longer be expected to go on paying, on this scale, what are, in effect, reparations to Germany. Speaking as chancellor of the exchequer, I grudge the money.'[60]

It was an unsustainable situation, with the growing financial cost of occupying Germany threatening the integrity of Britain's standing as a world power.[61] Yet the British were all too aware of the need to maintain their position in Germany. For one, there were the obvious humanitarian concerns that Save Europe Now had raised. These linked to more pragmatic considerations: the cost of allowing the situation in Germany to spiral out of control, whether it be a new brand of fascism or the spread of disease, could not be countenanced. In the spring of 1946, there were also escalating fears that German workers might embrace communism over liberal democracy, as a number of strikes and hunger marches rocked the Ruhr while large numbers of Communist Party candidates were voted onto works councils.[62] As Deputy Governor of the American Zone Lucius D. Clay remarked, there was no choice 'between being a communist on 1,500 calories or a believer in democracy on 1,000'.[63]

Attlee's government knew that only a balanced German economy that legitimately functioned as a single economic unit could minimize Britain's expenditure. But as inter-Allied disagreements in Germany intensified, this seemed to be an increasingly implausible aspiration.[64] The Foreign Office, previously unwilling to give up on the 'Big Three' framework, began to consider plans for an alternative approach to Germany which would break away from the stipulations of the Potsdam Agreement and end Britain's precarious alliance with the Soviet Union.[65] The proposed 'Western option', outlined by the staunchly anti-communist Ernest Bevin at a cabinet meeting in early May 1946, would aim to offset the cost of food imports through increasing the amount of goods exported from Germany.[66] It proposed a more rapid transfer of power back to the Germans and the reconstruction of the country's severely hamstrung industrial economy. The danger of the Soviet Union, Bevin suggested, had become 'as great as, and possibly even greater than, that of a revived Germany'.[67]

In the summer of 1946, British policymakers reached something of a consensus, privately accepting the need for this new approach in Germany. It then became a question of diplomacy as Bevin led the charge in trying to bring the Americans on board. In July, at the Paris Conference of Foreign Ministers, he openly declared Britain's intention to organize their Zone 'in such a manner that no further liability shall fall on the British taxpayer'. This announcement came in the midst of heated negotiations with the US, who remained unwilling to cede to Britain's demands that their burden be drastically lessened. At one point, Bevin suggested that the British might have to consider withdrawing from Germany altogether unless the costs of occupation were reduced.[68] It was likely a bluff: the foreign secretary was reluctant to endure the loss of status that such a move would entail, let alone the strategic risks involved. But it reveals quite how desperate the British were for a change of strategy in Germany only a year after Potsdam.

At the same time, domestic pressure on the Attlee administration was mounting. In July 1946 the Ministry of Food was forced to announce the introduction of bread rationing across the UK – something that had been assiduously avoided during both world

Right-wing extremist Eleonora Tennant (centre) parades around
Westminster protesting against the introduction of bread rationing
to the UK in July 1946.

wars.* In many ways, bread rationing was a policy which acquiesced
to SEN's calls for more government action and popular sacrifice.
But rather than being evidence of support for Gollancz, the news
was greeted with widespread outrage. In the House of Commons,
leader of the opposition Winston Churchill, sensing a chance to
put one over on the government, described the policy as 'one of the
gravest announcements that I have ever heard made in the House
in the time of peace'.[69] According to the *Daily Mail*, bread rationing
was 'the most hated measure ever to have been presented to the
people of this country'.[70] There were complaints from the British
Housewives League, who proclaimed to be in 'outright revolt'
against the bread ration.[71] At the furthest extreme of the debate,

---

* This rationing, as with the entire era of British post-war austerity (1945–
51), was primarily about maintaining the country's dollar reserves. These
were needed to pay for imports from North America and to service the
American loan.

the arch-Germanophobe Eleonora Tennant took direct action: she and two associates strode around Westminster wearing sandwich posters describing the MPs who voted for bread rationing as 'Criminals, Dictators, Contemptible and Public Menaces'.[72]

This heated public response ultimately warned the government off any further imposition on the ration book, despite the ongoing efforts of Gollancz and his supporters.[73] Whatever the ethical desirability and practical necessity of the policy, it was a public relations disaster, which served to intensify anti-German sentiment across Britain.

*

The growing evidence of widespread distress, malnutrition and mass dislocation in Germany struck at the heart of the moral and practical dilemmas underpinning the Allied occupation. In the summer of 1945, the Potsdam Agreement had outlined a stringent economic settlement, based on the prospect of ongoing cooperation between the 'Big Three'. Yet relations with the Soviets rapidly soured – with Britain and the Soviet Union, not the Americans, taking the first steps on the path towards a cold war. At the same time, unprecedented problems across Europe during the autumn and winter of 1945–6 made a mockery of the ambitious Allied plans for restructuring the German economy. In less than a year, the Potsdam Agreement had been rendered more or less defunct.

Britain was in a fix: financially crippled by six years of war and further hamstrung by the relentlessly escalating costs of its occupation of Germany, it was now facing a threat to domestic consumption previously thought unimaginable. For Britain's leading policymakers it was an untenable position. As time went on, the Attlee administration came to accept that the revival of Germany's economy in order to offset the cost of importing foodstuffs was unavoidable. This marked a clear shift away from the plans agreed between the Allies at the end of the war. The Soviets remained vehemently opposed to a policy they saw as opening the door to a German resurgence that might threaten their security, and it only worsened the growing tensions between East and West soured yet further. But the British felt they had no choice: if the Soviets weren't prepared to reshuffle their priorities away from securing reparations, then Britain would have to keep footing the bill for the food imports required to stave off total disaster.

That summer, Ernest Bevin was locked in negotiations with the US secretary of state, James F. Byrnes, in an attempt to find a diplomatic solution to Britain's predicament. With hindsight, we can see the foreign secretary's strategic manoeuvres as the starting gun of a conflict between East and West that would consume Europe for the next forty years. Eventually persuading Washington to pursue the 'Western option' in Germany was arguably Britain's final act as a major world power: in time, it was the Americans and the Soviets who would make the running in the nascent Cold War.

But this secret evolution of Britain's policy towards Germany hardly figured in media portrayals of the occupation, where attention remained fixed on the 'German Problem' as it had been understood at the end of the war. During the first year of the peace, the main focus of most British observers had been the prosecution of Nazis and the eradication of Germany's military power, as well as the scandal over fratting. Even when Gollancz's Save Europe Now campaign raised awareness of the refugee crisis, the most common response was one of indifference, underpinned by the sense that the Germans had brought it upon themselves. In fact, a peak of public and media interest in the crisis came in July 1946 with the announcement of the introduction of bread rationing – an iniquity that seemed to many unbefitting of a victor.

It is clear that swathes of the British media and public remained highly sceptical of anything resembling rapprochement towards their wartime enemy, even in the face of widespread suffering or even simply on the grounds of economic necessity. At the same time, it *was* evident – to government ministers, to journalists and to the country at large – that Britain's attempt to 'win the peace' had entered troubled waters. In February 1946 Selkirk

Panton warned readers of his column in the *Daily Express* that the German people were 'feeling sorry for themselves' and had 'learnt nothing from the war and their defeat'. After six years 'at our throats' and nine months 'at our feet', the German was now 'at our breakfast table, clamouring for bread'.[74]

Part Three

ALL IS NOT WELL

13

Germany Under Control

In June 1946 Sholto Douglas, the new military governor of the British Zone, stepped onto the stage of the Dominion Theatre in London's West End. It was a venue accustomed to the glitz and glamour of musicians and film stars – fifteen years earlier Charlie Chaplin had stood on the same stage during the UK premiere of his film *City Lights*. In contrast, Douglas, a heavy-set, pipe-smoking RAF veteran, wasn't the archetypical showman; but this wasn't the archetypical show.

'We cannot proceed with our great task in Germany without the support and help of the British people', Douglas announced to a crowd of more than 3,000 attendees. The audience included the mayors of each London borough, a scattering of minor celebrities, and friends and families of personnel on active service in the British Zone.[1] The 'magnificent work' of the Control Commission was, he continued, 'an achievement of which the whole British people may be proud'. Yet it seemed to him, in light of the flurry of negative stories in the popular press about occupied Germany, as if these successes were 'not always properly appreciated at home'. Douglas, who had recently taken over command for the Zone from Field Marshal Montgomery, was speaking at the opening ceremony of 'Germany Under Control', a public exhibition that aimed to 'show the work, aims and achievements' of the occupying forces.[2]

*

The growth of public relations as a facet of governance during the twentieth century is noteworthy and visible across both democracies and dictatorships. The extension of the right to vote, coupled with the greatly expanding role of the state, encouraged politicians to pay greater attention to mass opinion.[3] Over the course of two world wars, the overlapping fields of PR and propaganda were increasingly regarded as vital to the maintenance of morale on the 'home front'.[4] In Britain, Attlee's Labour government applied these lessons to peacetime and considered public relations an essential part of implementing their radical programme of social reform.[5] The turn to 'spin' also took place in post-war Germany, where the Control Commission formed its own Public Relations/ Information Services Control Group (PR/ISC), which was tasked with managing the public image of the occupation forces.[6] The group was headed by Major General W. H. Alexander Bishop, a former deputy director of the Political Warfare Executive – Britain's clandestine wartime propaganda operation.[7]

In the first instance, PR/ISC was given the job of communicating all manner of messages to the German people as part of their re-education, from evidence of Nazi crimes to basic information about the rules and regulations of the military government. But officials reasoned there would also be considerable interest in the fate of Germany back in Britain and realized it would be their job to 'manage' the information that made its way across the North Sea.[8] It was clear, one official noted, that news about the occupation was a 'closed shop' in which 'the entire picture of the military government in this Zone reaches the man in the street as a result of what he sees on the screen, what he hears on his radio and what he reads in his newspaper'.[9] With proper official oversight, it might be possible to ensure that 'the aims, achievements and difficulties of military government in the British Zone are properly presented to the public'.

In August 1945 a detailed public relations strategy was drawn up to define the character of information allowed to flow back to

Britain. The stated objective of the PR/ISC was to encourage a 'fair and accurate picture of military government operations'; implicitly, it was to stem the dissemination of news stories which would encourage popular protest or media criticism.[10] One Information Services official, Captain George W. Houghton, candidly remarked that this PR strategy was intended to 'help the press to put over the right stuff' and to 'prevent the correspondents having to search in inappropriate quarters and thus produce inaccuracies and get on to undesirable subjects'.[11]

In more concrete terms, Major Twist of the military government warned Information Services staff that, because the predominant feeling of the British public was still 'to hell with the Germans; let's put our own house in order first!', they should be wary of painting too bright a picture.[12] In addition, any message that might incorrectly suggest that 'controlling Germany is a simple matter' could spark 'an outcry from the folks at home for the troops to come back'. There was also to be no hint that anything like normal life was resuming in Germany, since this would also likely cause outrage and misunderstanding.

PR/ISC officials recognized that 'nine tenths of news... has to emanate from official sources' and, as such, they could exert a formidable amount of influence over the content of news reports.[13] In the case of the ever popular newsreels, imposing this sort of editorial oversight was fairly straightforward. The dependence of newsreel production companies on the authorities for film footage made them especially amenable to official control. As a result, the PR/ISC aimed to use the films issued by *Pathé*, *Gaumont-British* and *British Movietone News* to publicize the work of the Control Commission.[14] But it was the newspapers, as a result of their soaring popularity, that would provide the most influential and up-to-date accounts of life in occupied Germany: total newspaper circulation in Britain, in what was a golden age of the press, surpassed 15 million copies daily.[15] According to the official guidelines, the PR/ISC was to supply correspondents, 'as the intermediaries between the occupation authorities and the public at home', with the 'most accurate and fullest information, compatible with the maintenance of security, for a properly balanced presentation of facts'.[16] In practice, however, things were a little different. British officials used press conferences and printed handouts to provide newspaper journalists with choreographed and officially vetted public statements. Moreover, access to official personnel for interviews was strictly controlled and offered the Control Commission another, even more direct means to put across their carefully composed public relations message.

This conventional modern media management operated alongside more intrusive attempts to curtail the freedom of the press. Journalists sent to the British Zone in the hope of 'finding the news' were, like all visitors, required to follow a specific tour schedule arranged by PR/ISC officials. The documentary records of several touring parties of journalists have survived and show that the specific routes, means of transportation, accommodation and schedules of events were planned in painstaking detail.[17] For the most part, these itineraries were prepared unilaterally and tour groups were assigned a 'conducting officer' whose job was effectively to enforce compliance with the preplanned programme. The same regulations also controlled other visiting parties to Germany, such as filmmakers, politicians or writers. In May 1946 the Conservative MP Godfrey Nicholson offered a scathing public critique of the Control Commission's public relations strategy. In the House of Commons, he questioned the restrictions placed upon journalists, describing the chaperoned visits as 'Cook's Tours' of 'very little use' and 'everything for which the expression "conducted tour" stands'.[18] Nicholson reserved special indignation for John Hynd, as head of the Control Office for Germany and Austria, who, he alleged, exercised 'complete censorship upon who shall go... and on what they shall do there'.

The exercise of official controls and regulations over the mass media was, of course, nothing new: the war itself had seen a great deal of cooperation between the British government and the press, especially regarding the conduct of frontline reporters. In post-war Germany the transition to peacetime reporting regulations was intentionally slow, and wartime restrictions, including the need for official accreditation, were preserved to the advantage of the spin doctors.[19] The official status of 'war correspondent' was not abolished until August 1946, and even after this date journalists were obliged to wear British military uniform. As Terence Prittie, Berlin correspondent for the *Manchester Guardian*, recalled: 'I lived virtually isolated from the people of Berlin, in a British requisitioned flat, eating British rations, using British transport facilities and British occupation currency, even initially wearing British uniform.'[20] Given the occupied's mistrust of the occupiers, visibly belonging to one of the victor nations and depending on its support severely constrained the professional independence of journalists.[21] In addition, while newspapers mostly continued to follow the practice of self-regulation established in wartime, the official censorship of news still remained a risk for uncooperative editors.[22] Norman Clark, chairman of the British Zone Correspondents Association, reckoned that the exceptional circumstances of reporting in post-war Germany made it 'the most difficult story in the world to cover'.[23]

In spite of all these efforts to stymie the freedom of the press, in the first months of the occupation a number of highly critical stories had reached the 'man in the street'. Furthermore, PR/ISC officials were justifiably anxious that the government's April 1946 budget, which would publicize the extent of Britain's expenditure in Germany for the first time, was likely to give the public 'a shock'.[24] Underpinning these immediate concerns were more ideological considerations: many of those in senior positions in the British Zone feared that, without adequate public pressure to stay the course, political leaders back in London might lose their appetite for maintaining the occupation. They also held a sincere conviction that the task in Germany was a momentous one deserving of wide acclaim: 'history books will record [the occupation of Germany] in centuries to come', remarked one public relations official, '[but] can it be placed on the record now?'[25]

*

A more proactive public relations strategy was required, one that would defend the integrity of the British occupiers and repair the damage done to their reputation by media attacks. And so it was that in late 1945, PR/ISC officials decided that the CCG should be permitted to 'tell its own story' through exhibitions, films and written publications. These 'in-house' productions – all of them subject to the editorial control of the British authorities – would help 'spin' the news emerging from Germany by presenting a more positive, optimistic vision of the occupation. The aim of the campaign was to 'produce informed public opinion' about the situation in Germany and to promote the legitimacy and efficiency of the Control Commission's approach.[26] These endeavours would be coupled with renewed attempts to use the BBC's output to shed favourable light on the CCG.

In December 1945 representatives of the Control Commission and the British Army of the Rhine settled on the idea of a public exhibition conducive to 'the enlightenment of the public at home in regard to the tasks and problems of the Control Commission'.[27] Their plans did not get off to an ideal start: the organizers had hoped to be able to open the exhibition during budget week in April 1946, thereby offering the British public an explanation for the huge financial outlay in Germany.[28] It was a prudent timeline, especially because, as it turned out, Hugh Dalton would use his budget speech in the Commons to fan the flames of discontent over the cost of the occupation. Yet various logistical problems delayed the opening of the exhibition until the summer, when it would be held in conjunction with the London Victory Celebrations commemorating the first anniversary of the end of the war in Europe.

On 7 June 1946 'Germany Under Control' opened in a former air raid shelter on New Oxford Street in central London. The opening ceremony at the Dominion Theatre featured speeches from Sholto Douglas, his deputy Brian Robertson, and John Hynd. Hynd, as the government minister with overall responsibility for the British Zone, was especially keen to highlight the various achievements of the occupation which, he suggested, were being accomplished with 'no less credit by our men and women in Germany than the military victory itself'. But in his concluding remarks, Hynd offered a starker message, warning against any potential repeat of the complacency that had seen the British leave Germany soon after the end of the First World War:

> Our military government and the Control Commission have worked miracles, but miracles have still to be achieved before order is fully restored and the objective of the Potsdam Agreement is realized... This time we must be sure. This time we must stay until we have finished the job.[29]

As for the exhibition itself, a 'Popular Room' held the main attractions. These included large physical exhibits such as a Volkswagen Beetle, sent over by Ivan Hirst in the hope of garnering some positive publicity for his efforts at Wolfsburg; examples of military equipment transformed into agricultural machinery; Himmler's death mask; saucepans made from Wehrmacht helmets; and a display comparing German and British rations on a set of scales.[30] Alongside this was the 'Information Room' where up-to-date statistics and reports received from the British Zone live by teleprinter illustrated the ongoing work of the Control Commission. A number of service personnel seconded from Germany were on hand to answer questions from attendees.[31]

In terms of narrative, the exhibition didn't shirk on detail. The full script of the exhibition's displays was over 12,000 words in length. It began with a chronological interpretation of German history and accompanying diagnosis of Nazism.[32] Developments in Germany between 1918 and 1945 were the subject of around one-third of the displays and were focused on condemning 'German military tradition'. The Nazi Party was characterized as 'an instrument of conspiracy and coercion' put into power 'by an evil alliance among fanatical Nazi revolutionaries and the most unrestrained German reactionaries and militarists'. The displays went on to explore the widespread popularity of Hitler and 'the inherent autocratic mind of the German'.

The remainder of the exhibition summarized the broad objectives and 'machinery of control' set out at Potsdam in 1945. Then, unsurprisingly, there was an extensive array of evidence assembled to support the idea that the British were 'winning the peace'. These ranged from details of various demilitarization, denazification and de-industrialization activities through to an outline of 'the economic problem', health policy, education reforms, re-education, civil service restructuring, police reorganization, the rebirth of democratic politics and even the rearrangement of the German fire services.[33] 'Germany Under Control' acknowledged the potential corrigibility of the German people under the watchful supervision of the British occupiers and venerated 'the British model' as an excellent and curative means to remove the 'Nazi taint' from the German state and society.

At the same time, in accordance with the accompanying London Victory Celebrations, the Second World War and the theme of national sacrifice in pursuit of victory took centre stage. Wartime symbols and artefacts were displayed to draw in crowds and challenge critical interpretations of the occupation. These included numerous exhibits that were somewhat peripheral to the overarching theme of occupying Germany, such as the bronze eagle from the Reich Chancellery, Hitler's personal standard and a full range of German medals issued by the Nazi Party.[34] There were even abortive plans to transport from Hitler's bunker the room in which he had committed suicide.

'Germany Under Control' attracted over 220,000 visitors before embarking on a tour of sixteen cities around the UK.[35] While this fell short of initial projections, partly owing to organizational deficiencies, the PR/ISC regarded it as a success.[36] In addition, press coverage augmented the scope of the exhibition's impact, a result of a number of national and local newspapers reproducing the information on display. Some reports even quoted lead organizer Brigadier Campbell's grandiose claim that 'the task undertaken by the Control Commission was the greatest enterprise this nation had ever set its hand to'.[37]

The exhibition's positive impact upon public perceptions of the occupation of Germany stemmed from a combination of an interesting set of artefacts, a coherent narrative and, perhaps most importantly, successful promotion. In the pursuit of popular backing for the CCG, the exhibition's organizers had embraced all the tools of modern public relations. They put together an eye-catching poster emphasizing the notion of turning 'swords into ploughshares', a press preview, BBC radio reports covering the opening ceremony, the production of the BBC's first television documentary – produced under the same title and transmitted on 18 September 1946 – and the presence of A-list celebrities such as Basil Radford and Michael Redgrave at the exhibition, even if members of the royal family declined to be associated 'with such a controversial subject'.[38]

It was clear, moreover, that the exhibition had caught the attention of influential members of the political and media establishment. An official report remarked on how 'certain sections of the public' had shown considerable interest, specifically mentioning MPs, journalists and lecturers.[39] The succinct outline of the aims of the occupation as set down at Potsdam, the successes to this point and the reasoning behind a long-term commitment of time and money even encouraged one visiting MP to request elements of the exhibition be retained for display in the Houses of Parliament.[40]

There were, however, obvious limitations to the effectiveness of this public relations exercise, not least its relatively modest scale. A single exhibition could hardly be expected to compete with the powerful aggregate influence of the most popular national newspapers. There were also a number of practical problems with 'Germany Under Control' as an exhibition, prompting one visitor to write to the organizers and complain that he 'found the whole show to be very dull'.[41] A more representative visitor survey suggested that some members of the general public were sceptical of official information presented in this manner and branded it 'propaganda'.[42] There were repeated complaints from visitors about the integrity of the facts on display, with some even expressing doubts about whether the Germans were actually starving. A significant design flaw may be to blame: an ambiguity in the arrangement of the exhibit comparing British food rations with their much more meagre German equivalents had actually left many visitors with the opposite impression. As a result, the exhibition's staff were regularly asked why the British people were paying taxes to provide their defeated foe with such generous allowances of food. A number of staff grew concerned that patrons seemed to be leaving the exhibition with little idea of what exactly Britain was gaining from the occupation.[43]

*

'Germany Under Control' was only one part of a much broader public relations campaign. Many officials felt that a more appropriate medium for explaining why the British were in Germany and what they were doing there was the documentary film.[44] Inspired by the Documentary Film Movement, PR/ISC officials – with the help of the Central Office of Information's Crown Film Unit – set about producing films for screening in cinemas and workplaces across the country.[45]

In March 1946 they had released their first cinematic portrayal of Germany under occupation, entitled *A Defeated People* (which we also encountered in Chapter Six). Humphrey Jennings's short documentary film attempted to deploy the patriotic appeal of this gifted director's filmmaking to the advantage of the Control Commission.[46] Despite its blunt portrayal of the extent of material destruction wreaked on Germany, the film left little room for sympathy; it emphasized the supposed collective guilt of the German people for 'the war they started' and sounded frank warnings about the dangers posed by a Nazi resurgence. The British occupiers, on the other hand, were characterized as magnanimous, pragmatic and self-interested: 'our military government – that is your husbands and sons – have to prod the Germans into putting their house in order'.[47]

In the press, reviewers generally responded positively. The *Yorkshire Post* described the CCG as 'working wonders', while the *Sunday Express* commended the film for presenting 'with the inescapable persuasion of visual impact the nature and complexities of the task facing the administrators'.[48] Yet *A Defeated People*'s most powerful message was of Germany's all-encompassing downfall. The footage of destroyed towns and cities, ravaged shipyards and factories, and a beleaguered people emphasized the annihilation of the country's military and economic power. The film ultimately amounted to a self-congratulatory reflection on the comprehensive nature of Britain's victory. This sense of Germany's utter defeat was reflected in many of the film's reviews. The *Daily Worker*'s film critic was taken aback by the powerful effect of its visual representation of utter devastation, while the *News Chronicle* remarked that 'you will never obtain from any written or spoken narrative such an effect of empty misery and crushed aggressiveness, of a country so lost it is ripe for anything'.[49]

Shot on location in the British Zone, *A Defeated People* is an impressive and artistically valuable film which exemplifies the PR/ISC's endeavour to engage public support and raise awareness of the British occupation. Yet much like 'Germany Under Control', its influence hardly competed with that of the popular press. The length of time taken to produce the film meant that, when it eventually came out, its positive portrayal of British efforts in Germany struggled to supplant the adverse public image of the occupiers that had already taken root. A subsequent PR/ISC report acknowledged that the publicity value of the CCG's first documentary feature had been impaired by delays.[50] Instead, the film stood as a testament to the war, the destruction of Germany and the principles agreed at Potsdam – a 'hard peace' fit for a sinful people.

*

The Public Relations Division of the CCG had two more cards up their sleeve. First was the BBC, specifically the network's prolific and ubiquitous radio programming. The production of radio shows was much less time-consuming and costly than capturing and editing motion pictures, and 'the wireless' remained incredibly popular. Radio was also a medium that in many ways lent itself to a more pedagogical and more informative style, as had been achieved to great effect during the war itself. But perhaps most importantly, the BBC, as a public broadcaster, was historically amenable to official oversight – especially with regard to British foreign policy.[51]

In late 1946 Sholto Douglas, as military governor, raised the idea of recording a series of BBC radio programmes on the occupation in response to 'the spate of criticisms of the Control Commission which have been appearing in British newspapers'.[52] He felt that these unfavourable judgments had emerged out of an 'ignorance of the real position' that risked souring public opinion against the occupation. John Hynd, head of the Control Office for Germany and Austria, welcomed the proposal and within a few weeks Douglas had recorded a talk for the BBC programme *World Affairs*, which would eventually be broadcast in January 1947.[53] In it Douglas responded directly to the criticisms of the CCG and asserted that the vast majority of his staff were hard-working men and women who 'have carried our good name to the four corners of the world. Many indeed have done so before. They are continuing that mission in Germany.' In the following months regular programmes aired documenting the work of the CCG, pressing home the importance of their activities while correcting supposed distortions in the press.

Another tactic employed by the PR/ISC was aimed at beating the newspapers at their own game. In September 1945 it launched the *British Zone Review* (*BZR*), an in-house magazine due to be published bi-weekly for the duration of the occupation.[54] The PR/ISC hoped to replicate the success of the *Post Office Magazine*, a comparable PR exercise that had begun life as an internal publication before gaining a large public readership in the 1930s.[55] The regularity and quick turnaround time of such an undertaking, combined with total editorial authority, offered a potentially powerful means of disseminating information. The *British Zone Review* would be distributed across Britain as well as among personnel in Germany. As a member of the magazine's editorial board noted, it was intended 'to be a really re-educative publication. By re-educative I do not only mean for the Germans, but also of the British attitude towards their own task in Germany.'[56]

The *BZR* was described as the CCG's 'shop window', offering readers a 'review of the activities of the Control Commission' in order to emphasize 'the difficulties of CCG's job and illustrate what the job is'.[57] The magazine featured an array of articles on all aspects of the occupation, some offering a light-hearted take on the experience of living and working in Germany and others presenting a more political take on the occupation. In addition, a number of regular columns featured items such as soldiers' letters, interviews with British journalists stationed in the Zone, profiles of German officials, articles by commanding officers, photograph compendiums and a padre's page.

From the very beginning BZR had a rather disorderly feel. Its unusual mixture of articles was united only by the fact that they were incessantly upbeat about the work of the Control Commission. A CCG official complained that while it was 'expressive of a certain friendliness', the publication lacked a clear identity, was 'encouraging rather than constructive' and ultimately 'devoid of a point of view'.[58] The head of the PR/ISC's Magazine Section was less tactful and criticized the publication for being 'simply cheap and often very crude propaganda on behalf of the Commission'.[59] The BZR's editorial board habitually discussed increasing the scope and refining the clarity of the magazine's message. Yet the publication's editor, John Moffat, remained wary, warning that by taking a firmer stance on the issues of the day 'the government might be accused of running a newspaper!'[60] In his view there were two types of propaganda, direct and indirect: 'the first is crude, the second discreet. The first often fails; the second always produces results. The "BZR" practises the second.'[61]

The magazine did indeed find some relative success within the British Zone, where the vast majority of its 20,000-copy print run was distributed.[62] This is perhaps unsurprising considering that the magazine was free and available to British troops starved of English-language reading material. But as a means of public relations within the UK, the BZR was an unmitigated disaster. Around 2,000 copies of each edition were sent to Britain, sold at a cost of sixpence by His Majesty's Stationery Office and the stationer W. H. Smith & Son. It was assumed that, as the publication became better known, this number would quickly increase. This proved to be a wildly optimistic assumption: sales barely managed to top 500 overall and some branches sold as few as 2 copies.[63] But Brigadier John Treadwell suggested that, since MPs, government officials and, most importantly, national newspaper editors received copies of the *BZR*, it exerted some influence on the public debate over post-war Germany.[64]

However, in light of the limited impact of Jennings's *A Defeated People* and the programmes broadcast on BBC radio, combined with the public's almost total unawareness of the *British Zone Review* in Britain itself, it looked increasingly as if the ambitions of the CCG's Public Relations Division to redirect public opinion about the work of the British occupiers were doomed to failure.

*

If any further proof of the PR/ISC's shortcomings was required, in July 1946 one of the country's most popular newspapers published the most damning and sustained attack on the British occupation to date. Trevor Blore's article in the *Daily Mirror* appeared under an uncompromising headline: '£160 million a year – to teach the Germans to despise us'.[65] Blore claimed that 'lavish supplies of inexpensive drinks and easy, but dirty, money' were causing 'widespread demoralization and corruption' among British staff in Germany. It was, he suggested, 'all so easy' for a sizeable proportion of staff to make huge profits and run amok. The piece identified the heavy drinking of service personnel as a major source of misbehaviour, alleging that 'any midday or evening' you could see 'small groups of British men and women, generally of civilian status, swigging champagne cocktails... at the double'. Blore expressed particular dismay at the spectacle of 'British women, some mere girls, carried out dead drunk under the eyes of the German servants'.

The article went on to criticize black market dealings that were rumoured to be common practice among officers and were alleged to have 'robbed' the British taxpayer of at least £15 million in the last year alone. These corrupt activities, Blore continued, had also encouraged a spate of thefts and murders – occurring almost on a daily basis – against which a 'hopelessly understaffed' British police force were battling. Finally, Blore poured scorn on the quality of the personnel hired by the Control Commission, who were said to be antagonizing the Germans rather than acting as representatives of British democracy. He took special effort to commend the 2nd Battalion of the Essex Regiment for having avoided the misconduct so prevalent among their civilian colleagues. According to Blore, these soldiers had maintained Britain's honour by marching through the town of Einbeck at frequent intervals with colours flying so as 'to remind the local citizens who won the war'.

The litany of failings outlined in the *Daily Mirror*'s 'report to the people', all of which came 'at the expense of the British taxpayer's pocket and Britain's prestige', had been exposed through the cooperation of a number of disgruntled and concerned personnel in Germany. The paper reprinted some of their letters, including one from an anonymous veteran of both world wars and both military occupations of Germany, warning that the same mistakes were being repeated: 'Some of the examples we set the Germans here are very like the way their own officers acted when in Paris, Brussels, Amsterdam and elsewhere! They fail to see any difference in OUR way of living'. The result, he believed, was that the Germans, who 'to their faces, submit to insults' from ill-behaved British personnel, were profiting 'behind their backs' as a result of such weakness.

Blore's exposé marked a shift in tone from earlier attacks on the British forces in Germany. While controversies like fratting had piqued the public's interest and the refugee crisis had exposed the frailties of the Potsdam Agreement, the claims made in the *Daily Mirror* were a more comprehensive questioning of Britain's entire endeavour. If the British Zone really was a swamp of ineptitude and bad behaviour, and the competence and probity of Britain's occupying force was called into question, how could the British possibly hope to re-educate and reform the Germans? In the course of the next year, as more and more stories of scandal emerged from the Zone, these doubts over Britain's ability to succeed in Germany would only intensify.

14

The Best of Everything

On 9 June 1946, only two days after the opening of the 'Germany Under Control' exhibition, assistant chaplain-general of the British Army of the Rhine, the Revd Geoffrey Druitt, conducted a service of dedication in Berlin before a congregation which included some of the most senior officers in the BAOR and Control Commission. It was a warm Whitsunday in the German capital and the assembled audience – mostly in formal military dress – may well have had their minds on other things: a drink in the local beer garden? A stroll down the Kurfürstendamm? Or perhaps another rendezvous with their favourite Fräulein? As Gerald Lenanton remarked in a letter home to his wife, the Rhine Army 'very sensibly do not work, even unofficially, on Sunday'.[1]

Druitt was, in his own words, 'out for trouble'.[2] In the months prior he had tried, through backchannels and tempered statements, to draw the attention of senior officers to what he saw as perhaps the gravest problem facing the British in Germany: the supposedly crumbling sense of morality among the occupiers themselves. Yet these admonitions had come to nought and now Druitt planned a 'bold and startling pronouncement'. Risking the wrath of his seniors, he had invited members of the British press to attend the service, in the hope of ensuring that his warnings would not be ignored. His sermon, 'You and Germany', was intended to be a moral wake-up call to even the most distracted members of the congregation. 'We must get our eyes open to the things that are really happening... we must see where we are and where we're heading for', he proclaimed.[3] In Druitt's view there seemed to be no end in sight to the torments and challenges facing the local population, which encouraged a sense of nothingness and hopelessness; and yet the British simply 'shrug our shoulders and say "They asked for it"'. The Germans, he continued, desperately needed 'mentally, morally and spiritually' to see something worthwhile on the horizon but instead were confronted with the moral corruption of the British occupation forces:

> A sad proportion of the occupying armies are playing a shameful part in encouraging the rot. Too many are exploiting for financial gain the material needs of this conquered people. Too many are prostituting their women and girls by giving way to lust and easy temptation. Unless it pulls itself together, Rhine Army, as well as other Britishers, will leave a shameful heritage behind in Germany. Germans have souls, and as the occupying Power for the British zone we shall have to answer to God for our stewardship. I tell you that it is a Frankenstein we are creating.

Aside from Druitt's error – he meant, of course, to invoke Frankenstein's monster – there was no mistaking the vehemence of his broadside against Britain's occupiers. He did not let up, calling out the ignominy of those directly responsible for the conduct of the Rhine Army and Control Commission and the potential dangers that lay ahead:

> If an agreed political policy has been impossible to find, what about a moral and spiritual policy? What about our individual example and leadership in things spiritual and moral? Have we not much to be ashamed of by reason of our spineless indifference to obvious opportunities and our horrid examples of carnal lust? What with one thing and another Germany will be the first to show the result of this

wrong attitude and she will become not a danger as a military Power but as a cesspool of Europe, and it will be big enough and deep enough to drown herself and her neighbours, make no mistake. To-day the problem of Germany is our problem. The weakness of Germany is our weakness. The sin of Germany is our sin.

*

Remarkably, Druitt's anguished public breast-beating prompted little in the way of immediate response. Whether owing to the threat of censorship or for other reasons, the journalists in attendance chose not to file the story – and there seem to have been few, if any, repercussions for Druitt himself. It was only two months later, in August 1946, when a copy of the sermon found its way to the editorial offices of *The Times*, that his accusations were published more widely.[4] In the *Manchester Guardian*, the paper's special correspondent concluded that 'few whose task it is to observe the manners of conquest in this unhappy country will consider that the Assistant Chaplain-General has exaggerated the moral dangers of the occupation of Germany'.[5]

By that point, the revelations merely added fuel to the fire. In July, Trevor Blore's *Daily Express* article had focused public and political attention upon the standards of the British occupiers. In the following weeks and months, the British public were presented with a growing litany of accounts documenting the occupation's alleged shortcomings. The British, and, in particular, the Control Commission, were accused of being over-staffed, corrupt, inefficient, overindulged with excessive supplies of food and drink, lacking the skills required for the job, being too soft towards the Germans and indifferent to the task at hand.

In the House of Commons, the newly elected Labour MP for Bexley, Major Ashley Bramall, made a maiden speech decrying the state of the administration in Germany.[6] He had recently returned from Germany himself, having spent the best part of a year as part of the British army of occupation, and his observations from his tour of duty were far from sanguine: 'We have all too many of the wrong people, whose one aim, in their life in Germany, is to have as good a time as possible and to enrich themselves as much as possible.' Bramall was not the only member of the Control Commission or Rhine Army to air his or her grievances. The letters of serving personnel sent back to family and friends – and on occasion to the British newspapers – were laden with pejorative references to the set-up in Germany. Gerald Lenanton wrote in exasperation to his wife:

you can have no idea of the state of confusion and disorganization of the Control Commission here. I have now some experience of governmental administration, and have never seen anything to beat it even in the worst days of the war and during bombing. I am reminded of Mark Twain's 'you don't have to be crazy to work in this joint, but it sure helps'.[7]

A month later he commented that he had heard the Control Commission referred to in passing as 'the only Lunatic Asylum in the world run by the lunatics themselves!'[8]

This spate of criticism – both public and private – did not escape the attention of the authorities in both Germany and London. Many senior officials feared that the accusations were more than simply idle gossip or misinformation. In December 1945 a senior official in the London-based Control Office for Germany and Austria had commissioned a report from a member of the Economic Division on the 'problems that will have to be resolved if the work of the Control Commission is not to end in disastrous failure'.[9] Foremost among them was said to be an urgent need to improve the quality and discipline of the British staff: 'What we definitely should try to avoid', he implored, 'is to attract people who, in turn, are attracted by stories of the unceasing stream of wines and liqueurs; of country rides and excursions.' In response, one concerned official described the statement as 'dynamite', recommending it be sent to 'the right place' for further consideration.[10]

Yet little had been achieved by February 1946 when a letter arrived in Whitehall, this time from an anonymous military government officer, which warned Control Office officials that the CCG was 'badly managed, over-staffed and lacking in sufficient understanding of its task'.[11] When Trevor Blore's article appeared in July, Deputy Military Governor Brian Robertson was forced to acknowledge that while 'making some allowance for journalistic colouring and exaggeration', he was 'not prepared to deny the general tenor of the allegations'.[12] In October, Patrick Dean, a senior official in the Control Office for Germany and Austria, remarked privately that while many members of the Control Commission were 'devoted to their jobs', there was no doubt that some were 'lazy, inefficient and sometimes corrupt'.[13]

The summer of 1946 also saw the Parliamentary Select Committee on Estimates conclude that the administration of the British Zone needed slimming down: 'The masses of paper on every desk in every British office one visits leaves one with the impression of harassed officials unable to reach reality through walls of files'.[14] An earlier review of policy from the outgoing commander-in-chief Field Marshal Montgomery had confirmed much the same thing, with a striking change of tone from a year earlier:

> the best people to deal with many of the difficulties which beset Germany to-day and await her in the future are not ourselves but the Germans. They know far better how to deal with their country's problems and they are not inferior to us either in intelligence or in determination.[15]

The British occupiers had never been without their critics back home, as seen in the scandal over fratting that had erupted within the first months of the peace. But a year on from VE Day, what had been intermittent criticism had now emerged as something closer to a chorus of disapproval. The British occupying forces had acquired a public reputation for excess, overindulgence, corruption and inefficiency that threatened to undermine Britain's reputation on the international stage. Suspicions were growing that there might be something seriously wrong in the British Zone.

*

It all raises the question: what was life *really* like for the thousands of Britons who now called Germany home? Let's start with the living arrangements laid on for Britain's force of occupiers. There were certainly more than adequate supplies of lodgings for the British, even as thousands of Germans were living hand to mouth in cellars and bomb sites. As we've already seen, the military authorities had requisitioned swathes of buildings in the towns and cities of the Zone. Thousands of houses and flats along with their furnishings were turned over to members of the Control Commission and British army officers. For the more senior personnel this often meant large multi-room residences complete with German servants. A brigadier general, for instance, was entitled to a dining room, a study, five bedrooms, a dressing room, a lounge for house workers, three bedrooms for German servants, three cloakrooms, a kitchen and two bathrooms. This entitlement was a particular cause of tension between occupiers and occupied, as large German families were sometimes turned out to accommodate a single British officer and his wife.[16] Meanwhile, all civilian staff regardless of rank were entitled to private accommodation. In the correspondence of Mary Bouman, the translator we met in Chapter Nine, she notes the strange sensation of living in the shadow of a home's previous inhabitants: 'What interests me most is going into these once private houses and sniffing around and receiving pleasant little shocks in the form of network table covers, thermometers at the windows, the solid looking candelabra vases with branches of fir stuck in them.'[17]

After the brief period of irregular, impromptu requisitioning by combat units at the end of the war, the British authorities established a formal process with strict regulations, forms and fixed compensation rates.[18] The Barrack and Quartering Service of the BAOR would assess the suitability of buildings before giving fourteen days' notice of evacuation, although in practice it could be much shorter. The responsibility for finding alternative accommodation then lay with the local German authorities, often something easier said than done given the severe housing shortages. Lieselotte H., for instance, was forced, along with her husband and parents, to live in accommodation without a bathroom, toilet or proper kitchen for eight years in Detmold.[19] Those who lost their homes received a monthly payment from the British for the use of accommodation and furnishings, but most felt this to be wholly inadequate – the sum usually being markedly lower than the rent payments on their new, temporary accommodation and often failing even to cover the costs of maintenance.

In practice, some flexibility in living arrangements was possible, such as allowing Germans access to gardens or even spare rooms, but this was entirely at the discretion of British tenants. These improvised arrangements sometimes paved the way for Anglo-German friendships: Helga K., who along with her family was obliged to live in rooms above a stable block when their house in Westphalia was requisitioned as a sergeants' mess, remembers that the 'polite and friendly' nature of the British officers eased her understandable discontent.[20] But most Germans responded to their plight with a sense of misery and often outright anger. These feelings could manifest themselves in scathing characterizations of British occupiers. BAOR children were often called '*Tommybrut*' ('Tommy brat') and the German wives of British men as '*Tommyhure*' ('Tommy whore').[21] In some instances, displaced Germans would simply ignore their occupiers or engage in underhand acts of resistance, such as dumping rubbish on their doorsteps. There were also instances where those who moved into German properties didn't help themselves: in 1946 four houses in a residential area of Bielefeld were requisitioned for individual soldiers, who proceeded to raise the Union Jack.[22]

Across the Zone, Germans who felt aggrieved established societies to press their case, such as the Notgemeinschaft der Besatzungsgeschädigten ('Emergency Association for Victims of the Occupation') in Herford. Their main complaints were inadequate rights, insufficient compensation and requisitioned

A solitary figure walks through a heavily devastated area of Hamburg
in 1945. Almost 50 per cent of the city's houses were destroyed by
huge Allied air raids.

properties lying vacant. These groups published provocative posters,
with phrases like '*Du sollst nicht begehren deines Nächsten Gut*'
('Thou shalt not covet thy neighbour's property') or 'My Home,
Your Castle'.[23] Such conflicts over requisitioning were by no means
restricted to the British Zone, although the extensive bomb damage
and high numbers of refugees in the area under British control did
exacerbate housing problems in comparison with other zones.

The news of mass requisitioning invoked the fury of Victor
Gollancz and his supporters back in Britain. It also inspired a
personal outcry from a rather unexpected source: in September
1946 the British military government requisitioned the home of
Frau Faust in the small village of Udorf. She happened to be the
mother-in-law of *Daily Mail* journalist Maurice Lane-Norcott who,
in addition to sending a heated letter to the British authorities
in Germany, made a number of public pronouncements on the
'spectacle of an elderly and seriously ill woman being forcibly
ejected from her home on a stretcher'.[24] An official report suggests
that Lane-Norcott had not ascertained all the facts: special

arrangements *had* been made for Frau Faust, allowing her to move to a nearby property. In the end, *The Times* featured a clarification from Lane-Norcott in which he acknowledged that the British had treated her with 'every possible kindness and consideration' – senior officials in London privately lamented 'a further example of irresponsible criticism' of the occupiers.[25]

But in the context of the war and the anti-German feeling that existed among many of the British staff in the Zone, there was generally little interest in the moral implications of requisitioning. Daphne Smith, who had arrived in Herford in June 1945, explained in a letter to her father that she and her friends 'tell each other that the good furniture & household articles were probably taken from occupied countries, but I don't think anyone really gives a damn where they came from'.[26] Rather, most were concerned with turning a house into a home. Smith remarked that it was 'quite amusing to see how some of the girls have made their billets quite homelike – flowers on the tables, bedside lamps, carpets, curtains, cooking themselves a bit of supper on the gas stove'. During her service in Germany she spent much of her downtime in and out of requisitioned accommodation: 'we invite each other to tea & get a great kick out of cooking new potatoes + green peas + fresh lettuce from the garden... laying them out on bright, fresh table-cloths, & dainty cups & saucers & plates... It's great fun.' Such comforts contrasted sharply with the ruins that dominated the landscape. In one letter to her parents, Mary Bouman remarked that it was 'a strange feeling to pass from utter desolation to the soft carpets, comfortable chairs, spacious restaurants and luxurious bedroom fittings of the modern hotel... it is like passing into another world'.[27]

It wasn't all luxurious, however. In most cases, the lower ranks of the British Army of the Rhine were confined to requisitioned barracks on military bases or large municipal buildings across the Zone. John Allan was living in a Nissen hut* on a 'Jerry Ack Ack site' overlooking the Kiel Canal which was, he complained to his wife, 'Bleak – Muddy – Decayed & what is worse Isolated in

---

* A prefabricated steel structure made from a half-cylindrical sheet of metal.

the middle of a flat, cold and unfriendly country'.[28] This was also the case for some unlucky members of the civilian staff: a woman from the Control Commission Welfare Committee cornered journalist Fenner Brockway and complained that despite being promised treatment as civilians her group were being 'militarized'. She and her colleagues were facing the prospect of moving from requisitioned flats to a 'badly-blitzed warehouse' where 800 men and women were to share facilities with the British army, as many as four to a room.[29] Likewise, the requisitioned accommodation was not always up to scratch: Mary Bouman was agitated when she found her accommodation 'in quite a dilapidated condition with no curtains at all at the windows'.[30] In 1947, when she eventually moved flats, she was compelled to take things into her own hands, not only bringing floor mats with her, but also asking the German caretaker to acquire 'some hooks, nails, wall plugs, flex etc' after she had 'failed to raise these trifles from our own people'.[31]

*

Alongside private accommodation the British had access to a myriad of exclusive clubs, hotels, cinemas, theatres, sports grounds and company messes. Furthermore, the Navy, Army and Air Force Institutes (best known simply as NAAFIs) oversaw the recreational needs of the British armed forces, from shops to launderettes. These facilities came in all shapes and sizes: in Hamburg, for instance, they ranged from the grand Atlantic Hotel to a small community hall, located in the city's Rahlstedt district, dubbed 'The Mailbag'.[32]

For the British occupiers these venues offered a wide variety of free entertainment and recreation – for most, a world away from what might be on offer back home. During the war the Entertainments National Service Association had offered troops a chance to relax and unwind, playing host to stars such as Vera Lynn and George Formby. These efforts were continued after 1945, with the establishment of the Combined Services Entertainment Unit (CSE).[33] A notable member of the CSE was up-and-coming actor Roger Moore, who had been conscripted in 1946 as part of the Royal Army Service Corps.[34] Not long after his arrival, Second

Lieutenant Moore's jeep had an 'altercation with a tree' near Neumünster, leaving him in hospital. He successfully lobbied for a transfer to the CSE and spent much of the next year organizing the tours of artists and comedians, including Frankie Howerd and Ivy Benson. Moore also starred as the lead in a stage production of *The Shop at Sly Corner*,* performing in Hamburg, Celle, Hanover, Cologne, Lübeck and Bremen.

Moore wasn't the only future star to spend time in the British Zone. Peter Sellers, who had joined the RAF during the war, was stationed in a former Luftwaffe camp in Gütersloh as part of the air force's own entertainment troupe, the Gang Show. It was in these days that Sellers began masquerading as a classic British military man, with full handlebar moustache, parted hair, lieutenant's bars, wings and ribbons.[35] In his disguise he would surprise unsuspecting soldiers and airmen; little did they know that they were witnessing the first iteration of two of Sellers' most enduring comic characters: *The Goon Show*'s Major Bloodnok and *Dr Strangelove*'s Group Captain Lionel Mandrake.

Others took advantage of the opportunities for winter sports, including at the Control Commission's own ski resort based at Winterberg in the Sauerland. For the less adventurous, football was the game of choice, either as a player or spectator. In July 1945 Liverpool FC became the first of a number of professional clubs to tour the British Zone and play exhibition matches against service teams – beating the 84th Group RAF XI 7–0 at Celle in front of nearly 8,000 spectators before drawing 3–3 with the Army XI in Hanover.[36] The British Army of the Rhine quickly put together a strong squad of professional players from within their own ranks: at the Inter-Allied Championship in the autumn of 1946 BAOR Combined Services XI could pick from a squad of thirty-nine that included twenty-two full internationals. In the final, held at the Olympiastadion, Berlin, they won 6–3 against a resilient Czech team in front of 40,000 spectators.[37]

---

* A thriller play by Edward Percy about an expat French antiques dealer and black marketeer. It was first performed in Brighton in 1941 and enjoyed a London run of 863 performances between April 1945 and May 1947.

British soldiers admire the scoreboard at the Olympiastadion, Berlin.
It reads 'Arsenal 19 Chelsea 0', 'Hienz [sic] 57' and 'Heil Stalin and
Churchill and Truman'.

The BAOR's first commander-in-chief, Field Marshal
Montgomery, was a convert to the beautiful game, having become
a fan of Portsmouth FC when stationed nearby during the war.[38] He
had personally intervened to encourage the Football Association
to arrange club tours as entertainment for the troops, intended as
tonic for what one newspaper report described as the 'fed-up-and-
far-from-home feeling' feared to be increasingly prevalent among
the men.[39] In the first year of the occupation, the BAOR XI faced
teams from the top divisions of the English and Scottish leagues
once a week; these visitors included Brentford, Everton, Arsenal,

Notts County and Queen's Park Rangers. They more than held their own: in October 1945 with the help of their centre forward, Seton Airlie, a Celtic player, BAOR beat Rangers 6–1 in Hanover.[40] In March 1946 BAOR Combined Services beat Manchester United in front of 25,000 servicemen at the Bahrenfeld Stadium in Hamburg while scores of locals perched atop nearby trees.[41] Perhaps unsurprisingly, Monty's own Portsmouth FC made the trip to Germany too, losing 3–1 to a Combined Services team at the Hindenburg Arena* in Hanover on 13 March 1946. Their trip was memorable due to a difficult journey home: all air transportation was suspended owing to bad weather, meaning a seventeen-hour drive followed by a sixteen-hour train journey finally saw them onto a cross-Channel boat.[42]

At weekends international teams toured the Zone, with the BAOR playing two matches in two days against a Scotland XI in November 1945. The second of these, in Hamburg, was in front of 40,000 spectators, including Monty himself. John William Booth, now based in Wilster, Schleswig-Holstein, had won tickets to see the game in his regiment's raffle and set off for the match complete with his haversack rations of two sandwiches: one cheese, one jam.[43] As part of his regular correspondence home he included a short match report:

> Although the kick off was still almost an hour and a half away, the one terraced side of the ground was packed beneath the four Union Jacks flying against the iron-grey sky. So we took up a position just to one side of a goal and settled down to wait... Then to a growing murmur from the crowd on the opposite side of the field and a frenzy of action from the few cameramen by the entrance, the teams

---

* This stadium (now the Eilenriedestadion) still functions today as the home ground of the reserve team of Bundesliga club Hannover 96. When the British arrived it was stripped of its name – the Hindenburg Kampfbahn (the Hindenburg Arena), honouring the man who had appointed Hitler as chancellor in 1933 – and renamed 'Stadion der Stadt Hannover'. However, British soldiers and football programme makers appear to have kept using the old name.

walked onto the pitch, two by two. The Combined Services in white shirts and dark shorts and the Scots in dark PT kit, sweaters and long pants... It was a far from clean encounter with the 'ref' having to warn two or three of the players, but, on the whole, quite good. The Scots were by far the better ball players but the Services somehow managed to make a 1–1 draw of it.

Matches against Germans, however, remained a point of contention. In the first months of the peace, troops did schedule a number of impromptu match-ups between British and German teams. George Pringle, a military government official based in Warendorf, near Münster, who spent much of his time helping to restart local textile mills, remembers picking his unit's XI in a game against a local village team in the summer of 1945, with 2,000 spectators there to witness a British army win.[44] Robert Souper played in a game between Charlie Troop of the Royal Artillery and a team of Germans near Hamburg.[45] It became, in his words, 'a little tense' and felt increasingly political as German spectators jeered British errors. In the end Souper felt that the match was a positive thing that brought British and Germans together over their shared love of football – and it may have helped that Charlie Troop won the game. Not everyone agreed: in January 1946, news that the 53rd Division had played two matches against German civilians led to an official investigation over concerns that it had contravened non-fraternization rules.[46]

*

It wasn't just the generous allocations of accommodation and entertainment that gave the occupiers a taste of the good life. British personnel were able to acquire quantities and varieties of food that their new neighbours – as well as friends and families back home – could only dream of. For the civilian staff of the Control Commission, the official ration was 2,800 calories per day, the same as British civilians and substantially higher than that allocated to the Germans, while members of the Rhine Army were afforded even bigger portions.[47] 'I just can't believe it,' wrote Edna Wearmouth on finding fresh white bread, 'if it weren't for the names on all the places, I'd never believe I was in Germany.'[48]

Beyond their standard ration, the British were offered exotic menus at low costs in their exclusive clubs, hotels and canteens – all prepared and served by German staff. A menu from the CCG Club in the small town of Lemgo near Bielefeld, for instance, offered diners shrimp cocktail, roast chicken with sautéed potatoes, champignons, grilled tomatoes and *ananas à l'américaine* with ice cream, accompanied with brandy, wine and coffee.[49] At the NAAFI 'Corner House' Club, one could expect a menu du jour of hors d'oeuvre 'Corner House', potage Mulligatawny, mixed grill, *macédoine de légumes, pommes frites, pêche Melba ou fromage et café.*[50] If a meal of such extravagance was not an everyday occurrence for most of the staff, items such as fruit and fresh cream, seldom obtainable in Britain, were now commonly available to members of the CCG and Rhine Army.

The supplies available often inspired incredulity: 'THE FOOD?!!! It's amazing!!' Edna Wearmouth exclaimed in one letter home to her father, 'in England, before the war, we never had anything like this'.[51] In another, she acknowledged the privilege of her situation: 'You know dad I cannot help but feeling how lucky I am. I'm out here just when things are short at home and I'm getting all the best of everything.'[52] Over the coming months these bounties of food stood out above all else: 'Gosh Dad, I think I'm in a dream!!...' Wearmouth wrote in the summer of 1947, 'candies, biscuits, tinned fruit and chocolate – well again, I can only say it's a dream! If I could only send it home.'[53] One Sunday in April she met her friend Enid in the Kirchlengern district of Herford and couldn't quite believe the feast she was offered: 'what food I ate!!!! After a huge lunch, for tea we had fried spam and toast, fried egg and bread and butter, peaches and cream, fruit loaf and biscuits.'[54] A couple of months later, at an engagement party, Wearmouth 'just gazed in wonder' at the provisions, 'huge turkeys and chickens all beautifully dressed; huge hams and cooked meats dressed, salads, eggs, savouries; then ice cream, trifles, and huge cakes of cream and chocolate, small fancies and a huge three tier white iced cake'.[55]

If there were occasional grumbles – such as Mary Bouman's complaints that too much mess food came out of tins, that 'we never see any green salad or such fresh things at all' and that in the midst of winter only 'microscopic' portions of meat were available – for the most part, the British realized their good fortune.[56] It was, after all, marked in comparison to the meagre supplies available to the locals. Without doubt, the allocation of food in post-war Germany reinforced the power dynamics of the occupation by ensuring the physical and psychological supremacy of the Allied occupiers. Edna Wearmouth even wondered whether it was a conscious attempt by the British authorities to 'show the Germans they were wrong when they broadcast that we were starving during the war'.[57] She, like so many of her colleagues, was moved to try to redress the imbalance herself, telling her father that she had 'taken to pinching bits and pieces from our Mess to feed some of the people'.[58]

*

There was, however, one luxury which outshone even the generous allowances of food available in the British Zone: the seemingly unceasing flow of alcohol. In the first instance, soldiers and civilian personnel were entitled to a very generous ration 'on the house', at times as much as a bottle of champagne and two bottles of spirits per week.[59] In April 1946 men of the 6th Guards Brigade in Hamburg were each provided with three bottles of German gin, half a bottle of cognac, two bottles of champagne and eight litres of beer each month.[60] Beyond that, extra supplies were available at incredibly low prices – through both official and unofficial channels. A bottle of cognac that might have a market value of five dollars was available for sixteen pence.[61] In Berlin, Brian Dillon, an officer serving with the 1st Battalion, Royal Norfolk Regiment, was able to buy a bottle of gin for two shillings or a bottle of champagne for one cigarette.[62] Lance Bombardier John Allan remarked in a letter to his wife that the price of a pint of beer, often as little as one and a half pence, would make his dad's eyes pop out.*[63]

Each week British staff queued at their local NAAFI, collecting their allocation of drinks before lunch. In her mess, Katharine Morris was idly awaiting her bowl of soup as she noticed the tables around her gradually filling up with bottles as the young women from the Textiles and Light Industry Division were 'nursing their allocations of gin and wine'.[64] John William Booth, who in November 1945 had been reassigned from the BAOR to the Control Commission, was routinely tasked with delivering '100s & 100s of bottles' of beer and gin to messes across the Zone.[65] Perhaps most tellingly, in the spring of 1946, when Germany was facing an

Lance Corporal Keesan and Private Kenny, both Glaswegians, serve beer at a NAAFI bar in late 1945. The British occupiers did not lack for drink.

---

* After a steep increase in prices during the war, a pint in a London pub would have cost at least ten times this amount.

impending famine, Mary Bouman remarked in a letter home that 'the only commodity of which there seems no lack is drink. We may have to starve at some future date but it hardly seems likely that we will go thirsty'.[66]

In the German capital Brian Dillon recalls long boozy nights, beginning in the Russian sector with a trip to the opera before a trip to the French sector for a spot of dinner at the officers' club, and finally retiring to the British sector for 'a bit of a piss-up'.[67] It was all too clear to him that 'everyone drank too much'. The vigorous drinking culture of the British Zone was perhaps most noticeable at the parties and dances which Control Commission and Rhine Army personnel held with astonishing regularity. In fact, Edna Wearmouth's experience suggests that avoiding alcohol was more of a challenge than acquiring it. She had arrived in Germany resolutely teetotal and faced much jovial derision as a result, but before long the conviviality of her new environment enticed her to sample the luxurious libations on offer:

> I had my first sip of champagne. They got a bottle and I had to have a little sip, just to say I'd tasted it. I didn't like it very much – it tasted rather like cider but I expected it to be marvellous but I thought it like Andrews liver salts!! Have you tasted it? I'll never make a booser [sic], will I?[68]

Beyond the prevalence of alcohol, there were many reasons why the consumption of drink became so pervasive. For many of the veteran soldiers who made up the Rhine Army, boozing to excess was undoubtedly a form of self-medication; after six years of war, 'battle fatigue', now known as post-traumatic stress disorder, was widespread. This was likely true for some new recruits too: the horrors of hunger, destruction and the spectre of disease that haunted post-war Germany were liable to encourage anyone to seek out some form of escape. There were also more practical rationales: Katharine Morris resolutely stuck to her rule about not drinking tap water, opting instead to take lager with her meals.[69] But perhaps the most significant cause was the plain tedium of everyday life. Stuck on bases and unable to return to friends and family, many of those serving in Germany were counting down the days until they were given their ticket home. As the writer and journalist Ethel Mannin remarked after touring the Zone, 'if you're sensitive and sympathetic you tend to drink from depression; if you are insensitive and indifferent you drink because you are bored'.[70]

Whatever the motivation, the heavy drinking culture among the British had serious repercussions. Across the Zone, and especially near army messes, well-oiled occupiers were involved in countless punch-ups, accused of smashing windows or digging up vegetable patches, and criticized for harassing their fellow Britons and Germans alike.[71] In Berlin, trouble ranged from overturned jeeps to disappearing soldiers. For Brian Dillon, stationed in the German capital, it meant repeated attempts to retrieve his men after they had strayed into the neighbouring Soviet sector and got themselves into difficulties.[72] One night a missing lance corporal was last seen on an infamous street of cafés and brothels, forcing Dillon to contact his opposite number in the Red Army. He was told in no uncertain terms that the missing man was not in Soviet custody on account of his lowly rank: 'Lance Corporal? Oh we don't bother arresting them, we just throw them in the river.' If some wayward British soldiers merely returned home with a sodden uniform and a hangover, others were not so lucky. Peter Wayne witnessed an altogether more tragic outcome: in Minden, his heavy-drinking sergeant major was killed when he drunkenly stumbled in front of an oncoming tram.[73]

The abundance of alcohol undoubtedly helped to fuel a sexually permissive culture within the British Zone, something already exposed during the scandal over 'fratting'. As we have seen, relationships between British men and German women were commonplace during the occupation, ranging from casual sex to more serious encounters. But while British women seldom engaged in such Anglo-German relations, impeded not only by official strictures but also the threat of severe moral censure, many of them did partake in amorous interactions with other members of the Allied occupation authorities.

Edna Wearmouth's correspondence hints that her time in occupied Germany was, to some extent, shaped by the atmosphere of permissiveness and sexual licence she had encountered. Wearmouth certainly received a great deal of attention from colleagues, with 'the men at the office' assuring her that she 'could have more escorts than Princess Elizabeth'.[74] But it wasn't all well received: she regularly criticized colleagues in the Control Commission and Rhine Army for getting 'rolling drunk' at every opportunity and creating an unwelcoming and, at times, uncomfortable atmosphere.[75] On one occasion, she described a 'usual do' during which, as ever, drunkenness and unruly behaviour were rife: 'I do wish they were different for I love dancing, and I often wish I could go to a nice dance out here, but I cannot stand these men'.[76] In the memoir Wearmouth wrote some years later, she is even more forthright, explaining how she and other women were subject to lurid tales and sexual advances from their male colleagues:

> I was getting less innocent by the day. In the office, especially since the arrival of beautiful Enid, Bert was chagrined to find that neither of us fell for his hunky handsomeness and he took a daily delight in trying to shock us by regaling us with tales of his sexual exploits and his various German mistresses who, he said, fell at his feet... He was a walking Karma Sutra [sic].[77]

In this, Wearmouth certainly wasn't alone. In advance of her arrival in the Zone, Joan Hyde, who would serve with the Public Health Division in Hamburg, was warned by a friend that 'the only thing which you will have to be prepared for is the fact that most of the men imagine CCG girls have come out only for one thing – to entertain them, and if they find you are not interested in being their mistress then you've had it!'[78]

*

In the midst of the shattered buildings and crippling shortages of post-war Germany, British occupiers were evidently more than well catered for. That's not to say that everyone was overly indulgent or that all the British staff took full advantage of their propitious circumstances. But an abundance of accommodation, entertainment, food, drink and much more besides was a material reality of the British Zone for the occupiers, and one which undoubtedly helped to fashion an atmosphere of excess. From this emerged stories of indiscipline that invited critical commentary in the newspapers and threatened an upsurge of public resentment towards what many felt was a distasteful display of extravagance at a time of austerity and general privation. In April 1947 E. G. Ayrton of County Down, Northern Ireland, wrote to the new chief of the Control Office for Germany and Austria, Lord Pakenham, to express her distaste at the stories she had heard about the occupiers.[79] She alleged that the British were 'living in the lap of luxury, food and wine', attending parties every night in their clubs and being endlessly driven around by clueless, ill-informed English chauffeurs. All the while, she warned, Britain's reputation was 'being dragged in the mud... no wonder the German's [sic] hate us.'

Amid a growing outcry back home, the British authorities in Germany were finally compelled to act. The BAOR organized a series of obligatory 'Leadership Courses' for servicemen and their civilian counterparts.[80] Moreover, General Richard McCreery,* who in March 1946 had taken over from Field Marshal Montgomery as general officer commander-in-chief, British Army of the Rhine, communicated his conviction that 'homelier' messes and a reduction in alcohol supplies would introduce a 'healthier atmosphere' among his troops.[81] There were also attempts to improve the quality of CCG staff, with more rigorous assessments of applicants and efforts to hire army veterans to key positions. Yet these changes did little to assuage the anxieties of government

---

* McCreery, who had commanded the 8th Army during the war, had been general officer commander-in-chief, British Forces of Occupation in Austria, until his transfer to Germany.

officials back in London. In September 1946 a private Foreign Office memo acknowledged the apparent inadequacies of the Control Commission, which it described as a 'highly-paid army of retired drain-inspectors, unsuccessful businessmen and idle ex-policemen'.[82] Not long after, the prime minister voiced his own concerns to Ernest Bevin:

> I am not happy about our set-up in Germany. There is widespread criticism in many quarters. There is also some misgiving as to the quality of some of the personnel in the Commission. It is admitted that some are first-class but there are, it is said, others whose conduct and quality is not up to standard... We must realise that there is a strong body of criticism which seems to be based on personal observations. Gollancz, who has been out there for some time and is emotional, but influential, is coming to see me this week. Others, including Montgomery, have told me all is not well.[83]

15

Money for Old Smokes

In the spring of 1946, sixty-five-year-old Maria Mülhens was undergoing medical treatment at a temporary residence in the city of Cologne. Her actual home, Röttgen Castle, an imposing building with walled grounds and a famous horse-racing stable, had been requisitioned and now functioned as the seat of the British military administration for North Rhine-Westphalia.[1] The end of the war had been a tumultuous period in her life: in early 1945 Maria's youngest son, Hans, had been killed in fighting near Wesel, and her husband, Peter, succumbed to illness only a few months later. This series of events saw Maria inherit a large family estate which included the famous Eau de Cologne 4711 aftershave company. This, of course, provided Maria with a fortune that allowed her to escape the deprivations facing her compatriots. But Maria's social standing also brought with it unwanted attention from Germany's new rulers.

One day in late March, two British men in civilian dress appeared at Frau Mülhens's door.[2] They had Control Commission patches tacked onto their sleeves and introduced themselves as British army colonels. The two men invited themselves in and sat down beside the ailing woman to discuss an urgent matter: the formula for her world-famous aftershave brand. Eau de Cologne 4711 was invented under a very different military occupation, when French soldiers had taken over Cologne during the

Revolutionary Wars of the late eighteenth century. As the legend goes, Wilhelm Mülhens received a secret recipe for an 'aqua mirabilis' as a wedding gift. He soon marketed it as a health drink and, subsequently, a fragrance.[3] The unusual name came from the French insistence that each house be numbered continuously throughout the city, rather than by street. Mülhens's abode at the time was designated 4711 Glockengasse.

Now, almost two centuries later, it was the British who came knocking. They insisted that Frau Mülhens hand over the secret recipe that she, and she alone, knew by heart.[4] According to an official report, the two men showed a 'heated determination to get their own way' and put 'insistent pressure' on the frail widow, in the form of 'threatening innuendo, cajolery and threats'. Frustrated by Frau Mülhens's reluctance to divulge the formula, the Control Commission representatives suggested moving the 4711 factory to England, offering the Mülhens family a 50 per cent stake in their own business, while assuring Frau Mülhens that all concerns about security would be 'taken care of'. Still she stood firm. The men's approach now became distinctly hostile. It would, they insisted, be in Frau Mülhens's 'best interests' to give them the formula. If she didn't cooperate, there would be 'unpleasant consequences'. But she gave no response. Well, they continued, the family business may have to be closed. Still she said nothing. If Frau Mülhens refused to help, she would be 'taken away'; a prison van was on standby. Silence. Finally, in a state of some distress, Maria Mülhens insisted on retiring to bed.

The two British colonels who left empty-handed were members of the British Intelligence Objectives Sub-Committee (BIOS). This shadowy organization had been established in 1945 to oversee the identification of technical assets and scientific data from the British Zone – from documents and patents to machinery and skilled personnel.[5] These seizures were classed as 'intellectual reparations', whereby industrial secrets and technological innovations were transferred without compensation from German businesses to the Allies.[6] As well as this direct transfer of knowledge, the British occupiers helped bring about a fundamental reform of German patent law. In July 1946 all German patents were declared royalty-free, and microfilm copies of the entire catalogue of the German patent office were handed over to the occupiers.[7] In the course of the Allied occupation, BIOS sent more than 10,000 technically adept industrialists and scientists into the British Zone to assess factories and other sites. They were to investigate German industry in their own areas of expertise, ranging from ceramics to electron microscopes, and write extensive reports on any relevant technological and scientific innovations.[8] These reports were published back in Britain, with copies weighing down library shelves across the country for the perusal of any interested parties.[9] Their recommendations were also sent on to T-Force, who actioned any necessary acquisitions.

In the case of Eau de Cologne 4711, BIOS team No. 1972 was made up of representatives of the perfumery and cosmetic industries – in fact, both men were employees of the Anglo-Dutch giant Unilever: R. L. Demuth was a consultant chemist for the firm, while A. W. Adam was manager of the Perfumery Branch as well as director of the Pears Soap company.[10] These were senior Unilever representatives paying a visit to one of the company's greatest pre-war competitors in the hope of securing priceless trade secrets – and all under the guise of the military government. Remarkably, despite the obvious ethical concerns of this arrangement, it was all above board.

The alleged use of gangland-style intimidation was, however, an entirely different matter. In August 1946 a *Daily Express* reporter got wind of the story, threatened publication, and sought immediate assurance from military government officials that the offending personnel were to be suspended. The Control Commission successfully rebuffed the allegations, contending that the men had never been members of their organization. While this was technically true, behind closed doors officials were concerned that BIOS investigators would be 'put in an invidious light' if this 'somewhat unorthodox [albeit] unsuccessful trade piracy' were made public.[11]

These fears were realized a few months later when the BBC's German Service correspondent David Graham broke the story.[12] His broadcast, 'Why Recovery Lags?', preceded further damning accounts in the November editions of both *Tribune* and the *New Statesman and Nation*, the latter under the headline 'Scandal in Germany'.[13] It was suggested that businessmen in British army uniforms were routinely coercing German officials into giving them trade secrets, all at the expense of British taxpayers. This industrial espionage was said to result from insufficient supervision by the British authorities who had 'helped to render catastrophic the predicament into which the international situation, and above all the world food shortage, have placed the British Zone'. The *New Statesman and Nation* went on to decry journalists and MPs for being 'too reticent' about the state of Britain's organization in Germany: while nobody wanted to castigate 'the evil of men doing a difficult job', here was clear proof of systemic corruption and 'maladministration' that could not be ignored.

These stories prompted questions in the House of Commons and even led to an official investigation.[14] The Board of Trade, who oversaw the BIOS programme, remained adamant that it was 'proper for [the BIOS team] to make the enquiries upon which unfavourable press comment has been made', and condemned Frau Mülhens's 'improper attitude'.[15] But the Control Commission disagreed and acknowledged in their own report that BIOS team No. 1972's behaviour was 'irregular'. There was, however, little to be done – these men were civilians, not servicemen. In the end, Gilmour Jenkins from the Public Relations Division cautioned his superiors 'to let the affair die a natural death'.[16] Back in London, however, John Hynd couldn't help himself from confronting Kingsley Martin, editor of the *New Statesman and Nation*, at a London drinks reception about the merits of the article. Martin later responded via letter, offering details of a lengthy investigation into the matter and reiterating his belief that the British Zone was a hotbed of corruption: 'It is not, as far as I can judge, a question of a few isolated cases, but of a system which is encouraging corruption both on a large and small scale.'[17]

*

In 1949 the criminal underworld of post-war Europe was immortalized in Carol Reed's film noir *The Third Man*. Orson

Welles plays Harry Lime, a kingpin racketeer in murky occupied Vienna during 'the classic period of the black market'.[18] The war, and its aftermath, had seen an upsurge in corruption and illicit trading across the continent. This included Britain where the 'spiv' had become a recurring character in news media, known for his purportedly unpatriotic and greedy activities of antisocial racketeering – albeit actions which were sometimes framed as those of the heroic outlaw.[19] But it was in Germany that the chaos and disorder which had accompanied the end of the fighting helped spawn perhaps the most active black market in the world.

The growth of corruption and black marketeering were particularly pronounced in the British Zone: the economic vulnerability of the region had produced acute poverty, hunger and a breakdown of societal norms of law and order, all of which catalysed a ubiquitous shift towards the barter economy. For many Germans there were few means of survival other than acquiring food and other basic resources through such trades. Yet for members of the occupation forces the trade of looted goods, knick-knacks, alcohol and much else besides was often altogether more opportunistic. Scores of Allied soldiers and civilian administrators seized the chance to enrich themselves during their time as occupiers.

From the semi-official carpetbagging of BIOS teams to more innocent everyday trades, a widespread belief took root that almost everybody in the British Zone was mixed up in some sort of racket. Since shortages and rationing remained a feature of everyday life in austerity Britain, the black market was a topic that aroused a great deal of interest.[20] In August 1945 the *Sunderland Daily Echo and Shipping Gazette* featured an article by Ferdinand Tuohy highlighting the 'racketeering in Germany' as a 'flaw of the occupation' that was damaging the 'prestige and self-respect' of the occupiers.[21] It was not long before more mainstream newspapers were reporting the not-so-secretive workings of Germany's shadow economy, where cigarettes had established themselves as the currency du jour.[22]

As Lieutenant-Colonel Byford-Jones wrote in *Berlin Twilight*, his account of life in post-war Berlin, in occupied Germany 'only an infinitesimal proportion of cigarettes were smoked': instead, most were passed from person to person at a profit.[23] Allied occupiers of all nations, provided with an official ration of free cigarettes, suddenly found themselves in the advantageous position of being de facto suppliers of capital – Germany's new central bank. They could, and did, spend their considerable supplies of Camels, Lucky Strikes and Players on goods and services, from Nazi paraphernalia to luxury cameras (3,000 cigarettes at September 1945 prices) and watches (1,400 cigarettes). But the black market was a complex beast with no fixed rules, as one young woman in the Economic Division of the British Control Commission tried to explain:

> What shall I say of the aforesaid market, except that it flourishes like the green bay tree and is an education to manipulate? Current rates of exchange go something like this – (the Mark is pegged at six pence) – 20 cigarettes = 100 Marks; 1 bar chocolate = 50; 1 bar soap = 20; 1 lb. coffee = 1 dachshund; 1 pair fully fashioned stockings = 30 cigarettes; 1 camera = 700 ditto (or thereabouts) = 1 bicycle = 1 pair binoculars = 1 electric coffee roaster and so on. The barter is terrific – and one can obtain anything from a pin to an elephant in approved parking grounds all over Berlin.[24]

It was no exaggeration: the range of goods and services available was quite astounding, from dental procedures and oil paintings to car engines and antique dressers.[25] In open squares, tree-lined parks and abandoned buildings across the Zone throngs of men and women laid out their wares to the onlooking crowds of British soldiers and Control Commission staff. A lack of language skills among the occupiers often meant that negotiations took place in a state of mutual confusion. In the German capital there was the further complexity of four occupying powers competing for the best deal. After one of Edna Wearmouth's colleagues was posted to Berlin, she explained in a letter that 'an evening spent in this lucrative pastime is usually most hilarious as you may imagine – Russians, French, Americans, English, German – all boiled up together, bargaining and bartering, swapping, selling and arguing in umpteen different languages.[26]

Among the British staff, there was a particular demand for watches, pens and, oddly enough, pets. Gerald Lenanton, chief of North German Timber Control, noted that 'every officer and about every third "other rank" seems to have collected a dog over here' – with most breeds available at the price of fifty cigarettes or less.[27] His colleague Rex Golding acquired an eighteen-month-old German shepherd that was said to have bitten six Germans, 'which nobody seems to mind except perhaps the Germans themselves'.[28] It was a sign of the times, however, that one would seldom see a cat roaming the streets. As one Berlin chef explained to a correspondent for the *Daily Mirror*, 'dress them neatly and they'll pass as rabbits… roast them and no one will notice the taste'.[29] As Katharine Morris grimly noted, rather than felines these days it was hungry human beings who poked around bins looking for morsels of food.[30]

British soldiers attempt to trade their cigarette lighter for an accordion at a barter exchange in Lüneburg.

Such small-scale trades – for Pomeranians or potatoes – became a widely practised and often unavoidable part of life for occupiers and occupied alike, even though they remained strictly prohibited. Mary Bouman seems to have been fairly reticent about engaging in such dealings, aware of the perceived immorality of using the black market.[31] Yet in preparation for a forthcoming trip to Bavaria, she stocked up on coffee, 'which one can barter for eggs, milk, vegetables etc'. 'I know it sounds very like Black Market', she wrote anxiously to her parents, 'but it isn't as though one makes a practice of it. It is just for pure convenience in my case.'[32] For others, sharing the fruits of victory with friends and family back in Britain was a sure-fire way to alleviate any sense of guilt about participating in illicit trades. Edna Wearmouth regularly sent home packages to her father. In April 1947 she sent '100 cigarettes; 6 oz St Bruno Flake pipe tobacco; 1 thermos flask; 5 tablets toilet soap; 2 pieces washing soap; fancy wooden box; big bottle "Coty" Eau de Cologne; small bottle "Evening in Paris" Eau de Cologne; red slippers; matches'.[33] 'Of course, I couldn't declare exactly what was inside', she explained candidly in an accompanying letter, 'for it would never have got to you.'

These routine barters also gave rise to a dish now synonymous with Germany. In 1949 a Berliner by the name of Herta Heuwer obtained curry powder from British soldiers based in the German capital – supposedly, and very plausibly, in return for alcohol.[34] When Herta sprinkled the spice over a fried sausage laden with ketchup, itself synonymous with the American soldiers based in Germany, the currywurst was born. Easy to make, cheap and, most importantly, actually quite tasty, it became an instant hit. At the time of writing, more than 800 million portions are sold in Germany every year.

It wasn't, however, all quite so innocent. In the autumn of 1946, the Independent Labour MP Denis Pritt and the Conservative MP Michael Astor sent letters to John Hynd seeking an investigation into serious allegations of fraud and corruption in Germany.[35] In fact, Scotland Yard had already been given the go-ahead to assemble a squad of forty detectives to investigate criminal activities among British personnel.[36] It was widely reported that these 'Sherlocks for Germany' would be tackling the 'underworld of smuggling, forgery, black marketeering and fraud'.[37] There was plenty to do: in the coming months and years they would uncover an unremitting stream of evidence documenting the profiteering and criminality plaguing the British Zone. In Berlin, detectives found black market rings trading everything from narcotics and penicillin to rare artworks and radioactive substances.[38] An official report from July 1946 suggested that illegal trading was so rife that it threatened to ruin what little remained of the financial and economic structure of all four zones.

Perhaps the most well-known scam became so widespread that it cost the British exchequer an estimated £59 million – an astonishing loss that even had to be accounted for in the 1947 budget.[39] British personnel were afforded a generous ration of fifty cigarettes per week, often supplemented with another sixty available for purchase at reduced prices and further supplies which routinely arrived from home.[40] These cigarettes, as Germany's new unofficial currency, could easily be traded for German Marks – the official currency, now largely worthless to the locals beyond buying newspapers. Yet Marks were still accepted at a fixed exchange rate in the British army's NAAFI stores, where this defunct money could be used to buy goods, including more cigarettes, or, indeed, savings certificates. The latter could be subsequently exchanged for pound sterling. The British government was exchanging valuable goods, often bought with dwindling dollar supplies, or hard currency for worthless paper notes acquired from the sale of cigarette rations – money for old smokes.

A story from one anonymous British soldier illustrates quite how profitable this money-making scheme could be: he turned 500 Gold Flake cigarettes into actual gold.[41] He had received the cigarettes for his birthday, a genuine gift that arrived just days after he'd given up the habit – so what was he to do with them? A quick trip to the Kaiser Allee secured him 5,000 Marks from a hairdresser and then a tip-off: get to the NAAFI and they will give you postal orders at forty Marks to the pound. For a man who had earned forty-two shillings and sixpence a week as a river bailiff before the war, £125 was quite a handsome return for an afternoon's work – just over a year's salary. But eager not to raise too much suspicion, he held on to some of his Marks, used some of them to buy more cigarettes and also continued to claim his weekly ration. In time, the wads of notes grew thicker and thicker:

> After a while I became worried. I hid the money in all kinds of places, in my kitbag, in old socks, in the lining of my tunic. The money began to get on my mind, and I couldn't sleep. I used to go into the latrine and count it. I remember one day counting, to my horror, eight thousand Marks. That came to £200, and I had never had more than £5 in my life. I decided that I must get rid of it, and at a faster rate. Don't forget, it represented nearly two years' peacetime wages.

This remarkable system of exchange was allowed to continue until August 1946, when a British Zone currency, British Armed Forces Special Vouchers (BAFSVs), was issued as a preventative measure.[42] These were essentially British army banknotes, although printed privately rather than by the Bank of England. In fact, the third series was produced by Waddingtons, perhaps better known for producing Monopoly money. In January 1948 BAFSVs were themselves temporarily withdrawn when it was realized that they too had acquired a value on the black market.[43]

For some it all seemed quite distasteful, especially considering the prevailing conditions for those Germans who were trading their last worldly possessions in the hope of a square meal. Edna Wearmouth came across one of the many thousands who had taken advantage of the scheme, complaining to her father about a 'most objectionable young man':

> I shall never forget that man. He boasted about all the money he's making out here, changing cigarettes for German Marks and selling them for English money... He said he'd never go

back to UK for he was having the time of his life out here. Never did a stroke of work, plenty of money, everything on the Black Market, plenty of drinks, plenty of parties – how Enid and I kept our mouths shut and refrained from spitting at him, I cannot imagine!!![44]

Yet others evidently embraced their reputation as scoundrels: in a letter to the prime minister, Eve Graham, a former member of the Control Commission, recalled attending a party during her time in Germany where a cake had been decorated with the three emblems of the CCG – a swan (for swanning around), a fiddle and a racquet.[45]

The 'Money for Old Smokes' scandal was just one of the innumerable black market tricks that flourished during the four years of military occupation. Inevitably, there followed a steady stream of criminal cases in which British personnel of all ranks were charged with various offences. In August 1946, for instance, five Control Commission officers were found guilty of trading cigarettes and coffee for money and jewellery.[46] In April 1947 Theodore Reid Hartwick, a grade one* official in the Control Commission, was imprisoned for six months and handed a £1,000 fine for forgery, the 'conversion of cigarettes intended for Displaced Persons and former POWs' for his own use, and illegal dealings with Germans.[47] Likewise, RAF officer J. Washbourne Ecart was found guilty by court martial of bartering cigarettes, flour, sugar, tea, tobacco and coffee for Marks.[48] Peter Stainer, described in the *Daily Mail* as a 'wealthy Briton' and 'Lord of 3 manors', was sentenced to four years of penal servitude and a £1,000 fine in July 1946 for his part in black market operations in Germany.[49] His official function had given him power over the provision of alcohol, which, along with other items, he would sell illicitly to Germans, incurring 'a serious loss of sterling' on the British Treasury. These are only a small sample of the hundreds of analogous cases that made it into the British newspapers.[50]

---

* This was the most senior level in the CCG hierarchy.

In fact, some of the most high-ranking officials of the British armed forces and Control Commission were implicated in corruption and wrongdoing. The authorities felt particularly pressed to investigate the disappearance of art, furniture and other valuable items from the estates of the German aristocracy. In July 1947 the *Daily Mail* reported on the lost treasures of Prince Ernst-Wolrad zu Schaumburg-Lippe's requisitioned Schloss Bückeburg.[51] This case implicated leading figures in the military government's administrative hierarchy, including Sholto Douglas, military governor of the British Zone since May 1946. It was alleged that Air Officer Commanding Vice-Marshal Sir Arthur Coningham, Permanent Under-Secretary of State for the Foreign Office (German Section) William Strang, chairman of the Economic Control Office for the British and American zones of Germany Lieutenant-General Sir Gordon Macready and Sholto Douglas's wife, Lady Douglas, had taken huge amounts of furniture, cutlery and other household items to add princely charm to their new

Deputy Military Governor Brian Robertson (left), Military Governor Sholto Douglas (centre) and Economic Advisor to the Control Commission Cecil Weir (right).

abodes across Germany, as well as Coningham's villa in Cannes.[52] These allegations would ultimately cut short Sholto Douglas's tenure as military governor.[53] In October 1947 he was replaced by his deputy, General Brian Robertson. That December an official report noted that 166 carpets, 155 paintings, 5 Gobelin tapestries and 2,993 pieces of silver were still missing – most of them were never found.

In some instances, the scale of the corruption and fraud went far beyond personal gain and instead approached something more akin to organized crime. During the spring of 1947, Chief Inspector Tom Hayward, a twenty-two-year veteran of the Met's Criminal Investigation Unit who had been tasked with investigating crimes in the British Zone, came across Harold Ryder.[54] A deputy controller in the Trade and Industry Division of the Control Commission, Ryder was eventually charged, alongside several colleagues and their German accomplices, with involvement in various types of racketeering.[55] These indictments ranged from the buying and selling of German goods, including cutlery sets and bicycles, to the unauthorized allocation of 3,500 tons of steel to German manufacturers. Ryder's trial commenced in June 1947 and drew a substantial amount of press interest. The hearing was widely regarded as symptomatic of the crooked dealings that British officials were habitually engaged in.[56]

In the end, Ryder and all the other defendants were acquitted, barring a single misdemeanour offence, and questions were raised within the Control Commission administration about the 'sensational' presentation of the case in the newspapers.[57] There were suggestions that the then deputy military governor, Brian Robertson, should publicly 'counter the misleading statements' in one of his regular press conferences.[58] Gilmour Jenkins from the Public Relations Division stepped in, arguing that since 'interest in this case has died down' it would be 'best to do nothing which might revive it'.[59] He was plainly aware that negative publicity of this sort could not be easily refuted and would only further besmirch the reputation of the Control Commission, even when the charges were ultimately unproven. However, Ryder appeared, accused of fraudulent activities, along with two fellow senior CCG officials and a number of German businessmen, in another trial on 17 June. This time, much to the curiosity of the British newspapers, Ryder was found guilty of corruptly receiving items, including diamonds, sapphires, firearms, cutlery, bicycles and a silver cigarette case, all in exchange for business advantages.[60] While this verdict would later be overturned upon appeal, with Ryder successfully claiming that these gifts were acquired in the 'ordinary course of friendship', the damage had been done – few papers bothered to cover the acquittal.[61]

There were scores of other serious racketeering cases; charges included drug trafficking and note forgery.[62] These cases included evidence that some of those tasked with 'winning the peace' were mixed up in schemes on a par with Harry Lime's in *The Third Man*. In the course of acquiring a new camera, William Peters came across a British airman who had turned the black market into big business.[63] Alongside his duties in the RAF, he was trading from his Berlin flat together with his German girlfriend, resplendent in her fur coat and jewels. From various commissions, the man estimated his weekly turnover to be something in the region of 1 million Marks – money that was routinely smuggled back to Britain in the form of diamonds whenever he had leave. It was no one-off: a top-secret Control Commission report explained that 'a large number of illegal trading groups existed in which many Allied officers appeared to participate'.[64] The report warned that black market activities presented 'a major threat to the German and perhaps even European economy and financial stability' as well as a 'threat to Allied prestige and morale which might eventually have political repercussions'.

In September 1948 the *Daily Mail* published a particularly outrageous story of corruption tied to Germany's black market that highlighted the shadowy underworld of post-war Europe.[65] It claimed that Scotland Yard were tracking a notorious underworld kingpin who was dealing in stolen army supplies, currency and Nazi loot. He had cost the taxpayer millions, while making himself a millionaire 'twenty times over'. He led a gang, most of whom were said to come from a public-school background, who used bribery and intimidation to manipulate members of the occupation forces. It was believed that 'high-ranking British officials' were involved, silenced with bribes ranging from £50,000 to £250,000, while others were threatened with violence through the trickster's ominous-sounding 'insurance department'. The gang's money trail was said to reach around the globe, much of it laundered through legitimate businesses or siphoned off into offshore accounts in Bermuda, while their leader was said to live a life of luxury in hotels across continental Europe. Whether or not the story was based on fact or fantasy, its apparent plausibility speaks volumes about the ubiquity of corruption in this period – and the growing reputation of occupied Germany, and the British Zone in particular, as Europe's Wild West.

*

Taken together, the impact of these scams – both small and large – was considerable. In the first instance, there was a financial cost to the British Treasury: as was frequently bemoaned by the popular press, it was the British taxpayer who often ended up footing the bill for such rackets and swindles. Perhaps even more significant was their effect on the British Zone itself. While a privileged few made merry on the profits of the shadow economy of trades and barter, most Germans – desperately doing whatever they could to stave off hunger – were left ever more impoverished. In broader terms, the German economy was never going to break out of its slow death spiral without a stable medium of exchange. Without an end to the ubiquitous corruption and criminality, there was little hope of any kind of recovery. In the meantime, the burden on the Allies to supply food and essential goods only increased.[66] Finally, there was the reputational cost for the occupiers themselves. As we've already seen, the British newspapers were only too happy to report on the scandalous corruption of Control Commission and Rhine Army staff – thereby helping to reinforce the image of a bunch of unprincipled opportunists dedicated to lining their own pockets. From the procurement of gold watches to the theft of royal jewels, the British Zone became irrevocably associated with corruption and crime. In July 1946 the *Daily Mirror* accused the British authorities of running amok in their 'Black Zone':

> Something must be done to tighten up the administration of affairs in the British Zone in Germany... It appears that there is no one who can effectively cope with the culprits who are dragging Great Britain's good name through the dirt. The cost of the occupation to the British taxpayer is £180 million a year, and if to this is added the moral cost in loss of prestige, the situation is seen to be one which we cannot afford to tolerate.[67]

16

They Drink *Kaffee* When
We Drink Tea

In her role as translator, Mary Bouman was assigned to Officers'
Mess No. 16 in Herford, which was frequented by both civilians
and members of the armed forces. As it was for all British staff, the
mess was the centre of Mary's daily life in Germany: a place where
meals were taken, rations were received, parties were held, mail
was collected and much more besides. Each day at noon obligatory
vitamin supplements were handed out, while in the evenings men
and women sat around writing letters, reading a good book, or
paging through one of the days-old newspapers brought over on
British transport ships. Within a few weeks of her arrival, Bouman
had befriended a number of colleagues including 'a very nice
Scottish Major' in his late forties, who liked to sit in the corner
and complete crosswords with astonishing rapidity.[1] They found
themselves agreeing on most things and arguing the toss with
other members of Mess No. 16, including those she described as
'"Socialists In Theory" types'.

Not all encounters in the mess, however, were quite so agreeable.
The continuing demobilization of members of the armed forces,
combined with the fact that – in most cases – Control Commission
contracts were renewed only on an annual basis, meant that
messes saw endless comings and goings. In early March 1946 two

new arrivals in the civilian staff of the Control Commission who had been assigned to Mess No. 16 made public their extremely low opinion of the efforts of the German staff who prepared and served the meals, and they tried to enlist the German-speaking Bouman's help in getting their message across. 'They are trying to take the food in hand', she reported to her parents, taking it upon themselves to 'invade the kitchen trying to show the Germans how to make things like baked custard (don't like it anyway) and other typically English dishes'.[2] 'They don't like how the toast is done, why no grill or toast racks?' She went on, 'In vain I'll try to explain to them that the Germans don't know much about the art of making toast or baked custards or puddings… But they say they must learn.' Such conduct not only reveals the tensions that could arise on occasion between Control Commission staff, but also provides a clear illustration of the contempt towards Germans displayed by some members of the occupying forces.

While the relationship between rulers and ruled was by no means straightforward or fixed, in many respects the British and the Germans lived different and separate lives. We have already seen how well provided for British personnel were in material terms – in their accommodation, entertainments and, above all, food. Such advantages set them apart from the Germans with whom they shared the Zone. This gulf also shaped the culture of the Zone, which in the opinion of some observers began to mimic the characteristics of the British Empire. For Mary Bouman it was shocking to see her colleagues treat the country 'as a sort of British colony and the Germans as a species of rather inferior natives'.[3]

*

Even after non-fraternization regulations were a thing of the past, it is remarkable how many British staff kept themselves to themselves – a trend that was reinforced by official provision. They had their own buses, shops and cinemas. Trains had separate carriages for British and Germans, while churches held services based on nationality.[4] At one Hamburg hairdresser, four of the twelve cubicles were designated as British-only. On one occasion a British woman was kept waiting for twenty minutes and the authorities stepped in: the following day the proprietor was warned that if it happened again the premises would be fully requisitioned – and all of a sudden eight cubicles were now off-limits to the locals.[5]

Deane Richardson worked in the Control Commission's Economic Division. She moved to Germany in March 1946 after spending two years as part of post-war planning staff of the British Mission in Washington DC. Richardson split most of her time between Lübeck and Berlin – and the most striking aspect of her time in Germany during 1946–7 was the sheer lack of contact with the very people that she was supposed to be governing:

> Our life was lived in another world from the German occupants of the city who were enduring extremes of cold and hunger during that year. Although I was certainly participating in the government of the country I had very few contacts with its people except for Mess servants. I went to work by bus run by the military government, ate either in a Mess or a club and did no shopping as there were so few shops even on the Kurfürstendamm.[6]

At opera houses and music halls, orchestras were often required to play their programme twice a day, once for the British and then again for Germans.[7] In other venues mixed audiences were allowed but strict seating segregation was enforced, separating 'British', 'British with Germans' and 'Germans', although everyone was expected to rise for 'God Save the King'. In November 1946 Daphne Smith and her friend Sheila managed to secure tickets for the Kassel Symphony Orchestra, who played the overture to Wagner's *Die Meistersinger von Nürnberg* and Beethoven's *Eroica* symphony to a packed house.[8] But as the musicians began to warm up, Smith found herself increasingly agitated by the behaviour of the few Germans in the audience. A few days later she wrote an incensed letter to her mother that encapsulated the underlying friction between occupier and occupied:

You find yourself hating them as they come in, all the family, chattering away, greeting friends & acquaintances, & generally behaving as if you just weren't there. They're all 'dolled' up, in their fur coats, & cheap perfume, and the men bow formally to the women, & it's all as if they weren't aware there was an occupation of Germany. Even when the king is played, they rise reluctantly, & fidget throughout, & sit down before the last notes are played. You know you're superior to them, & that for all their indifferences you've got the upper hand. But you feel they are scarcely aware of your existence, let alone your existence as a controller & governor of their country. You find yourself wishing for something tangible to demonstrate that superiority, a display of military power or something.

It is, of course, hardly surprising that this kind of antagonism persisted well into the peace. This was an inevitable legacy of the war itself, so prominent in the minds of the many of those who made up the British staff. After six years of brutal fighting, which had seen widespread bombing of British cities, large-scale loss of life and major social upheavals, few were inclined to immediately forgive and forget. These memories were augmented in many cases by longer-standing antagonisms, stretching back to the outbreak of the First World War or beyond, and state-led propaganda campaigns. For years, whether it was through the writings of Lord Vansittart or the rhetoric of leading politicians, the British people had been subjected to the idea that the Germans were not just their enemy, but a wicked and malign people. These ideas were only hardened with the exposure of the crimes of the Holocaust. The notion that all Germans were potentially dangerous was then further reinforced in official guidelines set out at the beginning of the occupation: it was only in October 1946, for instance, that the British authorities finally revoked the order obliging Germans to step off the pavement and give 'right of way' to British personnel.[9] Likewise, the stories of *Werwolf* guerrillas and the insistence of many British officers that women under their charge needed male escorts at night did little to reduce the sense of paranoia.[10] The socialist writer Fenner Brockway had a disconcerting realization while touring Germany as a war correspondent in 1946. At the end of a meal at Berlin's Hotel am Zoo, Brockway was met with incredulity when he asked his British army officer dining companions about leaving a tip: 'Tipping? Tip Germans! A year ago we were trying to kill them. You don't think we now tip those we failed to get?'[11]

For most of the British staff, their most common contact with the locals was with those who worked as subordinates: waiters, cooks, cleaners, maids, gardeners, boilermen and such. These relationships reinforced the lowly position of Germans in the social hierarchy of the Zone. This inequality also manifested itself in the material reality of life in Germany after the war. The unequal allotment of housing and food meant that the local population was often in a state of near-destitution, appearing weaker, dirtier and altogether more dishevelled than their Allied rulers. It all helped to sustain a growing belief in British superiority among the occupation staff. Not only had they won the war, but now they ruled supreme over their defeated foe. After seeing a major slapping a young German boy, one soldier in the Green Howards reflected that 'none of us could have cared a bit for that little boy... they had been public enemy number one. So now we commandeered their horses, commandeered their Mercedes, commandeered their women. I would reckon sixty or seventy per cent of young Englishmen in Germany thought that way. Most of us were for having a bloody good time and believed we could get away with anything.'[12]

A final aspect of the great divide between occupiers and occupied was language. The British are rarely renowned for their command of foreign languages and this inadequacy was much in evidence in post-war Germany. There were, of course, those like Mary Bouman and Peter Wayne who had a personal connection to Germany and spoke the language fluently. But they were exceptions rather than the rule, and their ability to speak the local language made them much sought after in the sprawling bureaucracy of the British Zone. Those who knew German often found themselves forced into unexpected translation tasks: when the two women barged into the kitchen of Mess No. 16 demanding toast, they tried to engage Mary Bouman as an interpreter – only for her to refuse on principle.

In fact, the number of British staff who had solid knowledge of the language was so small that German secretaries often found themselves thrust into positions of considerable influence as bilingual translators. The situation was far from ideal and the British authorities sought to encourage more language learning among their staff. Alongside the basic phrasebooks they were given prior to arrival, German lessons were available for those interested. But for most, their vocabulary barely stretched beyond 'Bier' and 'Fräulein' – and interactions with the locals, even those related to official business, were conducted either through interpreters or wild gesticulation.[13] It all helped to create the impression of a starkly divided culture.[14] The writer and journalist Ethel Mannin, an acute and principled observer of the international scene since the 1930s with impressive anti-imperialist and anti-fascist credentials, was shocked to encounter 'two worlds' in her *German Journey*. Mannin wrote that 'it could be South Africa and the Europeans and "non-Europeans"… or India at the height of the British Raj'.[15]

*

Such attitudes, however, do not tell the whole story. Amid the disorder and uncertainty of post-war Europe, the social worlds of former enemies were unavoidably entangled. For all the formal segregation of occupiers and occupied, in the course of their everyday activities – whether travel or work or leisure – interaction between Britons and Germans (some of it jovial and friendly) was obviously inevitable. Nor did every member of the BAOR or CCG view their defeated enemy with the brutal disdain of Fenner Brockway's dining companions or Mary Bouman's toast-demanding mess-mates. More generous-minded souls seized the opportunity to engage rewardingly with Germany's people and culture and grew fond of their new environment.

As we've seen, several thousand Anglo-German marriages resulted from these interactions, a living embodiment of the rehabilitation of Germans in the eyes of some Britons. There were also cases where British occupiers befriended the locals in the course of their work and formed lifelong friendships. Ivan Hirst's German housekeeper recalled that the man overseeing the rebuilding of Volkswagen was modest and humble, and 'immensely disliked the performance made by some of the English, being rude to their German domestic staff'.[16] It was this attitude of mutual respect that helped Hirst recruit such a devoted workforce at the Wolfsburg car plant.

At a more quotidian level, personal papers and memoirs reveal an eagerness on the part of some occupiers to take language lessons – an activity that positively encouraged interactions with the locals. In her first letter home, Edna Wearmouth declared that she was 'just dying to learn German and be able to speak to them'.[17] She took language lessons with Hans Thol, the former resident of her lodgings who now lived in the cellar of the house along with his wife, Anneliese, and their four-year-old son. So keen was Katharine Morris to become fluent that she had as many as three German lessons a day: in the morning with a clerk in the office, at lunch with a neighbour and in the evening with an opera singer.[18] In her travels around Hamburg, she always carried her copy of *Grimms' Fairy Tales* in the original German, occasionally attracting the curiosity of passers-by.

Another driving motivation for joining the Control Commission was the opportunity to travel around Europe. With the required leave and transportation, it was possible to visit Brussels, Paris, Stockholm or Copenhagen for a few days. But more often trips were taken within Germany itself, whether city breaks in Hamburg, Cologne or Berlin or day trips to see the Möhne Dam, scene of the famous Dambusters Raid of May 1943. For many young women in particular, the time they spent in the British Zone was their first taste of independence away from the strictures of the parental home and the traditional gender roles of mid-century Britain.[19] Edna Wearmouth, who had never been abroad before, was adamant that she would 'make the most of every minute' and welcomed the opportunity to explore the countryside with particular enthusiasm.[20] She filled photo albums with pictures of natural landmarks, which she captioned with historical information or details of local legends, such as the Pied Piper.[21] Her discovery that Germany was a place of natural beauty or, to quote one caption, 'like walking through a fairy tale', was a very pleasant surprise and challenged the widespread preconception that this was a land of bombed-out ruins and concentration camps.[22] 'I can never rave enough about the beauty of Germany,' she wrote to her father. 'You will wonder, I've no doubt, at the way I tell you that every place is lovely – but it's true. There are so many lovely places.'[23]

Officially, members of the occupying forces were banned from travelling on public transport and staying in German homes, but the British authorities could do little to stop it. In the summer of 1947, Wearmouth described to her father an illicit trip on a German bus, during which she and her friends were 'chatting away to all the Germans and before long we had the whole blinking bus talking to us. Everyone was roaring and laughing at our broken German, but we carried on a lively conversation all the way.'[24] She also made a memorable visit to Fulda in the American Zone, staying in the family home of her German friend Günther. Having arrived with ample provisions of food for her hosts, she received a warm welcome and a cup of *Kaffee*, which, Wearmouth explained to her father, was what Germans had when 'we drink tea'.

*

From the beginning of 1946, with almost all the non-fraternization rules lifted, interactions with the Germans became all the more common. Local customs – especially unfamiliar foodstuffs or festivities – were often a source of friendly puzzlement. Christmas was a particular focus for cross-cultural exchanges, as Britons and Germans came together in celebration and worship. Mary Bouman embraced the traditions associated with the season in Germany, enjoying a 'Christmas with an English and German flavour', and describing how 'the fir garlands with Lametta made by the German staff vie with the garish paper decorations supplied by NAAFI'.[25]

She exchanged presents with local residents, gifting them alcohol, crayons and cocoa, and, in her self-appointed role as unofficial cultural ambassador, even sought to introduce the peculiarly British culinary customs of Christmas cake and mince pies. In the early years of the occupation, there could be no better gift than food.

The Christmas cheer went both ways: two of the German typists in Joan Hyde's unit of the Public Health Division penned a poem in imperfect English, poking fun at the oddities of the British who ran their office:

> Next door, 29, is working Major Prosserlein,
> He does not like his work without a song,
> Yours is my heart, come along
>
> ...
>
> Please, this time one copy only,
> That's our Mr Maloney, his German is quite well,
> But sometimes we are talking a little bit schnell.[26]

British Tommies entertain a group of young Germans in Lower Saxony.

Often it was the local children who became the centre of attention. In Germany, Christmas had taken on a very different and less festive feel over the last few years; at the height of the war the country's famous toy manufacturers in Nuremberg had halted production.[27] Now, though some of their factories were restarting, most toys were sold abroad – primarily to the United States – while the majority of German families had to prioritize food and fuel over Christmas presents. As one German magazine put it in December 1946, 'Father Christmas has been bombed out!'[28]

Whether because they missed their own children, they felt a paternalistic duty or they simply wished to give local kids something to smile about, British staff often took it upon themselves to provide some Christmas cheer and entertainment. In September 1946 Gerald Lenanton began putting aside his sugar and chocolate rations in preparation for a Christmas party for local children.[29] The following month his wife sent a selection of toys for the occasion – although Lenanton felt moved to remove a model submarine as he did not think 'it right that in 1947 German children should treasure models of what anyone might mistake for a U-Boat'.[30] While plans were said to be 'developing along the lines of a French farce', on 23 December around fifty 'very poor', 'fatherless' and 'poorly dressed' German children were treated to cakes and sausage rolls. They then enjoyed a performance of Kasperle, the German version of Punch and Judy, and finally – as was often the case on such occasions – a British officer arrived dressed as Father Christmas to hand out gifts.[31]

In December 1948 Mary Bouman helped at two children's Christmas parties, where the puzzling traditions of Christmas crackers and English party games were the order of the day. As she told her parents, they provided an unexpected but not unwelcome change of pace:

> The Germans I don't think ever went in for children's Christmas parties as we know them. Their idea is to sit round a table... and sing carols over and over again with serious solemn faces and then get up and recite long intricate verses to Father Christmas. Any idea of a good romp or games

seems unknown. But how they loved it when we showed them the way.[32]

Bouman helped dish out cakes and cocoa to more than 500 German children, who were also entertained with a puppet show and showered with gifts from Father Christmas. The presents consisted mainly of oranges, biscuits and chocolates, although one little girl, aged around four or five, was astonished to find a grapefruit at the bottom of her bag. It was a sign of the times when she turned to an older boy to enquire what exactly this mysterious object was. He solemnly assured her it was a lemon. 'ICH HABE EINE ZITRONE! ICH HABE EINE ZITRONE!',* she enthusiastically called out while jumping up and down.

These stories of friendship and camaraderie illustrate the kinds of person-to-person reconciliation that arose organically from social interaction taking place in the British Zone. British men and women were coming to recognize that not all Germans were quite so wicked as had been made out in recent years. There is a certain charm to the encounters between Britons and Germans which took place in this unique social world; they seemed to offer a glimmer of hope for a future where national rivalries might be felt less fiercely.

From 1947 onwards these kinds of interactions were positively encouraged by the British authorities. Take, for example, the work of the British military government's chief sports officer, John G. Dixon, who transformed the character of physical education in the Zone.[33] Dixon, a keen admirer of German culture and history, was dismayed at the lack of PE classes on offer to German children and the 'over-directed, mechanically and meekly performed techniques' performed in those that were taking place. He arranged trips for German physical education teachers to the UK, where they were to learn the most modern techniques of sporting instruction.

---

* 'I'VE GOT A LEMON! I'VE GOT A LEMON!'

But there is no doubt that the prevailing culture of the British Zone remained one of division rather than unity. The occupiers, as a result of their material advantages and status, could not help but be part of a ruling class. Even well-meaning interactions were marked by this: British personnel not only had the authority and rations to put on Christmas parties, but were often inspired by a kind of didactic zeal to teach the Germans how to have a good time.

This image of the British Zone as a land of 'haves' and 'have-nots' was certainly the impression that made its way back to Britain. Victor Gollancz, Fenner Brockway and others who had spent the war contesting Vansittartism were now quick to condemn what they saw as the imperialist attitudes prevalent in Britain's newest unofficial colony.[34] In the *Manchester Guardian*, Gollancz – himself a long-standing opponent of the British Empire – criticized the culture of the British Zone:

> Though there are many fine exceptions, the general attitude varies from a disgusting offensiveness, through indifference often identifiable with oblivion, to that humane and almost unconsciously superior paternalism which is characteristic of the 'white' attitude to 'natives'... The plain fact is that there are two worlds in Germany today, the world of the conquered and the world of the conquerors. They meet at the peripheries, but their hearts beat in inhuman isolation.[35]

Yet for some commentators the idea of running the British Zone as a colony had its merits. Broadly speaking, even on the brink of an era of rapid decolonization, the empire was a source of pride for many in Britain: so, might imperial rule be the ideal means of 'winning the peace' in Germany? Colonel Ralph Glynn, the Tory MP for Abingdon, certainly thought so. He declared in the House of Commons that 'the model which the Germans would most easily understand and which would train them until they undertake responsibility would be our colonial form of government'.[36] From the government benches Labour MP Richard

Crossman criticized what he perceived as a troubling evolution in the thinking of 'hard peace' advocates:

> I cannot help feeling that many hon. Members of this House, and many of the general public, are still suffering from the propaganda of the war. They move from 'Vansittartism' to something which is equally wrong at the moment, an attitude of treating Germans as a potential colonial people.[37]

17

The Hamburg Project

In 1946 Hamburg's *Rathaus* ('town hall') was one of the few buildings in the city centre that remained largely intact. Its distinctive turquoise roof and large clocktower, standing at over 100 metres tall, dominated a skyline of otherwise burnt and broken buildings. In front was a large marketplace which during the Third Reich was known as Adolf-Hitler-Platz. It now once again went by its pre-war name of Rathausmarkt, although only after British plans to rename it General-Ross-Platz in honour of the commander of the garrison troops of the 53rd Welsh Division had been shelved.[1] At round 11 a.m. on 27 June the area was a hive of noise and activity. Alongside the normal whirl of trucks, cars, trams, bicycles and pedestrians, a large crowd amassed in front of the town hall's main gates. As protestors scuffled with the local police, words that had not been sung in public for many months broke out spontaneously: '*Deutschland, Deutschland über alles, Über alles in der Welt...*' ('Germany, Germany above all, Above all in the world').

The previous year Allied occupiers had banned the German national anthem, the *Deutschlandlied* ('The Song of Germany').* For the crowd to sing it, and especially its opening two verses proclaiming Germany to be 'above all in the world', was a

---

* Germany would remain officially without a national anthem until the West German government reintroduced the *Deutschlandlied* in 1952. However, only the third verse was to be used when it was sung in a public context, the first two verses – with their overtly nationalist sentiments – being omitted.

deliberate provocation aimed squarely at the new rulers of their city. The locals were objecting to the 'Hamburg Project', an attempt to construct a British military government headquarters in the Harvestehude district of the city. Yet the concerns of the protestors also went far deeper: more than a year after the war had ended, Hamburgers still lived in squalid conditions and were unable to find adequate supplies of just about anything.

Despite this, the British pressed on with their grand building plans, which revealed their intention to remain in Germany for the long term. Their construction projects brought to the surface some of the tensions between rulers and ruled that had developed since the end of the war. Though now largely forgotten, the story of the 'Hamburg Project' illustrates the precarious position of the British occupation in the summer of 1946.

*

The immense scale of destruction in the major towns and cities of the British Zone had left the Control Commission without an identifiable headquarters. Military government offices and compounds were dotted around the countryside in smaller towns like Minden, Lübbecke, Herford and Detmold, where a larger supply of intact buildings had been available. It was hardly the most efficient way to run what amounted to a government. In response, the 'Hamburg Project' was intended to streamline this dispersed administration through the creation of a centralized HQ in the British Zone's largest city. This would hopefully curb the spiralling manpower costs of maintaining an occupation army and civil administration in Germany, thereby countering one of the major sources of criticism back home.[2]

Hamburg itself had sustained cataclysmic levels of damage from Allied area bombing during the war. At the end of the conflict there were an estimated 35.8 million cubic metres of rubble across the city, enough to fill a train of freight cars as long as the Earth's circumference; in slightly more comprehensible terms, 54 per cent of *all* buildings were damaged or destroyed.[3] Perhaps the clearest sense of the scale of destruction comes from first-hand accounts:

in April 1946 Mary Bouman wrote home to her parents, telling them of her sadness at the sight of 'poor old Hamburg' where the ruins were 'on too vast a scale to cope with'.[4]

This level of devastation had an impact on all aspects of life. There was, above all, a critical shortage of housing: huge air raids had damaged 79.5 per cent of available stock, with 49.2 per cent totally destroyed.[5] The same was true of municipal buildings: of the 451 schools that had stood in 1938, more than 200 were now being used for non-educational purposes, 64 billeted British soldiers, and over 150 were totally or heavily damaged.[6] In a city of 100,000 school-age children the strain on the remaining forty or so schools was unimaginable. Likewise, around 40 per cent of medical buildings had been rendered unusable. As a result of returning evacuees and refugees from the east, the city's population swelled, making the shortage of adequate shelter ever more acute.[7] By 1946 there was a growing population of homeless people in the city, while thousands of others lived in cellars or prefabricated Nissen huts.[8]

In the midst of what was an unfolding social catastrophe, British occupiers had already confiscated a substantial number of buildings for their own purposes: almost all the intact hotels, cinemas and theatres were requisitioned, alongside houses and flats, as living quarters. An introductory booklet for newcomers to the city handed out by Army Welfare Services listed two theatres, a concert hall, four cinemas, a café, a rest centre, eleven social clubs, a golf club, a rowing club, two swimming baths, numerous hairdressers, and various sports grounds fitted out for everything from fencing to horse-riding.[9] In the city centre the occupiers were allocated twenty separate bus routes as well as British-only carriages on the city's S-Bahn (suburban railway network), which they could travel on free of charge.[10]

Meanwhile, tens of historic buildings had been transformed. The music hall became 'Broadcasting House', while the Passage Kino in Mönckebergstraße was the 'Chevalier Cinema'. In the cellars of the town hall, the Ratsweinkeller was rechristened the 'Ship & Dragon Club'. The Reemtsma Villa, a grand 1930s residence which had previously ranked as one of the most expensive private dwellings in Europe, now housed an exclusive 'Officers Country Club'. Then

The Victory Club, Hamburg. This huge British-only club and hotel
featured numerous dance halls, theatres and restaurants.

there was the ostentatiously named 'Victory Club', located in the
Deutschlandhaus on Dammtorstraße. In 1944 a bombing raid had
largely destroyed the famous 'Ufa Palace', a 2,667-seat cinema that,
at the time, was Europe's largest. In May 1945 the remains of the
building were requisitioned and reconstructed as a British-only
club and hotel.[11] Here, 14,000 meals were served every day, and
across its seven floors British patrons could expect to find dance
halls, games and reading rooms, gift shops, ballrooms, theatres
and even a beer tavern. 'The huge Victory Club in Hamburg,' wrote
Victor Gollancz, 'which might house thousands of cellar-dwelling
Germans, blazes away by night in the ruined and darkened city.'[12]

This requisitioning was undertaken without a great deal of
consideration for those who were being evicted. Within the first
eighteen months of the occupation, the British requisitioned 9 per
cent of Hamburg's living space, despite the fact that their share
of the total population was a mere 1.8 per cent.[13] The 'Hamburg
Project' was designed to consolidate these earlier endeavours by
building something approaching a 'British Quarter' that could
accommodate a substantial proportion of the occupation staff.

One secret memorandum even described it as the creation of a 'British colony'.[14]

British planners masterminded a scheme that would involve the repair and modification of existing offices in the *Altstadt* ('old town') as well as the construction on the north-west banks of the Außenalster of numerous twelve- and eight-storey residential flats, theatres, shops, hotels and clubs – all for the exclusive use of British forces.[15] This ambitious building project would require over 35,000 German labourers and was projected for completion in the autumn of 1947. These plans would come at a considerable cost to the local population since they involved the demolition of around 750 badly needed houses and the requisitioning of many more. As a result, more than 30,000 people would need to be rehoused, which itself necessitated a programme of repairs to damaged houses throughout the city – all in order to accommodate as few as 5,000 British officers and their families.[16] As one newspaper reporter later commented, the initiation of such a project while thousands of Germans were living without adequate shelter or food was the very definition of 'asking for trouble'.[17]

*

In May 1946, once objections within the Control Commission regarding logistics and manpower were overcome, the 'Hamburg Project' was finally given the go-ahead. In mid-June a press release informed both the local population and the British media about the building programme.[18] Officials emphasized that the areas earmarked for demolition were already heavily devastated, that nobody would be removed until alternative accommodation was made available and that the plan would ultimately help to improve the efficiency of the Control Commission. In Britain, the reaction was muted, to say the least. There was little interest in the technicalities of the British Zone's amorphous administration, despite the ongoing outcry at spiralling costs and glaring inefficiencies. For the population of Hamburg, however, the news of further mass requisitioning prompted intense public anger. On 27 June this discontent came to a head when around eighty women marched on the *Rathaus* and called for support from the mayor in their protests.[19] They were soon joined by as many as 4,000 people who, according to the CCG's Public Safety Branch's official report, became 'truculent' and teetered on the edge of outright insurrection.

Around the front of the town hall two semicircles of German policemen in military tunics and Jäger shako peaked caps waited nervously with their arms linked. They looked out onto a sea of men in hats, young boys in dusty suit jackets, women in raincoats. Above the mass of people, pockets of protestors were perched atop trucks, cars, lamp-posts or balustrades. Towards the front, a combined force of teenagers and older women were causing a ruckus as the crowd broke out into songs and chants. At around 11:20 a.m., there was a half-hearted attempt to storm the town hall and British officers ordered the iron gates locked shut. Inside, a delegation of six women were meeting with Mayor Rudolf Petersen and British officials. They demanded more assistance for those faced with eviction and a stricter adherence to the promise of providing them with at least three weeks' notice.

While local Hamburg police had been given the job of holding the front line, members of the British Army of the Rhine were dotted in pockets around the square. In one corner, a member of the Royal Military Police abruptly confronted a middle-aged man in a long beige trench coat. Within seconds, a handful of British military policemen in their olive-green uniforms, distinctive red dress caps and white belt, sash, gaiters and pistol holster had congregated around him. Elsewhere, a man in a baggy black suit and hat was being force-marched at speed through the crowd, a British soldier at his back. A few onlookers momentarily stopped and turned, gesturing as if they might try to intervene, but within seconds the man was bundled into the back of an army truck. Inside the *Rathaus* itself, young typists could be seen perched upon windowsills, peering down at the protesters.

At some point a German policeman entered the mayor's office, warning him that the crowd was refusing to leave unless he showed his face. Petersen, 'white moustache bristling, hands grasping the lapels of his Savile Row suit', walked out upon the balcony and addressed the protestors to a chorus of cheers and boos.[20] Afterwards, good to their word, the crowd soon dispersed and the whole incident was over by midday, even if some were heard to proclaim 'we will come again'.

In the end, only eleven arrests were made. While some rebellious youths were said to have 'knocked off a few hats', the atmosphere had been calmed without resort to violence. A week later ten demonstrators were sentenced to a combined twenty-seven years in prison or youth prison. Meanwhile, further discussions were held with city authorities about relieving the burden on those who were worst affected by the 'Hamburg Project', which aimed to stave off accusations that the British had 'broken their word'.[21] It was a minor consolation for people facing the prospect of losing their homes, but there were no further protests.

*

What are we to make of this public disturbance? In light of the British attempts to instil the values of democracy in Germany, it might have been regarded as a good sign. In the months since the end of the war, the Allied occupiers had begun to slowly rebuild the country's political institutions. The British had identified two basic defects in the Weimar electoral system: first, an overemphasis on political parties, which severed the basic link between the electoral candidate and their constituency of voters, and, second, a form of proportional representation that routinely produced unstable coalition governments.[22] The British military government sought to adapt German electoral law. They incorporated the constituency principle with each elector having two votes for two representatives in parliament: the first directly tied to individual candidates for the local constituency and the second a vote for a political party; these second votes were tallied up and seats awarded to candidates on a regional list according to the proportion of votes cast for each party. In addition, the British insisted on annual elections for a third of all local councillors and, eventually, encouraged the inclusion of a 5 per cent threshold for parliamentary representation. Most of these changes would leave a legacy and remained as part of the system adopted by the Federal Republic in 1949 – although the unpopular practice of annual local elections was quietly discarded.

Harold Ingrams, on a year's secondment from the Colonial Office as head of the CCG's Administration and Local Government Branch, had entered Germany aspiring to eradicate 'the ghastly doctrine of the Nazis' and help the 'redemption and regeneration of Germany'.[23] At the heart of his work lay a fervent belief in the model of British democracy: 'we adhered to all in the German system which we thought would work democratically... but we wanted to inculcate the spirit of British local government'.[24] As he explained to colleagues in February 1946, 'we are trying to beat the swastika into the parish pump and the parish council does not go to war'.[25] Yet Ingrams ultimately realized that the path to democracy would be gradual and heavily reliant on compromises. He would abandon, for instance, his attempt to introduce first-past-the-post voting in favour of a modified system of proportional representation that was more acceptable to the Germans.[26]

The slow evolution of a new German democracy began in the summer of 1945, as political parties were once again permitted across all four zones in order 'to foster the growth of a democratic spirit in Germany and to prepare for the holding of elections at a later date'.* In the British Zone, the undertaking saw 8,100 local councils established by April 1946, where men and women 'uncompromised by Nazism' from 'all sections of the population' were able to shape their own country's destiny.[27] This grounding in local politics was intended to begin a long-term process towards democratic governance on a larger scale, even if national-level politics was not anticipated for some years yet.

In Hamburg, Rudolf Petersen, a successful businessman, was appointed mayor only seven days after Germany's final surrender.

---

* It was an allowance that came with strict regulations: parties had to deposit their programme with the occupation authorities, submit periodical reports on activities, provide full details of funding, seek permission for all public meetings, provide copies of all political literature to the Information Control branch, and were prohibited the use of uniforms, badges, emblems and armbands. See Balfour and Mair, *Four Power Control*, pp. 203–4.

He had since joined a new political party, the Christian Democratic Union* (CDU).[28] At the time of the protest, 'Old P', as the mayor was colloquially known, stood as *the* figurehead of political representation in the city. In raising their concerns through the correct channels, holding their political representatives to account and demanding action without resorting to violence, the protestors in Hamburg's main square had demonstrated the emergence of a 'democratic spirit'. Their action certainly didn't arouse a great deal of concern among the British authorities: the events warranted only a single paragraph in the Public Safety Branch daily report, alongside rumours of a communist-inspired hunger march and numerous armed robberies at nearby farms.[29]

Yet back in Britain the events of 27 June prompted some rather dramatic headlines: 'GERMANS RIOT IN HAMBURG', exclaimed the *Daily Mail*, while the *Daily Sketch* went with 'GERMAN CROWD CHANTS "UBER ALLES"'. Almost all the national dailies covered the story and many, including the *Daily Herald*, the *News Chronicle* and the *Daily Mail*, gave it front-page billing.[30] These reports gave meticulous details of the hostile chants and songs supposedly belted out by the crowd: 'We Are Not in Concentration Camps Now', 'Why Don't You Finish the Hunger Blockade' and 'We Are Not Indians – We Are Germans'. If such revelations were shocking, the alleged singing of both the German national anthem and the Nazi anthem, the *Horst-Wessel-Lied* had even graver connotations. In the *Daily Express* it was alleged that Free Hamburg, 'a new fascist-youth organization', had circulated chain letters labelling the mayor and city council as 'Jews, and the tools of Jews'. The *Express* also suggested that the demonstration was simply 'against Britain' and alleged that crowds had revived the old First World War slogan '*Gott strafe England*' ('May God punish England'). It also noted with incredulity that a 'German matron' had called an officer of the BAOR a '*Schweinhund*', literally meaning 'pig-dog' but in colloquial German closer to 'bastard'. In the *Daily Mail* readers were warned that 'anti-British feeling' was

---

* The CDU was an interdenominational (Catholic and Protestant) centre-right party founded in Berlin in June 1945.

becoming apparent across the Zone, in some areas approaching a 'dangerous level'. Their readership could draw only one conclusion: German nationalism was once again resurgent.

Yet for those in Britain who had long advocated a more conciliatory approach to Germany after the war, the events of June 1946 confirmed their own critical assessments of the occupiers – and the pressing need for a change of tack. In late 1946 the noted social reformer Lord Beveridge visited the Zone and wrote in his *Urgent Message from Germany* that the conditions of life for Germans were 'intolerable'.[31] The failed policies of the British administration were, he felt, partly to blame, foremost among them the 'Hamburg Project', which had made 'a desperate situation worse'.[32] Fenner Brockway agreed, writing in his *German Diary* of the same year that turning 30,000 Germans onto the streets and confiscating their belongings had 'caused a wave of resentment more bitter than any since the Occupation began'.[33]

German civilians in Hamburg queue up for soup rations in March 1946.

In the House of Commons, Victor Gollancz's great ally Richard Stokes led the charge. Stokes, Labour MP for Ipswich, had made his name as a principled opponent of the area bombing of German civilians during the war. Now, continuing his crusade against the 'hard peace' of 1945, he raised the 'Hamburg Project' as an example of the British Zone's rank mismanagement.[34] It was, he argued, an 'atrocity' to dispossess people 'who have been bombed to blazes' of their houses and few remaining possessions for the benefit of the 'British Raj'. Stokes made his distaste for the imperial culture of the Control Commission authorities abundantly clear:

Are we to see, in the midst of this devastation and in a state of things where men and women have not enough money to buy food for their families, have nowhere to live but holes in the ground and nothing in the shape of a prospect of industrial development, what? A great big gin palace in the middle of Hamburg? For what? For what I call the Hamburg Poona, for the British Raj?[35]

If the British authorities went ahead with the plans, Stokes concluded, it would only serve to further damage British prestige and undermine the overriding objective of the occupation – which, in his mind, was to liberate the German people from oppression:

Is this to be done when everybody is suffering from cold and hunger, and is it to be surrounded with soldiers carrying fixed bayonets and marching up and down outside? Is that the way to treat a population who should regard us as liberators and not as conquerors? We went there to liberate them from a beastly disease and now that we have done it we are behaving in exactly the same way as the beast did. This is precisely the sort of thing that the Nazis did.

In hindsight, we can see how this range of responses was representative of British attitudes towards the fate of post-war Germany. For some, the angry reaction of local residents prompted fears that fascism was resurfacing, while others perceived this scheme as a symbol of the moral bankruptcy and imperialist ethos of the occupation itself. Either way, the protest did little to ease the growing sense of dismay at the conduct of the British occupiers. The scandalous stories of drunkenness, unruly behaviour, objectionable sexual liaisons and an out-of-control black market had all taken their toll – and now the ability of the British to rule their Zone of Germany justly and competently was called into question.

*

In the end, no occupiers ever moved into the Grindel high-rise flats that stand to this day in Harvestehude.* By the end of 1946, the British authorities in Germany had decided to shelve the 'Hamburg Project' on account of what was euphemistically described as 'supply issues'.[36] The real reasons were manifold. A lack of adequate supplies of labour and materials were certainly a consideration, especially with the onset of winter. There were also obvious anxieties over the response of the locals after the events of the summer; it was becoming increasingly clear that policies could not simply be handed down without some consideration of the public mood. In the aftermath of the protests, the military commander of Hamburg remarked that 'a year ago we would have requisitioned almost without comment on a scale which resulted in Germans sleeping on the floor' before lamenting that 'this is no longer possible'.[37] But perhaps the most important factor in the decision to abandon the 'Hamburg Project' was the prospect of a more rapid reconstruction of Germany's political and economic life. In the aftermath of Bevin's negotiations with the Americans that summer, new plans materialized calling for the merger of the British and American zones – and eventually a much quicker renewal of western Germany than previously envisioned. It inevitably put proposals for a central HQ on the back burner.

---

* The British abandoned the project with only the foundations laid. It was not until 1948 that the local government decided to restart construction and built twelve high-rise modernist blocks for residential use.

In the British Zone the outcry over the 'Hamburg Project' added fuel to the fire of growing German hostility towards the conduct of the occupiers after a wave of hunger marches and strikes had previously hit the region.[38] It was quickly becoming clear that the attempt to 'win the peace' was anything but straightforward. In the first year of the occupation, the British employed much expense and energy – not to mention goodwill of the local population – in pursuit of the aims set out at Potsdam. Yet it had become apparent to those in charge that the agreements made in 1945 were not fit for purpose. The breakdown of relations with the Soviet Union, the influx of refugees and the ever worsening shortages of food and shelter were putting a financial strain on the British exchequer that simply could not be maintained. The Potsdam Agreement, conceived at a time of heightened anti-German feeling, bore increasingly little relation to the realities of building a democracy in the shadow of Nazism.

Not long after the Hamburg protests, Margarita Ostermann met with a number of CCG colleagues at the Atlantic Club. Over lunch, the talk turned to the plight of the Germans and, in particular, whether it was morally right that these beleaguered people should have their few worldly possessions confiscated at a moment's notice. She noticed over the course of the conversation that her companions, many of whom had undoubtedly harboured strong anti-German prejudices prior to their arrival in the Zone, were exhibiting signs of a transformation. It struck her how 'contact with the Germans does something to all these men, they feel responsible and defend them against the lack of understanding'.[39] Now, in the place of tired clichés about the 'unchanging German', most of her colleagues agreed that Germany 'must be given a chance by us and not utterly crushed or kept in the present state'.

This was certainly the attitude taken by Hamburg's new regional commissioner, Henry Vaughan Berry, who took up his position against the background of the vociferous protests of June 1946. Berry immediately voiced his own opposition to the 'Hamburg Project' and soon came to be respected among the city's political elites and trade unions as a fair-minded, effective governor.[40] He pushed for improved Anglo-German dialogue as a means not only of bringing about more effective governance, but also as a process of long-term reconciliation. Berry was adamant that, in order to succeed, the British occupiers needed 'to impress [their] ideas' upon the Germans through discussion, rather than simply imposing their rule.[41]

18

Operation Union

In mid-August 1946 the passenger ship SS *Empire Halladale* approached Cuxhaven, a harbour located at the mouth of the Elbe around 60 miles (97 kilometres) from the centre of Hamburg. The *Empire Halladale* had started life as a Hamburg Süd ocean liner under the name *Antonio Delfino*, built in 1921 to ferry passengers between South America and Germany. But after a period of war service with the Kriegsmarine, the ship was captured by the Royal Navy and renamed before being handed over to the Ministry of Transport as part of the reparations settlement. Now it was one of the two troopships that regularly made the forty-two-hour crossing from Tilbury Docks in London to the British Zone.[1] But this was no ordinary sailing: as the *Empire Halladale* was moored to the dockside, a huddle of Rhine Army officers and press photographers crowded the decked concourse below while a military band started up.

The assembled observers were not, as one might expect, ready to greet a new division of uniformed personnel or even a group of Westminster bigwigs. Rather, they watched as a parade of women in fashionable hats and stylish overcoats disembarked with an assemblage of unwieldy bags and, in many instances, carrying small children. Slightly older boys and girls walked down the gangway unaided, no doubt excited and intimidated at the fuss being made of them. These were the first wives and children of serving Rhine Army soldiers allowed to enter Germany as part of 'Operation

Union'. As they stepped onto dry land, they could see before them a large banner which read 'Welcome to the British Zone'. It was now home for this group of intrepid civilians.

Over the course of the next few months several thousand British civilians took up residence in the towns and cities of north-west Germany. They were propelled into an extraordinary existence alongside the chaos and dislocation that still marked much of the Zone. These forces families were provided with requisitioned flats, extra rations and special privileges. They were cast as representatives of the British people and tasked with providing a slice of domestic bliss amid the uncertainties of post-war Europe. Many senior staff in the British administration hoped that the presence of women and children would bring renewed order and discipline to a mission that was in danger of spiralling out of control. In the end, however, things turned out rather differently.

*

The public image of British personnel in Germany had been severely tainted by the various scandals of the past year. The seemingly wayward exploits of Britain's occupiers stood in sharp contrast with the veterans of the war, who were now increasingly venerated as heroes. For those in charge, the willingness of soldiers and civilian administrators to brazenly disregard regulations was concerning. But perhaps even more of a concern was the reputational cost: the growing media and public outcry about the state of affairs in Germany risked generating calls for radical changes in policy or perhaps even a full withdrawal. As the 'Germany Under Control' exhibition had demonstrated, both military top brass and government ministers were convinced that their work in Germany could ultimately only succeed with the backing of the British people. In their public utterances leading officials now invoked cautionary tales of the post-1918 peace. This time, they reasoned, Britain must finish the job or risk another war.

It was in this context that Sholto Douglas, as commander-in-chief of the Zone, felt obliged to do something to stop the rot. While public relations efforts continued, he encouraged officials of the Rhine Army to introduce a new and somewhat unconventional measure aimed squarely at encouraging more reputable behaviour from their staff: bringing over their wives and children.

There was, of course, a clear sentimental case for reuniting service families, many of whom had been separated for several years. In November 1945 letters appeared in the *Daily Telegraph* asking when the 'wretched army wife' will 'cease to be looked on as her husband's "excess luggage" to be left lying about indefinitely'.[2] The British authorities in Germany also openly acknowledged more pragmatic motivations. In the first place, they hoped that reuniting families would make the occupation more of a desirable posting. This, in turn, would encourage conscientious, hard-working individuals to join the British Army of the Rhine and the Control Commission, as well as persuading those already in Germany to stay on longer.[3] In addition, the British government believed that appeasing service wives would help to prevent potential 'bring the boys back home' sentiment from establishing a foothold in Britain.[4] But without doubt, the decision to allow wives and families to move to Germany was primarily designed to introduce a moralizing force to the British Zone, a direct response to the scandal surrounding non-fraternization and the wider malaise the occupiers found themselves in.

Throughout the public outcry over 'fratting', various commentators had raised the prospect of sending wives and families to Germany as a check on the corruptible men of the Rhine Army and Control Commission.[5] As one army padre delicately put it, British women would bring 'contentment' among the men, helping 'to form a centre of public opinion within the units' and 'generally exercise a steadying influence'.[6] Their impact could even extend to the work of the occupation itself: wives and families were envisaged as ambassadors of the 'British way of life' who could make a telling difference to the ultimate success of re-educating the German people. In a letter to *The Times*, a representative of the Church of England's Moral Welfare Council suggested that the future of Europe depended on the success of the occupation 'and to that... the British families may contribute a very great deal'.[7] 'Operation Union', then, was born out of a belief that the presence of British women and children in itself would act as a moral and perhaps literal brake on the more distasteful aspects of occupation life, thereby preventing British forces from becoming embroiled in further public scandals.

*

In 1945 concerns over difficult living conditions in Germany had rendered unthinkable the idea of wives and children joining service personnel in the Zone. A number of British personnel, some of whom doubtless had ulterior motives, publicly voiced their support for the cautious – and well-meaning – approach taken by officials.[8] But in the spring of 1946, when the crippling food shortages of the 'Battle of the Winter' began to ease, discussions were held at the highest levels of government regarding the possibility of relocating British wives to Germany.[9] In August, after a number of false starts owing to a lack of basic supplies and adequate housing, 'Operation Union' finally got underway.[10] This was significantly later than it was for American families, who had been arriving in Germany since the beginning of 1946 – an illustration of the uniquely challenging conditions found in the British Zone. In the French Zone, by contrast, some wives and children had joined their husbands and fathers almost as soon as the war was over, aided by the Zone's geographical proximity to France.[11]

British 'Married Families' – the official designation, which also included betrothed couples – were to be given passage to Germany, provided with furnished accommodation, rations, entertainment and more, and fully integrated into the occupation administration. There were also schemes to bring out the families of RAF and Royal Navy servicemen. Notably, no provision was made for male partners of women serving with the ATS or the Control Commission.*

On 15 August the first eighty-seven women arrived in Cuxhaven as designated 'pathfinders' who were tasked with testing the

---

* Likewise, considering the prejudices of the time, there was no acknowledgement of same-sex relationships. Despite this, numerous testimonies indicate that gay relationships were a feature of life in the British Zone.

arrangements before thousands of others made the same trip.[12] Upon arrival, this group of wives and fiancées were handed Union Jack lapel badges, ostensibly for purposes of identification, before being sent on their way via train or army car to various locations across the Zone.[13] Captain Matthew Evelyn Wood, charged with conducting the British wives to their destinations across Germany, reckoned he must be 'the ugliest officer in BAOR' to be considered such a safe chaperone.[14]

Yet for many involved it was no time for humour. Full of nervous excitement at the prospect of seeing their partners for the first time in months, they looked out of railway carriages and army transports on a spectacle of unimaginable destruction. In Cuxhaven scuttled ships dotted the waterfront, while gangs of emaciated children surrounded the British trains in the hope that a kindly passenger might throw them some chocolate or a morsel of bread. As they left the harbour, these British civilians passed through a landscape of craters, bombed-out buildings and appalling hardships. It was a world away from even the starkest realities of life in post-war Britain.

In the subsequent weeks and months, hundreds of women and children travelled to Germany aboard the SS *Empire Halladale* and SS *Empire Trooper* – and their passage inspired a great deal of interest back in Britain. The newspapers published numerous photographs and personal stories, all of which emphasized the novelty of travelling abroad.[15] The *Daily Mail* reported that the women had received a series of immunizations prior to enjoying their 'last English meal for some time', which consisted of 'cereals, bacon and eggs (real), marmalade and toast, roast beef and Yorkshire pudding'.[16] In the regional papers there was a perceptible degree of pride that local women were among the first wives to venture to Germany.[17]

Perhaps with an eye to stimulating a positive response from the media, the British authorities made sure that the women travelled in some style and that their arrival was greeted with suitably patriotic fanfare. *The Times* reported that 'welcome surprises for women long accustomed to ration restrictions and an austere diet' were to be expected on board the transport ships.[18] These included a choice of six wines available with meals consisting of white bread, crisp rolls, ice cream, soup, turbot, chicken, roast *and* boiled potatoes, green peas, pineapples and coffee, along with new toys for the children.[19] The sounds of 'military bands on a flag-bedecked dockside' greeted families upon their arrival in Cuxhaven. Their onward trains were stocked with cigarettes, sweets and magazines, while – in the midst of crippling transport shortages across Germany – everyone was allocated a corner seat, meaning that there were just four people in every six-person compartment.

In the newspapers this red-carpet treatment was covered at great length. *The Times* praised the 'marvellous organization' of the whole venture.[20] *Gaumont-British* and *British Movietone News* each produced two newsreels, evidently sourced from the same officially sanctioned footage, documenting the journey of the wives and children.[21] These films captured the poignant moments when families were reunited in Germany, where they would live 'surrounded by ex-enemies'. But not everyone was happy: Elizabeth Crookston of Weston-super-Mare wrote to the *Daily Telegraph* to complain about the displays of jingoism associated with 'Operation Union':

> All the publicity and ostentation over BAOR wives going to Germany is none of our seeking; all we require and demand is a passage out there. The fuss over the journey and our arrival is entirely unnecessary; moreover, to me it is positively humiliating and infuriating. We are not children or imbeciles, and are able to take care of ourselves... If, as seems imperative in England to-day, we have to be accompanied by "incidental music," then please remember that we have not asked for it.[22]

Yet these British women and children, whether they liked it or not, had entered an extraordinary social environment as representatives of a conquering army. As we have seen, the hierarchical power dynamics of military occupation were particularly acute in the British Zone. In fact, official messaging made no attempt to hide the divisions that would exist between these 'Married Families' and German society, even promoting their special role as British ambassadors. A specially prepared message from the prime minister, read out to the women as they disembarked, highlighted this diplomatic role:

> I know you will realize that each and every one of you has an important mission to perform on behalf of your country. The British soldier has been rightly called 'our best ambassador'. You can also do much to bring a wholesome influence on the German people by your example. You are going as representatives of the British people, and your behaviour and that of your children will demonstrate to the Germans the innate decency and honesty of the British and of their way of life. I know that you will show the virtues of good manners, of honest dealing and of tactful consideration... I hope that your stay in Germany will bring you happiness and that it will impress upon the minds of the Germans memories of a thoughtful, humane and generous people whose way of life is one to emulate.[23]

When the first groups arrived at Cuxhaven, commander-in-chief Sholto Douglas attended in person and conveyed a similar message: 'it is by your bearing and conduct that the Germans will form their opinion of the British way of life in which we all believe'.[24]

Nowhere is their newfound status clearer than in the remarkable *Pathé* newsreel *Where BAOR Wives Will Live*, released in August 1946.[25] The film, produced with the support of the British authorities, provided viewers with an idea of the types of communal flats that families inhabited in places such as Hamburg and Hanover. It advertised these 'comfortably-furnished and well-heated' abodes, alongside new NAAFI stores, a club in Brunswick that would provide 'recreational, social and helpful amenities', and the British-only writing and reading rooms of the Hotel Lorenz 'where Hitler used to stay'. The newsreel goes on to document a personal experience of 'Operation Union', interviewing Sergeant Major Putland, stationed in Germany, and his wife, still in Luton, who were soon to be reunited in Bad Oeynhausen. But it is the final segment of the film, devoted to the Control Commission's 'requisition quartering team', which stands out in dramatic style: a British officer is shown knocking on the door of a German woman, gesturing to explain that the flat will be 'taken over for a British wife', touring the flat, and pointing out the furniture that will also be requisitioned. The young mother, shocked and distraught, comforts her perplexed son as she confronts the reality of losing her house and most of her belongings. The narrator continues to explain the positive implications for British families in Germany.

*

As part of 'Operation Union', the British authorities hoped to shield the wives and children of Rhine Army personnel from the severe shortages that confronted their German neighbours. They also reckoned that a private's wife should have as good a quality of life as a colonel's, so they sought to provide all 'Married Families' with a newly furnished house or self-contained flat complete with kitchen and bathroom, food, fuel and laundry. Alongside generous Auxiliary Territorial Service food rations, families were given 100 cigarettes and 115 grams (4 oz) of sweets or chocolate per week; extra foodstuffs, wine, spirits and household goods were available from the NAAFI store (free from purchase tax[*]). These provisions would have left families more than comfortably supplied.

In the *Daily Mirror*, Marguerite Peacocke described the 'undreamed-of luxury' that would be found 'when the Joneses go to Germany'.[26] They would get 'twice as much as they do at home of most of the things which are rationed in Britain', including meat, sugar, preserves, fat, butter, tea, bread and cheese. There would also be clubs, cinemas and other entertainments on hand, while

---

[*] This had been introduced to Britain in 1940 and increased the cost of 'luxury goods' by a third.

the military would provide recreational transport, usually in the form of chauffeured cars. And the perks didn't end there: British families would be able to hire German domestic labour, which was affordable even to those who wouldn't normally have dreamt of such an extravagance. These families would live in much greater comfort, and at much less expense, than at home – although women were advised to bring their own sheets owing to a severe shortage in the British Zone.

For the children, schooling would be provided by the British Forces Education Service (BFES). The BFES offered nursery, primary and secondary education, and more than 200 teachers arrived from Britain in November 1946.[27] Most of the British schools were located in requisitioned houses and the conditions as winter approached were far from ideal: frozen water pipes, improvised equipment and unsuitable furnishings were just some of the many complaints found in school logbooks.[28] By August 1947 there were eighty-five schools in the Zone, 3,500 students and 220 teachers.[29] Among them was a secondary boarding school, the Prince Rupert School in the North Sea coastal town of Wilhelmshaven. The BFES was considered an educational experiment, not only because of the difficult conditions, but also the unique setting. Here was an opportunity to learn about 'the whole life and history of another nation with new things to see at every turn'. Optimistically, it would sow the seeds 'of a future relationship between these two nations which will contrast favourably with the relationship in the past thirty-five years'.[30] In the *Times Educational Supplement*, the chairman of the Teachers' Selection Board even wondered if the British children in Germany would become 'the light cavalry, not so much of an army of occupation, as of an army of mutual understanding'.[31]

With the prospect of families relocating to Germany, the British media displayed a heightened sense of interest in the day-to-day experiences of life there. In three articles published over the course of a week, the *Daily Mail* explained that British women would likely find furnishings in German private homes to be 'solid and Victorian, but clumsy' and the rooms 'probably dark and over-filled with furniture, pictures and dust-collecting objects'.[32] On the street, they would see 'more and better silk stockings', 'better complexions' and 'an almost complete avoidance of facial make-up', while their children 'will have to become accustomed to traffic on the right of the road and the fact that German drivers are usually ruthless regarding pedestrians'.

In July 1946, writing in the *Aberdeen Press and Journal*, John Flett reasoned that British women would be surprised at the good-quality housing they could come to expect in 'pleasant German holiday resorts... scarcely touched by the war' and that they would enjoy the mild spring weather.[33] On the other hand, they would also be faced with 'vast tracts of the most appalling devastation' that 'can scarcely be called pleasant' and would likely see hunger and near-starvation in the streets. Flett continued, rather unsympathetically, that while British food rations would be more than sufficient, these women would have limited opportunities for leisure: 'untidy, dirty, the rubble of shattered houses piled high on either side, these German streets offer no adventure for the shopper'. Amusements would consist mainly of theatres and cinemas 'far less attractive than our own' and cafés serving 'incredibly bad German beer'. It was inevitable that social life would 'have something of a colonial flavour', detached from the untrustworthy Germans:

> These people are still poles apart from ourselves. Their ideas are even to-day strongly coloured by the propaganda of Hitlerism. They feel no responsibility for the war, or for the crimes committed by their armies or their leaders.

*

It is perhaps no surprise that the stories of untold luxury provided to British families in Germany provoked opposition from unmarried members of the Control Commission and British Army of the Rhine. Many felt they were being handed a raw deal. The *Daily Mail* featured the complaints of a self-styled 'service bachelor' who had to live in army barracks: he accused the British wives of being 'spoiled darlings'.[34] But it was members of the Control Commission, most of whom lived in the requisitioned accommodation that was now being reassigned to wives and families, who felt most aggrieved. Mary Bouman wrote home to her parents to express her outrage at the excessive comforts afforded to the British wives and families:

> If they move in anywhere the house is always redecorated and put into full repair... I suppose it is one result of the acute housing shortage in England. What could be better than to come out here, have a house and all found for you and ready to move into. No wonder families are coming out at an increasing rate.[35]

Bouman felt it was hardly fair that the authorities were pandering to these women, while 'those who do the work here' were merely an afterthought: 'in almost everything they come first and we come second'.[36] This frustration at the elevated status of 'Married Families' even inspired a group of Control Commission staff to voice their protests publicly in the *Daily Mirror* and the *Manchester Guardian*. They complained that they were losing their requisitioned furniture and lodgings to the British families who were being 'pampered and petted all the way'.[37]

While British officials had hoped that allowing the wives and children of serving soldiers to relocate to Germany would transform the battered public image of their occupation, things did not quite go according to plan. The press portrayal of 'Married Families' as overindulged became firmly entrenched back home and played upon the everyday concerns of families in post-war Britain. A number of the bestselling newspapers concluded that all this luxury was an insult to their hard-pressed readers. The *Daily Mirror* poured scorn on the 'biggest BAOR family' who had left their 'little house' in Reading for a fourteen-room mansion in Detmold 'complete with servant, cook and governess for the children'.[38] The paper also published a letter from an anonymous British army captain, now serving in India after a period in occupied Germany, informing readers about the 'appalling' situation he had left behind: 'Men, women and children are dying in the streets while fat, bloated, snobbish wives of Control Commission officers sit back in the house of some evicted family whose underfed daughter is a slave for a meagre wage... Never in all my life have I been so ashamed of being English'.[39]

Likewise, the *Daily Mail* expressed outrage at the fact that German women who had married British servicemen were also provided with 'a higher standard of living than the British housewife at home'.[40] The NAAFI stores were said to be piled high with unrationed goods 'which have long been unobtainable in Britain' including 'face powders of the quality not seen in Britain for years'. A few weeks later, one *Daily Mail* reader wrote a letter to the editor suggesting that the provision of that calibre of food, 'which even in ordinary times would rank as luxury fare', and such clearly 'preferential treatment' were 'calculated to fan the growing flame of discontent among all the harassed and unfairly treated housewives of Britain'.[41]

These reports had an obvious impact on their readers and soon the prime minister was receiving scores of letters complaining about the iniquities of 'Operation Union'. One British housewife, J. N. Walton, wrote to Attlee warning that the requisitioning of German houses to accommodate British families was a 'crime against humanity' and not befitting a Labour administration.[42] She quoted extensively from a letter which had appeared in the *Manchester Guardian*, suggesting the British in Germany were living surrounded by a 'wall of quite unnecessary luxury'.[43] Their conduct, Mrs Walton concluded, contravened the prime minister's own exhortation to demonstrate the 'innate decency' of the 'British way of life' and would 'leave a bitter legacy in the minds of the German people'. In another private correspondence to the prime minister, concerned citizen Ernest E. Laws warned that the disdainful attitude of British families in Germany would preclude any chance of Britain ever 'winning the peace':

I write to you as principal director of policy and co-ordinator of Foreign Office, War Office and other interested departments to beg you to withdraw forces families from these Zones and repatriate them… Nazism is not dead: every act of arrogance and exploitation revives it; and the war is lost.[44]

In October 1946 *The Times* published a letter from a group of influential women, including philanthropist Dame Elizabeth Cadbury, social reformer Margery Fry and women's rights activist Baroness Pethick-Lawrence.[45] These women recorded their 'surprise and anxiety at the ideas and methods displayed in the arrangements for the British wives'. They condemned the endeavour to supply British families in Germany with comforts such as extra rations, special shops and 'special transport facilities to save the British wife from sitting near a German'. These luxuries came, they insisted, at great cost to the local populace. They argued that requisitioning German property in a context of high infant mortality, hunger oedema, outbreaks of tuberculosis and general human suffering was exacerbating a growing humanitarian tragedy that could only further damage 'British popularity and prestige'. The following day, a supportive letter from Clementine Churchill, wife of the former prime minister, appeared in the same newspaper. She suggested that great numbers of 'thoughtful people' would surely agree.[46]

This moralistic appeal from privileged circles ruffled some feathers. Quite understandably, the wives of British personnel were none too pleased at such a derogatory portrayal of their supposed moral failings. It even inspired some to defend themselves. An anonymous 'BAOR Wife' wrote a response in *The Times* addressed to these 'distinguished women': she asked flippantly whether any of them had husbands in the British Army of the Rhine and defended the right of women such as herself to have a happy family life.[47] The tales of luxury, she added, had been overstated: while there might be cheap champagne at the NAAFI, this was merely 'one of the few fruits of victory' for women who were 'examples of all that an ambassador should be'. Ruth Elford, who was intending to join her husband in Germany in the near future, also wrote a stern letter to *The Times* in defence of the British women in the Zone.[48] It was, she thought, hypocritical to lambast fraternization with the Germans and then also attack the scheme to bring out their families simply 'because it means requisitioning a few houses from the German people'.

In late August, *Yorkshire Post* reporter Joe Illingworth also leapt to the defence of the British families in Germany and rejected the 'spoiled darlings' tag that had now become commonplace.[49] He suggested there was a 'tacit unformulated assumption at the back of some people's minds' that wives were 'coming out to have a good time and form a decorative social background to life in Germany'. Rather, he argued, these women were accomplishing important work. For example, York resident Mrs Hartley, a graduate of Leeds University, was organizing the educational syllabus for British children in the Zone. The *Yorkshire Post* remained a staunch defender of 'Operation Union', in part due to the large numbers of local women and children who went to Germany to join their husbands and fathers. In another article the paper insisted that the 'Married Families' were fine ambassadors for Britain, even as they faced the unimaginable difficulties of life in a war-torn enemy country. Cyril Dunn's report included a story about the steely determination of British women to get on with their lives in the midst of adversity:

> A kind of passive war, confined to the minor skirmish, is going on for possession of the pavements in Celle. German mothers with prams obstruct the way, trying to make British mothers with prams detour into the road. 'I got fed up with this,' a young Scotswoman said to me, 'and one day I just pushed straight on, until our prams touched. We stood there, glowering at each other over our prams, until the German woman gave way. She yelled something at me. I supposed it was horrid.'[50]

Dunn's story also assured readers that 'life for British wives in the British Zone is much more real and earnest than is generally supposed', emphasizing that shortages and everyday hardships were commonplace. He reported how one exasperated British army wife had exclaimed 'all this stuff about Pampered Darlings makes us *boil!*'

It was certainly true that things were not quite as comfortable for British families in the Zone as many of the papers had made out.

In the early weeks of 'Operation Union' the authorities struggled to provide both the accommodation that was required and furniture to go with it. Even the *Daily Mail* acknowledged that 'all is not easy for the BAOR wife': while the early arrivals had been 'impressed by their pampered, much publicized and generally efficiently organized journey from England to Germany', they were now finding that the administration was 'beginning to creak'.[51] 'BAOR wives in tears', exclaimed the *Nottingham Evening Post*, explaining that some women had been 'ordered into "piggeries"' without tables, carpets or mattresses.[52]

All things considered, 'Operation Union' was not going to plan. The hope had been that the arrival of British women and children would apply a salve to the administration's many trials and tribulations, but it seemed to be achieving little beyond the (sometimes limited) personal contentment of those involved. Meanwhile, the feeling grew among the British public that these civilians had been handed a share of the excessive luxury now associated with the Zone, further exacerbating discontent back home. For some it was further proof of the paternalistic, divisive mode of British rule in Germany; for others, it was just an infuriating spectacle.

As it happens, 'Operation Union' soon ran aground. In December 1946 the first cold snap of winter struck and the British Zone's ramshackle transport network quickly and literally came to a halt. In the coming months coal supplies and food stocks were expected to run perilously low, and British army commanders were concerned that major cities like Hamburg would face starvation and complete societal collapse. The British authorities had little choice but to rapidly reduce the number of wives and children permitted to relocate to Germany.[53] As conditions in the Zone rapidly deteriorated, 'Operation Union' was brought to an end – for the time being.*

---

* In the early summer of 1947, as conditions in the Zone began to improve for Germans and Britons alike, the passage of British families became significantly easier – and, in time, decidedly less controversial. By June 1950 there would be more than 30,000 British family members in Germany, complete with access to a network of schools and other amenities that would remain in service for decades to come.

Part Four

GET OUT NOW!

19

A Looming Shadow of Catastrophe

In March 1947 a group of men could be seen valiantly attempting to clear a snow-covered road near the quaint Cotswold hilltop town of Stow-on-the-Wold. They were wrapped up in layers of heavy clothing, most of them in long military coats and peaked caps. This group consisted of some of the many thousands of German prisoners of war who were still held captive in Britain and used as labourers as part of the reparations settlement. Among them was Klaus Behr, who had been detained at Springhill Camp, near Chipping Campden, since his capture in September 1944.[1] 'The Englishmen think that there hasn't been such a hard winter in fifty years,' he wrote in his diary, 'at the moment one feels like a personified icicle'.

The winter of 1946–7 was indeed one of the coldest on record. But freezing weather wasn't Britain's only concern. Clement Attlee's Labour government was facing a series of crises that threatened to undermine the country's economic solvency and international standing.[2] From Germany to India, Britain's foreign policy woes and economic vulnerabilities came suddenly and chaotically to a head. In February, Chancellor of the Exchequer Hugh Dalton remarked in his diary that there was 'a looming shadow of catastrophe' stalking the country. 'The frosts, snows and fogs… continue unabated, and whoever is trying to be funny in arranging all this is rather overdoing the joke', he continued. 'The most satisfactory place, these days, is in bed!'[3]

*

In September 1945 the US terminated the Lend–Lease Act that had funded Britain's war effort, instigating tense negotiations over a new American loan. Then, in December, the two governments reached a hard-pressed deal that would write off British debts and provide a loan of 4.4 billion US dollars. In return, the British agreed to ratify the Bretton Woods Agreement,* which defined the value of all currencies, including sterling, in relation to the dollar. Bretton Woods confirmed America's position as the world's economic powerhouse and opened up the world's markets to American capital. Signing up to the agreement was the price of Britain remaining solvent: the escalating costs of the country's overseas commitments and the crippling budgetary constraints at home combined to force the government's hand. Yet the new loan did not spell an end to the country's financial woes. Attlee's government was still forced to reassess the nation's foreign policy obligations, not least across its sprawling and increasingly costly empire.[4] The war had invigorated anti-colonial movements across the world and the costs associated with maintaining British rule soon spiralled out of control.[5]

In India, Britain lost control over the devolution of power, and the push towards independence was growing stronger by the day. As the prospect of retaining the British Raj ebbed away, military and economic advisors remained adamant that Britain retain its access to Indian resources of manpower and air bases.[6]

In the Middle East, there was also significant resistance to British power and authority: since the 1930s large numbers of Jewish migrants, many of them escaping Nazi terror, had arrived in Palestine, a British mandate[†] after July 1920.[7] This prompted resentment from the local Arab population and led to a period

---

* The Bretton Woods Conference was held in New Hampshire in July 1944 to regulate the post-war financial and monetary order. It established the World Bank and the International Monetary Fund.

† In 1920 Britain was assigned the Mandate for Palestine by the League of Nations. It required Britain establish a 'national home for the Jewish people' alongside the Palestinian Arabs, as per the Balfour Declaration of 1918.

of instability and violence in the Arab Revolt of 1936–9 – and ultimately stricter British controls on Jewish settlement. Now, in the aftermath of the Holocaust, international pressure on Britain to allow more Jewish migration to Palestine intensified. It created tension between the British military government in Germany and the relatively small but significant number of German Jewish Holocaust survivors in the Zone. Official policy recognized this group as nationals of Germany rather than a separate Jewish nation. In April 1946 Norbert Wollheim, secretary of the Central Committee of Jewish Survivors, attending the unveiling of a memorial at Bergen-Belsen one year after the camp's liberation, denounced the British for their inaction during the war and poor treatment of Holocaust survivors in its aftermath.[8]

As the British unsuccessfully tried to control a combustible situation in Palestine, Harry S. Truman's White House publicly supported the Zionists without offering any material help to maintain order. Clement Attlee lamented that the Americans 'forever lay heavy burdens on us without lifting a little finger to help'.[9] Zionist groups took up arms against the local Arab population as well as the British, which created a major security concern and another burden on Britain's limited resources. All British personnel in Palestine were provided with armed guards, while officials were sequestered in protected security zones, called 'Bevingrads' after the foreign secretary. Zionist insurgents carried out a campaign of sabotage that included the bombing of the King David Hotel (where the British had their headquarters) in Jerusalem in July 1946, killing ninety-one people. At the peak of the violence in 1946–7, 100,000 men – around 10 per cent of the entire British armed forces – were occupying a territory the size of Wales at an annual cost of around £40 million.[10]

Meanwhile, Britain's relations with the Soviet Union had soured considerably. Stalin had established a firm grip over Eastern Europe and was now making claims on the former Italian colonies in North Africa. He demanded a new agreement over access to the strategically important Turkish Straits and, in early 1946, failed to withdraw troops from Iran as previously agreed.[11]

To many British observers, it seemed that Moscow was moving away from the wartime alliance and towards outright antagonism.* Britain's limited supplies of money and manpower were thus further stretched. In Greece, the British were spending millions on financial aid as well as shipments of troops and equipment in order to prop up a royalist government entangled in a fight against communist insurgency. As a matter of military strategy, the British would not countenance the prospect of communist victory in the Greek Civil War, an outcome which threatened to extend Stalin's influence into the Mediterranean. But this military and financial support to Greece represented yet another financial drain.

And then, of course, there was Germany. In the eighteen months since the end of the war, the British had been pilloried in the press over their conduct as occupiers and the spiralling financial costs of the occupation. The price of importing food to stave off famine, combined with the innumerable challenges of maintaining a semblance of order amid the still-ongoing refugee crisis, created a growing sense of despair.

Overall, the British were in a tricky position. They were anxious to maintain their position as a major world power and committed to working with the Americans to limit the spread of Soviet communism, yet they found themselves without the requisite financial or manpower resources to do so.† And then came the winter.

*

In the early months of 1947, a series of Atlantic depressions brought snow and blizzards to the British Isles and much of Europe. A perilous situation had somehow got worse. 'Christ, it's bleeding

---

* There were also more positive signs, at least for those who wanted to look: the Soviets had, after all, calmed revolutionary left-wing groups in France and Italy, while also keeping out of the conflict between royalists and communists in Greece.

† It led some from within the Labour Party to advocate a 'Third Way' on international affairs, rejecting Soviet or American hegemony in favour of some sort of European bloc.

cold,' wrote the Oxford undergraduate Kingsley Amis to his friend Philip Larkin.[12] Not elegant, perhaps, but pretty well on the nose. During the first few months of 1947, Britain froze.

On 29 January, Elmstone in East Kent recorded a temperature of -21.3 degrees Celsius. In February the observatory at Kew recorded a twenty-one-day stretch without sunshine, while the mean maximum temperature recorded at the Greenwich Observatory was the lowest for over a century.[13] From Durham to Derbyshire sporadic heavy snowfalls created snowdrifts of up to ten or twelve feet.[14] Roads were blocked, not just with ice and snow but also abandoned vehicles, further hampering road clearances.[15] The railways fared slightly better, although disruptions and accidents were commonplace: on 29 January, a fireman working on the 6:23 a.m. Huddersfield to Bradford service leant out of his cab window and was knocked out cold by an enormous icicle hanging from a bridge. Over the course of several weeks fuel supplies dwindled, causing domestic shortages and power cuts which brought British manufacturing to its knees. In less than a month, more than a million people lost their jobs. It was truly a bleak midwinter.

In Germany the cold weather was felt all the more keenly. Nora Heather, stationed in the Rahlstedt area of Hamburg, took daily temperature readings and on only a single day between 1 December 1946 and 15 March 1947 did the mercury rise above zero – on occasion dropping as low as -22 degrees Celsius.[16] In January her accommodation block was left without power or heat for two days a week because of shortages. She had only the provision of an extra British army blanket and a rabbit skin jacket to compensate. Inevitably the water pipes froze and 'each day a fresh ring of ice formed around the bath', so Heather's housemaid Hertha was sent off to bring buckets of water from a nearby mess.

In Hamburg the Elbe froze over, providing some with the opportunity to ice-skate and others with a more direct route to the warmth of the Atlantic Club. But it certainly wasn't all fun and games. Katharine Morris remembers walking up to her ninth-floor apartment in the midst of another power cut and passing an exhausted porter, only to find her roommate wrapped in a fur coat, valiantly attempting to fix the ladders in her nylons by candlelight.[17] Soon, Morris was herself routinely wearing jumpers, cardigans, long bed socks and scarves over the top of her pyjamas. One morning, after waking up without heat, water or electricity, she rushed to the canteen in the same manner 'as people escape from a burning building'. 'Cradling a cup of tea in my hands to warm them,' she wrote, 'I foresaw a day of complaints and contrivances, of mounting hardship for everyone'. In the end, Katharine Morris was rather lucky: she was temporarily relocated, alongside another woman, to a small single room in the Reichshof Hotel. They took it in turns to sleep on the sofa in front of a small window habitually obscured by a sheet of ice.

In the small town of Büren, near Paderborn, Edward Rich began his service with the Control Commission that January. As a veteran of the British military mission to Iraq, he found the wintry weather to be an almighty shock:

I have no idea of the number of degrees of frost that we endured that winter but it was cold enough for the snow to freeze as it fell and remain frozen for days on the trees and bushes and even on the telegraph lines, which were often an inch thick in congealed snow and which took on an unusual beauty for such an unsightly object of modern utility.[18]

He was thrown firmly into the deep end of administrative duties. The weather cut him off from mail, rations and officialdom for weeks at a time while he faced all manner of tasks: supervising the allocation and price of food, arranging coke for heating the hospital, housing refugees despite the protestations of local householders, helping a group of Jehovah's Witnesses who had survived the Holocaust, advising timber-felling for reparations and reforestation programmes, controlling poachers among the local British army detachments who were killing deer in nearby forests, overseeing religious processions, and curtailing attempts of German bureaucrats to 'feather their own nests'. To cap it all off, Rich was now the local magistrate with sentencing powers of up to three months' imprisonment. 'I had been just a month in Germany, a cold unhappy month and with a sense of frustration and the incompatibility of my surroundings', he wrote in his memoir. 'I was more than once on the point of throwing in my hand and scuttling home for England'.

For all the hardships and deprivations forced upon the British occupiers, the impact of the winter on the German residents of the British Zone was much worse. This was a population that had been without adequate food supplies for the best part of two years and many of them still lacked proper housing or clothing fit for winter. In the early months of 1947, available rations dropped as low as 700 calories per person per day in parts of the Ruhr, approximate to that given out in the concentration camps by the Nazis.[19] Coal shortages made it harder to heat homes and further exposed the local population to the mercies of the cold. The 'Hungerwinter' of 1947 claimed the lives of thousands of Germans. Many froze to death in their own beds, weakened after months of deprivation and exposure.[20]

*

In the face of these overlapping crises, the need for a change in Britain's foreign policy was all too clear. The Attlee administration set about reducing expenditure, including drastic cuts to military spending and overseas deployments.[21] In Germany, change was already on the agenda. During the summer of 1946, Bevin had pushed the Americans towards the 'Western option': reconstruction in the Western zones of Germany that would allow for economic recovery and lessen the burden on the British taxpayer. That September, US Secretary of State James F. Byrnes finally acquiesced, and, in his famous 'Stuttgart Speech', he outlined America's intention to remain in Europe for the foreseeable future.[22] The British willingly accepted Byrnes's proposal for an economic fusion of the British and American zones into what became known as the Bizone. This was a clear and unmistakeable break with the Potsdam Agreement. It signalled that the Western powers were willing to go it alone in post-war Germany – even if they still outwardly declared their ongoing commitment to the 1945 settlement in principle.

This development instigated a sharp shift in British policy that allowed power to be gradually given back to the Germans. An important first step was the establishment of the Zonal Advisory Council in 1946, a German-run body consisting of administrative heads of the various *Länder*, political parties and trade unions. While the body was supervised by British administrators and lacked an executive function, it offered the German people the means to influence the political decisions of the occupiers.[23] Likewise, the creation of an Economic Advisory Board also showed that Britain was willing to move from close and intensive control towards a more supervisory form of occupation. Now, in January 1947, there was a further handover of power back into German hands as the Anglo-American Bizone – or 'Bizonia' as some called it – came into existence. In line with the new Ordinance 57, the British authorities handed executive power back to the Germans in their Zone at the *Länder* level and below. This included responsibility for law and order, local government, education policy, elections and public health, following on from German-run denazification panels that had been in action since the previous year.[24] There were also significant changes in the economic management of the Zone. A case in point is North German Coal Control, which would be dissolved in November 1947 and its authority over this all-important area of the German economy handed to the German-run Deutsche Kohlenbergbau-Leitung ('German Coal Mining Administration').[*] As Kreis Resident Officer Edward Rich remarked, 'to the ordinary official of the CCG, the effect of the Ordinance was that, where previously we have ordered the Germans to do this or not do that, we now had to advise them what to do'.[25]

As a symbol of this radical shift in relations between occupiers

---

[*] This German-run body still received policy guidance from a UK–US Coal Control Group and remained answerable to the British and American military governors.

and occupied, in January 1947 commander-in-chief Sholto Douglas wrote in the *British Zone Review* that 'through personal contact and free discussion, the Germans will gain a fuller appreciation of the British way of thought, and conversely the British will reach a better understanding of the German mental outlook'.[26] Anglo-German discussion groups soon sprang up across the Zone, at first limited to thirty participants with the most controversial topics studiously avoided – although current events such as housing issues, food supplies, education reform, or recent musical releases were fair game. By 1948 there were several thousand such groups, including twenty-five in Hamburg alone. Two of the most notable were the Hamburg International Club, which catered for eighteen- to thirty-year-olds, and the elite Hamburg Anglo-German Club, modelled on the classic English gentleman's club and at which the city's regional commissioner Henry Vaughan Berry was a regular attendee.

The introduction of Ordinance 57 also cut short some of the Control Commission's most ambitious plans. For one, attempts to democratize and decentralize the German civil service were permanently shelved.[27] German political elites had resisted removing the party alignment of civil servants: for many, this proposal seemed an open invitation for former Nazis to work under a cloak of secrecy. British efforts to dissolve the traditional distinction between *Beamte* (a more privileged civil servant, with special legal status) and *Angestellte* (a contracted employee of the state without the same rights) also did not advance.

In addition, plans to radically reform the structure of the German police force were ended. While the Control Commission had retrained some German police officers, attempts to democratize the forces under their direction conclusively failed. The British were uneasy with the German convention of political intervention, whether it came from *Länder* officials or elected police chiefs. Yet to the German authorities, Britain's model of an unelected chief constable without an executive superior seemed authoritarian. In 1947, when powers over policing returned to German hands, little had changed.

Lance Corporal Richardson of the Corps of Military Police (right)
seeks directions from three Berlin policemen.

Likewise, the amorphous concept of 're-education', so
prominent in the minds of many British planners at the beginning
of the occupation, now faded into relative obscurity. In German
schools the conservative character of the teaching profession had
impeded British attempts at reform: without German cooperation,
few of the ambitious plans for restructuring the school system were
ever realized.[28] While Nazi-era curricula and, to a limited extent,
teachers had been removed, the British plans for wholesale changes
were abandoned.[29] In the end, the most quantifiable results were
efforts to improve the status of teacher training instruction and a
campaign to ensure the survival of private schools. In the Zone's
universities progress was even harder to achieve: while the range of
subjects on offer was slightly expanded, the Control Commission
failed to do away with the status of professors as civil servants and
was similarly unable to disband the student organizations that it
had identified as hotbeds of German nationalism.[30]

There were more obvious successes when it came to managing
the German media. In September 1945 the British authorities in

Hamburg – with the assistance of BBC radio engineers – set up Nordwestdeutscher Rundfunk (NWDR, 'North-west German Broadcasting').[31] This radio station was modelled on the BBC, complete with a charter, and, from October 1946, had a former head of the BBC German Service, Hugh Carleton Greene, as its first director-general. The station had a more relaxed tone than earlier German radio and eventually even allowed some criticism of the occupation authorities to be aired. It also became widely admired for its music broadcasting. In 1955 NWDR was split into Norddeutscher Rundfunk, responsible for Lower Saxony, Schleswig-Holstein and Hamburg, and Westdeutscher Rundfunk, covering North Rhine-Westphalia.

The Control Commission's post-war licensing system also gave rise to a number of hugely important periodicals and newspapers. This includes the now world-famous *Die Welt*, which began life in Hamburg as the official newspaper of the British military government and was modelled on *The Times*.[32] There is also the remarkable story of twenty-one-year-old John Chaloner, an information officer based in Hanover who cut a rather swashbuckling figure. Chaloner toured the British Zone in a roadster requisitioned from the former Nazi Foreign Minister Joachim von Ribbentrop – and laid the foundations for one of the world's most respected news publications.[33]

In 1945 Chaloner began the complex work of restarting newspaper production in the area around Hanover and, in March 1946, decided to create a new magazine.[34] Five issues of *Diese Woche* appeared later that year, filled with a mix of original journalism and translated articles from popular British and American weeklies. This was no easy task: producing a magazine required everything from ink and paper to printing machines, and from string for tying bundles, to German staff and a delivery network. Through a combination of determination and unbridled resourcefulness, whether they were sourcing newsprint from the UK or acquiring a fleet of bicycles, Chaloner and his team made it work. *Diese Woche* immediately found an audience – the first edition ran to 15,000 copies.

The popularity of *Diese Woche*, and other British-led publications, stemmed in part from a surplus of cash in circulation, since so many goods were acquired through the black market barter economy. Because of a relative lack of alternative reading material available, newspapers filled a gap in the market.* Yet the Public Relations/Information Services Control Group was less than impressed and reprimanded the young entrepreneur for exceeding his authority. Senior officers were said to be incensed at his publishing articles critical of the occupation authorities, something that Chaloner felt was 'the natural role of the so-called free press'.[35]

Chaloner was barred from further involvement with the magazine, but it was not closed down. Instead, the licence simply passed to *Diese Woche*'s German editor, Rudolf Augstein, himself only twenty-two years old. In January 1947 Augstein renamed the magazine *Der Spiegel* and it soon had a print run of more than 50,000. Each edition featured incisive, thought-provoking journalism. Heinz Norden, editor-in-chief of *Heute*,† remarked that the publication '*bläst wie ein frischer Wind durch das deutsche Zeitungswesen*' ('blows like a fresh wind through the German press').[36] And so began a news magazine that is still internationally admired for its probing investigative reporting – something that, in the words of one historian, would prove as influential in securing a free and independent press in the Federal Republic as any other action taken during the occupation.[37]

*

In a practical sense, the Bizone didn't radically alter the structure of the occupation: the British and American zones were still distinct entities, even if their economic administration was now a common endeavour. There was a limited transfer of staffing responsibilities, including a number of hand-picked British recruits who were sent to work in the American Zone. They included Edna Wearmouth,

---

* In the years 1944–7, very few German books were published, owing to paper shortages and licence requirements; see Bark, Dennis L. and Gress, David R., *A History of West Germany*, pp. 155, 160.
† An illustrated magazine set up in the American Zone, which ceased production in 1951.

who moved to Frankfurt in June 1947 and was eager to tell her father all about the oddities of the Americans she had met:

> They have funny customs. Everything is eaten with only a fork and they mix sweet and savoury. For instance, for breakfast we had bacon with fried sort of cakie stuff and maple syrup poured over with prunes and raisins!!... There's every kind of fresh fruit drinks and the famous Coca-Cola! You will have heard of this typical American drink which they sell as we sell ices – from shops, streets etc. It's ice-cold lemonade with a faint ginger flavour and very refreshing.[38]

A few weeks later, she was less convinced: 'The Americans are very queer and I'm only now forming an opinion of them. I should say that they are definitely anti-British and resent our moving into their Zone. They are all for show and rather boastful.'[39]

In the short term, the establishment of the Bizone also did little to reduce British expenditure in Germany, while simultaneously drastically exacerbating tensions with the Soviets. In part as a response to this policy, the Soviet Zone would undergo a more overt 'Sovietization' from 1947 onwards. This followed on from the forcible merger of the Social Democratic Party of Germany and the Communist Party of Germany to form the German Socialist Unity Party (Sozialistische Einheitspartei Deutschlands, or SED)* in April 1946.

The Bizone was, nevertheless, a momentous step in reinstituting German executive power and an important precondition for kick-starting the Zone's flailing economy. Above all, the British had secured American participation in the rehabilitation of Germany in international affairs, which Ernest Bevin felt was a 'juncture of great political importance'.[40] Ultimately, it was the beginning of a strategy of containment that would eventually result in Germany being divided between East and West.[41]

---

* In October 1949, the Marxist–Leninist SED would become the ruling party of the German Democratic Republic.

In April 1947 John Hynd was replaced as chancellor of the Duchy of Lancaster by Lord Frank Pakenham, granting him overall responsibility for the British Zone. Pakenham was a more senior political figure and his overriding priority was the reduction of costs in Germany, starting with the integration of the Control Office for Germany and Austria into the Foreign Office*.[42] There was little obscuring the uphill task that faced Pakenham in the British Zone: upon taking ministerial office, he was sent a letter from a concerned member of the public, E. S. Biddough, who sought to draw Pakenham's attention 'to a few of the many things that is making the CCG a by-word, a matter of scorn to the German population'.[43] The Control Commission was, she insisted, full of 'loafers' who were the 'worst possible type to represent England'; 'only the people capable of upholding the prestige of the British empire' should be allowed to remain.

Lord Pakenham, who in April 1947 was made chancellor of the Duchy of Lancaster, surveys a map of the British Zone of Germany.

---

* COGA was henceforth Foreign Office (German Section).

*

In January 1947, just as the Bizone came into being, Britain's political and military chiefs made another historic decision: the final go-ahead was given for the development of a British atomic bomb. In August 1946 the Americans had unilaterally terminated an agreement on atomic research with the UK and Canada – a potential breakdown in defence cooperation. In many ways, an iron law of diplomacy since the Second World War has been that the possession of nuclear weapons affords some degree of independence when it comes to foreign policy. Ernest Bevin implicitly understood this, and he had personally turned the tide of British discussions on the development of the bomb. In October 1946 the foreign secretary arrived at a crucial meeting on the matter after a summer of tiresome negotiations with the Americans remained fresh in his mind. As he explained to his colleagues:

> I don't want any other foreign secretary of this country to be talked at by a secretary of state in the United States as I have just had in my discussions with Mr Byrnes. We have got to have this thing over here whatever the costs... We've got to have the bloody Union Jack flying on top of it.[44]

Then, over the course of a single week, between 14 and 20 February, the Attlee administration made several more momentous foreign policy calls. First of all, the cabinet finally decided to refer the crisis in Palestine back to the United Nations. It was a gamble based on the idea that the pro-Palestinian majority at the UN might give Britain a favourable settlement.[45] But more than that it was an admission of impotency: the British could not handle the chaos that had been unleashed in the Middle East and they lacked the capacity to regain control. This dynamic played out very publicly between July and September 1947, when 4,500 Jewish refugees onboard a converted US packet steamer, the *Exodus 1947*, were prevented from landing in Palestine by the Royal Navy.[46] What followed was a protracted and highly publicized spectacle, as the British sought to return these migrants, most of whom were Holocaust survivors, to Europe. While the *Exodus 1947* had set off from France, all its passengers were forcibly redirected to Hamburg, where they were resettled in displaced persons camps in Lower Saxony – much to the outrage of Zionist sympathizers around the world.* In September 1947 the UN Special Committee on Palestine reported in favour of partition and the plan was adopted by a UN resolution in November. The British did not feel able to support the UN partition plan because it did not have the support of both Jews and Arabs (who had rejected it). The British decided unilaterally that their mandate would end in May 1948 and that they would withdraw all British personnel. In their wake, they left a war between Arabs and Jews and, ultimately, the new state of Israel.

Also in February 1947, Attlee announced that the British were to leave India. Lord Mountbatten was appointed as viceroy and pushed through a rapid and violent partition which brought the two self-governing nations of India and Pakistan into existence that August. Partition was the start of a process of decolonization that, over the next decade and a half, would result in the dismantling of most of Britain's global empire.

Finally, the cabinet confirmed their decision to end aid to Greece and Turkey by 31 March, radically reducing Britain's foreign obligations. This was a significant test of the American commitment to Europe and it heralded a major strategic realignment. Crucially, the US domestic political scene had changed, as mid-term elections brought an anti-Soviet Republican majority to Congress.[47] This shift combined with the power vacuum left in Greece and Turkey and prompted President Truman to step in: his speech on 12 March laid out the foundations of what would become known as the Truman Doctrine – a policy of containment aimed towards the Soviet Union.[48] Not only would the US hold the line against the spread of communism in Greece and Turkey, but across the entire world.

---

* Within two years, almost all of these 4,500 refugees had emigrated to the new state of Israel.

The Truman Doctrine was a precursor to the ambitious European Recovery Program, better known as the Marshall Plan. In early June 1947 US Secretary of State George C. Marshall announced that billions of dollars of US aid would soon be available to countries across Europe. This significant influx of capital was designed to spark a post-war recovery and open up trade barriers. These measures were also aimed at securing America's hegemonic position in the world's economy while helping to stop the spread of Soviet communism. Britain, France and the Western zones of Germany would be the three biggest recipients of American aid. Taken together, the Truman Doctrine and the Marshall Plan firmly cemented America's commitment to Europe, eased British financial anxieties and marked a major escalation of the Cold War. This new strategy had profound implications for the occupation of Germany: it would boost the restoration of the Western zones, establishing them as a bulwark in the fight against communism and spearheading a division of the country between East and West.[49]

Over the course of just a few days, Attlee and Bevin set in motion a realignment of Britain's strategic priorities across the world. The 'special relationship' with America now became the focus of Britain's diplomatic efforts, all in the context of straitened finances and a crusade against the Soviet Union. Through it, the British were to maintain their position in Germany. It was hoped that, in time, the Western zones could be turned from an economic burden into a strategic outpost of the new Cold War.

20

Complete Chaos, Germany

From 1945–7, influential journalist Frank Owen regularly used his column in the *Daily Mail* to pour scorn on the British occupiers. Owen, who had co-authored the famous anti-appeasement pamphlet *Guilty Men*, described the British Zone as 'one large malodorous rubbish heap' situated outside one's house upon which a family of beggars were living at the homeowner's expense.[1] That expense was an eye-watering £80 million a year, a figure that was soon to rise even higher. The CCG, known colloquially as 'Complete Chaos, Germany', was an 'unwieldy, over-staffed and file-bound' bureaucracy that could only be negotiated efficiently through bribery. In Owen's view, this fastidious pencil-pushing staff of incompetents, unable to find employment back home, were 'discrediting the good name of Britain'.

In the summer of 1947, Owen took up the reins as editor of the *Mail* and soon used his influence to publish even more commentary that was critical of the British occupation. There was, as we've already seen, plenty of fuel to keep this particular fire burning. In early August the paper published a scathing cartoon showing Clement Attlee as a mother bird feeding dollars to the already vastly overfed 'British Zone in Germany' cuckoo in the 'British Economy' nest.[2] This invasive bird was sapping the nation's resources and starving the fledgling chicks, each labelled 'import-export gap', 'food shortage' and the nearly lifeless 'consumer'. It was a blunt attack on the Labour government and marked the beginning of a determined campaign against the continuation of Britain's presence in Germany.

A week later Douglas Jay, the Labour MP for Battersea North, publicly touted the idea of abandoning the military occupation, commenting at a public meeting that the expenditure in Germany was too high for Britain to bear.[3] Jay warned that if the Americans weren't prepared to cover more of the costs, Britain should notify them of the intention to evacuate by the end of the year. At the time this idea garnered little in the way of a response, but within just a few weeks the notion that Britain should get out of Germany took the British press by storm.

*

While the series of historic foreign policy decisions of 1946–7 more or less ensured Britain's determination to stay the course in Germany, this was not entirely obvious to most observers. It was only in January 1948 that the British government made their diplomatic priorities clear, when Ernest Bevin launched an anti-Soviet crusade in the House of Commons and, subsequently, on the BBC.[4] The delay was born of pragmatism and ongoing Cold War diplomacy over the question of who would take the blame for the failure of the Potsdam Agreement, as well as how the British public would respond to such a radical foreign policy change.[5]

This lag in the broadcast of Britain's new Cold War orientation helped perpetuate an ever more pronounced gulf between publicly espoused policy towards Germany and the actual outlook of leading British politicians.[6] There was, in other words, little assurance in the summer of 1947 that Britain's troubling financial predicament and international overstretch were entirely resolved. Then, in August, the temporary convertibility of sterling to the dollar brought about Britain's second balance of payments crisis since the end of the war.[*]

---

[*] The terms of the American loan of July 1946 had allowed for the convertibility of sterling to dollars, beginning in July 1947. In practice, countries that had sterling balances from buying British exports were now able to exchange them for dollars. After six weeks of Britain's limited dollar reserves dwindling yet further, the government was forced to suspend convertibility. For more on the crisis, see Cairncross, Alec, *Years of Recovery: British Economic Policy 1945–51* (London; New York: 1985), pp. 121–64.

That month, the British press began to call for radical action, with much of their attention focused on Germany: if the British occupiers were only making things worse, then why keep them there? If there were any arena from which Britain should withdraw, they reasoned, then surely this was it.

At the end of July the *Daily Telegraph* featured an article documenting the high-ranking CCG officials who had given up their positions in frustration at the organization's incompetence.[7] The Control Commission, they lamented, had no clear policy except thwarting all 'initiative and personal zeal'. In the first week of August, the paper's editorial highlighted Deputy Military Governor Brian Robertson's recent admission that his staff had encountered complications in their task 'to extend the empire of true democracy, of peace and of decency', and suggested that it should prompt 'disquiet and questioning'.[8] Meanwhile, more letters appeared in *The Times* from disgruntled occupation staff questioning the efficiency of the Control Commission: the administration was said to be far too large and filled with incompetent individuals, while superiors did nothing to rectify the situation.[9] On 11 August, Brian Connell, the *Daily Mail*'s Germany correspondent, described the CCG as an 'amateur team' of 'aloof administrators' who 'have committed the unforgivable crime of getting neither respect nor results from their two years' efforts'.[10] Connell, who claimed to know an administrator who had failed to meet a single German after four months in his job, warned that the British were risking the revival of Nazism:

> Missing by the very method of its recruitment either the result-by-example integrity of the long-term Civil Servant or the practical efficiency of the new managerial type, Britain's Control Commission neither administers Germany nor controls it. While the dead hand of its amateur bureaucrats in their parallel administrations lies heavy on the land, the nominal passing of executive power since the beginning of the year from the palsied hand in the velvet glove of the British to the nerveless paws of the Germans has resulted

in official and economic activity dissolving in a sea of utter corruption... The British are now paying £2.10s per head to provide £100 million of bread grains while the Germans weep crocodile tears that we are deliberately starving them [yet] without any question something like seventy per cent of the Germans are getting food as good as in England – and in many cases more varied... In the uneasy lull which lies over Germany today, half a million heads are being raised to sniff the changing air. Merchants, professional men, the middle class and the myriad minor aristocracy, who thought Hitler slightly vulgar, and have taken good care not to 'collaborate' with us, sense their turn is coming... At their shoulders stand the snubbed, humiliated, resentful survivors of the regular officers' corps... [who] offer their organising ability, their administrative efficiency and their talent for engrossing discipline in the midst of anarchy... Many people may recall that this is just about where Hitler came in.

Two days later Frank Owen's editorial campaign in the *Daily Mail* continued. He castigated the government's decision to spend an estimated 11 per cent of the American loan on feeding the German people, all the while running up an enormous bill for the costs of the British administration.[11] The prospect of waiting to offset these costs until October, when it was hoped the Level of German Industry plan would be revised, was met with a soon-to-be familiar refrain: 'The plain man says: "Get out now! We cannot afford to wait until then!"'[12]

A week later, on 21 August, the *Mail* published an incendiary report into allegations that British troops had looted £200,000 worth of jewels, gold and other valuables from the Grand Duchess of Mecklenburg at gunpoint.[13] The same day, Owen wrote another editorial decrying the British occupiers as a 'Disgrace to Britain'.[14] The British occupation of Germany was 'one problem which must be handled now with speed and decision' and 'because of the shame it is bringing upon the British name' it 'should be ended forthwith'. The British had entered Germany with the 'intention of restoring order, exacting punishment and teaching the Germans the high standards of the British way of life'. Yet the result was 'wholly discreditable to ourselves', the task being 'physically and financially beyond our own powers' and 'morally far beyond the powers of those we sent there to handle it'. The total cost of the occupation, including administrative overheads, the upkeep of the BAOR soldiers, black market losses and food exports, was estimated to be £228 million per year and the labours of 124,000 personnel. The moral costs were said to be 'even more appalling', from the lowest ranks, where 'mounting figures of venereal disease... tell their own story', to the highest, where 'the grossest corruption pervades the organization':

> Hardly a day passes but we read with shame of British officers of field rank and over in Germany being charged with corruption, looting or some similar offence... Racketeering and blackmail have become part of the daily practice of large numbers of the occupying forces, both military and civilian. These things must be exposed, and the *Daily Mail* intends to expose them. They are making the name of Britain stink in Europe. The inevitable conclusion is that we must bring these men home, for our own good and theirs... The longer the decision is delayed the worse it will be for us. We must get out of Germany NOW. We cannot afford to remain there.

*

It was not long before leading officials in the Foreign Office and the Control Commission raised concerns over a seemingly orchestrated 'Get Out of Germany' campaign 'proceeding with increasing virulence'.[15] They were anxious that such attacks could damage the morale of the British staff in Germany, further enrage the local population and ultimately derail the military occupation. Eric Underwood, head of the German Information Department at the Foreign Office, noted that 'enlightened opinion... is perfectly aware that a panic evacuation would be in the real interests of neither ourselves nor the Germans, but in such cases the unenlightened cannot be ignored'. Underwood suggested a government spokesperson should stress 'that we will not permit our temporary embarrassments to invalidate our long-term responsibilities in Germany'. This, he hoped, 'would have a salutary effect on opinion in this country and in Germany too'.

In the meantime, Lord Pakenham, as the new minister with responsibility for Germany, sprang into action. He was provided with daily briefings about the *Daily Mail*'s critical campaign and proceeded to write to the paper's owner, Viscount Rothermere, as well as his editor. Pakenham complained that the paper's claims from 21 August were a 'gross exaggeration' that must not have been seen by either man prior to publication.[16] He also reminded Frank Owen of his personal promise to get in touch 'before launching out along those lines' and proposed a friendly meeting to discuss the matter further. Owen rebuffed his offer in no uncertain terms:

The only thing astonishing about the *Daily Mail* article is that it was not published a long time ago. It contains no exaggerations at all, and you need not believe that it was done without my knowledge – on the contrary, I initiated it. As a matter of hard fact, we have evidence in this office which, if published, would result in a number of high-ranking officers being placed under immediate arrest for court martial. The charge is looting, and on a massive scale. It will astonish a good deal more if the Director of Public Prosecutions does not move on the matter. If you are not aware of these facts, I suggest you look into them, because they are likely to explode an almighty scandal.[17]

On 4 September, Lord Beaverbrook's *Daily Express* published its own exposé of the British Zone under the incendiary headline: 'BRING HOME THESE MEN! CORRUPT, LAZY, THEY DISCREDIT OUR RULE'.[18] John Deane Potter's article warned that Germany, far from a democracy, was turning towards communism and fascism. He even quoted a joke, originally delivered by a

German comic, poking fun at the predicament: 'are you not warmed by the democratic sun? It's a funny thing about that sun, it turns some of us red and some of us brown again'. Potter argued that it was clear the British authorities were to blame; they had far too many 'maggots feeding on the corpse of defeated Germany' among their ranks and 'the reason why democracy is a laughing stock in Germany today is due to 20,000 Britons called CCG (BE). The best of them admit ruefully this stands for Complete Chaos Guaranteed (By Experts).'

In his merciless critique, Potter went on to paint a picture of what he saw as the 'typical Control Commission official', the 'Civilian Officer Spiv'. A failed salesman, Spiv had come to Germany in the face of a panic over demobilization. He maintained his artificial standard of living through the black market and spent most of his time gallivanting around the German countryside. He liked it there because 'it provided everything that a man of his mentality could want': unlimited drink, from champagne to beer, cheap food, and German women to wait on him in any capacity. Mrs Spiv had, of course, joined him in the British Zone and, provided with a grand house and several servants, enjoyed the fruits of victory just as much.

As for the Control Commission, Potter lambasted a culture of 'laziness and corruption', of enjoying comforts at the Atlantic Hotel and profiting from the old-boy racketeering network which pervaded the Zone. This was 'Britain's newest Colonial Service', but with a much inferior staff and only one fear: exposure in the press.* The article went on to document numerous stories of alleged dishonesty and folly, such as ordering anti-freeze for air-cooled VWs, which were only adding to the British taxpayer's hefty bill. Potter concluded that the British should leave Germany before it was too late: 'I think it is high time, for the sake of Britain and the future of Europe, that the Spivs were sent home – and quickly. Brought back to work – while they are still capable of it.'

---

* Potter even quoted a public relations official who lamented the weakening of press censorship.

These accusations caused uproar among some members of the British staff. Mary Bouman described it as a 'malicious and humourless article' and suggested that Potter 'evidently never went near where work was being done and got his copy solely from bars'.[19] At the Cologne Club on New Year's Eve 1947 one of the fancy dress costumes was 'Mrs Spiv', laden with fox furs and flashy jewellery – a witty if somewhat self-defeating riposte considering the character of the accusations.[20] The upper echelons of the British administration suggested contacting the *Express*'s editor, Arthur Christiansen, in order to point out various factual errors and exaggerations in John Deane Potter's article.[21] The news that the entire report had featured prominently on Soviet-controlled Berlin Radio presented a further possible means of persuasion: one Foreign Office official acerbically noted that Christiansen 'may derive some satisfaction from the contribution which his paper has made to our ally's propaganda machine'.[22] But in the aftermath of Frank Owen's straight-bat response, it was reasoned that '[not] much good can come from intervening with newspaper editors or proprietors. The only real answer is to take the offensive ourselves.'[23]

*

Military Governor Sholto Douglas and Foreign Secretary Ernest Bevin were both tasked with writing 'private' letters defending the Control Commission and the Rhine Army and asserting that 'the vast majority... tackle their Augean task' with 'industry and conscientiousness'.[24] The official line was that while corruption and misconduct had occurred, only a small number of 'black sheep' were to blame.[25] The Public Relations Division intended for these letters to be published and placed them in routine orders where the press were 'likely to get hold of [them]'.[26] In October 1947 this scheme paid off as they appeared in a number of national newspapers.[27]

Their publication did little to stop the press campaign. Several more articles appeared, slating the conduct of the British authorities in Germany and suggesting they should be brought home immediately. The *Daily Graphic* questioned spending '£80,000,000 on misfits', while Rex North claimed in the *Sunday Pictorial* that the Control Commission members were motivated by cheap drink, plentiful food and easy living rather than the important task in hand.[28] In the *Daily Mirror*, the authors of the 'Live Letters' column, responding to correspondence about where potential reductions in government expenditure could be found, explained:

> Laddie, we can give 'em plenty! For instance, get out of Palestine next week. Then get out of Germany; that would save a packet. It is to us Old Codgers little short of lunacy to spend £80,000,000 a year helping Germany to prepare for another war on us (which is what we did in 1918 and are doing now. Anyway, we can't afford the money).[29]

By October, senior officials in Germany were anxious that the campaign, albeit 'in a less hysterical form', had even reached the correspondence columns of *The Times*.[30] That month the Control Commission issued a 'morality memo' to all members of staff in Germany, warning them of the potentially disastrous consequences of 'any departure from high standards' in the face of the allegations circulating in the press. The memorandum was an implicit acknowledgement that there was substance to the claims. Inevitably, this admission angered some members of the CCG, who felt it unduly accusatory, and the memo soon found its way into the hands of journalists.[31] Public Relations officials were aghast, with one lamenting privately that 'any efforts to uphold the prestige of CCG personnel must of course fail in their effect if they are torpedoed by such ill-advised memoranda as that which the press seized upon with unholy glee'.[32] They said it was 'indicative of a weak administration' to 'seek to blame all for the sins of the few', adding that this 'sort of stupidity hardly helps us to offset doubts in the minds of the public at home about CCG'.[33]

There was also a more practical response to the 'Get Out Now!' campaign, as officials in Germany sought to curtail the excesses of occupation life once and for all. In the spring of 1947, as power was handed back to the Germans, the Control Commission staff were reduced by around 6,000, or about 25 per cent, leaving 20,000 in place. Over the following two years, further reductions in staff numbers, as well as specific attempts to root out troublemakers, would result in the number of CCG employees reaching as few as 12,000.[34] Much has been made in previous historical accounts of the British Zone being overstaffed compared to the other three zones of occupation, but these claims are probably exaggerated, and disparities explicable on account of differences in organizational structure.[35] What we can say is that Control Commission staffing levels were considerably higher than was strictly necessary. Reducing the number of CCG staff in 1947 was possible due to the handover of a great deal of responsibility to the Germans. If the British had pursued a similar strategy from the very beginning of the occupation, then the manpower and financial burden of the occupation would certainly have been eased.

Furthermore, the CCG's complex administrative structure was simplified, and the introduction of language tests and other stipulations improved the quality of the hiring process. The *Manchester Guardian* concluded that 'even the Commission's best friends would agree that this reshuffle is overdue'. According to Edward Rich, who had joined the CCG as a Kreis resident officer in January 1947, these changes helped to instil a sense of anxiety among the staff: after being greeted in a hostile fashion by a number of his new colleagues, Rich realized 'that one's arrival was often regarded with extreme suspicion as the man in the chair's immediate reaction was that his sins had found him out and here was his successor'.[36]

A more general change of strategy arose from political imperatives and would significantly alter the shape of the British administration. In October 1947 the Select Committee on Estimates published a report on the occupation that concluded that 'the burden of supporting the German in peace is proving as irksome as the burden of defeating him in war'.[37] It recommended urgent changes, including more emphasis on German recovery, further economic reintegration of the Western zones, a statement of policy on the length of the occupation, increased German responsibility for the economy, and a prioritization of food imports. As we have seen, many of these policies were already in motion thanks to Bevin's efforts in establishing the Bizone.

*

There was undoubtedly an element of truth in many of the allegations made during the summer of 1947, although we also shouldn't lose sight of the fact that the popular papers had an axe to grind. Many of Britain's influential press barons were outspoken opponents of the Labour government and were all too happy to take aim at the apparent shortcomings of the administration, whether in its domestic policies or in its conduct of the occupation of Germany.* These excoriating attacks on the British occupiers were also, in some sense, characteristic of the popular press, with its deeply ingrained predilection for sensationalism and scandal. The relentless Germanophobia that accompanied much of the critical coverage had long-standing origins – and populist appeal. Media coverage of the occupation also reflected more wide-ranging contemporary anxieties: as Britain sought to establish its place in world affairs in the aftermath of the Second World War, there were growing concerns in some quarters that the country might have entered a period of terminal decline. As a result, problems such as the black market or corruption, experienced across all four occupation zones, were framed as distinctly British shortcomings.

In hindsight, the political repercussions of the 'Get Out Now!' campaign were minor. Even in the face of the many and various costs associated with maintaining the occupation, the Attlee government had already set out its stall when it came to the British Zone. Events might have been quite different had the press onslaught come a year earlier: amid the tense Anglo-American negotiations over the future of Western Germany, public demands for a British evacuation in 1946 might have radically altered the history of the early Cold War.

---

* As a case in point, Lord Beaverbrook's *Daily Express* had run the infamous headline warning that a Labour victory would lead to the imposition of a 'Gestapo in Britain' during the 1945 election campaign.

Yet despite its failure to force a hurried evacuation from Germany, this media campaign still marks a hugely important moment in the history of the British occupation. While the accusations in the British newspapers may have presented a slightly skewed portrait of the occupation, there is no doubting their influence.* The 'Get Out Now!' campaign marked the high point of domestic interest in post-war Germany and, as such, it helped to crystallize a remarkably unfavourable public image of the occupiers. By the end of 1947 it seemed to many in Britain that the occupation of Germany was a blight on the country's international standing: a waste of time and energy that merely exposed the country's growing weakness on the world stage. Over the next two years, it was an unflattering reputation that the British occupiers would struggle to shake off.

---

* The press was experiencing a boom in popularity at this time, with total circulation of national newspapers calculated at over 15 million: it is estimated that 87 per cent of the adult population read a daily newspaper by 1950. Middle-market (*Daily Mail* (2,076,000)) and mass-market titles (*Daily Mirror* (3,702,000); *Daily Express* (3,855,000)) represented the bulk of this circulation, whereas the 'quality' press had a much more limited output (*The Manchester Guardian* (126,000); *The Times* (268,000); *The Financial Times* (71,000)). In addition, it is estimated that the circulation of the regional press was over 6.5 million. These figures, which are for the end of 1947, were compiled by the Royal Commission on the Press 1947–9.

21

The London Programme

In early 1948 pioneering documentary filmmaker Arthur Elton witnessed the deprivations that still ravaged much of the British Zone. 'The cold is intense; the rations of the German staff are not being honoured in Cologne and it is rare for less than two of the team to be in bed with "flu"', he wrote to his liaison in the Foreign Office. 'As a consequence the hourly labour is becoming mutinous; they are plagued by thieving, roving street-gangs attack the cars, the discomforts are acute.'[1] Elton, who had helped shape the Documentary Film Movement in the 1930s, was now working as a producer for the government's own film-making division, the Crown Film Unit. That spring, he went to Germany to shoot a new documentary about the British occupation, *A School in Cologne*, which highlighted the work of the occupiers in reforming the country's education system.[2] It presented a gloomy picture of life in post-war Germany: the opening scenes show a row of children's feet dangling above their schoolroom floor, some in ragged shoes and others barefoot; above them, a leaking roof lets rainwater trickle down into a bucket placed beside the odd assortment of desks and tables. Meanwhile, across the city, young boys and girls play amid rubble and broken military machinery while others scavenge for coal and basic supplies. 'This is Cologne in the third winter after the war,' notes the sombre narrator. The job was said to be 'far from finished'.

If conditions had improved since the bitter winter of the previous year, the systemic lack of food, fuel and transport remained – and was now coupled with a growing impatience for change among the local population. In the Ruhr, once the industrial heartland of Germany, workers were beginning to take action in the face of the perpetual hunger and poor working conditions that they had faced since 1945. In the second week of January 1948, around 60,000 workers went on strike in Essen, Solingen and elsewhere, prompting frantic American officials to suggest – without foundation – that German workers were being directed by Moscow to undermine the Marshall Plan.[3] In his own report to the Foreign Office, Elton concluded with a cautionary note: 'I think we shall be lucky if we get the film out of Cologne this week before there is a total breakdown in the Ruhr Area, either because of the lack of food supplies or because of strikes, or both'.[4]

A School in Cologne was part of a renewed public relations effort to create more 'positive publicity to counteract the abuse of CCG personnel' which had peaked in the summer of 1947.[5] It was no easy task. As one Control Commission member commented, the organization had become something of an 'Aunt Sally',* with its work 'always in danger of being used as a "wet weather story"' – especially because public curiosity 'in its less high forms' was particularly hungry for criticism and intrigue.[6] There were also challenging material considerations: in the context of the growing conflict between East and West, more and more government funding was redirected to anti-Soviet propaganda. The Central Office of Information, along with the British Council and the covert Information Research Department, was increasingly bound up in these endeavours and less interested in news about Germany itself.[7] In particular, the Public Relations Division of the Control Commission was hit hard by budget cuts.[8] At the height of the 'Get Out of Germany' campaign, a suggestion to produce a film

---

* A traditional pub game similar to a coconut shy but played in teams, with an 'Aunt Sally' doll as their target.

explaining why the occupation was so expensive had been shelved after it was deemed too costly.[9]

The result of this PR strategy was a series of fairly unremarkable films, most of which barely made a dent in public perceptions of the occupation. Alongside *A School in Cologne*, the British occupiers produced a film documenting the reformed German police force, entitled *Trained to Serve*.[10] This production contrasted the history of the German policing under Nazism, when the totalitarian character of the police and arbitrary arrests by the Gestapo were universally feared, with the change that had arisen under the supervision of the Public Safety Branch of the Control Commission. The police were commended for becoming 'servants of the people' rather than their masters.

Another film, *K.R.O. – Germany 1947*, focused on the work of a Kreis resident officer, the Control Commission's 'man on the ground'.[11] It followed the daily activities of a noble and considerate, but above all effective, British administrator and offered a glimpse into the work that the British were doing 'in order that the German people may learn how best to help themselves'. German people are overwhelmingly portrayed as weak, destitute and dependent on the paternal figure of the KRO as they encounter food and housing shortages, an influx of refugees, the black market, idle industry and a broken education system. Its message was clear: this was an important job that must be seen through to the end.

The curious character of these films, as well as the British public's waning concern with events in post-war Germany, is such that all three failed to secure a theatrical release. Instead, *K.R.O. – Germany 1947* was listed alongside *How to Make Pickles* in the Monthly Film Bulletin's record of new educational films, available for viewing from selected libraries and film institutes.[12]

*

Just as the British people were gradually losing faith – and interest – in the British occupation, significant shifts were happening behind the scenes. While the establishment of the Bizone in January 1947 had done little, as yet, to reduce Britain's outlay in Germany, it did pave the way for a new approach to the occupation. Gradually, the punitive four-power policies laid down at Potsdam were disappearing. In their place came an attempt to build up the German-run administrative infrastructure and the economy of the British and American zones.

In February 1947 Control Council Law No. 46 liquidated the state of Prussia, a polity castigated as 'a bearer of militarism and reaction'.[13] It would turn out to be one of the final four-power decisions made in Germany. That month the Soviet representative at the Control Council in Berlin voiced his country's distrust of the fusion between the British and American zones. They considered the Bizone to be a short-sighted, unilateral break from the common policies agreed in 1945 and a blatant attempt to utilize Germany for the benefit of Western monopolistic capital.[14]

In the summer of 1947, the Americans finally rescinded JCS 1067, a document that had guided their own occupation policy since the end of the war and which was imbued with the legacy of the Morgenthau Plan: it had expressly forbidden 'steps looking toward the economic rehabilitation of Germany [or] designed to maintain or strengthen the German economy'.[15] Soon after, the British and Americans agreed to a revised Level of Industry plan in the Bizone that substantially increased production across heavy industry and other sectors of the economy.*

The decision to revive German industry didn't go down well with the British media. In November a *Pathé* newsreel wondered whether 'some new world-shaking warmonger' might 'arise from the rubble' of Berlin.[16] On Armistice Day, William Barkley's column in the *Express* featured a choice headline: 'Watch Out, They'll Cheat Us Yet!'[17] It warned that the restoration of Germany was short-sighted:

I lose no sleep worrying about Germany going down into the abyss. Nor does it disturb me that Germany is cut in two

---

* Under this new arrangement, production could reach 100 per cent of the level attained in 1936, rather than 70 per cent as previously agreed; see Oppen, Beate R. von, *Documents on Germany under Occupation*, pp. 239–45.

parts. I wish it were 22. How poignant are the memories of November 11, 1918. The clouds that had hung over us since the early years of the century were dispelled. Then, as the world was recovering, the cry went up that Europe could not prosper until Germany was rebuilt. So she was rebuilt, and another generation was convulsed in re-smashing her... Some British Tories, and Socialists, too, who make a humane appeal to uplift Germany, nourish the ulterior motive of building a barrier against Bolshevism as the false guide Hitler proposed... Keep fresh the memory of the German crimes.

Nevertheless, the Western powers pressed on. In December 1947 Ernest Bevin explained to the House of Commons that the London meeting of the Council of Foreign Ministers had ended without any agreement on the future of Germany. It was the fifth meeting of the body that had been formed to carry the wartime alliance into the post-war era. The failure of these talks signalled the collapse of four-power diplomacy and set the path towards a break with the 'noble experiment' of the Control Council.[18] In his speech Bevin challenged the apparent obstructionism of his Soviet counterpart and indicated Britain's desire to continue with their plans for rebuilding the German economy:

> if there is to be no settlement between the Four Powers we cannot go on for ever with the burden of cost this represents, with Western Europe in chaos, and with no means of redress. If we are to succeed there must be an acceptance that we British are peace-loving people with nothing else but a desire for a just settlement... we are going to push on to raise the German standard of life in accordance with our promises, to rehabilitate their industries, to keep to the new level of industry, always remembering that we must not push Germany ahead of the liberated countries.[19]

In January 1948 Bevin presented the cabinet with his policy for a Western Union – part of which included the creation of a democratic, Westward-looking sovereign West German state.[20] A number of public pronouncements soon followed, marking a major shift away from fear-mongering over the resurgence of German nationalism and towards a focus on halting the spread of Soviet communism. While reverence for the Soviet Union's wartime exploits still maintained a hold on much of the British media and public, perceptions were slowly changing. In February 1948 a Soviet-backed coup in Czechoslovakia helped to engage popular support in Britain for the mounting political crusade against the USSR.[21]

In the aftermath of Bevin's declaration of Britain's new focus on countering the Soviet Union, practical changes were introduced in Germany. For one, the British authorities quietly declared denazification to be complete, with all further remedial action now in the hands of the German *Länder*.[22] It was a political decision: as the nascent Cold War came to dominate British policy in Germany, the impulse to continue a wholesale examination of German society and pursue war crimes prosecutions quickly diminished.[23] It was a decision mirrored in the other Western zones.[24]

Over the course of the next year, there would be a dismantling of the legal machinery relating to war crimes.[25] No one claimed that all of those guilty of crimes during the Third Reich had been brought to justice – far from it. Many thousands of perpetrators, including some occupying senior positions in the Third Reich's murderous regime, went unpunished, while others were handed paltry fines or short prison sentences. Towards the end, denazification slowly turned into a means of rehabilitating former Nazis, and lenient penalties freed individuals to take an active part in a society where professional expertise now trumped the political taint of historic associations.[26] That isn't to suggest that denazification was merely a box-ticking exercise: for the many thousands of Germans who were subjected to internment or prosecution, the consequences of their Nazi associations were very real. More broadly, the denazification programme helped to establish the authority of the Allies and to institute a partial reconstruction of German society.[27] Yet, while there is little doubt that Germany was indeed more or less 'denazified' by the end of the 1940s, it probably had much more to do with the experiences of 1945 – military defeat, national humiliation and the privations and chaos that ensued – than the erratic and ultimately truncated work of the British.[28]

This development was part of a gradual winding-down of the military government's rule, which eventually led to the complete handover of power to the Germans themselves. In February 1948 the British and Americans created a central administration in the Bizone under the Frankfurt Charter. This included a high court and a central bank, laying the groundwork for the establishment of a West German federal state.[29] The Attlee government had rejected calls to withdraw from the British Zone of Germany in the summer of 1947, but it was now obvious that the occupation was to be brought to an end much sooner than anyone had anticipated.

*

The final part of Bevin's ambitious plan was to expand the Western Union: at the first session of the London Six-Power Conference, held between 23 February and 6 March, the British and Americans made progress in their efforts to get France on side.[30] On 17 March, Britain, France, Belgium, Luxembourg and the Netherlands announced the Treaty of Brussels – a precursor to the establishment of the North Atlantic Treaty Organization (NATO) the following year. This decision was made without the Soviets, who were excluded from the London conference, meaning it was quite clearly in violation of the Potsdam Agreement. In the Soviet Union the news was denounced as the capitalist nations of the West abandoning democratization in favour of preserving monopolistic capitalism.[31] By way of response, the head of the Soviet military administration in Germany, Marshal Sokolovsky, walked out of the Allied Control Council in protest. On 20 April the second session of the London Six-Power Conference pressed ahead to finalize plans for a free and democratic West Germany, to be known officially as the Federal Republic of Germany. This would fuse the US, British *and* French Zones into a single entity, with a constituent assembly to be established by 1 September

1948. The Western powers would, however, maintain supervision over German industry through the International Authority of the Ruhr, as well as completing work towards demilitarization and disarmament and retaining a military presence within the Federal Republic itself.

At the end of June, Ernest Bevin rose in the House of Commons to deliver the news of the so-called 'London Programme'.[32] It was clear, he suggested, that the occupying powers had failed to enact a common policy in Germany. The issue at hand was: why not? According to the foreign secretary, the blame lay squarely at the Soviet door: having refused to adhere to the Potsdam Agreement on reparations, Stalin had forced the British to spend more than £200 million on food and raw materials for Germany since 1945. In Bevin's reading, it had left the Western powers with no choice:

we could not leave this great Western area, for which the United States, France and ourselves were responsible, as a slum – a great human slum – because all the resources capable of contributing to the standard of life not only of Germany but of Europe were lying there unrehabilitated and unrestored. We had to do something.

To some, however, it all seemed rather hollow. Victor Gollancz had long rejected the imposition of a military government on defeated Germany and favoured the restoration of German statehood in its entirety. He had also, of course, long campaigned for more to be done to help the beleaguered people of the British Zone. Yet in July 1948 he wrote to the *Manchester Guardian*, remarking that he was left 'feeling sick at heart in the very hour [we] are being fulfilled'.[33] For Gollancz, taking a more 'sentimental' attitude towards the German people was foremost a moral choice, not a political one. The self-serving realpolitik displayed by Allied leaders was simply further proof of the West's decay:

Is it because it is right to be decent to human beings as such that a wave of sentimental pro-Germanism... is now swelling? No: it is because in the changed circumstances the Russians are more dangerous to us than the Germans, and therefore it is the Germans we must woo as potential allies in a dreaded conflict… In three short years the pariah nation, held criminally responsible, as a whole, for Auschwitz and Buchenwald, has become, as a whole, 'Christian and civilized' – with Auschwitz and Buchenwald forgotten. In 1945, they were to be fed 'as a matter of policy': in 1948 they are to be 'treated' as Christian and civilized because 'our interests converge'.

Part Five

CHANGING
ENEMIES

22

Bad Nenndorf

On 10 April 1948 a man wearing a fawn mackintosh, dark trousers, brown shoes, and a paper bag over his head staggered into a Hamburg barracks, manacled to a British soldier. While a sentry was holding a fixed bayonet two feet from his back, this mysterious figure hobbled across the base before being led into a nearby prison block.[1] The following day, freed from the constraints of his impromptu hood, he appeared as a witness in a trial that threatened to expose the secretive and brutal work of British intelligence in occupied Germany.

The man in question was Robert Buttlar-Brandenfels, a German spy whose wartime activities remain mysterious to this day.[2] In May 1945 he appeared in the British Zone and, posing as a British subject, sought to persuade I Corps HQ to send him to London; a minor aristocrat, he claimed to have worked as a Soviet spy before being arrested by the Gestapo in 1943. At least the second part of the story was true, and after two years in a Berlin prison it was only the arrival of the Red Army that saved him from almost certain execution. Buttlar-Brandenfels, who went by several aliases including Karl Jensson, Karl Hilger, Robert Hellman, Karl Hjerring and simply Hjerrberg, was now offering his services as an intelligence asset to the British. In early August 1945 he was given clearance to travel to Croydon Airport in London, although upon arrival he was detained by the Home Office. In the coming months he was repeatedly interrogated by British intelligence, who doubted his story: a Security Service file suggests that 'all who had dealings with his case concluded that he was a compulsive liar with a significant inventive capacity'.[3] The following year Buttlar-Brandenfels was transferred back to Germany, first to No. 4 Civilian Internment Camp at Recklinghausen and then, in November, to a place that would soon be regarded with terror and loathing: No. 74 Combined Services Detailed Interrogation Centre at Bad Nenndorf.

The building in Bad Nenndorf that housed No. 74 Combined Services
Detailed Interrogation Centre.

This shadowy man – seemingly willing to work for the British government – was one of hundreds of prisoners subject to cruel and dehumanizing treatment at the hands of their British captors. In his courtroom testimony Buttlar-Brandenfels explained how on one occasion he had his jacket, boots and blankets confiscated before being forced to scrub the walls of his empty concrete punishment cell for seventy-two hours. This room was entirely bare, without any radiator, furniture or even windowpanes as temperatures plummeted to -25 degrees Celsius.[4] His limp was the result of losing four toes to frostbite that winter.

At Bad Nenndorf, he alleged, the British were running a regime of torture where humiliation, physical distress and intimidation were intended to break prisoners. As one interrogator had explained quite shamelessly, his captors did not 'care a damn whether you leave this place on a stretcher or in a hearse'. In his two years in the hands of the Gestapo, Buttlar-Brandenfels reckoned he had received no treatment remotely comparable to that he experienced during his time in British captivity.

*

To understand exactly why the British occupation authorities were running a secret interrogation centre in the heart of Germany, we must turn to the broader history of the intelligence services. In the course of the war, senior figures in the British military and government had come to appreciate the value of espionage operations. Yet it was unclear what role spies could or should play in a modern democracy during peacetime, and there were also disagreements over exactly what threats were most urgent in the post-war world. In occupied Germany, Britain's spies carved out a new role for themselves.[5]

As the war came to a close, the Joint Intelligence Committee envisioned a great deal of work for the intelligence services in the British Zone. It would centre on locating and arresting many thousands of Germans as part of denazification, as well as keeping tabs on clandestine networks of ardent Nazis and the much-feared Werewolves.[6] The chief of the Secret Intelligence Service (SIS, also known as MI6), Stewart Menzies, even wondered whether some sort of 'Black and Tan' paramilitary force, as had been employed to such savage effect in Ireland in 1920–1, might be required. This provocative idea was ultimately shelved, but proposals for a substantial intelligence organization were given the green light.

The Control Commission created its own Intelligence Division of more than 1,200 officers under the command of Brigadier J. S. 'Tubby' Lethbridge.[7] They outnumbered both SIS and MI5, who had their own spy networks in the British Zone alongside the individual intelligence arms of the army, navy and air force. In some cases, British spies also went undercover as members of the Control Commission or even entire parts of its extensive bureaucracy.[8] In one instance a division of clandestine SIS agents established the suspiciously boring-sounding 'No. 1 Planning and Evaluation Unit'. Reportedly, when one member was asked what they actually did, their reply was simply that 'in the morning we plan and in the afternoon we evaluate what we planned in the morning'.[9] Britain wasn't alone: post-war Germany soon became the front line of the intelligence war, as all the world's major powers created substantial intelligence operations in the ruins of the Third Reich. In time, Berlin became known as the *Agentensumpf*, or 'spy swamp'.

What was this gargantuan network of spies and support staff expected to achieve? The answer is opaque: Britain's clandestine activities in Germany remain, to this day, a closely guarded secret. The Information Division's entire archive was destroyed.[10] But various leaks, released files and personal recollections outline the main preoccupations of British spooks during the Allied occupation.

In the first place, intelligence officers were involved in the complicated work of tracking down fugitives as part of the machinery of denazification, work which included processing and, on occasion, interrogating suspect prisoners. It also meant countering any subversive elements that might prove a headache to the occupiers. While the feared Werewolf movement had proved weaker and more ineffective than anticipated, pockets of resistance to Allied rule still remained. In the winter of 1945–6, the Intelligence Division and their American counterparts launched a counterinsurgency programme, codenamed Operation Nursery.[11] In a series of raids, more than 800 unrepentant Nazis were arrested, many of whom, as the operation's name suggested, were former members of the Hitler Youth. There were a number of similar actions over the course of the occupation, including Operation Selection Board and Operation Dry Martini. Whether the latter was shaken or stirred remains unclear, though it is a good question: Ian Fleming, author of the James Bond stories, was himself working as part of British intelligence in Germany.[12] But while these activities were eye-catching and often well publicized, there was little in the way of an actual insurgency to counter. It has been suggested that the shocking tales of underground Nazi cells developing new biological weapons or planning uprisings that intermittently made it into the British newspapers were a deliberate, self-aggrandizing exaggeration on the part of the security services.[13]

In addition, the Intelligence Division, as well as its SIS and MI5 counterparts in Germany, was engaged in more traditional espionage. British agents, working alongside the T-Force organization, helped to secure technical and scientific information that advanced Anglo-American research into guided missiles, aviation technology and nuclear weaponry.[14] This was a real asset, said to have been the biggest transfer of mass intelligence from one country to another – an estimated $5 billion worth of patents and technological secrets alone. There were clandestine human intelligence operations too: the British were eager to turn Nazi scientists and spies to their own advantage. Wernher von Braun, an aerospace engineer central to the V-2 rocket programme, was picked up by the British in the hope of securing his cooperation.[15] This operation caused some controversy in the popular newspapers, considering von Braun's complicity in the use of slave labour. In the end, however, he opted for a more lucrative American offer, becoming a central figure in NASA's space exploration programme.

If von Braun got away, there's no hiding the array of unsavoury characters the British did work alongside in their hunt for secrets. One of the greatest scandals of the post-war era is the extent to which all sides were willing to disregard evidence of historical war crimes in the pursuit of new intelligence assets. British authorities arrested SS Major Horst Kopkow in 1945 and he seemed willing to cooperate. A leading figure in the Third Reich's Security Police, Kopkow was responsible for counter-sabotage and counter-espionage.[16] This included action against British agents, around 150 of whom are thought to have been executed under his command. Yet Kopkow evaded justice: when Allied war crimes investigators instigated his prosecution, British intelligence protected him. In March 1948 he was released, ostensibly on account of insufficient evidence but also on the grounds of his 'special employment under an "I" agency here'. The agency in question was SIS, who proceeded to fake Kopkow's death and provide him with a false identity that allowed him to continue his work as an informant and counter-espionage asset for the British under the alias Peter Cordes.[17] In the first instance, he provided information about the Red Orchestra network of anti-Nazi resistance groups. At some point, in the late 1940s or early 1950s, he even moved back to Germany, where he embarked on a successful career in the textile industry. It was a job provided by his spymasters back in London to whom Peter Cordes, aka Horst Kopkow, reported on a regular basis.[18] He lived without fear of prosecution until his death in 1996.[19]

Another striking story comes from the very beginning of the occupation. In May 1945 the British captured an entire division of Ukrainian SS soldiers, the 14th Waffen Grenadier Division of the SS (also known as the 1st Galician Division). This unit had been established under the orders of Heinrich Himmler, and some of its members are believed to have participated in massacres of Jews and other civilians.* Yet in anticipation of a potential war with the Soviet Union, the British (under pressure from the Vatican) refused to repatriate the fiercely anti-communist men of the 1st Galician Division. Instead, the unit was maintained as a fighting force, complete with arms and its own officers, in prisoner-of-war camps in Austria and, subsequently, the Italian resort town of Rimini.[20] In 1947 around 8,000 of these men – some of whom had been personally honoured by Himmler – were given passage to the UK and settled into civilian life. In 2001 an ITV documentary revealed that 1,500 of them were still there, which prompted a Scotland Yard investigation into war criminals living in Britain.[21]

The true magnitude of Britain's cooperation with former Nazis may never be known, especially because most of the relevant

---

* This allegedly includes the suppression of the 1944 Warsaw uprising as well as the murder of British and American airmen in Slovakia; see Cobain, Ian, 'Yard reopens inquiry into former Nazi soldiers still alive in Britain', *The Guardian*, 4 February 2006; Margolian, Howard, *Unauthorized Entry: The Truth About Nazi War Criminals in Canada, 1946–1956*, (Toronto; Buffalo; London: 2000), pp. 133–4.

archival files were either destroyed or retained by the government. Yet these examples paint a troubling picture, one that raises another searching question: in the eyes of the intelligence services, who was the real enemy in post-war Germany?

There is no doubt that much of this work sought to establish networks of informants and spies that could help maintain control in the British Zone. The Control Commission's Intelligence Division developed a 'Central Personality Index' which listed thousands of supposedly subversive elements, while the Censorship Branch worked at Herford, Hamburg, Peine and Bonn to monitor civilian mail and telecommunications.[22] In other words, a great deal of effort was put into keeping tabs on German society: political trends, the development of political parties, the general morale of the population, the work of trade unions, applicants for state posts, youth movements, universities and churches all came under the scrutiny of British intelligence. Hundreds of informers were recruited and often kept loyal through the most precious of commodities in Germany: food. As one SIS officer pointedly remarked to his colleagues, an agent codenamed 'Cook' knew very well 'on which side her 500 grammes of bread are buttered'.[23]

But for many in the security services the primary focus of the post-war peace was always the Soviet Union. The British intelligence community had a long-standing anti-Soviet outlook, unhindered by the complexities of public relations or international diplomacy. In Germany, much of their security work involved blatant political repression, primarily aimed against the German Communist Party.[24] In addition, many spies began acquiring assets and expertise that might help them in any future East–West conflict: turning networks of reliably anti-communist Nazi spies quickly became a priority. Likewise, part of the race for Nazi secrets involved an explicit denial programme, Operation Matchbox, whereby German scientists and technicians who were of no great use to the Western Allies were nevertheless picked up to keep them from the Soviets.[25] When Bevin and Attlee publicly signalled their intentions to counter the Soviet Union at the beginning of 1948, Britain's spymasters were already well set.

In time, as tensions ratcheted up further, SIS began running agents into the East from Germany. In 1948 George James was recruited into Naval Intelligence while working as part of the British-led minesweeping operations. For weeks on end all kinds of peculiar individuals would turn up at his house in the British Zone. They crouched over maps in the cellar as his wife silently delivered pot after pot of fresh coffee.[26] These were the planning stages of a clandestine ferry service from the Danish island of Bornholm under the command of Kriegsmarine veteran Hans-Helmut Klose, who would use his work with the German Mine Sweeping Administration as cover. Operation Jungle, which ran from 1949–55, attempted to get spies into Estonia and Latvia using captured high-speed German boats.[27]

These kinds of missions were high-risk and carried with them the potential to further unsettle a delicate political situation if discovered. Furthermore, and unknown to the intelligence services, Soviet spies had infiltrated much of the British state: Leo Long, a senior member of MI14 (the intelligence arm of the War Office), tasked with getting agents into the East, was in fact himself working for the Soviets after being recruited by Anthony Blunt.[28] In addition, a senior figure in the CCG's Press Department was later found to have been working for Soviet Intelligence.[29] Commander Anthony Courtney, a senior Naval Intelligence representative in Germany, later commented that the extent of Soviet penetration in the Foreign Office meant that attempts to infiltrate the Soviet Union were doomed from the very start.[30]

A more sure-fire means of acquiring information, and without the risk of sending British agents to their deaths, was the retrieval and detailed interrogation of Russian emigrés and defectors. Grigori Aleksandrovich Tokaev was the most high-profile asset in this class: an expert in Soviet rocket science and aeronautics, he defected to the British sector of Berlin in November 1947.[31] But even this approach had its problems, including the risk of taking in Soviet plants and the ever-present danger of public exposure at a time of great political sensitivity. There were growing anxieties in London that press reports on these activities could leave some with the impression that the British, rather than facilitating carefully selected defections, 'condone unlimited non-selective and competitive body snatching'.[32]

*

At the heart of much of this intelligence work – be it processing prisoners, turning Nazi agents or rooting out Soviet spies – was detention and interrogation. As we've already seen, the British maintained a network of civilian internment camps where apparent subversives or those suspected of war crimes could be held. Yet there was another, more secretive camp, reserved for the highest-priority suspects: the Combined Services Detailed Interrogation Centre, or CSDIC. Initially housed in the Tower of London, this shadowy organization had been created in March 1939 and was staffed by German-speaking officers from all three branches of the armed forces.[33] In anticipation of the forthcoming war, the CSDIC was envisioned as a place for interrogating enemy prisoners. It worked in parallel with the Prisoner of War Interrogation Section and MI5's Camp 020, better known as the 'London Cage'.[34] In the course of the war, British interrogators developed new techniques for extracting information from prisoners, including the employment of microphones in cells, the use of experimental drugs and, most commonly, brutal and violent interrogations.[35] These were, in deed if not name, torture centres.

As the war came to a close, the CSDIC had grown far beyond its ten-cell premises in the Tower of London and had centres across the world: Trent Park mansion in London's northern suburbs, Latimer House and Wilton Park in Buckinghamshire, as well as complexes in Cairo, Beirut, Algiers, Naples, Rome and Delhi.[36] Now intelligence officers set their sights on establishing a new centre in the British Zone of occupied Germany.

On 1 August 1945 the sleepy spa town of Bad Nenndorf in Lower Saxony awoke to the sound of trucks, and citizens peered out of their windows to see scores of British army soldiers disembarking.[37] Large swathes of the town were requisitioned and over 1,000 Germans lost access to their homes as reels of barbed wire were quickly unfurled along an outer perimeter. Inside, several streets of buildings and houses were put entirely at the disposal of the CSDIC. At their centre stood the town's famous bathhouse, the Winckler-Bad, a curved, ivy-covered building on the corner of Bahnhofstraße and Poststraße, which was best known for administering therapeutic mudbaths. But now the former baths were to be used as interrogation cells for the CSDIC's newest camp: No. 74.

In fact, it was one of four interrogation centres operating across the British Zone and Berlin. One was housed in a former Gestapo detention centre; all were completely unknown to the outside world.[38] A veteran of the London Cage, Colonel Robin 'Tin Eye' Stephens, was tasked with running Bad Nenndorf. Over the course of the war, Stephens had pioneered new and brutal techniques for forcing confessions, including the use of stress positions,* and was quoted as saying that those who could break a man were born, not made.[39] Over the next two years, 'Tin Eye' and his team of twenty interrogators would test this macabre theory on hundreds of prisoners, whose lives would become a living hell.

The daily routine at Bad Nenndorf went something like this: at 4:30 a.m. prisoners had to get up and for the remainder of the day no one was allowed to lie or sit down; anyone who broke this rule would have their food allowance restricted. The already tiny portions of food, one of the warders later noted, 'consisted mainly of slops', usually potatoes and greens that had not been drained properly.[40] When one prisoner complained that they were going to starve, the camp doctor responded perfunctorily: 'Yes, it looks like you are.' Throughout the day, inmates were marched at the double through the corridors for repeated interrogation sessions. In the course of these examinations prisoners were beaten, whipped and forced to sit or stand in cold water for hours.[41] Some prisoners were forced into stress positions or made to stand to attention for

---

* Forcing prisoners to stand to attention for hours on end, sometimes in handcuffs or shackles, in order to place enormous strain on a small number of muscles and cause intense pain.

twelve hours at a time; others were tied up and beaten. If inmates were thought to be uncooperative, as in the case of Robert Buttlar-Brandenfels, they would be taken to the bare Cell 12 and forced to scrub the walls for hours on end. In freezing conditions, buckets of water were thrown over them. This routine of interrogations and punishments would continue until 9:30 p.m. when the men were forced to remove all outer clothing and await inspection, often resulting in aggressive confrontations or physical abuse. Then a few inmates were instructed to fetch pails of sewage, which were on occasion dumped onto the prisoners' clothing. Finally, each man was provided with two blankets and allowed to lie down on bare wooden beds from which several slats had been removed. The lights remained on at all times and twice a night prisoners were forced to stand to attention for twenty minutes, reciting name and number.

These chilling torture methods were never meant to be revealed. This camp was a closely guarded secret, designed to service the vast intelligence operation in post-war Germany by supplying information acquired through methods of intimidation, ritual humiliation and sheer brutality. But it was only a matter of time until news got out. Local residents were plainly aware that something quite terrible was happening in their small town. Ingrid Groth, then a seven-year-old resident of Bad Nenndorf, later remarked that 'sometimes, you could hear the screams'.[42] By the end of 1946, Dr Wolfgang Günther, chief medical officer of the Civilian Internee Hospital in Rotenburg, was growing concerned at the steady stream of patients who were arriving in British army trucks from Bad Nenndorf.[43] The men were dirty, confused, often emaciated, and were usually sporting numerous injuries and wounds. Above all, these men were terrified. In December, Günther wrote a report documenting his disquiet, but British army intelligence quickly warned him to mind his own business. Large numbers of injured men, sometimes unceremoniously dumped at the front of the hospital, continued to arrive. By spring, one appeared on average every three days.[44]

On 17 February 1947 medical orderly Joseph Krauth helped carry a stretcher bearing thirty-eight-year-old Franz Osterreicher from a British army lorry at the front of the hospital.[45] Osterreicher was a suspected Soviet agent who had entered the British Zone with a false ID card. Under interrogation at Bad Nenndorf it turned out that he had simply been visiting a romantic partner and, as a gay man, lied to protect himself from prosecution. In post-war Germany the Allied occupiers had retained the repressive existing laws prohibiting homosexuality; in fact, some LGBT inmates of concentration camps liberated in 1945 were not released but instead expected to see out the remainder of their sentences in a regular prison.* Upon his arrival at Rotenburg, it was obvious from his condition that the camp and its guards had taken a brutal toll on the innocent man. He was filthy, cold, unable to speak and too emaciated to be weighed. He had frostbite and, according to Dr Günther's notes, his body 'was without the slightest reserve of resistance against infection'. A few hours later Franz Osterreicher was pronounced dead.

Then, four days later, another man by the name of Walter Bergmann arrived in a similar state, seriously malnourished, Dr Günther estimated that this man weighed about 40 kilograms (6 stone 3 pounds) – approximately half of his weight upon admittance to Bad Nenndorf the previous September. Despite the best efforts of the medical staff to revive him, Bergmann would also die at the hospital within days. Günther decided it was time to act regardless of the consequences. He contacted Major James Morgan-Jones, the British commandant of the nearby Fallingbostel Civil Internment Camp, who agreed to visit him at Rotenburg Hospital and meet some of the surviving Bad Nenndorf prisoners now under his care.[46] The British major was appalled. He noted that one man was so emaciated that he looked like an inmate of Bergen-Belsen. In the following weeks Morgan-Jones and a number of other observers wrote reports that made their way up through the Control Commission hierarchy. Eventually,

---

* In 1950 the more repressive Nazi-era additions to the existing legal ban on homosexuality were removed in East Germany, but retained in the Federal Republic until the late 1960s.

news reached the Intelligence Division chief Brigadier 'Tubby' Lethbridge, who was warned that sooner or later these stories were 'bound to come to the notice of the press or parliament'.[47]

Around the same time, a chaplain at the nearby Fallingbostel CIC told the bishop of Hildesheim about rumours of ill-treatment and torture at Bad Nenndorf.[48] The news reached Cardinal Bernard Griffin, head of the Catholic Church in England and Wales, and the Labour MP Richard Stokes. Stokes was a committed Catholic, a staunch socialist and a long-term ally of Victor Gollancz. In late March 1947 Stokes turned up unannounced at the gates of Bad Nenndorf and demanded admittance, giving the British sentries little option but to accommodate him. The details of Stokes's tour of the facility are sketchy and it is unclear how much his access around the camp was managed; the only record is the account he provided in the House of Commons.[49] 'I always find that if I bump into MI5 I find something dirty,' he proclaimed, warning that there was 'something funny going on' at Bad Nenndorf. While he found no evidence of physical torture, he saw that the vast majority of the sixty-five male inmates were in solitary confinement and in cells without heating as temperatures outside hovered around twelve degrees below zero. Stokes was not entirely convinced by his guide's reassurance that the conditions in the centre were 'the very worst that had happened' and insistence that they 'would never happen again'.

The following month commander-in-chief of the British Zone Sholto Douglas ordered a court of inquiry into Bad Nenndorf. It quickly concluded that the treatment of inmates at the camp was not only wrong but potentially illegal, finding at least two credible cases of manslaughter.[50] The matter was handed over to civilian police, namely the Control Commission's man from Scotland Yard, Tom Hayward. He had recently arrived from London and was tasked with investigating the various criminal misdemeanours allegedly committed by British personnel in Germany. He could hardly have expected that his first major case would be an investigation into a secret torture camp. In June 1947 Hayward completed a 130-page report that remains the most comprehensive examination of what took place there.[51] It highlights numerous failings and wrongdoings committed, including the removal and theft of personal belongings, the inadequacy of clothing and footwear provided to inmates, the intimidatory atmosphere, threats of death and torture, physical assaults, arbitrary punishments, wholly insufficient medical care, meagre rations and unnecessarily long periods of detention without release or trial.

In London there was consternation at the prospect of the publicity which might arise from any criminal proceedings. According to Hector McNeill, minister of state at the Foreign Office, it would be 'a propaganda stick with which the Russians will beat us for a long time'.[52] There was, in fact, no doubt that the Soviets already knew of No. 74 Combined Services Detailed Interrogation Centre at Bad Nenndorf: McNeill's secretary was the as yet undiscovered Soviet agent Guy Burgess, one of the Cambridge spies.[53] But with the word already out, and considering the shocking nature of the indictments listed in Hayward's report, the Control Commission had little choice but to act. In July 1947 the camp was shut down and Colonel Stephens was placed under arrest. As overall commander of the centre he was court-martialled alongside Captain John Smith, Bad Nenndorf's medical officer, and Richard Langham, an interrogator. Another man, Frank Edmunds, was also charged, but he had already left the army and, after protracted legal proceedings, was found to be no longer subject to military law.[54] In December, Richard Stokes once again used his parliamentary standing to ask how many deaths from ill-treatment had occurred at Bad Nenndorf.[55] In his response, Foreign Secretary Bevin was forced to admit on record that judicial proceedings were now pending. The story featured in the *Daily Express* the following day.[56]

*

In anticipation of a further flurry of press interest, the British government made arrangements for these trials to be held partially in camera, that is, behind closed doors. It was feared that British interrogation methods would be revealed, that the reputation of the intelligence services would be put at risk and that the existence of other interrogation centres in Germany, those not even disclosed to the Red Cross, would come to light.[57] There was also concern that intelligence assets would be exposed, hence the complex security arrangements including the hood provided to Robert Buttlar-Brandenfels.

In March 1948 the first court martial was held across two locations: first, Hanover in the British Zone and, subsequently, Chelsea in London. Interrogator Richard Langham was accused of two counts of disgraceful conduct of a cruel kind. A German witness for the prosecution accused Langham of beating him up and burning him with cigarette ends. Even with the reporting restrictions, these proceedings were covered extensively in the British newspapers. In the *Daily Express*, one report highlighted that Raymond Short, the camp's intelligence officer, remarked that it was 'quite proper' to threaten inmates that their families would be killed.[58] Remarkably, despite the overwhelming evidence of abuse, Langham was acquitted on the grounds that he was acting 'under a sense of duty and without any sadistic motive' and that, ultimately, he was not responsible for the 'certain amount of violence' that had been administered.[59]

In April, Captain John Smith, the camp's medical officer, was brought to court and charged with the manslaughter of Franz Osterreicher and Walter Bergmann along with a score of charges of professional neglect. Smith accepted that conditions at the camp were horrific but claimed that he had no knowledge of the cruelties that were meted out.[60] At the same time, his defence lawyers routinely questioned the integrity of the witnesses. Smith described Robert Buttlar-Brandenfels and a former SS soldier who also took the stand as 'charmers', 'trained liars', 'deceivers' and 'Nazis'.[61] It was undoubtedly a powerful hand to play: even if in the eyes of the law all were entitled to justice and fair treatment, ex-SS members hardly made star witnesses. In the end, Smith was acquitted of both manslaughter charges and over half of the professional neglect claims, and his only punishment was dismissal from the armed forces.

Finally, there was the court martial of Colonel 'Tin Eye' Stephens, who was charged with four counts of disgraceful conduct of a cruel kind and ill-treatment of prisoners. In the run-up to his trial, Stephens's lawyer complained that he had been put under arrest with humiliating restrictions, while all the time his name was being dragged through the mud in open court.[62] In response to the charges, Stephens's legal team threatened the British government: this trial, they made clear, would cover a much wider field of intelligence work, including their client's role in the London Cage during the war, and would shine a light upon the value of intelligence gained at Bad Nenndorf.[63] In a final act of bravado, Stephens's representatives issued writs against various senior members of the British occupation staff, including former commander-in-chief Sholto Douglas and bigwigs from across the secret services.[64] If Stephens was going down, he was going to bring the entire edifice of British intelligence work in Germany with him.

The government was alarmed enough that it decided the trial should be held entirely in camera, on the shaky grounds that 'secret and non-secret matter would be so interwoven in evidence that it would be impracticable to adopt the arrangement for partial camera which had been in force in the earlier trials'.[65] This was an extraordinary act of suppression: it would be sixty years until the transcript of the hearing was declassified, largely due to the tireless work of investigative journalist Ian Cobain.[66] We now know that Stephens claimed he was simply unaware that the prisoners at Bad Nenndorf had been subject to such horrors, adding that he had been preoccupied writing a memoir of his wartime exploits as head of the London Cage.[67] In spite of extensive evidence of the cruel and inhumane tortures inflicted under his command at Bad Nenndorf, Stephens was also acquitted of all charges.

In the aftermath of the trial, the deputy director general of MI5, Guy Liddell, wrote in his diary of his delight at the verdict.[68] In August, Stephens restarted his career with MI5 and was whisked off to the West African coast where he worked as a liaison officer until his retirement in 1960; he had attained the honorary rank of brigadier.[69] In Germany, the No. 74 Combined Services Detailed Interrogation Centre at Bad Nenndorf was replaced with the No. 10 Disposal Centre, and revised regulations were introduced to safeguard against any repeat of the crimes disclosed in the three court martial trials. Some improvements certainly were implemented, although it is startling to discover that eleven of the eighteen interrogators employed at No. 10 Disposal Centre in 1948 had previously worked at No. 74 CSDIC.[70] Remarkably, German newspapers featured a number of positive appraisals: *Die Zeit* considered the very existence of the trials to be a triumph for democracy and a process that revealed what had gone on at Bad Nenndorf.[71]

Meanwhile, former detainees who sought compensation from the British authorities received short shrift. In March 1948 the wife of Ernest Fallen de Droog, a former inmate at Bad Nenndorf, wrote to the Foreign Office to demand recompense for her husband's brutal treatment and the loss of his personal belongings.[72] De Droog was a veteran of the Spanish Civil War and a long-time intelligence asset who worked for the British between 1938 and 1941 before he was suspected of defecting.[73] In 1945 he was arrested and spent four months at Bad Nenndorf, where no evidence was found to support the accusation that he was a traitor. De Droog would spend the next seven and a half months in Rotenburg Hospital with neuritis and post-traumatic epilepsy. When he was asked to assess de Droog's claim for compensation, a Control Commission official concluded that it was 'difficult to say whether the four months he spent in Bad Nenndorf were entirely responsible for his "moral and physical ruin"'.[74] It was further alleged that the man's wife was simply seeking to take advantage of the press attention given to Bad Nenndorf and concluded that there was no cause for further action.[75] In private correspondence, officials lamented how British prisoners who had suffered at the hands of the Nazis had received no compensation. Others worried that accepting the claim would set a dangerous precedent: 'In my opinion, once we have paid compensation to one recent inmate of Bad Nenndorf, we shall get a flood of demands for compensation.'[76]

The Bad Nenndorf trials had briefly hit the headlines, but the secrets of Britain's expansive intelligence networks remained largely hidden from public view. It would be several decades before the torture camp at the heart of the British Zone was finally exposed. Instead, as the Cold War came into view, successive governments came to accept SIS and MI5 as vital components of the British state. In Germany, intelligence had become an essential front line in the fight against the Soviet Union. Over time, the nation's spooks were increasingly valued as a means of maintaining Britain's power on the world stage, not least because of the relative inexperience of the Americans in this arena: the CIA was founded only in 1947. The lack of outcry over the crimes committed at Bad Nenndorf was mainly a product of the British government's use of legal loopholes to hide the truth from public view. But it was also, in part, down to a quirk of historical timing: just as Robin 'Tin Eye' Stephens was taking the stand, events in Berlin had captured the world's attention.

23

Berlin

In late June 1948 Don Bradman was batting at Lord's for the final time in his illustrious cricketing career. It was a fine summer's day and, after England only narrowly avoided the follow-on that morning, the game was Australia's for the taking. In the session after lunch, Bradman and Barnes built a 174-run partnership, the kind befitting a team that would become known as 'The Invincibles'. Australia went on to win the series 4–0. About 500 miles away, Pip Coan was on board a Dakota transport plane flying from Wunstorf in the British Zone of occupied Germany to Berlin.[1] At the end of the war, Coan had decided to stay on in the army, and had recently taken a Regular Officers course with the Royal Army Service Corps at Blandford Camp in Dorset. In anticipation of his subsequent posting, he left his pregnant wife and young child under the temporary care of his brother in London. Then, with only a single day's notice, Coan was unexpectedly called to the German capital – and his family was not allowed to join him.

Soviet troops had stopped all British, French and American traffic by road, rail and canals into the German capital, which, although divided between the four Allied powers, was situated deep inside the Soviet Zone. In the summer of 1945, the Western Allies had failed to secure in writing any specific rights of access to Berlin and now found themselves in a weak position, legally and materially.[2] The British quickly launched Operation Knicker to temporarily supply the cut-off BAOR garrison in the city through an airlift, while the politicians worked out a long-term solution.

Pip Coan immediately set off from London Liverpool Street on a train to Harwich and, from there, a transport ship sailing to the British Zone. As the most junior officer on board, he was quickly designated 'baggage officer' – in his recollections, he suggests 'regimental mule' might have been more appropriate. When he finally reached Germany, Coan made his way to the RAF base at Wunstorf in Lower Saxony where he boarded a Dakota headed for Gatow, Berlin. Owing to the roar of the plane's twin propeller engines, the pilot suggested he move up towards the cockpit and listen to the radio. As he approached, Coan could make out the distinctive Hampshire burr of the BBC's cricket commentator, John Arlott: '... meanwhile, the Don bats on'. As Australia continued to pile on the runs in front of nearly 30,000 spectators at Lord's, no one, least of all Pip Coan, could predict how events would unfold in the German capital. Was this the start of another war?

*

Tensions between the Soviet Union and the Western Allies had been growing steadily since the end of the war and were felt both at a diplomatic level and in Germany itself. In early 1948, as the Cold War came into full view, it was palpable to everyone that the uneasy peace which had existed in the last few years was precarious. An anti-communist position was now well established within the highest ranks of the British military and government, not least in Bevin's Foreign Office. In the Zone itself, Brian Robertson, who had succeeded Sholto Douglas as commander-in-chief in November 1947, articulated this new, aggressive posturing at a dinner with his French and American counterparts in April 1948: 'if we keep on talking indefinitely', he warned, 'we might wake up some fine morning to find the Hammer and Sickle already on the Rhine'.[3]

In March 1948 Mary Bouman wrote home from Germany and reported that the 'political situation at the moment seems fraught with ominous possibilities'.[4] Later that month, the Soviets announced the first restrictions on military and passenger traffic between Berlin and the Western zones. It was an attempt to pressure the Allies to retreat from their ambitious plans for the reconstruction of western Germany. Then, on 1 April, Soviet guards halted two American trains, headed for the German capital, at Helmstedt, just inside the British Zone. They demanded to search the trains and check travellers' documents, but Allied officers refused and a standoff ensued. Jean Eastham, a member of the ATS and part of the British garrison in Berlin, was on board and remembers being taken along with some officers to a nearby villa: 'We were given a meal then we were put on three buses and taken to the Autobahn where they kept us waiting for another three hours. Finally, they let us through but they wouldn't release the truck with our kit so we arrived without our luggage. It was all very exciting.'[5]

This was the beginning of the April Crisis, or the Little Airlift, when Soviet officials made periodic alterations to the Allied access arrangements for Berlin – and in the process created intermittent moments of chaos. The British immediately halted all train journeys and opted instead to bring in passengers and supplies by air. In response, the Soviet air force began sporadically intercepting British planes mid-flight, flying intentionally close to impede their path, a tactic known to military pilots as 'buzzing'. On 5 April a British European Airways Viking aircraft was flying between London and Berlin with a stop in Hamburg. This was a commercial flight, with ten passengers and four crew on board, most of whom were civilians.[6] As the airliner reached Berlin in the early afternoon, it descended to around 1,000 feet, made a gentle left-hand turn, and prepared its landing gear for touchdown. Then, seemingly out of nowhere, a Soviet Yak-3 fighter aircraft appeared from behind and, according to eyewitnesses, dived beneath the unwieldy passenger airliner before climbing sharply. At the midpoint of this bold manoeuvre, the Yak's starboard wing clipped the port wing of the Viking, which caused both to break off. The two planes crashed. There were no survivors in the 'Gatow air disaster'.

It was the kind of accident that could easily have turned simmering tensions into all-out warfare. This was certainly on the minds of some back in London, including Winston Churchill. According to the American ambassador, Britain's wartime leader was convinced that the US should exploit their monopoly over atomic weapons: 'He believes that now is the time, promptly, to tell the Soviets that if they do not retire from Berlin and abandon eastern Germany, withdrawing to the Polish frontier, we will raze their cities. It is further his view that we cannot appease, conciliate or provoke the Soviets; that the only vocabulary they understand is force.'[7] The rhetoric was eerily similar to that used in relation to Germany only years earlier.

From the Americans came a more restrained, but still potentially inflammatory, plan to break through the Soviet blockade by force. The military governor of the US Zone, General Lucius D. Clay, proposed an Anglo-American convoy of tanks, troops and lorries that would push past the Soviet border guards on the roads into Berlin.[8] Yet his British counterpart, Brian Robertson, warned that just a handful of Russian tanks could block their path – or even instigate a shooting match which an exposed convoy of British and American soldiers would have little hope of winning.

Instead, it was the British who led the way in the developing crisis over access to Berlin. In the first place, Attlee and his cabinet established three guiding principles: to maintain the Western position in the German capital, to keep the peace, and to hold firm with the implementation of the London Programme. This approach ruled out abandoning Berlin but also any acts of aggression that might start a war. It also limited the likelihood of successful negotiations, considering that the Soviets were wholly committed to stopping the Western plans for the reconstruction of Germany. In the following weeks, as intermittent disruptions continued and both sides seemed no closer to compromise, the crisis gained momentum. Mary Bouman wrote once more to her parents, lamenting the anxiety that stalked everyone in Germany: 'I suppose it is too much to expect to be able to live a decent quiet existence in these times.'[9]

Then, in June, events in Berlin escalated with unnerving speed. On 16 June the Soviet representative walked out of the city's governing body, the Allied Kommandatura. It was a piece of political theatre that signalled the resolve of the Soviets to stand firm. The following evening, Private Chris Howland was finishing his shift at the British Forces Network radio station* in Hamburg when two British military policemen appeared.[10] They handed him a sealed envelope and informed him that they would all be staying in the studio until the following morning, when he would be asked to read its contents over the radio at 6:30 a.m. during the *Wakey-Wakey* show. A bemused Howland waited all night and then announced to his audience news of a currency reform. The Deutsche Mark (DM) would become legal tender across the British, French and American zones in just three days' time, rendering all previous currency invalid. This would pave the way towards a more stable economy and assist ambitious reconstruction plans.[11] On 20 July all Germans would be able to exchange 65 Reichsmark (RM) for 40 DM at ration card-issuing offices and, a month later, 60 RM for another 20 DM. But beyond this first 60 DM allocation, the old currency became more or less worthless: 1,000 RM was worth only 65 DM. The reform essentially wiped out all public and private debt overnight – as well as the black market. On the eve of the currency exchange, a group of forty men paraded at Cologne Central Station with a placard that read 'RETRAINING FOR BLACK MARKET TRADERS'.[12]

The currency reform was a provocative move that inevitably angered the Soviets. They had not been informed of a change which risked a wave of inflation in the Soviet Zone, where the old German currency remained legal tender. Over the course of the next few days, the Soviet authorities rushed to introduce a new currency of their own, colloquially known as the 'Ostmark'. But, more significantly, the USSR instigated a series of retaliatory

---

* While the channel catered to the British occupiers, its music selections (mainly British chart hits) were very popular with German audiences. Howland would later briefly host a German-language show on Nordwestdeutscher Rundfunk.

actions that came to a head on 24 June when all rail, road and water connections into Berlin from the Western zones were entirely and conclusively cut. It was the beginning of the Berlin Blockade.

To regain access to the city, the Western Allies were invited to negotiate with the Soviet Union, who proposed the resumption of four-power control over Germany in preparation for a new unified German government and the eventual withdrawal of the occupiers.[13] As far as the British and Americans were concerned, this offer was a blatant attempt to undermine the Western Union and perhaps even usher in a communist Germany.[14] The final hopes of a diplomatic solution were dashed.

While American policymakers and military commanders were as yet undecided on the best course of action, it was again left to the British to spearhead the Western response. Foreign Secretary Bevin and his military advisors in the Zone pushed for an ambitious airlift, to supply not only the Western garrisons in Berlin, but the people of the city too.[15] It was a monumental undertaking, something that had never been attempted on such a scale; many feared it would fail. Yet without any obvious alternatives and few diplomatic channels still open, the British and Americans had to chance their arm – and their airmen. On 26 June the first transport aircraft carrying supplies for Berliners took off and within days scores of British troops, including Pip Coan, were put to work.

Bevin appeared in the House of Commons where he defiantly announced to the cheers of both benches that the British intended to maintain supply routes into the German capital: 'We recognize that as a result of these decisions a grave situation might arise. Should such a situation arise, we shall ask the House to face it. His Majesty's Government and the Western Allies can see no alternative between that and surrender, and none of us can accept surrender.'[16] The Americans were also increasingly bombastic, promising resources to step up the airlift while making it abundantly clear that the Western powers were no longer willing to negotiate. In a clear signal of intent, the British government accepted an offer to accommodate a fleet of American heavy bombers in Britain, and in mid-July two groups of B-29s arrived.[17] It was a bold act of military posturing: these were the same class of aircraft that had dropped atomic bombs on Japan.[18] A few days later, Mary Bouman wrote a letter from the British Zone once again, the tenor of her correspondence growing more anxious by the day: 'most people seem to think there will have to be a show-down in the not too distant future'.[19]

*

Remarkably, all-out war was averted. Rather, over the course of the next thirteen months, thousands of British, American and German men and women worked around the clock to supply the Western sectors of Berlin by air. In raw terms, it was an astonishing achievement: more than 266,000 flights brought 2.25 million tons of supplies of food, fuel, newsprint and more.[20] By the summer of 1949, a plane was landing or taking off every sixty seconds and more than 8,000 tons of supplies were brought in each day – far exceeding the 5,620 tons estimated as a minimum for the city's 2.25 million inhabitants.

But things weren't always so efficient. In the early days, the airlift was marked by chaos as pilots, planes, loaders, air traffic controllers and the whole assemblage of support staff scrambled into action. On his first night on duty, pilot Dickie Arscott slept on a billiards table, and Francis Daw had to make do with the floor at RAF Wunstorf.[21] But there were more serious concerns too: in those first few weeks pilots often found flight plans to be disordered and mismanaged. Only strict air corridors were available to British and American planes, but there was little clarity on the regulations and technical details of flying in such a narrow area of sky. It was some time before strict rules over altitudes, turning points and communications allowed for a more orderly convoy of planes. Even the official report on the airlift noted that 'it is not derogatory to state that the first phases of the mission were marked with a high degree of confusion in the handling of air traffic'.[22] Even as things improved, there was nothing that could stop the occasional accident: 101 servicemen died during the Berlin Airlift, 40 of whom were British.

The British flew most of their planes from a former Luftwaffe air base at Wunstorf, near Hanover, to the airfield at Gatow in south-western Berlin.[23] It was a forty-five-minute trip each way. The pilots received a weather briefing prior to take-off: good conditions in Berlin meant three-minute intervals between planes, and five minutes if the visibility was poor. Upon arrival, planes were guided in by ground-controlled approach, a relatively new radar-based technology. There was no room for error and no space for second tries. If a pilot missed their slot, they simply turned back or, if necessary, made an emergency landing at a nearby relief airfield.

Then it was time for men like Pip Coan to get to work. He was an airstrip officer at Gatow and oversaw the monumental ground operation required to offload planes and have them back in the air as soon as possible.[24] While pilots nipped into the Malcolm

An RAF ground crew loads spare wheels onto a Dakota transport
aircraft during the Berlin Airlift.

Club for a cup of coffee, Coan, along with his teams of German labourers and British soldiers, moved supplies onto lorries, then into hangars and, finally, into the city itself. Supplies ranged from sacks of coal and tinned food to Volkswagen cars and, on one occasion, an entire baker's oven. Even faced with such awkward loads, by July 1949 the average ground time in Berlin was just thirty-two minutes per plane.[25]

It was exhausting work for everyone involved and downtime was much sought after No. 99 Squadron RAF pilot, Bob Cherry, recalls that the mess at Wunstorf was open 24/7, with tired pilots and navigators enjoying a tipple at all times of the day alongside a post-operational meal of eggs and bacon.[26] On occasion, longer periods of leave allowed for a trip home to see family or a night out in Hanover with members of the Control Commission, whom Cherry remembers as living 'like fighting cocks'. But for members of the CCG and Rhine Army actually based in Berlin, gone were the luxuries of the occupier: these months were spent eating liver, smoked haddock and canned food as, unlike the Americans, the British were provided with the same rations as German civilians.[27] According to one member of the garrison, invitations to dinner at an American mess became a much sought-after commodity.

The difficulties of an airlift on such a grand scale were not lost on British commanders, who, behind the scenes, drew up a series of evacuation plans for the Britons based in the German capital. 'Operation Pickle', which had subsidiary plans entitled 'Operation Pickle Cabbage' and 'Operation Pickle Onion', was part of the broader – and altogether more serious sounding – 'Operation Chivalrous'.[28] In the aftermath of the sudden withdrawal from India, British officers in Germany set to work compiling detailed lists of the service personnel and their family members, and identifying those who would need housing or medical assistance.[29] These plans remained top secret: the occupiers did not want to cause alarm with any hint that the Allies were planning to leave.[30] Yet there were some evacuations: 15,000 German children and sickly Berliners were brought out of the city in British planes.

In the end, there was no need for any major divergence from the strategy adopted in the summer of 1948. Faced with innumerable hurdles, not least the challenge of supplying Berlin through the winter, British and American pilots performed admirably. In May 1949, as it became clear that the Western powers would not be forced to withdraw from Berlin, the Soviets lifted the blockade. While the airlift technically continued until August and built up the city's surplus in case of future action, the first great confrontation of the Cold War was over.

*

The Berlin Airlift was a great victory for the Western powers, especially in public relations terms: the British and Americans had stood firm in the face of apparent Soviet aggression and come out on top. At the same time, it was now clearer than ever that the Americans would take the lead in European affairs. The British, through a combination of soft power diplomacy and anti-Soviet posturing, had navigated a way through the assorted crises of the early Cold War. But now they were destined to take a step back as the two superpowers confronted one another across the continent – and the entire world.

In Britain, the press and newsreels enthusiastically adopted the anti-Soviet outlook of leading politicians and military leaders. There was no longer any patience for wartime sympathy towards the Red Army, who was now firmly recast as the enemy and a great threat to the peace.[31] But what did it all mean for the future of Germany? For the Western powers, the path was now clear: their focus shifted from the historic 'German Problem' to the Cold War. With the Potsdam Agreement finally and conclusively cast aside, it was time to complete the work of the London Programme. A new West German state would soon come into being, a political and economic bulwark against the Soviet Union. Its creation represented a complete shift in thinking about Germany. A country long condemned as a malign force at the heart of Europe was now suddenly hailed as an ally in the fight against communism. This was realpolitik at its most blatant, an act of political convenience which required a complete about-turn in British foreign policy and rowed back on years of state-led anti-German propaganda.

In December 1948 Attlee's cabinet approved a new set of policies that would end the occupation. In the short term, demilitarization and reparations, in the form of dismantling factories and military installations, were to continue. Furthermore, under the terms of the 'Ruhr Statute', Europe's industrial heartland would be put under international supervision. But the formal structures of the military government were to be disassembled and replaced with a military security board and the Allied High Commission, both working under the terms of the Occupation Statute. This meant that the Western Allies could intervene in matters of foreign policy, trade and constitutional conventions if and when required. The settlement also allowed for British, American and French troops to remain in West Germany. Otherwise, however, the Germans would be free to run their own affairs as a sovereign nation.

Yet this total transformation of Britain's policy towards Germany was not absorbed and accepted unanimously by the British media and public. While the Berlin Airlift might have helped shift opinion on the Soviet Union, it did little to revise long-held views on the Germans.[32] As would become clear in the final year of the occupation, many in Britain viewed the rapid resurrection of West Germany with a great deal of scepticism and, in some cases, outright fear.

24

Don't Let's Be Beastly
to the British

In April 1949 the *Daily Mail*'s reporter Tom Pocock reported his astonishment at the evening entertainment offered at a 'smart Hamburg restaurant where no Briton can afford to eat'.[1] The well-fed diners were said to be laughing and slapping their thighs along to the resident choir, who had a new twist on an old classic: 'Don't Let's Be Beastly to the British'. This Coward-inspired song was, at least according to Pocock, a fair reflection of the changes that had taken place in recent months – the Germans, he lamented, knew that the British were 'no longer capable of being beastly to them'. If there was any doubt in the minds of readers, Pocock went on to describe his meeting with a local businessman of 'the type that put Hitler into power'. The unnamed man was said to have spurned the journalist's offer of a British cigarette and opted instead to smoke his own cigar. If that wasn't symbolic enough, he went on to explain that while four years ago the Germans had no hope, now things were very different: 'My country is rising again – more fast than you know. Your country is going down. We Germans will be masters of Europe again in twenty years'.

This was most likely a fanciful or at least exaggerated account designed to arouse the ire of British readers enduring yet another year of austerity while they heard murmurings of an impending 'economic miracle' in Germany. But fabricated or not, Pocock's account reflects British anxieties about Germany's apparent resurgence. Since 1947, British and American policymakers had pursued policies with the aim of rapidly rebuilding the country's economy and establishing a new sovereign West German state. It was a momentous step, coming only two years after the beginning of an occupation that many in Britain had expected to last for several decades.

It wasn't long before food rations grew and goods flooded the shops. After several years of crippling shortages and deprivation in the Zone, things were undoubtedly looking up for most Germans. But not everyone in Britain was feeling quite so optimistic. While British and American pilots were working night and day to supply beleaguered Berliners with food and coal, Britain once again erupted into a civil war of words over the future of Germany. Three of the country's most popular newspapers, the *Daily Mail*, the *Daily Express* and the *Daily Mirror*, greeted the prospect of Germany's revival as a threat. In time, even some of the country's more highbrow publications, including the *Manchester Guardian*, *The Times* and the *Daily Telegraph*, succumbed to similarly Germanophobic rhetoric.

At the root of these anxieties stood the problematic legacy of the Allied occupation itself, which came under scrutiny as it came to an end. By now, official policy towards Germany had shifted from retribution to rapprochement, thereby implicitly declaring the occupation to have been a success. Yet much of the British press, including many prominent opinion-formers, had come to the opposite conclusion: it seemed as if the military government had achieved little beyond diminishing Britain's reputation on the world stage. As the Control Commission was handing over the reins of power, widespread doubts remained as to whether the British had indeed 'won the peace'.

*

In the summer of 1948, the authorization of higher industrial output, combined with the introduction of a functioning currency, the implementation of tax reform, and the curtailment of certain price and consumption controls, reinvigorated the economy of the Western zones.[2] That year also saw the introduction of the Marshall Plan, which brought with it a supply of credit and, more importantly, stability to the West German economy.[3] Now, the once-pervasive black market gradually disappeared, absenteeism dropped dramatically and shops filled up with consumer goods.

But just as British policymakers were moving full-steam ahead with economic reconstruction, a remnant from the summer of 1945 reared its head and exposed many of the wider public's anxieties about Germany. At Potsdam, dismantling had been devised as a means of acquiring reparations in kind while simultaneously reducing Germany's industrial and military potential.[4] As early as 1946 the removal of industrial capacity and the loss of jobs at a time of widespread shortages provoked an incensed reaction in Germany, prompted criticism from the country's emerging political leaders and even led to a number of strikes at factories targeted for demolition.[5] In Britain, representatives of the 'soft peace' lobby denounced dismantling as a policy first and foremost about vengeance.[6] In November 1947 the *Manchester Guardian* published a letter from Victor Gollancz and Labour MP Richard Stokes in which they described the policy as a 'crime against humanity'.[7]

Very little dismantling had actually been carried out in the British Zone before 1948.[8] But perversely enough it was then, just as the Western Allies were commencing West German industrial reconstruction, that dismantling efforts were finally stepped up – with official support continuing largely unabated for the next two years. By the end of 1949, more than 600 industrial installations had been dismantled across the three Western zones.[9] It was an obviously contradictory position that stemmed primarily from Anglo-American assent to French demands for the inhibition of Germany's military potential.[10] This burst of dismantling set the stage for a renewed series of German protests that would cast a shadow over the final months of the occupation.[11] For the teams of dismantlers, both British and German, obstruction, verbal abuse and physical attacks quickly became a regular occurrence, necessitating the provision of armed troops to oversee operations.[12] The occupation authorities grew increasingly uneasy and publicly warned that 'resistance against dismantling workers is resistance against a military government order'.[13] In a number of cases, German workers who refused to complete their allotted tasks were hauled off to British military government courts.

In turn, these protests provoked an incensed response in many of the British papers. 'Ruhr Workers Defy British', ran the *Express* in January 1949. It claimed that German workers who didn't disobey orders were branded 'traitors of the Reich' and 'British lackeys' by their compatriots.[14] According to an editorial in *The Times*, dismantling had opened up the Germans to 'irresponsible demagogy'.[15] By June 1949 even the *Manchester Guardian* saw cause for concern: an editorial suggested that German opposition to a policy earnestly endeavouring to safeguard Europe stemmed from political manipulation of renascent nationalism.[16] The letters pages of *The Times* even threatened a return to the antagonistic debates over the 'German Problem'. Journalist and writer Stuart R. de la Mahotière wrote passionately in support of dismantling. He argued that the Germans were 'clever propagandists' with 'insidious' arguments who attempted to 'befog our reason with sentiment, as they did after the First World War'.[17] He even suggested that the German people's agitation against dismantling was only the first step towards another attempt to conquer Europe. It was rhetoric unambiguously reminiscent of *Black Record*, and, fittingly, it incited a response from Victor Gollancz, who once again attacked the dismantling policy as an unfair attempt to impede the German recovery.[18]

*

The disagreements about dismantling were by no means the only example of the British media's growing anxiety over Germany's economic recovery. In the first months of 1949, the press sounded repeated warnings that German industry in the British Zone was indeed getting 'back on its feet', which prompted fears over revived competition. In January, Brian Connell, writing in the *Daily Mail*, suggested that 'the German drive to balance her economy and recapture her export markets is going to cause Great Britain a lot of trouble'.[19] In the paper's editorial, 'Made in Germany', Frank Owen struck a similar tone:

For more than three and a half years Britain has had a good run as the leading industrial nation outside the United States. Germany and Japan, her two biggest pre-war trade competitors, were down and out... But now the horizon is no longer clear. Another sun is rising – or re-rising, Germany, our formidable former enemy, is beginning to emerge again as a no less formidable trade competitor.[20]

Owen even went on to wonder whether Germany's revitalized economy would once again facilitate a political and military resurgence, as had happened in the aftermath of the First World War:

If the recovery of German industry means the recovery of German war power, it would be a matter for the Military Security Board, who should not neglect it. The Western Allies should keep a wary eye on Germany – remembering that forewarned is forearmed.

The following month, trade union leaders and manufacturers publicly censured the Attlee government for allowing allegedly 'unfair' trade methods to persist in the Western zones.[21] They suggested that American subsidization of the German economy, coupled with artificially low labour costs, threatened British prospects on the world market. That Britain was also benefitting hugely from the Marshall Plan – it eventually pocketed the biggest share of any European nation – was conspicuously absent from this analysis. Nevertheless, these complaints were eventually voiced in the Commons, where President of the Board of Trade Harold Wilson and the foreign secretary both sought to reassure business and union leaders that Germany would be stopped from 'muscling in' on British export markets.[22] At the same time, Deputy President of the Board of Trade John Edwards downplayed the threat of a German speed-up by claiming that 'unfair competition' was 'not yet a serious menace'.[23]

Such reassurances did little to halt the tide of unease at the news from western Germany. The ever popular newsreels continued to document with a sense of foreboding the restoration of German cities, the success of the currency reform and the revival of industry.[24] In June 1949 a *Pathé News* film entitled *'Made In Germany' – Out to Capture World Market* highlighted Hamburg's trade fair as proof that 'German industry has almost completed its comeback'.[25] It reported that 'Germany's varied products today challenge British goods all over the world', with the two countries clashing 'head on' in their export trade. The examples of optical lenses and cameras were used to illustrate an area were German firms now dominated a formerly British market: 'Germany's dilemma today is Britain's danger signal tomorrow'.

If these concerns over the future of international trade and Britain's competitiveness on the world market were somewhat abstract, they were complemented with more concrete appeals to the common man – and in the 1940s, nothing was more compelling than food. In 1949 news reached British shores that the Germans were enjoying an abundance of luxurious meals, complete with fine wines, fresh vegetables, piles of meat and more – and, as we've heard, maybe even singing along to anti-British songs. In March, David Walker described his experience of Düsseldorf in the *Daily Mirror*: he reported that the locals could choose between steak and eggs, sausages, Hungarian goulash, fresh onions or turtle soup, all with generous helpings of beer, cigarettes and whisky.[26] In June, the experiences of the *Daily Express*'s science reporter, Chapman Pincher, received mention in the paper's editorial.[27] After he arrived in Munich, a banking error forced him to live 'as a German' and use local currency rather than service vouchers. Chapman, preparing to 'rough it', was astonished to find 'a menu fifteen inches deep, with a choice of ninety-three separate dishes' in the crowded Humplmayr's restaurant. It included twenty-one meat courses, such as a gigantic porterhouse steak that would have counted as a British family's fortnightly meat ration. This was in 'Hitler's own city', which had been 'ruined and conquered just four years ago'.

The same month, Bill Arthur visited Cologne and presented a goading picture of Germany's allegedly newfound extravagance and luxury to the *Mirror*'s readership.[28] Arthur, a businessman by trade, had visited his long-term friend Wilhelm Schmidt several times since 1945 and, as had become customary, carefully prepared a selection of groceries to help Schmidt and his wife, Elli, make ends meet. This time, however, he was greeted with laughter: '"Food for me?" he said, "listen, I will show you something. We have everything. Just you come and eat with us Germans." And from then on, I did – and I mean EAT.' There were, Arthur reported, grand portions of steak, pork chops, fish, eggs, trays loaded with Havana cigars, and cigarettes, as much butter as you pleased – the options were apparently endless: 'many Germans that I saw are eating well. The food is there for them – if they work. And the factories are open from 7 a.m. till 6 p.m. They're working like beavers. The shops have chocolate, sweets, cream cakes and other luxuries. I even saw nylons. In my 1,350-mile tour I found post-war Germany flowing with milk and honey.' It was now Arthur who was expecting delivery of a food package from his German friend upon his arrival back in austerity-hit Britain. He even planned to return to Germany with his wife to provide her with 'a good square meal'. The article, complete with a Bismarckian caricature of an overindulgent German, struck at the heart of British anxieties about having lost the peace: the tables had turned and now it was the beleaguered British who apparently needed saving from undernourishment.

Later that year, a story of administrative oversight corroborated these exact fears. The Ministry of Food, in recognition of the food gifts sent to Britain from America and elsewhere in the preceding years, decided to stamp all international letters with 'Thank You for Food Gifts'. Unthinkingly, this gesture of appreciation was also included on the many thousands of letters sent to the British Zone of occupied Germany. This was, of course, entirely misleading – the British government had spent millions providing food for the German people since 1945 and had certainly not received food gifts *from* Germany. It produced a misunderstanding that Conservative MP John Boyd-Carpenter even voiced in a Commons debate: 'For all our troubles and difficulties we are still a great power with a great responsibility in the world, and to see our country, even though in a trifling thing, appearing to demean itself in the eyes of those with whom recently we were at war and over whom we were victorious, seems to be a wrong thing to do.'[29] Likewise, a number of local newspapers picked up on the story, including the *Hull Daily Mail*, whose editorial pessimistically described the 'ironic transformation' which now saw Germany sending 'hungry Britain' food parcels.[30] It was an utterly false claim, but, as they say, when the legend becomes fact, print the legend: this particular interpretation of events clearly struck a chord with the country's prevailing self-critical mood.

25

A Fourth Reich?

On 6 October 1945 a civilian car under military police escort pulled up to a smart set of modernist office buildings in the centre of Cologne. From one of the upper window ledges an enormous Union Jack flag extended out over the street below and shadowed a large white billboard that read 'HEADQUARTERS MILITARY GOVERNMENT – Regierungsbezirk Köln'.[1] A German man in his late sixties stepped out of the car and made his way up to a room on the third floor. Inside, he was met by a line of three officers from the British military government, each in their khaki uniform and accompanying leather Sam Browne belt. On his left sat Colin Lawson, acting commander of Cologne; on the right, Colonel Charrington; and in the centre, Brigadier John Barraclough, military governor of the entire North Rhine province. There was no preamble, no handshake, no trace of politeness. Rather, as the man peered around the room looking for a seat, the moustachioed Brigadier Barraclough simply bellowed: 'REMAIN STANDING'.

Without a moment's pause, the brigadier began reading in English from the short memorandum that lay before him, while after each passage an interpreter translated the words into German:

I am not satisfied with the progress which has been made in Cologne in connection with the repair of buildings and the clearance of the streets and the general task of preparing for the coming winter... with proper supervision and energy on your part, more could have been done to deal with these problems than has, in fact, been done... In my opinion you have failed in your duty to the people of Cologne.[2]

The man remained emotionless, staring blankly and silently with his hands clasped as the brigadier continued: 'You are therefore dismissed to-day from your appointment as *Oberbürgermeister* ('mayor') of Cologne... you will leave Cologne as soon as possible... you will take no further part in the administration or public life of Cologne or any other part of the North Rhine Province... You will not indulge either directly or indirectly in any political activity whatever'. When Barraclough had finished, he pushed the letter across the desk. While still standing, the man silently reached inside his jacket, retrieved a fountain pen and leant over to sign his name: 'Konrad Adenauer'.

In the hectic days of spring 1945, American soldiers had liberated Cologne and set about installing German civilians they deemed trustworthy, reliably anti-Nazi and, above all, capable into positions of municipal power. All across the country, people with local experience and know-how were urgently needed to help restore some semblance of stability, from clearing streets to repairing power supplies. In this instance, word reached the approaching Americans of an ambitious and energetic politician named Adenauer. As a member of the pre-war Catholic Centre Party, he had been *Oberbürgermeister* between 1917 and 1933 before being dismissed as Hitler took power. There was no questioning his political credentials: during the Third Reich, Adenauer had kept a low profile and was still arrested twice as an opponent of the Nazi regime. By the war's end, he was the obvious choice to oversee Cologne's reconstruction and returned to the mayoralty in the weeks before the British military government formally took control of the city.

It was the second time Konrad Adenauer had dealt with a British occupation. As mayor after the First World War, he had come under the direction of the first British Army of the Rhine – a legacy that would contribute directly to his downfall. In July 1945 General Charles Ferguson, a retired veteran of that military government, wrote a scathing memorandum for the Control Commission:

> He gave no trouble whatever, and carried out our orders without question and with efficiency. His demeanour was stiff (as was ours) and correct – but he made no pretence of anything but hatred of the British. He would carry out the orders, he said, because there was nothing else to be done, but we must not imagine that it was from any loyalty to or affection for us – 'We will never forget. If it takes us five or ten or fifty years, we will never rest until we get our revenge' – This outburst came more than once, when on some occasion his feelings got the better of his discretion. I am certain that this was genuinely his real attitude towards us, and that he hated us with intense bitterness.[3]

In early October, Brigadier John Barraclough, the senior officer in the area, decided to act and ordered British military police to 'produce' Adenauer.[4] They tracked him down to the outskirts of Remagen and escorted Adenauer's car back to Cologne, where he was unceremoniously given his marching orders. This was something of a surprise: Adenauer did, after all, hold the level of popular support required for the job and there was no doubting his anti-Nazi convictions. Above all, he had the experience and political acumen needed to help the battered city of Cologne through what was sure to be a difficult winter.

The official file on the matter offers few concrete reasons as to why Barraclough made the call, only the generic language of government bureaucracy justifying his dismissal on operational grounds. General Ferguson's rather far-fetched accusations offer some of the only clues as to why the British turned on Adenauer so decisively. But was the word of a retired general really enough to warrant the removal of a respected politician at a time of great uncertainty? Rather, it seems highly likely that Ferguson's memorandum was commissioned in order to hide the real reasons for Adenauer's dismissal: a personal animosity on behalf of Barraclough as well as a growing anxiety over the mayor's apparent willingness to talk back. In the weeks prior, Barraclough had openly complained about Adenauer's requests for more coal and building materials to help the civilian population. There also may have been political interference: Adenauer, once of the Centre Party and now a leading figure in the newly founded CDU, was firmly of the political centre-right. Leading Labour politicians in Britain may well have favoured the advancement of their social democratic allies in the Social Democratic Party (Sozialdemokratische Partei Deutschlands, SPD), and perhaps even ordered Adenauer's dismissal from London.

For whatever reason, at the start of October the British not only removed Adenauer from office but also banned him from all political activity and prohibited him from entering the city. Barraclough even rejected a request for an exemption on the grounds that Adenauer's wife, Auguste, was undergoing regular treatment for a serious illness at a Cologne hospital.[5] 'If we give permission to Adenauer to come in with his wife', wrote the brigadier, 'we shall find that the lady required medical attention five days out of six'.[6] It was only when she was later admitted to hospital and described as 'dangerously ill' – as a result of complications from a suicide attempt in 1944 while under Gestapo imprisonment – that the British finally relented.[7]

It was obvious to many of Barraclough's colleagues that he had made a grave and vindictive error. Lieutenant-Colonel Alan Prior, a senior commander in Cologne, returned from his honeymoon to news of Adenauer's dismissal and was enraged. A few days later he confronted Barraclough at a drinks party held at the Villa Hügel: 'You really are a stupid man. You know nothing of civil affairs or the conduct of politics. You have performed the most incredibly stupid act against a man who before Hitler stood high among German politicians. You are unfit for your job.'[8] It was the end of Lieutenant-Colonel Prior's army career. However, in something of a tacit acknowledgement of their error, the military government withdrew the order banning Adenauer from political activity two months later. But he never did return to his position as mayor. Much bigger plans were afoot.

*

From 1946 onwards there had been a gradual shift towards the restoration of political institutions in the Western zones. British and American administrators held the first local elections that same year, as democratic forms were gradually reintroduced. The Western powers licensed political parties, excluding those on the far right, and the political scene that emerged was not hugely dissimilar to elsewhere in Europe: two workers parties, the socialist SPD and the Communist Party of Germany (KPD), faced off against the bourgeois parties, most prominent of whom were the CDU and the Free Democratic Party (Freie Demokratische Partei, FDP).[9]

The two main parties had considerably contrasting ties to the pre-war era. For the SPD, membership and party structures were resurrected from the Weimar Republic.[10] On the other hand, the CDU, along with its Bavarian sister party, the CSU (Christlich-Soziale Union, Christian Social Union), was an entirely new political formation: a united Christian party from the political middle ground.[11] Its development stemmed from the complicity of the Protestant and Catholic parties during the rise of the Nazi Party and consigned the once-powerful Catholic Centre Party to the dustbin of history.

Likewise, the political ideologies of the two major forces in West German politics were markedly different. In the Western zones the SPD became an anti-communist social democratic force, much like Attlee's Labour Party.[12] The party's new leader, Kurt Schumacher, had spent ten years in a Nazi concentration camp and now harboured hopes for a new social democratic German state.[13] He advocated for the nationalization of the Ruhr industries and a break with capitalism in favour of economic planning. Conversely, the CDU's political programme was less clear-cut. In time, it would adopt the social market economy (*soziale Marktwirtschaft*) developed by the future minister of economic affairs (and future

West German chancellor) Ludwig Erhard – which rejected the class divisions that had long defined European politics and openly embraced capitalism.[14]

In the four years since his dismissal, Adenauer had become leader of the nascent CDU and helped turn it into a powerful political machine. Adenauer's reputation reached beyond Cologne and he became nationally renowned for his hard work, energy and unquestionable political instincts.[15] In the summer of 1948, he was made chairman of the Parliamentary Council that drafted West Germany's new constitution, the *Grundgesetz für die Bundesrepublik Deutschland* ('the Basic Law for the Federal Republic of Germany'). It was a sign of his growing authority in the politics of the new era, an era which he believed should be oriented around the free market and organized along federal lines.

On 12 May 1949, just days after the Berlin Blockade came to an end, the Basic Law was ratified, and it became law eleven days later. From that point all eyes turned to the first democratic election campaign in Germany since the 1930s. The Federal Republic would test its new form of parliamentary democracy that was based on proportional representation through a double vote: half of the deputies were elected through direct constituency votes and the other half chosen from party lists according to the national result. This system was designed to exclude extremist parties, with 5-percent vote threshold for representation and an explicit constitutional prohibition of anti-democratic parties.[16] The 1949 election saw the SPD and CDU face off and each present differing conceptions of Germany's past and future. But they found common ground in their shared desire to completely eliminate the remaining vestiges of military occupation, including the much-hated dismantling, as soon as possible.

Back in Britain, the election – instead of being hailed a symbolic achievement marking the revival of German democracy – was met with scepticism. *Picture Post* published an extensive, if quasi-scientific, survey of German voters.[17] It suggested there was a great deal of uncertainty regarding Germany's political future, as outspoken nationalists and former Nazis vied with democrats, socialists and communists for claims on the recent past and responsibility for the future. In the *Daily Mail*, a report on the 'road back' to democracy in Germany described the election as an 'unreal battle' between parties set to have a 'tough time' convincing the German people that representative government would work.[18] All the parties were said to be pledging 'to frenzied applause' their intention to pursue German unity, to reclaim land that now lay in Poland, to end dismantling, to stop paying the costs of occupation[19] and to create a new German army – all regarded by the *Mail* as 'portents for the future'. The article even suggested that 'one of the most sinister aspects of German political life over the past months' was said to be the 'former Nazis, professional officers and the strong body of ultra-nationalists' who were 'biding their time in the background' and 'may yet become the principal force in Germany again'.

This kind of rhetoric about the supposedly dictatorial character of Germany's prospective democracy wasn't confined to the popular press. In the *Manchester Guardian* numerous reports warned of a resurgence of anti-Semitism and Nazism.[20] The emergence of the German Party (Deutsche Partei, DP) under the leadership of Hans-Christoph Seebohm came under particular scrutiny. This marginal political force was said to appeal to those who had 'suffered' under denazification, to call for a 'renewal' of the German Reich and to contend that the war's victims had died for Germany's future.[21] In one editorial, the *Guardian* suggested that there was more than enough reason to view the new Germany with 'a very alert and sceptical eye' because it was by no means certain that it would develop into a 'tolerant, just social democracy'.[22] The attempts of Otto Strasser to re-enter the political fray also inspired comment under the headline 'Seeds of trouble: Scepticism as to the New German State'.[23] Strasser, a prominent early member of the Nazi Party now exiled in Canada, was claimed to be working in alliance with the League for Germany's Renewal (otherwise known as the League of German Rebirth).[24] The article went on to allege that the Western orientation of Germany had obscured the clarity of the Allied vision 'so that the nationalist, anti-democratic tendencies in Germany are judged from the point of view of whether or not they are anti-Russian'. While, for the *Guardian*, this was not yet a Nazi revival, it was eerily reminiscent of 1925 and 'the causes from which Nazism sprang'.

These anxieties were augmented by a number of official reports: in July the Institute of Jewish Affairs in New York reported that anti-Semitism was one of 'the strongest characteristics' of present-day Germany. Likewise, an American-led survey into the German media raised fears that a 'pro-Nazi press' was reviving.[25] In August, British Military Governor Brian Robertson felt compelled to warn the Germans to curb the revival of Nazism and to 'protect Democratic institutions from attack'.[26] It inspired an editorial in the *Daily Mirror* cautioning against sentimentality or any erroneous belief in shortcuts to democracy, and calling for action by the Western powers if the Germans failed to stop the 'menace of Nazi nationalism' themselves.[27]

*

These allegations of a resurgence of political extremism were undoubtedly a sensationalist account of a momentous election campaign. In fact, they probably reveal more about the prevailing mood in Britain than Germany. Scarcely beneath the surface lay a broader anxiety: had the British lost the peace?

West Germany held its first federal election on 14 August and the same week *The Times* hosted a revealing exchange between veterans of the wartime debate over the 'German Problem'. No one, it seemed, was satisfied with how the occupation had played out. Victor Gollancz pessimistically suggested that 'on the morrow of the elections the German picture is darker, from a European point of view, than at any time since the end of the war'.[28] Even in the midst of the humanitarian crisis, he argued, there had been hope for a resolution of the 'German Problem'. But now he contended that the Allies, in eschewing his 'soft peace' approach, had spurned the only chance of fabricating a sustainable peace:

> Do we want a Germany steeped in hatred and thirsting for revenge?… if not, time is desperately short – a matter not

of years or months but of weeks and days. I have no wish to rehearse the whole tragic story of the Allied occupation. Just because the wickedness of Nazism had been so extreme and so corrupting, there was one chance and one chance only of our victory bringing health: and that was for the victors, in spite of every precedent, to be guided by what some would describe as Christian ethics and others as the elementary insights of commonplace psychology. We threw the chance away.

In the coming weeks numerous correspondents wrote impassioned letters to *The Times* and the *Manchester Guardian* about exactly what had gone wrong in the British Zone.[29] Among their number, somewhat inevitably, was Lord Vansittart, who warned that the present trajectory in Germany was simply another form of appeasement: 'The policy of concession has been tried throughout the century under various names... and has so far cost 50 million lives'.[30] Vansittart added that it was abundantly clear that the occupation had failed to enact the 'hard peace' policies he had long advocated, thereby allowing Germany to rise once more without atonement or reprimand. It led him to a sombre conclusion: 'Britain has been ruined by Germany.'

While the British newspapers were debating the country's apparent shortcomings, the people of West Germany went to the polls. Despite the recent advances of social democratic forces across Europe, the first West German elections saw an unexpected success for Adenauer's CDU and ushered in a centre–right coalition with the FDP and the DP.[31] On 15 September 1949 Konrad Adenauer was nominated as the first chancellor of the Federal Republic of Germany, a position that he would hold until 1963. It heralded a new political age.[32]

Adenauer's electoral success was met with a flurry of invective and trepidation from much of the British media, who questioned the integrity of his democratic convictions and envisaged a worrying future for Europe. At the end of August, the *Daily Telegraph* voiced scepticism about democracy's prospects in Germany:

When we hear of the projected reappearance of Nazi organs with many of their old associates, when we perceive again that curious kink in the German character which causes them to select Britain as the chief target of abuse, we are bound to ask what form of nationalism we are to expect, whether the new form of democracy will go the way of the Weimar form, and whether, in fact, what is emerging in Germany is a democracy without democrats.[33]

A fortnight later the paper reiterated its concerns in another editorial, asserting that Hitler had come to power because of the inherent failings of the Germans and their political leaders.[34] Amid 'recrudescent nationalism' and the 'reinstatement of prominent ex-Nazis' in Germany, the British people ought to wonder whether these new democrats 'will be any more successful than their predecessors from 1848 onwards':

> Extremists on the Right are all the bolder because their nationalistic mouthings against the Allies are echoed by the nominal moderates of the Social Democrat and Christian Democrat parties. If these two large parties continue as they did during the election campaign to attack the occupying powers for purely demagogic purposes, they will certainly find themselves outbidden by the self-appointed heirs of Hitler and Goebbels.

This scepticism was particularly palpable among those who had hoped the socialist Kurt Schumacher's SPD would gain power. The *Manchester Guardian*'s editorial was concerned by the rightward direction of German politics, especially at the prospect of small far-right parties taking part in Adenauer's coalition.[35] The election result was said to be still further proof that 'British policy in Germany has suffered a lamentable failure'.[36]

On the other hand, the *Daily Mail* was momentarily buoyed by the victory of a right-wing party, and its editorial demonstrated an uncharacteristic degree of sympathy towards the challenges that faced the new German government.[37] The following week the paper's Germany correspondent Brian Connell interviewed Adenauer himself, who used the platform to laud the democratic faith of the German people and his government's intention to put a halt to both right-wing radicalism and unfair economic competition.[38] Yet the *Mail*'s politically orientated change of heart had its limits: a Kenneth Ames article referred to the 'new Reich of Adenauer': on a recent visit to Germany, Ames claimed to have seen anti-British slogans chalked on the walls and witnessed a German train conductor 'not looking unlike the late Heinrich Himmler' impudently enforce obscure ticketing regulations – supposedly a sign of nascent authoritarianism.[39] The paper's efforts to extol the virtues of Adenauer's new government were also, plainly, not appreciated among some of the paper's readership, with one concerned correspondent arguing that it was 'no time to haul down the British flag':

A CDU campaign poster from the 1949 election featuring Konrad Adenauer. It reads 'With Adenauer for the peace, the freedom and the unity of Germany therefore CDU.'

The Germans have been responsible in the past 100 years for three minor and three major wars, with the loss of millions of dead and millions wounded. These wars have been fought with increasing ferocity and brutality the last including torture and the mass massacre of prisoners. Maybe we'll soon be apologising to the Germans for winning the war.[40]

In a similar vein, but with an even greater platform, the *Daily Express*'s foreign correspondent Charles Wighton made disparaging allusions to the Third Reich, while excoriating Adenauer as a nationalist:

> Black-uniformed German police sprang to attention with a military salute as a long, black limousine edged on to the Godesberg-Koenigswinter Rhine ferry this afternoon... The limousine's elderly passenger was seventy-three-year-old Dr Konrad Adenauer... For the second time in twenty-five years the Germans have chosen a septuagenarian, a retired professional man to be their leader. The first time it was a General – the senile Hindenburg, who prepared the way for Hitler. Now it is ex-lawyer and civil servant Adenauer... a reactionary nationalist... under today's fashionable cloak of democracy.[41]

Adenauer was accused of holding prejudices dating back as far as his opposition to the first British Army of the Rhine in 1919, augmented by his removal as the mayor of Cologne in 1945. As a result, the government he was forming was expected to succumb to reactionary ideas:

> Now in three weeks' time anti-British, grim, difficult Dr Adenauer will take office as Minister President (prime minister) of the new German Federal Republic. His government will be anti-Socialist, and committed to leave the Ruhr war arsenal in the possession of still formidable German big business. Under strong pressure from widely

differing wings of the Christian Democrats, Dr Adenauer is almost bound to follow the only policy acceptable to all – 100 per cent anti-Allied, and against the occupation.

*

On 21 September 1949 Allied military governors were replaced by High Commissioners, which marked the de facto end of the post-war occupation. The Petersburg Agreement of November 1949 would further expand the political independence of West Germany, until the Bonn–Paris Conventions of May 1955 formally concluded the Allied occupation. In the British Zone, Brian Robertson became the first civilian High Commissioner, now working under the authority of the Foreign Office. The Allied High Commission convened at the Hotel Petersberg on the outskirts of Bonn and supervised the Federal Republic of Germany's first steps as a self-governing nation. Across the British Zone a skeleton staff of civilians oversaw the rebirth of German politics, albeit with little actual power. By the time Colonel Edward Rich left Germany in 1952, he was responsible for an area the size of Yorkshire and spent most of his time sorting out intermittent disputes between locals and the British army over requisitioning or damages inflicted during training exercises.[42]

In November 1949 the city of Bonn was chosen as the country's new capital city. A small, sleepy municipality on the Rhine that many felt inadequate for the task, it was selected precisely because of a new German political trend: impermanence. By avoiding a major city like Frankfurt, West German politicians were living in the hope that their country would be united in the near future and Berlin would be restored to its former glory as capital.[43] In hindsight, this was a forlorn dream: in October 1949 the creation of the German Democratic Republic in the Soviet Zone struck a formal division within Germany that would endure for the next forty years.

Back in Britain, the controversial policy of dismantling once again dominated news from the newly sovereign West Germany. The policy of breaking up industrial concerns was still being actively pursued even as most of the British occupiers returned home. It led, predictably, to yet more protests. In September the story of British officers who were allegedly attacked while trying to complete dismantling duties at the Ruhr-Chemie synthetic oil plant in Oberhausen provoked a particularly incensed reaction. A number of the papers published a picture of an overturned car and castigated the German protestors for their violent actions. In response, Frank Owen in the *Daily Mail* published an editorial entitled 'Lest We Forget' that painted the German people as historically uncivilized and warlike:

> Europe is faced once more with an age-old question: can the Germans be either civilized or controlled? So far the answer has always been 'no'... German nationalism, that terrible thing which has brought fire, slaughter and uncounted suffering to Europe, is again resurgent. German bellies are full, so German bullying begins. Two British Control Commission officials are beaten up by 200 Germans. Nazi newspapers are on the way back. Workmen strike against the dismantling of war plants.[44]

Owen's incendiary editorial went over familiar ground, reciting a pocket history of both world wars to emphasize the long-standing deceitfulness of the German people. The only solution, it concluded, was a firmer hand:

> What are we to do with the Germans? It is easier to say what we should not do. It is futile, for example, to send troops into the place where the British officials were attacked and withdraw them the same day. We dare not be soft with the Germans. We want them in the European community, but not at the price of failing to remember their dreadful deeds. Three words should be in our minds: LEST WE FORGET.

In the *Daily Mirror*, William Connor wrote 'the story behind the picture that shocked Britain' under the headline 'THESE

GERMANS...'[45] German workers completing dismantling assign-
ments were said to have been greeted with graffiti reading 'JUDAS!
THERE'S A PLACE ON THE GALLOWS FOR YOU!' For Connor,
this was indicative of 'the anger and bitterness' felt by Germany
'against her conquerors'.

Connor went on to paint a troubling picture of the threat posed
by Germany's economic and political revival. In the first place, he
informed his readers that factories and plants of the Ruhr, Europe's
'greatest industrial centre', were in much better shape than most
people in Britain assumed. This, he warned, not only heralded the
revival of economic competition, but also offered the potential for
a military resurgence:

> Five years ago this area was under the hail of Allied bombers...
> Great havoc crashed down upon these towns and famous
> works like Krupps [*sic*] at Essen were practically wiped out.
> But not all were destroyed, nothing like it... The truth is that
> Germany is alive and stirring again, and nowhere more than
> in the iron guts of the Ruhr. There her heart beats strongly, the
> clump! Thump! Clump! Of the knocked-out gladiator getting
> ready to climb back into the arena again. Germany without
> the Ruhr is like a clock without a spring – or rather, a gun
> without a trigger. And Germany, unwound or unloaded, is a
> state unbearable to the industrious, patriotic and martial Hun.

Connor railed against the attempts of German industrialists
to prevent further dismantling, alleging they were unabashed
militarists who had unquestionably supported Hitler's regime.
Above all, as Germans, they were intrinsically predisposed to war
and aggression:

> They cry out 'the task now is to save German economy
> and the German workers from a still greater misery which
> would be of absolutely no economical advantage to any
> other country in the world. May our warning not fall on
> deaf ears!' Deaf ears! I seem to remember some deaf ears

during the seven deadly years from 1932 to 1939 when the German Ruhr worked night and day to re-arm Germany for the most atrocious war in history... It may be that these Geldmachers, these Spolders and these Wenzels are all certified as being free from the Nazi taint. But whatever our denazification courts declare, the record of the German race as a whole shows that they do not care very much for people of other lands.

In Connor's mind it was now unquestionable that the Allied occupation had been a lamentable failure:

Nationalism is aflame again in the midst of this immensely formidable nation, which cannot be cut out of the heart of Europe. Somehow, we have got to live with these aggressive and unrepentant people. But nowhere did I hear expressions of regret or much conciliation from the Germans... Dismantling inflames their anger, stokes their frustration and burns away the last hopes of reconciliation. This job should have been done three years ago, and it should have been completed while defeat was fresh upon them. As it is, any old excuse will do to defame the Allies... What is certain is that Jerry (like Annie) still wants to get his gun.

William Connor's rhetoric is an extreme iteration of the Germanophobia that had been sustained, and in some instances even augmented, since 1945. His anxious analysis ran contrary to British policy at the end of the decade, but Connor was by no means a lone voice.[46] While Allied policymakers had firmly turned their backs on the antagonistic relations of the recent past, much of the popular media continued to replicate the bombastic rhetoric of wartime. As the occupation came to an end, any notion that Britain had 'won the peace' was firmly rejected. Rather, the autumn of 1949 was a time for sombre reflection upon the dangers that lay ahead from the new Germany – and the failure of the British occupiers to secure a different outcome.

That September, Sefton Delmer's *Daily Express* column entitled 'Can Germany Harm Us?' just about summed up the popular mood.[47] Delmer warned his readers that the 'Spirit of the Swastika' had returned once more and that the German people had made it clear during the election that they 'hanker for a return of the drum-thumping, head-rolling leadership of Adolf Hitler or some other like him'. This, he went on, continued as West Germany's first parliament was established with its ostensible support 'for the strong-arm squads who beat up Germans working for the British' that was intended to appeal 'to the Nazi that lurks in every German's heart'. Delmer concluded on a pessimistic note:

In my view, it is already too late for any scolding or appeasement – though no doubt our experts will try out plenty of both. When the new West German government is formed under Dr Adenauer this week, Germany will have been safely launched on the road to Nazism... The Germans resent dismantling. They resent the presence of the Allied Control Commission, whether it is in mufti or in uniform. They resent the Ruhr authority, the new international administration of this vital industrial area. They resent the presence of our soldiers. They will organize resistance – passive and active. In the name of patriotism the government and the German public will once more connive at terrorism and violence. As a consequence, power will pass to the terrorists and chauvinists. And I don't care what they call themselves, they will be the same old Nazis again... The new chapter in German history beginning this week is another Nazi chapter.

26

So Long, Farewell,
Auf Wiedersehen, Goodbye

In the spring of 1949, British cinema-goers flocked to see *It's Not Cricket*, the latest slapstick outing from the comic duo Basil Radford and Naunton Wayne.[1] The pair was best known for playing buffoonish cricket-obsessives, most famously in Alfred Hitchcock's *The Lady Vanishes*. Their latest role, as the film's title suggests, was little different. There was, however, a new twist to this story: Radford and Wayne starred as two British intelligence officers serving in post-war Germany.

It's Not Cricket depicts the occupation forces in a strikingly unflattering light, a final self-deprecating monument to the years of scandal and criticism that had beset the British Zone.

The film's opening credits explain to viewers that after the war 'Germany was famous for two things – Zones and Drones', and that this was 'the regrettable story of two Drones who didn't even know their Zones. It starts in Germany, gets nowhere and stops at nothing'. As far as the plot is concerned, it is characteristically convoluted and features various mishaps and mistakes. The amiable buffoons Major Bright and Captain Early are busy completing their pools coupon prior to going home to England on leave when news of an escaped Nazi war criminal, Otto Fisch, is announced. The two officers pay the news little attention and impatiently wait for their batman to arrive: 'he's probably doing a spot of fraternising'.

1949 film poster for *It's Not Cricket* starring
Basil Radford and Naunton Wayne.

In fact, Fisch has attacked their orderly and taken his place in disguise, but the hapless Bright and Early fail to notice this.

They continue on their way and greet a soon-to-be-demobilized colleague at the station with a telling refrain: 'oh poor you, back to the stress and strain of civvy street'. Once on their train, headed for the Channel crossing, they make conversation with a brigadier:

Brig. Falcon: You gentlemen are in the Intelligence Corps, I presume?

Maj. Bright: Yes, rather so.

Brig. Falcon: What are you doing about Fisch?

Maj. Bright: Well, it's nothing to do with us, sir.

Capt. Early: No, no, the Catering Corps looks after that, sir.

Maj. Bright: Plenty of it in the mess, I must say.

Capt. Early: Too much if you ask me, sir!

Upon their arrival in England, the fugitive Fisch is finally recognized but manages to escape – leading to Bright's and Early's dismissal from the service. Following this, the pair decide to start a detective agency in London, whereupon they again stumble upon Fisch in the course of their work. The fugitive Nazi, played by Maurice Denham, is a rank caricature with a short temper, shifty demeanour and miserable expression. Fisch has made contact with a secret network in England – cue a series of comical 'Heil Hitlers'. The dénouement involves a cricket match in which a ball containing a stolen diamond is unwittingly used. Fisch, spectating from behind the sightscreen, is unable to comprehend this 'very dull game' and rushes onto the field to retrieve the ball. 'What does he think he's playing at?' asks one puzzled observer. 'Whatever it is, it's not cricket,' retorts Major Bright. Eventually the diamond is recovered, but the buffoonery is not quite complete – in the final scene, Bright and Early unsuspectingly hire a newly disguised Fisch as their office assistant.

The film perfectly captures the public image of the British occupiers that had emerged by the end of the 1940s: these were not high-minded victors or glorious conquerors but blundering fools. After all the grandiose plans for coming to terms with the so-called 'German Problem', the occupation ultimately had failed to live up to anyone's expectations. This was no liberation of an 'Other Germany' from totalitarian oppression, nor a wholly successful and magnanimous rehabilitation of the German people. It wasn't even perceived as the concluding chapter in a heroic narrative about victory in two world wars. In Germany the British had seemingly achieved little beyond damaging their own reputation through ineptitude and immorality.

This damning portrayal of the occupation as a humiliating failure was, of course, a reflection of more deep-seated insecurities about Britain's place in the world.[2] In the first four years of the peace, events in Germany exposed the nation's financial and moral weaknesses. These failings had been excoriated by the popular press in harshly critical coverage which perpetuated a downbeat self-image of a nation in decline. Britain was, it seemed, unable to maintain its international commitments or even command respect among vanquished enemies.[3] The patriotic fervour and grand aspirations that had greeted the end of the war were an increasingly distant memory.

*

On 27 September 1949 Mary Bouman woke to find a bunch of red roses alongside her morning tea, a thoughtful and unexpected birthday gift from the German caretaker of her billet.[4] By then, Bouman had been in the British Zone as part of the Control Commission for three and a half years, working in Herford as a translator in the Legal Division. It had been an eventful time, to say the least, and her birthday would be no different. After breakfast, she rushed to the local registry office to act as a witness at the marriage of a German woman she had befriended. To mark the occasion, Bouman purchased a number of wedding gifts including a bottle of gin, dessert spoons and, by express request, a set of women's underwear. After toasts in honour of the newly-weds,

A notice in front of the Brandenburg Gate, Berlin. By the end of 1949 most of the British staff in Germany had returned home.

Bouman returned to her office to find a pile of her own presents from colleagues and friends, which included a cigarette holder and a set of books. That evening, to cap off the celebrations, Bouman was treated to dinner at the Bath Club in Bad Salzuflen: 'a fitting end to a memorable day'.

It was, as it turned out, a fitting end to a memorable few years: the same week it was confirmed that she would be returning to Britain in a fortnight's time. The news came as no surprise, considering that the military occupation was coming to an end, but nevertheless was bittersweet. For Bouman, the last few years had been personally fulfilling, while also leaving her wondering if the British had achieved anything much at all. In a letter home to her parents, she reflected with some regret on the legacy of her time in Germany:

> I shall be most sorry to leave for a number of reasons but there is a complete 'run-down' of everything here now and the best days have undoubtedly gone. I shall miss my independence, the service, the friends who remain, the ease of entertaining and the odd glass of sherry or liqueur. I should have liked to have been included in the new set-up in Frankfurt or Bonn or wherever it will be and watch the new German government at work, but there is evidently no room in the new establishments for people who speak the language and know the country and people. Only the unimaginative civil servant is wanted who doesn't know the language and never will. If we hadn't had so many of this type to run Germany after the collapse we should have got further and had more success in our administration of the country and have made a greater impression on the Germans themselves. I can't help feeling a great opportunity has been lost because the wrong types have come out here.

Bouman was one of the many thousands of British men and women who served in Germany between 1945 and 1949. Of course, each had their own experience of the military occupation – and when it came time to say *Auf Wiedersehen* ('goodbye'), their responses were just as diverse. In the summer of 1947, after just over a year's service in Germany, Katharine Morris decided to spend her weekend leave in the attractive town of Preetz in Schleswig-Holstein with a church group.[5] When she returned to Hamburg, Morris felt an acute sense of estrangement, a realization that her life in Germany was quite peculiar. 'What was I doing here?' she wrote in her memoir. 'Why was I here in this alien country with my insatiable religiosity, spending my time in the service of strangers who had no claim upon me, while those [memories] of my own people at home were muted by distance, dimmed by the fascination of these unfamiliar scenes?' The following day, a cable arrived that would change all that. It was from her parents, who told Morris that it was time for her to return home. As their only surviving child, and as a daughter, it was expected that her primary responsibility was to her family:

I had been living with the history of my time. Now, conditioned by all the centuries of women's responsibility to the family, I must return home. While I accepted this as inevitable, and in my heart had anticipated such a summons, now that it came it was a wrench full of pain, coming as it did at a time of fulfilment, when an alternative road full of promise seemed to open ahead of me (that dream of Berlin!) But for me there could be no alternatives now.

In other cases, the return home sparked more mixed feelings. In December 1946, after three and a half years with the ATS and over a year in the British Zone, Daphne Smith was released from service. 'It is quite a solemn thought that this will be my last letter from Germany', she wrote to her mother, 'I'm already beginning to get nostalgic about the army. It's been great fun. But now, as Monica Dickens says, the party is over. So Civvy St here I come!'[6]

Henry Vaughan Berry, regional commissioner for Hamburg since 1946, became Britain's representative at the International Authority of the Ruhr in May 1949, shortly before receiving his knighthood. This organization oversaw the German coal and steel industries until 1951, when it was superseded by the European Coal and Steel Community, a forerunner of the European Union. When Berry died in 1979, his wife received a letter from German Chancellor Helmut Schmidt, who had been a student in Hamburg during the 1940s: 'It is with deep personal regret that I have learned about the death of Sir Henry. I will always remember the interesting and inspiring hours I spent in Sir Henry's house in Hamburg, Germany and I personally lost a friend'.[7] These words stand as a vivid testimony to the best kind of interpersonal reconciliation that took place across all levels of German society between 1945 and 1949; while friendship certainly wasn't the only mode of engagement between occupiers and occupied, the military government did see many Britons and Germans come together as friends rather than former enemies. From marriages to working partnerships, these bonds would serve as a foundation for a more peaceable Anglo-German relationship in the decades to come.

For many, especially soldiers serving in the British Army of the Rhine, demobilization papers were received with glee. After years of fighting, followed by months of boredom in the British Zone, the return to family and friends couldn't come soon enough. 'I have really had a very gay time out here over Xmas and the New Year, but I do so want to be home', wrote Henry Hughes to his mother in January 1946.[8] His mess's New Year's Eve party had gone on until 5:30 a.m., which was inconvenient for Captain Hughes, who took over as duty officer only two hours later. But the ongoing delay in his demobilization proved all the more irksome: 'I can't say I feel particularly interested in my work, and am far more concerned with counting the days'. Finally, at the end of February, he was able to celebrate the award of his 'bowler hat' with friends and family at Selsdon Park Hotel in Croydon.[9] For John William Booth the wait was even longer: 'I think I shall need two month's recuperation after the gosh-darned waiting of these "home-stretch" months', he wrote in February 1946.[10] He was left in eager anticipation until the good news finally came that spring: 'Yes folks, it's a "RED LETTER DAY" – without further ado let me spread the glad tidings – D-Day for my leaving the beautiful city of Bad Oeynhausen has been officially proclaimed... Sunday 28th April 1946! Seventeen days to go!'[11]

The handover of power in 1949 wasn't the end of the story as far as the Rhine Army was concerned: until 2020, when the final British base was handed over to the Bundeswehr, the British Army would maintain a sizeable presence in north-west Germany. In towns and cities across the former British Zone and the British sector of Berlin as many as 50,000 British troops and their families lived side by side with German civilians. It was an arrangement which saw Britain and the Federal Republic stand together as allies in the Cold War. This legacy of the occupation also had a unique social history: after the end of the occupation, these British enclaves in Germany forged a distinctive community and embodied the shift from foe to friend.

*

What should we make of Britain's attempt to 'win the peace' in Germany? As we have seen, many British observers at the time, some of them with their own political agendas, condemned the occupation as a lamentable failure. For British policymakers, however, 1949 marked the end of a troubling few years of uncertainty. In the face of the Cold War and severe financial constraints, Britain's foreign policy towards Germany had moved from outright antagonism to alliance in extremely short order. This would prove to be a hugely significant shift in modern British, European and world history: the West's strategic realignment in Germany was the genesis of a new global order in the aftermath of the Second World War. It set the stage for a division of the continent that lasted for the next forty years but also safeguarded a relative stability in European affairs for the first time in a generation.

As far as Bevin and Attlee were concerned, the occupation could be regarded as an outright success. It had been a demanding task, involving the taking of a series of difficult decisions which, they believed, would protect Britain's interests in Europe and set West Germany on a path towards peace and prosperity. In the dark days of the immediate post-war era the British staved off total catastrophe, restored order, and set the foundations for a stable nation state to emerge. In many ways, the unfolding of events since 1949 would appear to endorse Bevin's and Attlee's view. In the years following the occupation, the Federal Republic offered no military threat and, in fact, became a part of the NATO alliance in 1955. The history of West Germany was certainly not 'another Nazi chapter' as some had feared but rather a story of a steady democracy, economic powerhouse and reliable ally. It has continued undiminished since the reunification of Germany in 1990.

This is the view most often put forward in the various attempts to tell the story of the military occupation to date.[12] In 1965 former commander-in-chief of the British Zone Brian Robertson, by then Lord Robertson of Oakridge, wrote an impassioned defence of the occupation in an academic journal. While the Western Allies had, in his opinion, started out with 'an entirely false picture in their minds', the hard work of those on the ground, the clear-sightedness of their commanders and what he concluded could only be divine intervention had allowed a 'miracle' to take place in Germany. In hindsight, he suggested, it was a vital juncture in the fight against the Soviet Union. This portrayal was repeated time and time again in the accounts of historians and former occupiers alike.[13]

An even more notable and ultimately insidious revival of interest in the occupation came at the height of the 'War on Terror'. In the run-up to the Iraq War, a number of British and American policymakers became interested in the history of post-war Germany as an exemplar for post-conflict strategies of rule. In a Cabinet Office paper on 'winning the peace' there were references to the apparent similarities of 2000s Iraq to 1940s Germany.[14] In February 2003, just weeks before the invasion began, President George W. Bush gave a speech at the American Enterprise Institute remarking that there 'was a time when many said that the cultures of Japan and Germany were incapable of sustaining democratic values... Some say the same of Iraq today. They are mistaken.'[15] Following the invasion, Sir Jeremy Greenstock, the

UK's special representative for Iraq, was even warned by a UN special representative not to 'over-emulate post-war Germany' as the Coalition Provisional Authority was zealously pursuing 'de-Ba'athification'.[16] This not-so-subtle nod to denazification aimed to remove the traces of Saddam Hussein's Ba'ath Party from Iraqi society. Like so much of the war in Iraq, the comparisons with occupied Germany were a disastrous misreading of the facts to suit political ends.

There were certainly numerous ways in which Britain's attempt to 'win the peace' in Germany left a sustainable, quantifiable and wholly positive legacy. *Der Spiegel* and Volkswagen are two clear examples of British occupiers taking the initiative and producing results. There were more systemic successes too: the British imprint on the German electoral system is plain to see, even if it perhaps owed more to the legacy of the Weimar Republic than the Administration and Local Government Branch of the Control Commission. Likewise, the efforts to demilitarize Germany proved effective. The good-natured hard work of members of the BAOR and CCG in rebuilding the education sector, establishing law courts, and much else besides should not be forgotten. Undoubtedly, a substantial proportion of the British staff were committed to the task in hand and sincerely wanted to build a better world in Germany. They would learn much about their former enemies – and themselves – in the process. Above all, there is no doubting the long-term strategic success of Britain's foreign policy decisions between 1945 and 1949: in grand historical terms, the peace was most certainly won.

It is instructive – and revealing – however, to take a granular view of the occupation between 1945 and 1949. In many instances a great deal of energy, manpower and precious financial resources was expended with no great and obvious reward. The Potsdam Agreement saw the Allies pursue contradictory or impracticable goals while being unable to reach any kind of compromise on potential modifications. For Britain, it created an unsustainable financial burden that necessitated a radical change of approach. And while Bevin and Attlee did successfully complete a diplomatic realignment vis-à-vis Germany, in the process Britain's newfound limitations as a world power were painfully exposed: it was clear that from this point on, any major British foreign policy aspirations would be dependent upon the approval and resources of Washington. Meanwhile, as the Cold War took centre stage, the nebulous plans for 're-educating' the Germans fell flat; other grand ambitions of reforming the German education system and civil service, or nationalizing heavy industry failed to come to fruition; and noble ambitions to 'denazify' the Zone were curtailed on political grounds. There is also an abundance of evidence to suggest that a substantial proportion of the British staff were simply not up to scratch, implicated, as they were, to differing degrees in the culture of corruption and excess that pervaded post-war Germany – as much a reputational problem as anything, but significant nonetheless. And amid the muddle, blunder and human frailty which characterized many of these shortcomings, we must not overlook the episodes imbued with prejudice, imperial arrogance and cruelty.

From the huge financial costs to the endless stream of scandals that engulfed the Zone, the occupation of Germany was not Britain's finest hour – but it was also clearly not as compromised as many critical observers made out. With the benefit of hindsight, we can see that the British Government's radical about-turn regarding Germany, transformed from enemy to ally in a few short years, was a momentous adjustment. It went against decades of previous policy, as British policymakers sought a path out of their troubling predicament in the aftermath of the Second World War. Following on from years of state-led anti-German propaganda and with no guarantee of success, it is hardly surprising that at the end of the 1940s the British media and wider public remained deeply sceptical of this bold change of tack. It would be years before questions over whether the British ought to have been more or less beastly to the Germans were finally laid to rest.

Acknowledgements

It was a rainy Manchester day in late 2013 when I first decided to try and learn more about Britain's relationship with Germany in the years immediately after the Second World War: how, I wondered, did the British and German people come to terms with the fifty years of mutual hostility and conflict that preceded their becoming neighbours, allies and even friends after 1945? Little did I know that almost ten years later I would be lucky enough to publish a book on the subject. If a week is a long time in politics (as events in February 1947 prove beyond any doubt), then a decade is certainly a long time in research. Over that time, I have become deeply indebted to family members, friends, colleagues and encouraging institutions for their enduring support and guidance.

This book simply would not exist without the financial support provided to me as an early career scholar and writer. I owe thanks to the Arts and Humanities Research Council, who funded my doctoral studies, as well as the German History Society, Cambridge University History Faculty, Kurt Hahn Trust, and Wolfson College, Cambridge, all of whom helped fund research trips. In the course of turning my PhD thesis into a book, I was also supported by The Society of Authors and the Authors' Foundation.

I am forever grateful for the assistance of librarians, archivists, and all the other staff at the British Library, Imperial War Museum, Churchill Archives Centre, National Archives, Cambridge University Library, British Film Institute, Harry S. Truman Library, and Chipping Campden History Society. A special mention goes to my colleagues at the National Army Museum, not only for their support as I was researching this book but also for welcoming me with open arms after I joined the museum as a historian in 2022. Finally, I must thank the Noël Coward Archive Trust for their permission to use the title of Coward's song: it is a testament to his abilities as a writer that, eighty years on, the phrase 'Don't Let's Be Beastly to the Germans' still so perfectly encapsulates British deliberations about Germany at the end of the Second World War.

In the course of researching and writing this book, a large number of colleagues and scholars have generously offered their time and expertise. First of all, my supervisors as a postgraduate student, Sir Richard J. Evans and Henning Grunwald, offered valuable critiques of my work as well as professional advice. I am also grateful for the constructive feedback of my PhD examiners, David Reynolds and Jan Rüger, which similarly helped to shape this book. I am, of course, thankful for the help of numerous other supportive scholars, including Jon Lawrence and Scott Anthony. Likewise, I owe a great deal to those who have laid the foundations for researching and understanding the British occupation of Germany: Anne Deighton, Christopher Knowles, Ian D. Turner, Bettina Blum, Camilo Erlichman, Ian Cobain, Patricia Meehan and countless others. I would also like to mention my undergraduate advisors, Jonathan Kwan and Chris Wrigley, who helped to direct my intellectual interests. Finally, I will be eternally indebted to the teachers and staff at Parrs Wood High School, where I learnt a great deal about history and much more besides.

I have found the process of turning scholarly research into a book both rewarding and challenging. It would, however, have been more or less impossible without the unstinting encouragement and guidance of my agent, Andrew Lownie, who took a chance on me as a new writer and remains incredibly supportive. Likewise, I am thankful for the faith shown by Head of Zeus and, in particular, my editor, Richard Milbank: this book is much richer for your enthusiastic and instructive feedback. I also owe gratitude to editorial assistants Aphra Le Levier-Bennett and Ellie Jardine, my copyeditor, Petra Bryce, and all the other people working behind the scenes to bring this book into being. Any errors that do remain are, of course, my sole responsibility.

My book also owes a tremendous amount to those who recorded their experiences of life in post-war Germany. While I will never meet Edna Wearmouth, Mary Bouman, Norman Skinner, Hans-Erich Nossack, Ilya Suster, or the tens of others whose stories and recollections of the late 1940s I have documented here, I will always feel a special affinity for them. There is untold joy in rediscovering long-lost letters or photograph albums which recount forgotten, ephemeral moments of the past, whether it be love affairs, treasured meals, or someone's first taste of champagne. Ultimately, it is these stories of ordinary people, with all their weird and wonderful ways, living in extraordinary times, who stand at the centre of everything I hope to achieve as a historian. I would like to think that this book has provided some of those who saw the British occupation of Germany first-hand with an opportunity to tell their tale.

Then, of course, there are those people in my own life who have made writing this book not only possible, but worthwhile. A huge, everlasting thanks to my parents, Sue and Graham, who encouraged me to pursue my ambitions and have always remained supportive. Likewise, my brother, Alex, who has always stood by me, and my niece, Izzy, who resolutely insisted on 'helping' with my research as she was herself learning the art of writing. I am also grateful to have such supportive in-laws: Yvonne, whom we miss dearly, and John have never failed to share their enthusiasm for my work. To Mark E. Smith, who is not appreciated but was always gonna make an appearance, cheers. To Dave at the Alma, Rowan at the Queens: thanks for all the searching questions.

I feel incredibly lucky to have such wonderful friends: Joe Burns, Michael Randle, Tom McGuinness, Beth Williams, Jonny McCullough, Rahul Patel, Ben Bray, Jens Åklundh, Perica Hadzi-Jovancic, Mike Vickers, Phil Daley, Ciara Higgins, Kaylie Cordingley, Abby Crookes, Helen Woerner, Rosie Raftery, along with many others, are some of the most fun, supportive people one could hope to know. Finally, all my love and admiration for my wife, Alexandra, to whom this book is dedicated. Thanks for your unwavering enthusiasm, support, friendship, advice, inspiration, and good humour, from both near and far. Alex is the most incredible intellectual companion, an insightful reader and a thoughtful critic, without whom writing this book would not have been possible – nor would I have had quite as much fun along the way.

Notes

Chapter One

1. Memoir, 'When All The Trees Were Green', Private Papers of Miss K M Morris, Documents.1159, Imperial War Museum Archive, London.
2. 'DB Station&Service AG: 100 Jahre Hamburger Hauptbahnhof', commemorative booklet, Deutsche Bahn, accessed 1 September 2021, www.bahnhof.de/site/shared/de/dateianhaenge/publikationen__broschueren/ub__personenbahnhoefe/100__jahre__hamburg__hbf.pdf
3. 'Supplement', *London Gazette*, 29 October 1945.
4. Memoir, 'When All The Trees Were Green', Morris Papers.
5. For more details, see Blum, Bettina, '"My Home, your Castle": British Requisitioning of German Homes in Westphalia' in Erlichman, Camilo and Knowles, Christopher (eds), *Transforming Occupation in the Western Zones of Germany: Politics, Everyday Life and Social Interactions, 1945–55* (London: 2018), pp. 115–32.
6. Spender, Stephen, *European Witness* (London: 1946), pp. 22–4.
7. Panayi, Panikos, *German Immigrants in Britain during the 19th Century* (Oxford: 1995).
8. Panayi, Panikos, *Enemy in Our Midst: Germans in Britain During the First World War* (Oxford: 1991), p. 153.
9. Panayi, *Enemy in Our Midst*, pp. 223–58.
10. Panayi, Panikos, *Prisoners of Britain: German Civilian and Combatant Internees During the First World War* (Manchester: 2012).
11. Stibbe, Matthew, *German Anglophobia and the Great War, 1914–1918* (Cambridge: 2006), pp. 33–8.
12. Stibbe, *German Anglophobia*, p. 18.
13. These were just some of the electioneering slogans put to use during the December 1918 general election campaign; see Neiberg, Michael S., *The Treaty of Versailles: A Concise History* (Oxford: 2017), p. 14.
14. Keynes, John Maynard, *The Economic Consequences of the Peace* (London: 1919).
15. Williamson, David G., *The British in Interwar Germany: The Reluctant Occupiers, 1919–30* (London: 2017), p. 134.
16. Simms, Brendan, *Britain's Europe: A Thousand Years of Conflict and Cooperation* (London: 2016), p. 150.

Chapter Two

1. Robbins, Ron Cynewulf, 'Finest Hour 112: Sixty Years On: The Atlantic Charter 1941-2001', International Churchill Society, accessed 13 January 2021, https://winstonchurchill.org/publications/finest-hour/finest-hour-112/sixty-years-on-the-atlantic-charter-1941-2001-1/.

2. Cairncross, Alec, *The Price of War: British Policy on German Reparations 1941–49* (Oxford: 1986), p. 18.

3. Baylis, John, 'British Wartime Thinking about a Post-War European Security Group', *Review of International Studies* 9, no. 4 (1983), pp. 265–81.

4. Vansittart, Robert, *The Mist Procession* (London: 1958), p. 16.

5. His most celebrated work was Vansittart, Robert, *The Singing Caravan: A Sufi Tale* (Newtown: 1932).

6. Rose, Norman, 'Vansittart, Robert Gilbert, Baron Vansittart (1881–1957)', *Oxford Dictionary of National Biography* (Oxford: 2004).

7. Rose, Norman, *Vansittart: Study of a Diplomat* (London: 1978), p. vii.

8. Vansittart, Robert, *Black Record: Germans Past and Present*, 15th ed. (London: 1941), p. ix. Citations refer to this edition unless otherwise stated.

9. Vansittart, *Black Record*, p. ix.

10. Lawson, Tom, *The Church of England and the Holocaust: Christianity, Memory and Nazism* (Cambridge: 2013), p. 117; Jones, Jill, 'Eradicating Nazism from the British Zone of Germany: Early policy and practice', *German History* 8, no. 2 (1990), pp. 145–62.

11. Official Report, Fifth Series, Parliamentary Debates, House of Commons, Vol. 351 (1939), 1 September 1939, Col. 125–39; Goldman, Aaron, 'Germans and Nazis: The Controversy over "Vansittartism" in Britain during the Second World War', *Journal of Contemporary History* 14, no. 1 (1979), p. 161.

12. Rose, *Vansittart*, pp. 244–7; Goldman, 'Germans and Nazis', pp. 162–4. The broadcasts received a considerable amount of attention in the press; see *Sunday Times*, 1 December 1940; *Sunday Times*, 8 December 1940; *Daily Mail*, 25 November 1940; *Daily Mail*, 6 December 1940; *Daily Telegraph*, 29 November 1940; *Daily Telegraph*, 3 December 1940; *Daily Telegraph*, 4 December 1940.

13. Vansittart, *Black Record*.

14. Rose, *Vansittart*, p. 247. These figures are from Vansittart's personal papers, Letter Vansittart to P. P. Howe, Hamish Hamilton, 27 January 1941, VNST II/1/10, Correspondence: January 1941 – November 1941, Correspondence with publishers and The Sunday Times about Vansittart's book 'Black Record', Churchill Archives Centre, Cambridge; Printing Numbers (Black Record), 26 August 1941, VNST II/1/10, Correspondence: January 1941 – November 1941, Correspondence with publishers and The Sunday Times about Vansittart's book 'Black Record', Churchill Archives Centre, Cambridge.

15. See Vansittart, Robert, *The Roots of the Trouble* (London: 1941).

16. Gollancz, Victor, *Shall Our Children Live or Die?: A Reply to Lord Vansittart on the German Problem* (London: 1942), p. 5.

17. Rose, *Vansittart*, p. 248.

18. Quoted in Chandler, Andrew, 'The Patronage of resistance: George Bell and the "Other Germany" during the Second World War' in Chandler, Andrew

(ed.), *The Church and Humanity: The Life and Work of George Bell, 1883–1958* (Farnham; Burlington, Vt: 2012), p. 97.

19. Gollancz, *Shall Our Children Live or Die?*, p. 95.
20. Glasgow, George, 'Sir Robert in Action', review of *Black Record* by Robert Vansittart, *Manchester Guardian*, 19 January 1941.
21. Wells, H. G., 'If We Do Not Strike Now We Deserve Disaster', *Daily Mail*, 3 September 1941.
22. 'Vansittart's Best', editorial, *Daily Mirror*, 2 December 1940.
23. Tombs, Isabelle, 'The Victory of Socialist "Vansittartism": Labour and the German Question, 1941–5', *Twentieth Century British History* 7, no. 3 (1996), p. 301, https://doi.org/10.1093/tcbh/7.3.287.
24. Olick, Jeffrey K., *In the House of the Hangman: The Agonies of German Defeat, 1943–1949* (Chicago: 2005), pp. 30, 44; Goldman, 'Germans and Nazis', p. 169; Rose, *Vansittart*, p. 258; Später, Jörg, *Vansittart: Britische Debatten über Deutsche und Nazis 1902-1945* (Göttingen: 2003); Dodd, A. H. 'Germany's Record – The Dangers of Distorting History', letter to the editor, *Manchester Guardian*, 6 December 1940; Laski, Harold J., *The Germans – Are They Human? A Reply to Sir Robert Vansittart* (London: 1941), pp. 3–4; Fraenkel, Heinrich, *Vansittart's Gift for Goebbels: A German Exile's Answer to Black Record* (London: 1941), p. 3.
25. Hickey, William [Tom Driberg], 'Pickled Eggs', *Daily Express*, 9 April 1941.
26. Bevan, Aneurin, 'Should We Blame the Whole German People', *Picture Post*, 17 July 1943.
27. Blunt, Alfred, 'Bishop of Bradford…', letter to the editor, *Picture Post*, 31 July 1943.
28. Gooch, G. P., 'Germany and Her Neighbours – Historian's Criticism of "Black Record"', letter to the editor, *Manchester Guardian*, 12 March 1941.
29. Hirst, Francis W., 'Germany's Past and Present – Blackening the Record', letter to the editor, *Manchester Guardian*, 5 February 1941.
30. Fraenkel, *Vansittart's Gift for Goebbels*; Olick, *In the House of the Hangman*, p. 46; Barkley, William, 'Bishop and Peer Duel About "Good" Germans', *Daily Express*, 11 March 1943; 'German People Not Guilty – TUC', *Daily Mirror*, 11 September 1943.
31. Goebbels, Joseph, *The Goebbels Diary*, trans. Lochner, L. P. (New York: 1948), pp. 93–4, 139, 226–7, 341–3.
32. Goldman, 'Germans and Nazis', p. 162.
33. Vansittart, *The Roots of the Trouble*; Vansittart, Robert, *Lessons of My Life* (London: 1943); Vansittart, Robert, *The German Octopus – 'Win the Peace' Pamphlet No.2* (London: 1945); Vansittart, Robert, *Bones of Contention* (London: 1945).

Chapter Three

1. Edwards, Ruth Dudley, *Victor Gollancz: A Biography* (London: 1987), p. 198.
2. Aster, Sidney, 'Appeasement: Before and After Revisionism', *Diplomacy and Statecraft* 19, no. 3 (2008), p. 446.
3. Edwards, *Victor Gollancz*, p. 359.
4. Gollancz, *Shall Our Children Live or Die?*.

5. Gollancz, *Shall Our Children Live or Die?*, pp. 12–3, 17, 23, 26–9, 33; Chandler, 'The Patronage', p. 98.
6. Gollancz, *Shall Our Children Live or Die?*, p. 33.
7. Gollancz, *Shall Our Children Live or Die?*, p. 23.
8. Gollancz, *Shall Our Children Live or Die?*, p. 3; Edwards, *Victor Gollancz*, p. 365.
9. Brown, Douglas, *Commonsense versus Vansittartism* (London: 1943), pp. 7, 19, 22. See also Diplomaticus [Konni Zilliacus], *Can the Tories Win the Peace? And How They Lost the Last One* (London: 1945); Pollitt, Harry, *How to Win the Peace* (London: 1944); Cole, G. D. H., *Europe, Russia, and the Future* (London: 1941), pp. 148, 152, 154; Saran, M., Eichler, W., Heidorn, W. and Specht, M. (eds), *Re-making Germany* (London: 1945); Fraenkel, Heinrich and Acland, Richard, *The Winning of the Peace* (London: 1942), p. 16; Brailsford, Henry Noel, *Our Settlement with Germany* (Harmondsworth: 1944), p. 20.
10. These arguments, many of which derived from the SPD's view of German history as articulated by exiled Germans, anticipated certain interpretations of the *Sonderweg* thesis.
11. Brown, *Commonsense*, p. 7.
12. Carr, Edward Hallett, *Conditions of Peace* (London: 1942), p. 211; Official Report, Fifth Series, Parliamentary Debates, House of Lords, Vol. 126 (1943), 10 March 1943, Col. 535–82; Lawson, *The Church of England and the Holocaust*, p. 172; Barkley, William, 'Bishop and Peer Duel About "Good" Germans', *Daily Express*, 11 March 1943.
13. For a comprehensive survey of Vansittartist ideas in wartime Britain, see Später, *Vansittart*.
14. Tell, Rolf, *The Eternal Ger-Maniac: Hitler and His Spiritual Ancestors* (London: 1942), pp. xii–xiii. There were also more official, clinical attempts to comprehend Nazism through psychology; see Pick, Daniel, *The Pursuit of the Nazi Mind: Hitler, Hess, and the Analysts* (Oxford: 2012).
15. Butler, Rohan, *The Roots of National Socialism* (London: 1941); Taylor, A. J. P., *The Course of German History: A Survey of the Development of Germany since 1815* (London: 1946). For historical accounts of this movement, and Tennant in particular, see Goldman, 'Germans and Nazis', p. 156; Griffiths, Richard, *Fellow Travellers of the Right: British Enthusiasts for Nazi Germany 1933–1939* (Oxford: 1983), pp. 182–6; Bacchetta, Paola and Power, Margaret, *Right-wing Women: From Conservatives to Extremists Around the World* (London; New York: 2003), pp. 186–7. For evidence of Tennant's tumultuous relationship with Vansittart himself, see Letter Vansittart to Mrs Steward, British Prisoners of War Relatives Association, 20 May 1944, VNST II/1/23, Correspondence about the 'Never Again' Association, Churchill Archives Centre, Cambridge.
16. This included the influential group of Conservative Party backbenchers who made up the Post-War Policy Group; see Weymouth, Anthony [Dr Ivo Geikie-Cobb] (ed.), *Germany: Disease and Treatment – Based on the Memoranda of the Post-War Policy Group* (London; New York: 1945). The author's identity was revealed in 'Obituaries', *Times*, 18 August 1953.
17. Rose, *Vansittart*, p. 260.
18. See Rose, *Vansittart*, p. 261, as well as examples below. For the BBC coverage, see *The Listener*, 19 October 1944; *The Listener*, 26 October 1944; *The Listener*, 7 December 1944.

19. 'Should We Blame the Whole German People?', *Picture Post*, 17 July 1943.

20. 'Lord Vansittart on the German Menace: The "Win the Peace" Movement', *Manchester Guardian*, 20 September 1943. Also see Später, *Vansittart*, pp. 183–5.

21. 'Winning the Peace – "German Army Must Go"', *Manchester Guardian*, 22 May 1943; Vansittart, Robert, 'Vansittartism Explained', *Daily Express*, 20 September 1943; Rose, *Vansittart*, p. 261.

22. Rose, *Vansittart*, p. 261.

23. 'Securing Europe From Germany – Danger of Using Ideological Spectacles – Lord Vansittart on Peace Aims', *The Scotsman*, 12 June 1943; 'How to Win the Peace – Lord Vansittart's Suggestions', *Birmingham Post*, 24 January 1944; Rose, *Vansittart*, p. 261.

24. Vansittart, *Bones of Contention*, p. 7.

25. 'Whip Hand 1944 – Lord Vansittart on Nazi Collapse', *Liverpool Daily Post*, 13 January 1944; '"Never Again" – Lord Vansittart's Object', *Manchester Guardian*, 13 January 1944.

26. 'German Aggression – "Never Again" Movement – Aims and Policy', *The Scotsman*, 19 January 1943; Draft Memorandum and Articles of Association, 27 July 1942, VNST II/1/23, Correspondence about the 'Never Again' Association, Churchill Archives Centre, Cambridge; Mr WJ Brown on the Things to Come, Never Again Luncheon (Grosvenor House), 6 April 1942, *British Movietone News*, newsreel, no. 42120, British Movietone News Digital Archive, www.movietone.com.

27. Letter Vansittart to Mrs Unwin, 2 July 1943, VNST II/1/23, Correspondence about the 'Never Again' Association, Churchill Archives Centre, Cambridge; 'Vansittartism', *Daily Telegraph*, 19 February 1942.

28. Vansittart, *Black Record*, pp. v, viii; Vansittart, *The Roots of the Trouble*, p. 9; Vansittart, Robert, 'Vansittartism', letter to the editor, *Manchester Guardian*, 3 August 1943; Vansittart, Robert, 'Should We Blame the Whole German People', *Picture Post*, 17 July 1943; Hickey, William [Tom Driberg], 'Hammer of Huns', *Daily Express*, 20 January 1941; Vansittart, Robert, 'Vansittartism', letter to the editor, *The Economist*, 17 January 1942; Vansittart, Robert, 'The Rise of Brutality', letter to the editor, *The Economist*, 31 January 1942; Vansittart, Robert, 'The German People', letter to the editor, *The Scotsman*, 11 June 1942.

29. Einzig, Paul, *Can We Win the Peace?* (London: 1942), pp. 8–9.

30. Vansittart, *Black Record*, pp. v–vi.

31. '"Let a Lancaster Drop the Non-Haters"', *Daily Express*, 24 September 1941.

32. 'The Rise of Brutality', *The Economist*, 27 December 1941.

33. Vansittart, Robert, *Black Record: Germans Past and Present*, 1st ed. (London: 1941), p. vi.

34. File report 1543, 'Germany After the War', December 1942, Mass-Observation Archive, University of Sussex, Brighton.

35. Goldman, 'Germans and Nazis', pp. 156–7. File report 1624, 'Private Opinion About the German People', March 1943, Mass-Observation Archive, University of Sussex, Brighton. This was, moreover, likely to be a conservative estimate, with investigators suggesting that some respondents had concealed their vitriol for Germany due to social desirability bias.

36. What To Do With Germany?, 16 February 1944, *March of Time*, outtakes, Film

ID: 2249, United States Holocaust Memorial Museum, https://collections. ushmm.org/search/catalog/irn1001713.

37. These claims come from the shop's own history, which lacks authenticating source material; see 'About Foyles', W & G Foyle Limited, accessed 21 April 2020, https://web.archive.org/web/20200422183518/https://www.foyles.co.uk/about-foyles.

38. Vansittart, *Black Record*, p. 53; Vansittart, Robert, 'Foreword', in Coole, W. W. and Potter, M. F., [Władysław Wszebór Kulski] (eds), *Thus Spake Germany*, 2nd ed. (London: 1941), p. xii; 'His Cure for Germany', *Daily Mail*, 2 March 1943.

39. Vansittart, Robert, 'What Shall We Do with Germany? There's Nothing to be Frightened of Says Lord Vansittart', *Sunday Express*, 28 November 1943; Vansittart, Robert, 'The Problem of Germany: A Discussion', *International Affairs* 21, no. 3 (1945), pp. 313–23.

40. 'Vansittart Says Third War Unless', *Daily Express*, 27 March 1943; Vansittart, *Bones of Contention*, pp. 48, 82.

41. Vansittart, *Bones of Contention*, p. 46.

42. Braunthal, Julius, *Need Germany Survive?* (London: 1943), p. 212.

43. Edwards, *Victor Gollancz*, p. 377.

Chapter Four

1. Morley, Sheridan, *A Talent to Amuse: A Life of Noël Coward* (London: 2016), pp. 301–2.

2. Shephard, Ben, *The Long Road Home: The Aftermath of the Second World War* (London: 2010), p. 125.

3. 'Don't Let's Be Beastly to the Germans', Noël Coward, Song, His Master's Voice, 1943.

4. 'What Our Readers Are Saying – "Vansittartism" Rhymed', letter to the editor, *Yorkshire Post*, 21 July 1943.

5. Nicholas, Siân, *The Echo of War: Home Front Propaganda and the Wartime BBC, 1939–45* (Manchester: 1996), p. 161.

6. Day, Barry, *The Letters of Noël Coward* (London: 2014), p. 434.

7. Lee, Sabine, *Victory in Europe: Britain and Germany since 1945* (Harlow: 2001), p. 14; Lach, Donald F., 'What They Would Do about Germany', *The Journal of Modern History* 17, no. 3 (1945), p. 227, www.jstor.org/stable/1898987; Gollancz, *Shall Our Children Live or Die?*, p. 124; Geyer, Curt, FitzGerald, Edward and Loeb, Walter, *Gollancz in German Wonderland* (London: 1942); Tombs, 'The Victory of Socialist "Vansittartism"', p. 296.

8. Cairncross, *The Price of War*, p. 45; Watt, Donald Cameron, *Britain Looks to Germany: British Opinion and Policy towards Germany since 1945* (London: 1965), p. 39; Reynolds, David, 'The Diplomacy of the Grand Alliance', in Bosworth, Richard J. B. and Maiolo, Joseph (eds), *The Cambridge History of the Second World War*, vol. 2, *Politics and Ideology* (Cambridge: 2015), pp. 301–23.

9. Balfour, Michael, 'Another Look at "Unconditional Surrender"', *International Affairs* 46, no. 4 (1970), pp. 719–36, https://doi.org/10.2307/2614534.

10. Baylis, 'British Wartime Thinking', p. 268.

11. Cairncross, *The Price of War*, pp. 35–6.
12. Szanajda, Andrew, *The Allies and the German Problem, 1941–1949: From Cooperation to Alternative Settlement* (Basingstoke: 2015), pp. 6–7.
13. Szanajda, *The Allies*, pp. 9–10.
14. Eubank, Keith, *Summit at Teheran* (New York: 1985), p. 314.
15. Reynolds, David, *Britannia Overruled: British Policy and World Power in the Twentieth Century* (London: 1991), p. 146.
16. Szanajda, *The Allies*, p. 12; Burridge, Trevor, 'Great Britain and the Dismemberment of Germany at the End of the Second World War', *The International History Review* 3, no. 4 (1981), p. 576.
17. Szanajda, *The Allies*, p. 16; Cairncross, *The Price of War*, p. 54.
18. Olick, *In the House of the Hangman*, p. 83. As they say, possession is nine-tenths of the law and even with details of reparations yet to be decided, it was obvious that having control over Germany's most heavily industrialized region could be beneficial.
19. Olick, *In the House of the Hangman*, pp. 83–5.
20. 'The Policy of Hate', *Time*, 2 October 1944.
21. Cairncross, *The Price of War*, p. 55; Olick, *In the House of the Hangman*, p. 29.
22. *Foreign Relations of the United States*, Diplomatic Papers, Conferences at Malta and Yalta, 1945, ed. Barron, Bryton (Washington: United States Government Printing Office, 1955), Document 290.
23. Reynolds, 'The Diplomacy of the Grand Alliance', p. 319.
24. Reynolds, *Britannia Overruled*, p. 147.
25. The exact details of this were set to be worked out by the Allied Reparations Commission in Moscow; see Farquharson, J. E., 'Anglo-American Policy on German Reparations from Yalta to Potsdam', *The English Historical Review* 112, no. 448 (1997), pp. 904–26.
26. Goldman, 'Germans and Nazis', pp. 156–7. File report 1624, 'Private Opinion About the German People', March 1943, Mass-Observation Archive, University of Sussex, Brighton; File report 2565, 'Attitudes to the German People', February 1948, Mass-Observation Archive, University of Sussex, Brighton.
27. Hynd Opening Speech, FO 1039/669 Control Office for Germany and Austria and Foreign Office: Control Commission for Germany (British Element), Economic Divisions: Records, CCG Exhibition London: Vol II, December 1945 – March 1946, National Archives, London.

Chapter Five

1. Reel 7, Cole, Norman (Oral History), Sound Recording, Catalogue Number 29540, Imperial War Museum Archive, London.
2. Beevor, Antony, *The Second World War* (London: 2012), p. 674.
3. Reel 7, Cole, Norman (Oral History).
4. Reel 7, Souper, Robert Reinagle (Oral History), Sound Recording, Catalogue Number 33336, Imperial War Museum Archive, London.
5. Bedessem, Edward N., *The U.S. Army Campaigns of World War II: Central Europe* (Washington: 1996), pp. 9–11.
6. Memoir, 'Private Skinner', Private Papers of N A Skinner, Documents.14502, Imperial War Museum Archive, London.

7. 'Musketeer', 'The 21st Army Group in North-West Europe – IV', *Royal United Services Institution Journal* 103, no. 610 (1958), pp. 230–42, https://doi.org/10.1080/03071845809433549.

8. Reel 7, Souper, Robert Reinagle (Oral History).

9. Memoir, 'Private Skinner', Skinner Papers.

10. Fritz, Stephen G., *Endkampf: Soldiers, Civilians, and the Death of the Third Reich* (Lexington: 2004), p. 36.

11. Reel 5, Chester, Charles (Oral History), Sound Recording, Catalogue Number 21030, Imperial War Museum Archive, London.

12. Bessel, Richard, *Germany 1945: From War to Peace* (London: 2009), pp. 19–25.

13. Bessel, *Germany 1945*, pp. 44–5.

14. 'Musketeer', 'The 21st Army Group', pp. 240–41.

15. Bessel, *Germany 1945*, p. 36.

16. Memoir, 'Private Skinner', Skinner Papers.

17. Marshall, Barbara, *The Origins of Post-War German Politics* (London: 1988), p. 6.

18. Donnison, Frank, *Civil Affairs and Military Government, North-West Europe 1944–1946* (London: 1961), pp. 195–6.

19. Bessel, *Germany 1945*, p. 170.

20. Marshall, *The Origins of Post-war German Politics*, pp. 5–7; Smith, Barbara, 'The Rules of Engagement: German Women and British Occupiers, 1945–1949' (Unpublished PhD dissertation, Wilfrid Laurier University: 2009), p. 24.

21. Donnison, *Civil Affairs and Military Government*, p. 208.

22. Donnison, *Civil Affairs and Military Government*, p. 218.

23. Bessel, *Germany 1945*, p. 180.

24. Reel 9, Wayne, Peter (Oral History), Sound Recording, Catalogue Number 30638, Imperial War Museum Archive, London.

25. Longden, Sean, *T-Force: The Race for Nazi War Secrets, 1945* (London: 2009).

26. Bessel, *Germany 1945*, pp. 116–18.

27. Bessel, *Germany 1945*, pp. 116–18; Naimark, Norman M., *The Russians in Germany: A History of the Soviet Zone of Occupation, 1945–1949* (Cambridge, Mass.; London: 1995).

28. Some, but by no means all, of these stories appeared in the British papers; see 'British Officer and Girl Shot In Berlin: Murder Suspected', *Times*, 5 November 1946; 'Shots in Flat: Control Commission Driver for Trial', *Manchester Guardian*, 17 November 1948; 'Control Commission Driver Acquitted', *Manchester Guardian*, 12 March 1948; 'British Official Murdered: Shot Dead in Germany', *Manchester Guardian*, 12 May 1949; 'British Officer and German Girl Shot', *Daily Mail*, 5 November 1946; 'Shot Girl: 2 Officers Held', *Daily Mail*, 7 August 1946; 'Bath Man Dead in Germany', *Bath Chronicle and Weekly Gazette*, 2 August 1947; 'Briton Accused of Murder in Germany', *Dundee Courier*, 17 January 1948; 'Fight in Flat in Germany', *Belfast News-Letter*, 17 January 1948; 'RAF Airman Charged with Rape', *Manchester Guardian*, 28 August 1946. Also see Longden, Sean, *To the Victor the Spoils: Soldiers' Lives from D-Day to VE-Day* (London: 2007). For the Soviet Zone, see Dack, Mikkel, 'Crimes Committed by Soviet Soldiers Against German Civilians, 1944–1945: A Historiographical Analysis', *Journal of Military and Strategic Studies* 10, no. 4 (2008), http://jmss.org/jmss/index.php/jmss/article/view/75; Anonyma, *Eine Frau in Berlin: Tagebuchaufzeichnungen vom 20. April bis 22.*

Juni 1945, 1st ed. published 1953 (Frankfurt am Main: 2003); Naimark, *The Russians in Germany*.

29. Longden, *To the Victor the Spoils*, pp. 140-41.
30. 'Shot German Girl', *Manchester Guardian*, 9 September 1949.
31. 'German Girl's Death: Story of Shooting in a Wood: Ex-Soldier's Alleged Statement', *Manchester Guardian*, 31 August 1949; 'Alleged 1945 Murder in Germany', *Times*, 31 August 1949.
32. 'In Brief', *Manchester Guardian*, 29 September 1949.
33. Bessel, *Germany 1945*, p. 256.
34. Bessel, *Germany 1945*, p. 256.
35. Bessel, *Germany 1945*, p. 262.
36. Bessel, *Germany 1945*, p. 263.
37. Mosley, Leonard O., *Report From Germany* (London: 1945), p. 72.
38. Mosley, *Report From Germany*, p. 70.
39. Mosley, *Report From Germany*, p. 69.
40. Mosley, *Report From Germany*, p. 81.
41. Bessel, *Germany 1945*, p. 145.
42. Bessel, *Germany 1945*, p. 173.
43. Treber, Leonie, *Mythos Trümmerfrauen: Von der Trümmerbeseitigung in der Kriegs- und Nachkriegszeit und der Entstehung eines deutschen Erinnerungsortes* (Essen: 2014).
44. Blum, '"My Home, your Castle"', p. 116.
45. The Foreign Office, *Instructions for British Servicemen in Germany, 1944* (Oxford: 2007).
46. For more details, see Biddiscombe, Perry, *Werwolf! The History of the National Socialist Guerrilla Movement, 1944-1946* (Toronto: 1998); Biddiscombe, Perry, *The Last Nazis: SS Werewolf Guerrilla Resistance in Europe 1944-1947* (Stroud: 2000).
47. Hodenberg, Christina von, 'Of German Fräuleins, Nazi Werewolves, and Iraqi Insurgents: The American Fascination with Hitler's Last Foray', *Central European History* 41, no. 1 (2008), p. 79. www.jstor.org/stable/20457312.
48. Marshall, *The Origins of Post-war German Politics*, p. 6.
49. Meehan, Patricia, *A Strange Enemy People: Germans under the British, 1945-1950* (London: 2001), p. 40.
50. Smith, 'The Rules of Engagement'; Stark, John Robert, 'The Overlooked Majority: German Women in the Four Zones of Occupied Germany, 1945-1949, a Comparative Study' (Unpublished PhD dissertation, Ohio State University: 2003).
51. Knowles, Christopher, *Winning the Peace: The British in Occupied Germany, 1945-1948* (London; New York: 2017), pp. 162-5.
52. MacDonogh, Giles, *After the Reich: From the Fall of Vienna to the Berlin Airlift* (London: 2008), p. 75.
53. Reel 2, Williams, William Richard (Oral History), Sound Recording, Catalogue Number 15437, Imperial War Museum Archive, London.
54. Quoted in Harding, Luke, '"I have never seen such horror in my life"', *The Guardian*, 14 April 2005, www.theguardian.com/world/2005/apr/14/secondworldwar.germany.
55. Reel 4, Sassoon, Agnes (Oral History), Sound Recording, Catalogue Number 9093, Imperial War Museum Archive, London.

56. See Welch, David, 'Atrocity Propaganda' in Cull, Nicholas John, Holbrook, David and Welch, David (eds), *Propaganda and Mass Persuasion: A Historical Encyclopedia, 1500 to the Present* (Santa Barbara: 2003), pp. 23–6.

57. Letter to mother, 23 April 1945, Private Papers of Miss J McFarlane, Documents.9550, Imperial War Museum Archive, London.

58. Holmila, Antero, *Reporting the Holocaust in the British, Swedish and Finnish Press, 1945–50* (Basingstoke; New York: 2011), p. 1.

59. 'Richard Dimbleby describes Belsen', archive broadcast, BBC, accessed 27 April 2023, www.bbc.co.uk/archive/richard-dimbleby-describes-belsen/zvw7cqt.

60. Jordan, Ulrike, '"A Mixture of Stubborn Resistance and Sudden Surrender": The British Media Report on the End of the War in Europe' in Jordan, Ulrike (ed.), *Conditions of Surrender: Britons and Germans Witness the End of the War* (London; New York: 1997), p. 43.

61. Haggith, Toby, 'The 1945 Documentary German Concentration Camps Factual Survey and the 70th Anniversary of the Liberation of the Camps', *The Holocaust in History and Memory* 7 (2014), pp. 181–97.

62. It would only be fully restored in 2014; see *Night Will Fall*, documentary film, directed by Andre Singer (2014; London: British Film Institute).

63. 'These are the Germans', *Daily Mail*, 19 April 1945; Proof Positive, 30 April 1945, *Gaumont-British News*, newsreel, Issue 1478, ITN Source Newsreels, www.itnsource.com/en; Reilly, Joanne, *Belsen in History and Memory* (London: 1997), pp. 71–4; Kushner, Tony, *The Holocaust and the Liberal Imagination: A Social and Cultural History* (Oxford: 1994), pp. 210, 215–21.

64. Holmila, *Reporting the Holocaust*, pp. 23–4, 194; Pronay, Nicholas, 'Defeated Germany in British Newsreels: 1944–45' in Short, K. R. M. and Dolezel, Stephan (eds), *Hitler's Fall: The Newsreel Witness* (London: 1988), pp. 28–49.

65. Balfour, Michael, *Propaganda in War: Organisations, Policies and Publics in Britain and Germany* (London: 1979), p. 302.

66. 'Peers Debate Atrocities: Vansittart Proposes Annual Repentance Day for Germany – British Dupes of the Lie that they "Didn't Know"', *Daily Express*, 2 May 1945.

67. Holmila, *Reporting the Holocaust*, p. 26.

68. Official Report, Fifth Series, Parliamentary Debates, House of Lords, Vol. 136 (1945), 1 May 1945, Col. 61–97.

69. Lord Vansittart on the German Atrocities (interview with Leslie Mitchell), 30 April 1945, *British Movietone News*, newsreel, no. 45700, British Movietone News Digital Archive, www.movietone.com.

70. Gordon Walker, Patrick, *The Lid Lifts* (London: 1945), p. 86.

71. Bessel, *Germany 1945*, p. 47.

72. Reel 6, Suster, Ilya (Oral History), Sound Recording, Catalogue Number 27774, Imperial War Museum Archive, London.

Chapter Six

1. Kynaston, David, *Austerity Britain, 1945–51* (London: 2007), p. 6.
2. 'Gwydir Street VE Day Party', Cambridgeshire Collection, Cambridge Central

Library, accessed 14 April 2021, https://capturingcambridge.org/petersfield/gwydir-street/gwydir-street-ve-day-party/.

3. Kynaston, *Austerity Britain*, p. 9.
4. Kynaston, *Austerity Britain*, p. 7.
5. Kynaston, *Austerity Britain*, pp. 8, 10.
6. Kynaston, *Austerity Britain*, p. 11.
7. Kynaston, *Austerity Britain*, p. 14.
8. Kynaston, *Austerity Britain*, p. 13.
9. Kynaston, *Austerity Britain*, p. 16.
10. Weight, Richard, *Patriots: National Identity in Britain, 1940–2000* (London: 2002), p. 104; *Daily Express*, 8 May 1945.
11. Weight, *Patriots*, p. 106.
12. Kynaston, *Austerity Britain*, p. 15.
13. Weight, *Patriots*, p. 107; *Daily Telegraph*, 5 May 1945.
14. 'Westminster Abbey and VE Day', Westminster Abbey, accessed 4 August 2021, www.westminster-abbey.org/about-the-abbey/history/ve-day-75.
15. 'Westminster Abbey. A short thanksgiving for victory', Westminster Abbey, accessed 4 August 2021, www.westminster-abbey.org/media/4109/ve-day-1945.pdf.
16. Weight, *Patriots*, p. 107; *Daily Telegraph*, 7 May 1945.
17. Victory in Europe (1945), newsreel, *British Pathé*, no. 1149.21, 14 May 1945, British Pathé Newsreel Archive, www.britishpathe.com/.
18. Beevor, *The Second World War*, pp. 758–60.
19. Kershaw, Ian, *The End: Germany, 1944–45* (London: 2011), p. 372.
20. Letter, 11 May 1945, Private Papers of Miss D E Smith, Documents.2379, Imperial War Museum Archive, London.
21. Letter, 7 May 1945, Smith Papers.
22. Memoir, 'Private Skinner', Skinner Papers.
23. Reel 5, Chester, Charles (Oral History).
24. Reels 1–8, Johnson, Peter William (Oral History), Sound Recording, Catalogue Number 3790, Imperial War Museum Archive, London.
25. Reel 10, Johnson, Peter William (Oral History).
26. Journal, McFarlane Papers.
27. Reel 7, Wayne, Peter (Oral History).
28. Reel 9, Wayne, Peter (Oral History).
29. Letter, 22 May 1945, Smith Papers.
30. Letter, 3 June 1945, Smith Papers.
31. Letter, 9 October 1945, Letters written by L/Cpl John William Booth, 2011-01-4, National Army Museum, London.
32. Letter to 'Ma', 23 September 1945, Letters written by Henry Ronald Hughes, 2014-10-27-73, National Army Museum, London.
33. '"Britain Must Stay Strong," Says Monty', *Daily Mirror*, 26 September 1945.
34. Spender, *European Witness*, pp. 22–4.
35. Diefendorf, Jeffry M., *In the Wake of the War: The Reconstruction of German Cities After World War II* (New York; Oxford: 1993), p. 126.; Peters, William, *In Germany Now: The Diary of a Soldier – A Diary of Impressions in Germany, August–December, 1945* (London: 1946), p. 8.
36. Berlin – Carcass City, 23 September 1946, *British Movietone News*, newsreel, Issue 47494, British Movietone News Digital Archive, www.movietone.com.

37. Calder, Angus, *The Myth of the Blitz* (London: 1991), pp. 234–44.
38. Aldgate, Anthony and Richards, Jeffrey, *Britain Can Take It: The British Cinema in the Second World War* (Oxford: 1986), pp. 218–43.
39. See Farquharson, J. E., *The Western Allies and the Politics of Food: Agrarian Management in Postwar Germany* (Leamington Spa: 1985).
40. Mary Bouman to her parents, 20 February 1946, Lübbecke, Private Papers of Miss M Bouman, Documents.16779, Imperial War Museum Archive, London.
41. Lee, *Victory in Europe*, p. 8.
42. Malzahn, Manfred, *Germany 1945–1949: A Sourcebook* (London: 2003), pp. 109–11.
43. Bessel, *Germany 1945*, p. 255.
44. Malzahn, *Germany 1945–1949*, pp. 129–31.
45. Malzahn, *Germany 1945–1949*, p.129.
46. Connor, Ian, *Refugees and Expellees in Post-War Germany* (Manchester: 2014), pp. 12–15.
47. Beevor, *The Second World War*, pp. 761–2.
48. Dickens, Arthur Geoffrey, *Lübeck Diary* (London: 1947), p. 45.
49. Cabinet Minutes, 3 April 1945, CAB 79/31/11, War Cabinet and Cabinet: Chiefs of Staff Committee: Minutes, National Archives, London.
50. Donnison, Frank, *Civil Affairs and Military Government, Central Organization and Planning* (London: 1966), pp. 113–14. It had been planned for the Control Commission to have more technical expertise among its staff, especially in the fields of agriculture and food distribution where problems were being felt so acutely; see Donnison, *Civil Affairs and Military Government*, p. 257.
51. Donnison, *Civil Affairs and Military Government*, pp. 263–8.
52. Cabinet Minutes, 16 May 1945, CAB 79/33/16, War Cabinet and Cabinet: Chiefs of Staff Committee: Minutes, National Archives, London.
53. Cabinet Minutes, 16 May 1945, CAB 79/33/16, War Cabinet and Cabinet: Chiefs of Staff Committee: Minutes, National Archives, London.
54. Letter, 5 June 1945, Smith Papers.

Chapter Seven

1. Mee, Jr, Charles L., *Meeting at Potsdam* (London: 1975), pp. 39–44; Astley, Joan Bright, *The Inner Circle: A View of War at the Top* (London: 1971), p. 209.
2. 'Obituary', *The Independent*, 28 January 2009; Astley, *The Inner Circle*, pp. 211–18.
3. Dobbs, Michael, *Six Months in 1945: From World War to Cold War* (London: 2012), pp. 335–6.
4. Astley, *The Inner Circle*, p. 214.
5. Quoted Mee, *Meeting at Potsdam*, p. 44; Astley, *The Inner Circle*, p. 215.
6. *Foreign Relations of the United States*, Diplomatic Papers, The Conference of Berlin (The Potsdam Conference), 1945, vol. II, ed. Dougall, Richardson, (Washington: United States Government Printing Office, 1960), Log of the President's Trip to the Conference July 6 to August 7, 1945, Document 710.
7. Dobbs, *Six Months in 1945*, pp. 324–5.
8. Mee, *Meeting at Potsdam*, pp. 28, 32.

9. Moran, Charles, *Churchill at War, 1940–1945* (New York: 2002), p. 313.
10. Feis, Herbert, *Between War and Peace: The Potsdam Conference* (Princeton, NJ: 1960), p. 181.
11. Mee, *Meeting at Potsdam*, p. 254.
12. Marshall, *The Origins of Post-war German Politics*, p. 8.
13. Dilks, David (ed.), *Alexander Cadogan / The Diaries of Sir Alexander Cadogan, O.M., 1938–1945* (London: 1971), p. 770.
14. Bew, John, *Citizen Clem: A Biography of Attlee* (London: 2017), p. 11.
15. Bew, *Citizen Clem*, p. 13.
16. Quoted in Bew, *Citizen Clem*, p. 413.
17. Ramsden, John, *Don't Mention the War: The British and Germans since 1890* (London: 2006), p. 266.
18. Bullock, Alan, *The Life and Times of Ernest Bevin*, vol. 3, *Ernest Bevin: Foreign Secretary 1945–1951* (New York; London: 1983), p. 856.
19. Letter, 26 July 1945, Smith Papers.
20. Bew, *Citizen Clem*, p. 353.
21. Harry S. Truman letter to Margaret Truman, 29 July 1945, Papers of Harry S. Truman Pertaining to Family, Business, and Personal Affairs, Harry S. Truman Library, Independence, Mo.
22. Mee, *Meeting at Potsdam*, p. 254.
23. Lee, *Victory in Europe*, p. 16.
24. Cairncross, *The Price of War*, p. 130.
25. Mee, *Meeting at Potsdam*, p. 256.
26. Mee, *Meeting at Potsdam*, p. 276.
27. *Times*, 2 August 1945.
28. Shaw, Tony, 'The British Popular Press and the Early Cold War', *History* 83, no. 269 (1998), p. 69, https://doi.org/10.1111/1468-229X.00063.
29. *Times*, 3 August 1945; *Daily Mirror*, 3 August 1945; BBB [Bernard Buckham], 'Whatever Happens We Stand by the Potsdam Decision', *Daily Mirror*, 5 October 1945.
30. Shaw, 'The British Popular Press and the Early Cold War', p. 70.
31. Bullock, *The Life and Times of Ernest Bevin*, vol. 3, p. 29.
32. Shaw, 'The British Popular Press and the Early Cold War', p. 70.
33. Quoted in Graham-Dixon, Francis, *The Allied Occupation of Germany: The Refugee Crisis, Denazification and the Path to Reconstruction* (London; New York: 2013), p. 39.
34. Gollancz, Victor, 'The German Settlement', *The Economist*, 11 August 1945; Crossman, R. H. S., 'Our Job In Germany', *New Statesman and Nation*, 8 September 1945. These articles were re-published in Gollancz, Victor, *Europe and Germany: Today and Tomorrow* (London: 1945).
35. Deighton, Anne, 'The "Frozen Front": The Labour Government, the Division of Germany and the Origins of the Cold War, 1945–7', *International Affairs* 63, no. 3 (1987), p. 450, https://doi.org/10.2307/2619245; Bullock, *The Life and Times of Ernest Bevin*, vol. 3, p. 29.
36. Marshall, *The Origins of Post-war German Politics*, p. i.
37. 'Proclamation No. 1 from the Control Council for Germany (Berlin, 30 August 1945)', *Official Gazette of the Control Council for Germany*, 29 October 1945.
38. Balfour, Michael and Mair, John, *Four Power Control in Germany and Austria 1945–1946* (Oxford: 1956), p. 96.

39. 'F.-M. Montgomery on Future of Germany', *Times*, 12 November 1945.
40. Letter, 15 May 1945, Letters written by L/Cpl John William Booth, 2011-01-4, National Army Museum, London.

Chapter Eight

1. 'Porta Westfalica-Barkhausen', History, KZ-Gedenkstätte Neuengamme, accessed 1 July 2021, www.kz-gedenkstaette-neuengamme.de/en/history/satellite-camps/satellite-camps/porta-westfalica-barkhausen/.
2. Reel 12, Wayne, Peter (Oral History).
3. Farquharson, J. E., 'The British Occupation of Germany 1945–6: A Badly Managed Disaster Area?' *German History* 11, no. 3 (1993), p. 328.
4. Overy, Richard, *The Bombing War: Europe 1939–1945* (London: 2014), p. 335.
5. Intelligence Report, 1 May 1945, FO 371/46730, Allied Control Commission: Policy in Occupied Germany: Post-Defeat Military Government Planning for Germany: Situation in Occupied Germany, Foreign Office: Political Departments: General Correspondence from 1906–1966, National Archives, London.
6. G. W. R. T., 'The Early Days', *British Zone Review* 1, no. 4, November 1945.
7. Chrystal, Paul, *British Army of the Rhine: The BAOR, 1945–1993* (Barnsley: 2018), p. 11.
8. Johnson, B. S. (ed.), *All Bull: The National Servicemen* (London: 1973).
9. Blum, '"My Home, your Castle"', p. 116; Balfour and Mair, *Four Power Control*, p. 94.
10. Lee, *Victory in Europe*, p. 17.
11. Marshall, *The Origins of Post-war German Politics*, p. 17; Pronay, Nicholas, 'Introduction – "To stamp out the whole tradition…"', in Pronay, Nicholas and Wilson, Nicholas (eds), *The Political Re-education of Germany and her Allies after World War II* (London; Sydney: 1985), p. 8.
12. Meehan, *A Strange Enemy People*, pp. 47–8.
13. Marshall, *The Origins of Post-war German Politics*, p. 21.
14. Farquharson, 'The British Occupation of Germany 1945–6', p. 327.
15. Reinisch, Jessica, *The Perils of Peace: The Public Health Crisis in Occupied Germany* (Oxford: 2013), pp. 10–14.
16. Reinisch, *The Perils of Peace*, pp. 286–7.
17. Cabinet Minutes, 24 February 1948, CAB 129/25/2, Cabinet: Memoranda (CP and C Series), National Archives, London; Cabinet Minutes, 4 June 1946, CAB 129/10/18, Cabinet: Memoranda (CP and C Series), National Archives, London. Also see Farquharson, 'The British Occupation of Germany 1945–6', p. 327; Marshall, *The Origins of Post-war German Politics*, p. 22.
18. Edna Wearmouth to her father, 15 March 1947, France/Germany, Private Papers of Miss E Wearmouth, Documents.5413, Imperial War Museum Archive, London.
19. Meehan, *A Strange Enemy People*, p. 60.
20. Quoted Meehan, *A Strange Enemy People*, p. 60.
21. See Meehan, *A Strange Enemy People*, p. 52; Letter from Maurice Dean, Foreign Office, 3 February 1947, FO 371/64240, Long-term staffing policy of the Control Commission for Germany, National Archives, London.

22. Spender, *European Witness*, p. 29, hinted at ten years; Dickens, *Lübeck Diary*, p. 123, suggested 'several years'; Beveridge, William, *An Urgent Message from Germany* (London: 1946), p. 18, simply said 'years'; Byford-Jones, Wilfred, *Berlin Twilight* (London; New York: 1947), p. 42, reported rumours of up to twenty years; Brinton, Henry, *Vengeance Is Dear* (London: 1946), p. 101, suggests, with some foresight, five to eight years; Minshall, Thomas H., *On Disarming Germany* (London; New York: 1945), p. 10, says the military occupation may last for 'five, ten, fifteen years or even more'; Morgan, J. H., *Assize of Arms: Being the Story of the Disarmament of Germany and Her Rearmament (1919–1939) in Two Volumes*, vol. 1, (London: 1945), p. xvii, says twenty-five years; Eisler, Robert and Hart, Robert George, *Winning The Peace: A Comprehensive Policy* (London: 1948), p. 7, wanted the occupation to last for 'a generation'.

23. Vansittart, 'The Problem of Germany', pp. 320–21; Brockway, Fenner, *German Diary* (London: 1946), p. 86.

24. Cabinet Minutes, 24 February 1948, CAB 129/25/2, Cabinet: Memoranda (CP and C Series), National Archives, London.

25. Balfour and Mair, *Four Power Control*, p. 96.

26. Marshall, *The Origins of Post-war German Politics*, p. 15.

27. Chaney, Sandra, *Nature of the Miracle Years: Conservation in West Germany, 1945–1975* (New York; London: 2008), pp. 67–8. By January 1947 more than 26,000 tons of wood had been exported to the UK, causing anxiety among the locals over the threat of deforestation.

Chapter Nine

1. Tetlow, Edwin, 'I Was There! Cossacks Welcomed Us as We Entered Berlin', *The War Illustrated*, 3 August 1945.

2. Memoir, John Rhys, Private Papers of J E Rhys, Documents.19794, Imperial War Museum Archive, London.

3. Born, Lester K., 'The Ministerial Collecting Center near Kassel, Germany', *The American Archivist*, 13, no. 3 (1950), pp. 237–58, www.jstor.org/stable/40288828.

4. Vansittart, Robert, 'Germany After the War – Aims of Occupation', letter to the editor, *Times*, 11 May 1945.

5. McCallum, Ronald Buchanan, *Public Opinion and the Last Peace* (Oxford: 1944); Minshall, *On Disarming Germany*.

6. 'Blowing Up Nazi Bombs', *Daily Mirror*, 23 August 1945.

7. 'Kiel: Graveyard of the German Navy', *Picture Post*, 6 October 1945.

8. Madsen, Chris, *The Royal Navy and German Naval Disarmament, 1942–1947* (London: 1998).

9. Reel 3, James, George Philip Henry (Oral History), Sound Recording, Catalogue Number 14837, Imperial War Museum Archive, London.

10. 'Obituary: John A. Bouman', *Standard-Sentinel*, 5 November 1958.

11. Dack, Mikkel, 'Questioning the Past: The Fragebogen and Everyday Denazification in Occupied Germany' (Unpublished PhD dissertation, University of Calgary: 2016).

12. Taylor, Frederick, *Exorcising Hitler: The Occupation and Denazification of Germany* (London; New York; Berlin: 2011), p. 311.

13. Taylor, *Exorcising Hitler*, p. 304.
14. Taylor, *Exorcising Hitler*, pp. 309–10.
15. Meehan, *A Strange Enemy People*, pp. 70–4; Beattie, Andrew H., *Allied Internment Camps in Occupied Germany: Extrajudicial Detention in the Name of Denazification, 1945–1950* (Cambridge: 2020), p. 176.
16. Beattie, *Allied Internment Camps*, pp. 21–2, 70, 77–8.
17. Hun Prisoners: How the Mighty Have Fallen, 22 November 1945, *British Movietone News*, newsreel, Issue 46223, British Movietone News Digital Archive, www.movietone.com.
18. Black, Monica, *A Demon-Haunted Land: Witches, Wonder Doctors, and the Ghosts of the Past in Post-WWII Germany* (New York: 2020).
19. Meehan, *A Strange Enemy People*, p. 108.
20. Quoted in Beattie, *Allied Internment Camps*, p. 88.
21. See Meehan, *A Strange Enemy People*, pp. 73–4.
22. Letter, Brian Robertson to Gilmour Jenkins, 21 October 1946, FO 1030/304, Control Commission for Germany (British Element): Various Private Office Papers and Administration and Local Government Branch Files, Correspondence DMG/Permanent Secretary: vol II, National Archives, London.
23. Bessel, *Germany 1945*, p. 187; Beattie, *Allied Internment Camps*, pp. 1, 64.
24. Beattie, *Allied Internment Camps*, p. 1.
25. Beattie, *Allied Internment Camps*, p. 85.
26. Quoted in Meehan, *A Strange Enemy People*, p. 207.
27. Longden, *T-Force*; Cobain, Ian, 'How T-Force abducted Germany's best brains for Britain', *Guardian*, 29 August 2007.
28. Reckitt, B. N., *Diary of Military Government in Germany 1945* (Ilfracombe: 1989), p. 71.
29. Lee, *Victory in Europe*, p. 16.
30. See Meehan, *A Strange Enemy People*, pp. 212–3.
31. 'Zur Geschichte des Produktionsstandortes Salzgitter', The history of the Salzgitter-Konzerns, Salzgitter AG Corporate Archives, accessed 1 January 2022, https://geschichte.salzgitter-ag.com/de/einzelne-geschaeftsbereiche-und-standorte/geschaeftsbereich-flachstahl/salzgitter/ungewisse-zukunft.html.
32. Cairncross, *The Price of War*, pp. 189–90.
33. See Van Hook, James C., *Rebuilding Germany: The Creation of the Social Market Economy, 1945–1957* (Cambridge: 2004), pp. 53–93.
34. Herbert, Ulrich, *A History of 20th-Century Germany*, trans. Fowkes, Ben (Oxford: 2019), p. 463; CAB 128/12/34, 31 May 1948, and CAB 128/13/28, 4 November 1948, Cabinet: Minutes (CM and CC Series), National Archives, London.
35. For a full discussion, see Farquharson, J. E., 'Land Reform in the British Zone, 1945–1947', *German History* 6, no. 1 (1988), pp. 35–56.
36. Herbert, *A History of 20th-Century Germany*, p. 465.
37. Watt, *Britain Looks to Germany*, p. 85.
38. For a good overview, see Lupa, Markus, *Changing Lanes under British Command: The Transformation of Volkswagen from a Factory into a Commercial Enterprise, 1945–1949* (Wolfsburg: 2011), p. 8; Turner, Ian, 'Das Volkswagenwerk – ein deutsches Unternehmen unter britischer Kontrolle'

in Foschepoth, Josef and Steininger, Rolf (eds), *Britische Deutschland- und Besatzungspolitik* (Paderborn: 1985), pp. 280–300.

39. Richter, Ralf, *Ivan Hirst: British Officer and Manager of Volkswagen's Postwar Recovery* (Wolfsburg: 2013), pp. 11–7.

40. Lupa, Markus, *The British and Their Works: The Volkswagenwerk and the occupying power 1945–1949* (Wolfsburg: 2005), p. 6.

41. Quoted in Parrissien, Steven, *The Life of the Automobile: A New History of the Motor Car* (London: 2013), p. 178.

42. Quoted in Parrissien, *The Life of the Automobile*, p. 179.

43. Lupa, *The British and Their Works*, p. 13.

44. Parrissien, *The Life of the Automobile*, p. 181.

45. Watt, *Britain Looks to Germany*, p. 71.

46. Pronay, 'Introduction', pp. 16–8, 23.

47. Euros, Glesni, 'The post-war British "re-education" policy for German universities and its application at the universities of Göttingen and Cologne (1945–1947)', *Research in Comparative and International Education* 11, no. 3 (2016), p. 249.

48. Pronay, 'Introduction', p. 21.

49. Pronay, 'Introduction', p. 2.

50. Pronay, 'Introduction', p. 23.

51. Watt, *Britain Looks to Germany*, pp. 72–3; Pronay, 'Introduction', p. 1.

52. Herbert, *A History of 20th-Century Germany*, p. 466.

53. Herbert, *A History of 20th-Century Germany*, p. 467.

54. Quoted in Phillips, David, *Educating the Germans: People and policy in the British zone of Germany, 1945–1949* (London: 2018), p. 113.

55. Quoted in Phillips, *Educating the Germans*, p. 112.

56. Quoted in Phillips, *Educating the Germans*, p. 112.

57. Watt, *Britain Looks to Germany*, pp. 80–1.

58. Quoted in Phillips, *Educating the Germans*, p. 122.

59. Herbert, *A History of 20th-Century Germany*, p. 465.

60. Howson, Peter, *Britain and the German Churches 1945–1950: The Role of the Religious Affairs Branch in the British Zone* (Woodbridge: 2021).

61. Meehan, *A Strange Enemy People*, p. 175.

62. 'Re-education of Germany', photograph, *Manchester Guardian*, 22 March 1946.

63. Lee, *Victory in Europe*, p. 17.

64. Pronay, 'Introduction', p. 27.

65. For breadth of support, see 'Re-education', editorial, *Manchester Guardian*, 13 February 1946; 'Democracy in Germany: The Need – and the Means – of Bringing about a Revival', *Manchester Guardian*, 14 June 1945.

66. Birley, Robert, 'Re-educating Germany', letter to the editor, *Times*, 8 May 1945; 'Re-education in the British Zone: 1,000,000 German Children Back at School', *Manchester Guardian*, 28 August 1945.

67. 'A Welcome Appointment', editorial, *Times*, 13 February 1947; 'Re-education – R. Birley to Advise', *Manchester Guardian*, 13 February 1947.

68. Young Germany – Narration by the Rt. Hon. Ellen Wilkinson – Minister of Education, 18 October 1945, *Pathé News*, newsreel, Issue 1153.2, British Pathé Archive, www.britishpathe.com/.

69. Marshall, *The Origins of Post-war German Politics*, pp. 68, 199.

70. Watt, *Britain Looks to Germany*, p. 79.
71. Reel 8, Souper, Robert Reinagle (Oral History).
72. Reckitt, *Diary of Military Government*, pp. 75–6.
73. Watt, *Britain Looks to Germany*, p. 79.
74. Biographical note, Private Papers of Miss M K Ostermann, Documents.15377, Imperial War Museum Archive, London.
75. 'Democratization and Decentralization of Local and Regional Government (Second Edition (Revised 1 Feb 46))', Booklet, FO 1013/725, Control Office for Germany and Austria and Foreign Office: Control Commission for Germany (British Element), North Rhine-Westphalia Region: Records, Military Government on administrative, local and regional government: democratisation and decentralisation, National Archives, London.

Chapter Ten

1. Longerich, Peter, *Heinrich Himmler: A Life* (Oxford: 2012), pp. 1–10.
2. For example, Crime Club, 4 June 1945, *Pathé News*, newsreel, Issue 1155.13, British Pathé Archive, www.britishpathe.com/.
3. The Belsen Trial Aka Belson Trial, 27 September 1945, *Pathé News*, newsreel, Issue 1165.14, British Pathé Archive, www.britishpathe.com/.
4. Guards Of The German Bergen-Belsen Concentration Camp Tried In Court 1945, 27 August 1945, *Gaumont-British News*, newsreel, Issue 1224, ITN Source Newsreels, www.itnsource.com/en.
5. Letter to his wife, 27 September 1945, Private Papers of Sir Gerald Lenanton, Documents.11120, Imperial War Museum Archive, London.
6. For example, Ashbrook, Harry, 'Belsen is a Bore to the Germans', *Daily Mirror*, 19 September 1945.
7. Bloxham, Donald, *Genocide on Trial: War Crimes Trials and the Formation of Holocaust History and Memory* (Oxford: 2001), pp. 99–100.
8. Sharman, Claire Louise, 'War Crimes Trials between Occupation and Integration: The Prosecution of Nazi War Criminals in the British Zone of Germany' (Unpublished PhD dissertation, University of Southampton: 2007), p. 79; '"Blonde Beastess" Has Confessed Her Guilt', *Daily Mirror*, 6 October 1945.
9. Bloxham, Donald, 'British War Crimes Trial Policy in Germany, 1945–1957: Implementation and Collapse', *The Journal of British Studies* 42, no. 1 (2003), p. 92, https://doi.org/10.1086/342687.
10. Sharman, 'War Crimes Trials', p. 3.
11. Quoted in Tusa, Ann and Tusa, John, *The Nuremberg Trial* (New York: 2010), p. 25.
12. Overy, Richard, 'The Nuremberg Trials', in Sands, Philippe (ed.), *From Nuremberg to The Hague: The Future of International Criminal Justice* (Cambridge: 2003), p. 3; Note by the Prime Minister, 1 November 1943, PREM 4/100/10, Treatment of Major War Criminals, Prime Minister's Office: Confidential Correspondence and Papers, National Archives, London; Diary Entry, 21 June 1945, KV 4/466, Diary of Guy Liddell, Deputy Director General of the Security Service, June to November 1945, National Archives, London.

13. Sharman, 'War Crimes Trials', p 4.
14. Vansittart, *Bones of Contention*, p. 48.
15. Sharman, 'War Crimes Trials', p. 58.
16. Sharman, 'War Crimes Trials', p. 51.
17. Sharman, 'War Crimes Trials', p. 93; Dale Jones, Priscilla, 'British Policy Towards German Crimes Against German Jews, 1939–1945', *The Leo Baeck Institute Yearbook* 36, no. 1 (1991), pp. 339–66, https://doi.org/10.1093/leobaeck/36.1.33.
18. Sharman, 'War Crimes Trials', pp. 104–5.
19. Sharman, 'War Crimes Trials', p. 90.
20. Sharman, 'War Crimes Trials', p. 54; Reichel, Peter, *Vergangenheitsbewältigung in Deutschland: Die Auseinandersetzung mit der NS-Diktatur in Politik und Justiz: Die Auseinandersetzung mit der NS-Diktatur von 1945 bis heute* (Munich: 2001), p. 109.
21. Lawson, *The Church of England and the Holocaust*, p. 144.
22. Sharman, 'War Crimes Trials', p. 82.
23. Sharman, 'War Crimes Trials', pp. 82, 84, 86, 88.
24. Holmila, *Reporting the Holocaust*, p. 85.
25. Overy, 'The Nuremberg Trials', p. 2.
26. Quoted in Holmila, *Reporting the Holocaust*, p. 78.
27. Bloxham, *Genocide on Trial*, p. 158.
28. Vansittart, Robert, *Events and Shadows: A Policy for the Remnants of a Century* (London; New York: 1947), p. 118.
29. *Daily Express*, 1 October 1946.
30. Sharman, 'War Crimes Trials', p. 27.
31. Bloxham, 'British War Crimes Trial Policy', p. 106.
32. Dale Jones, 'British Policy Towards German Crimes', p. 546.
33. Sharman, 'War Crimes Trials', p. 50.
34. Dale Jones, 'British Policy Towards German Crimes'.
35. Dale Jones, 'British Policy Towards German Crimes'.
36. Sharples, Caroline, 'What Do You Do With A Dead Nazi? Allied Policy on the Execution and Disposal of War Criminals, 1945–55', in Erlichman, Camilo and Knowles, Christopher (eds), *Transforming Occupation in the Western Zones of Germany: Politics, Everyday Life and Social Interactions, 1945–55* (London: 2018), pp. 97–112.
37. Sharples, 'What Do You Do With A Dead Nazi?', p. 100.
38. Sharman, 'War Crimes Trials', p. 121.
39. Pierrepoint, Albert, *Executioner: Pierrepoint* (London: 1974).
40. Pierrepoint, *Executioner: Pierrepoint*, pp. 141–3.
41. Pierrepoint, *Executioner: Pierrepoint*, pp. 141–3.
42. Sharman, 'War Crimes Trials', p. 122.
43. 'Wolfenbüttel Prison Memorial', Gedenkstättenportal zu Orten der Erinnerung in Europa, accessed 19 March 2023, www.memorialmuseums.org/eng/staettens/view/44/Wolfenb%C3%BCttel-Prison-Memorial; Official Report, Fifth Series, Parliamentary Debates, House of Commons, Vol. 470 (1949), 5 December 1945, Col. 1524.
44. Official Report, Fifth Series, Parliamentary Debates, House of Commons, Vol. 470 (1949), 5 December 1945, Col. 1524.
45. Sharples, 'What Do You Do With A Dead Nazi?', p. 103.

46. Sharples, 'What Do You Do With A Dead Nazi?', pp. 103–4.
47. Sharples, 'What Do You Do With A Dead Nazi?', pp. 103–4.
48. Sharples, 'What Do You Do With A Dead Nazi?', pp. 100, 121.
49. Marrus, Michael R., 'The Holocaust at Nuremberg', *Yad Vashem Studies* 26 (1998), pp. 4–45.
50. Overy, 'The Nuremberg Trials', p. 2.
51. Holmila, *Reporting the Holocaust*, p. 84; Kushner, *The Holocaust and the Liberal Imagination*; Bloxham, *Genocide on Trial*.
52. Sharman, 'War Crimes Trials', p. 54.
53. Sharman, 'War Crimes Trials', p. 104. There were doubts in some quarters regarding the death of Hitler, with allegations in the British press that he had instead fled Berlin in the final days of the war soon taking root. Yet British authorities in Germany quickly rejected this theory, verifying his death in May 1945. For more see Evans, Richard J., *The Hitler Conspiracies* (New York: 2020), pp. 165–211.
54. Sharman, 'War Crimes Trials', pp. 104–5.
55. Sharman, 'War Crimes Trials', p. 89.
56. Sharman, 'War Crimes Trials', p. 90.
57. Sharman, 'War Crimes Trials', p. 97.
58. Sharman, 'War Crimes Trials', pp. 93–5.
59. Sharman, 'War Crimes Trials', p. 100.
60. Sharman, 'War Crimes Trials', p. 103.
61. PREM 8/391, Command Paper (CM) (46) 94th Conclusions, 4 November 1946, Prime Minister's Office: Correspondence and Papers, 1945–1951, Trial of German Industrialists before an International Military Tribunal, National Archives, London.
62. Bloxham, 'British War Crimes Trial Policy', p. 107.

Chapter Eleven

1. Meehan, *A Strange Enemy People*, p. 48.
2. Marshall, *The Origins of Post-war German Politics*, p. 6.
3. The Foreign Office, *Instructions for British Servicemen in Germany*, p. 63.
4. 'Enemy Told: This is Why We Ignore You', *Daily Mail*, 11 June 1945.
5. 'Hamburg's Divided Beaches', *Manchester Guardian*, 23 May 1945.
6. 'Definitely Wallflowers', photograph, *Daily Mirror*, 28 May 1945. The same photo was also published in the *Daily Mail*, alongside another image showing the roped-off British-only area of a Hamburg beach. British soldiers, the caption explained, were strictly obeying non-fraternization orders; see 'Non-fraternisation in 2 Scenes', photograph, *Daily Mail*, 28 May 1945.
7. Weber-Newth, Inge, 'Bilateral Relations: British Soldiers and German Women', in Ryan, Louise and Webster, Wendy (eds), *Gendering Migration: Masculinity, Femininity and Ethnicity in Post-War Britain* (Aldershot: 2008), p. 56.
8. INF 6/401 Crown Film Unit Productions, Trained To Serve, National Archives, London.
9. 'Sophie's Choice', New Zealand Police Association, accessed 20 March 2023, www.policeassn.org.nz/news/sophies-choices#/.
10. Knowles, *Winning the Peace*, pp. 121–4, 164–8, 181.

11. Carruthers, Susan L., *The Good Occupation: American Soldiers and the Hazards of Peace* (Cambridge, Mass.: 2016), p. 115.

12. Deluce, Daniel, 'Fratting is Rife in the Reich', *Liverpool Daily Post*, 13 June 1945.

13. 'Two BLA Officers Accused', *Daily Mail*, 15 June 1945; '"Black Market" Trial for 3 Officers', *Daily Mirror*, 29 December 1945; 'Officer Charged With Fraternization', *Times*, 5 July 1945; 'Fraternisation Sentence', *Manchester Guardian*, 2 August 1945.

14. 'Fraternisation Court-Martial', *Daily Telegraph*, 5 July 1945.

15. 'Pocket Cartoon', cartoon, *Daily Express*, 10 July 1945.

16. Neb, 'Cartoon', cartoon, *Daily Mail*, 16 July 1945.

17. 'Picture Gallery – So This is Fraternisation!', photograph, *Daily Mail*, 17 July 1945.

18. 'The Greatest Year in History', *Picture Post*, 5 January 1946.

19. '"…Down a Shady Lane…"', *Birmingham Daily Gazette*, 19 July 1945.

20. Maxwell, Henry, 'Fraternisation', letter to the editor, *Times*, 24 July 1945.

21. 'Fratting? I'd Rather Have Beef', *Aberdeen Press and Journal*, 10 January 1946.

22. '£14 fine for Fratting', *Daily Mail*, 1 June 1945.

23. '"Tommy" is Curious – That's Why He Talks', *Daily Mirror*, 14 July 1945.

24. 'Heroes Abroad Send Heartbreak Letters Home – "Stop Our Wives Fraternising", "Girls Queue Up To Go Out With Wops,"' *People*, 29 July 1945.

25. Quoted in Meehan, *A Strange Enemy People*, p. 52.

26. Kirby, E. 'Fraternisation', letter to the editor, *Birmingham Mail*, 30 July 1945; 'Allied Help for Germans in Emergency Only', *Manchester Guardian*, 28 July 1945; 'Wives Doubts About "Frat" – Soldiers' Protest Meetings – Prefer Cricket – or Beer', *Dundee Courier*, 28 July 1945; 'Frat Protest by Troops', *Daily Express*, 28 July 1945; 'BLA Troops Protest', *Daily Mail*, 28 July 1945.

27. 'It's "Eyes Front" – and No Whistling', *Daily Mirror*, 7 July 1945.

28. 'Fraternisation Court-Martial', *Daily Telegraph*, 5 July 1945.

29. Quoted in Carruthers, *The Good Occupation*, p. 115.

30. Price, Evadne, 'We Must Hate or Lose the Peace – German Women Fooling the Troops', *People*, 18 March 1945. This explanation was also common in the American public discourse on fraternization; see Carruthers, *The Good Occupation*, p. 114.

31. Price, Evadne, 'Here's the Truth About This Fraternisation Problem – Thousand People Write to Tell Evadne Price', *People*, 18 November 1945.

32. '"Frat" Lure', *Daily Mirror*, 22 June 1945; 'German Staff to be Exiled', *Daily Mail*, 22 June 1945.

33. Lane-Norcott, Maurice, *Daily Mail*, 17 July 1945.

34. 'Horror Camps – "Fraternising is Terrible"', *Western Daily Press*, 14 July 1945.

35. 'Major Guilty of Fraternising', *Sunday Post*, 12 August 1945.

36. Three Bewildered Young Ladies, 'On Fraternisation', letter to the editor, *Liverpool Echo*, 13 July 1945.

37. 'Blitz Veterans Did Not Fraternise', *Birmingham Mail*, 16 July 1945; 'In No Mood to Fraternise', *Aberdeen Press and Journal*, 17 July 1945.

38. 'Desert Rats Won't Fraternise', *Daily Express*, 25 June 1945. This claim was plainly false.

39. Calman, Montague, 'A Tommy Says No Frat', letter to the editor, *Whitstable Times and Herne Bay Herald*, 30 June 1945.

40. 'Allied Help for Germans in Emergency Only', *Manchester Guardian*, 28

July 1945; 'Wives Doubts About "Frat" – Soldiers' Protest Meetings – Prefer Cricket – or Beer', *Dundee Courier*, 28 July 1945; 'Frat Protest by Troops', *Daily Express*, 28 July 1945; 'BLA Troops Protest', *Daily Mail*, 28 July 1945.

41. WATCHING, 'Fraternisation', letter to the editor, *Lancashire Evening Post*, 24 July 1945.

42. Indignant, 'Letters', letter to the editor, *Daily Mail*, 31 July 1945.

43. Cutts, M., letter to the editor, *People*, 29 July 1945.

44. This was also suggested in Walker, *The Lid Lifts*, pp. 84–5.

45. Illingworth, Joe, 'Fraternisation Can't Be Stopped', *Liverpool Daily Post*, 23 May 1945.

46. 'Fratting', editorial, *Daily Mail*, 4 June 1945.

47. 'Fraternization in Germany', *Times*, 9 July 1945.

48. See 'Notes on the Present Situation', 6 July 1945, in Yasamee, H. J. and Great Britain Foreign and Commonwealth Office, *Documents on British Policy Overseas*, vol. 1, *Conference at Potsdam, July–August 1945* (London: HMSO, 1984), p. 71.

49. 'Troops May Speak to Little Germans', *Manchester Guardian*, 12 June 1945.

50. Fraternising Wins the Day, 2 August 1945, *Gaumont-British News*, newsreel, Ref BGX409300122, ITN Source Newsreels, www.itnsource.com/en; Fraternising – Frat Ban On – Frat Ban Off..., 2 August 1945, *Pathé News*, newsreel, Issue 1161.01, British Pathé Archive, www.britishpathe.com/; Berlin Today, 2 August 1945, *British Movietone News*, newsreel, Issue 45960, British Movietone News Digital Archive, www.movietone.com.

51. To begin with these latter modifications also produced a great deal of confusion, which was recounted in the British press; see 'Berlin "Frat" Chaos', *Daily Mirror*, 16 July 1945; 'Heard the 9 O'C News – And Fraternised', *Daily Mail*, 16 July 1945; 'Muddle in Relaxing Ban Causes Berlin Comedy', *Daily Telegraph*, 16 July 1945.

52. 'Nazi Victory Number One', *Daily Mail*, 18 July 1945; 'Fratting a Nazi Victory, He Thinks', *Daily Mirror*, 18 July 1945.

53. 'Common Sense Prevails', editorial, *Manchester Guardian*, 16 July 1945.

54. Cook, Gertrude B., 'Fraternisation', letter to the editor, *Manchester Guardian*, 27 August 1945.

55. 'Marriages to German Girls', *Manchester Guardian*, 24 August 1946; 'Waiting List for German Brides', *Manchester Guardian*, 17 September 1946; 'In Brief', *Daily Mirror*, 10 December 1946.

56. FO 1030/174 Control Commission for Germany (British Element): Various Private Office Papers and Administration and Local Government Branch Files, Marriages with Ex-enemy Nationals, National Archives, London. Soldiers were also required to obtain permission from a senior commander, while German women were subject to a 'security examination' and required a 'certificate of good character' from a mayor or equivalent official; see Weber-Newth, Inge and Steinert, Johannes-Dieter, *German Migrants in Post-War Britain: An Enemy Embrace* (Oxford; New York: 2006), p. 163; Weber-Newth, 'Bilateral Relations', pp. 53–70.

57. Knowles, *Winning the Peace*, pp. 199, 226.

58. 'Herbert Will Marry German Girl He Has Never Seen', *Daily Mirror*, 10 May 1948.

59. Kleinau, Elke and Schmid, Rafaela, '"Occupation Children" in Germany after

World War II – Problems and Coping Strategies', *Children & Society* 33 (2019), pp. 239–52, https://doi.org/10.1111/chso.12323.

60. Lee, Sabine, *Children Born of War in the Twentieth Century* (Manchester: 2017), pp. 85–6.
61. Report, 'Civilian Venereal Diseases in British Zone of Germany', Public Health Branch, October 1945, FO 1032/697, Economic and Industrial Planning Staff and Control Office for Germany and Austria and Successor: Control Commission for Germany (British Element), Military Sections and Headquarters Secretariat: VD control in British Zone, National Archives, London.
62. Stark, 'The Overlooked Majority', pp. 389–90.
63. Dichter, Heather, 'Game Plan for Democracy: Sport and Youth in Occupied West Germany', in Erlichman, Camilo and Knowles, Christopher (eds), *Transforming Occupation in the Western Zones of Germany: Politics, Everyday Life and Social Interactions, 1945–55* (London: 2018.), p. 142.
64. Carruthers, *The Good Occupation*, pp. 111–50.
65. *A Foreign Affair*, film, directed by Billy Wilder, starring Marlene Dietrich (1948; Hollywood, CA: Paramount Pictures); Carruthers, *The Good Occupation*, p. 279.
66. FO 936/749 Control Office for Germany and Austria and Foreign Office, German Section: Establishments: Files, Miscellaneous complaints: General Public, 1946–51, National Archives, London.
67. Letter J. H. Webster to Private Secretary of the prime minister, 10 May 1948, FO 936/749 Control Office for Germany and Austria and Foreign Office, German Section: Establishments: Files, Miscellaneous complaints: General Public, 1946–51, National Archives, London.

Chapter Twelve

1. Bray, Charles, 'Retribution', *Daily Herald*, 24 August 1945.
2. Clark, Norman, '25,000 Seek Food Every Day', *News Chronicle*, 24 August 1945.
3. Frank, Matthew, *Expelling the Germans: British Opinion and Post-1945 Population Transfer in Context* (Oxford: 2007).
4. It remains a controversial policy to this day; see Mazower, Mark, *Dark Continent: Europe's Twentieth Century* (London: 1999); Naimark, Norman, *Fires of Hatred: Ethnic Cleansing in Twentieth-Century Europe* (Cambridge, Mass.; London: 2002).
5. Douglas, R. M., *Orderly and Humane: The Expulsion of the Germans after the Second World War* (New Haven, Conn.: 2012).
6. Winterberg, Sonya, *Wir sind die Wolfskinder: Verlassen in Ostpreußen* (Munich: 2014).
7. Douglas, *Orderly and Humane*, pp. 25–6.
8. Graham-Dixon, *The Allied Occupation of Germany*, p. 136.
9. Douglas, *Orderly and Humane*, p. 90.
10. Graham-Dixon, *The Allied Occupation of Germany*, p. 140.
11. Douglas, *Orderly and Humane*, p. 151.
12. Quoted in Douglas, *Orderly and Humane*, p. 150.

13. Frank, Matthew, 'The New Morality – Victor Gollancz, "Save Europe Now" and the German Refugee Crisis, 1945–46', *Twentieth Century British History* 17, no. 2 (2006), p. 233. The war with Japan was officially over on 15 August.
14. Frank, 'The New Morality', p. 237; Edwards, *Victor Gollancz*.
15. Frank, 'The New Morality', p. 238.
16. Frank, 'The New Morality', p. 233.
17. Gollancz, Victor, *Our Threatened Values* (London: 1946); Frank, 'The New Morality', p. 236.
18. Edwards, *Victor Gollancz*, p. 423.
19. Frank, 'The New Morality', p. 238.
20. Frank, 'The New Morality', pp. 239–40.
21. Frank, 'The New Morality', p. 240.
22. Frank, 'The New Morality', p. 240; Gollancz, Victor (Chairman) and Rathbone, Eleanor F. (Vice-Chairman), 'Save Europe Now', letter to the editor, *Manchester Guardian*, 22 December 1945; Duff, Peggy, *Left, Left, Left: A Personal Account of Six Protest Campaigns, 1945–65* (London: 1971), p. 17.
23. Frank, 'The New Morality', p. 243.
24. Frank, 'The New Morality', pp. 243–4.; Edwards, *Victor Gollancz*, p. 414.
25. Edwards, *Victor Gollancz*, p. 415.
26. Edwards, *Victor Gollancz*, p. 449.
27. Farquharson, J. E., '"Emotional but Influential": Victor Gollancz, Richard Stokes and the British Zone of Germany, 1945–9', *Journal of Contemporary History* 22, no. 3 (1987), p. 514, https://doi.org/10.1177/002200948702200308; Frank, 'The New Morality', pp. 242–3; Official Report, Fifth Series, Parliamentary Debates, House of Commons, Vol. 414 (1945), 26 October 1945, Col. 2351–454.
28. Frank, 'The New Morality', p. 246.
29. Frank, 'The New Morality', p. 255.
30. Frank, 'The New Morality', p. 236.
31. Rose, P. G., 'Food Supplies', letter to the editor, *Times*, 22 February 1946.
32. Frank, 'The New Morality', p. 242.
33. BBB [Bernard Buckham], 'Feed the Brutes?', *Daily Mirror*, 5 October 1945.
34. Low, David, 'Shall We Feed the Germans?', cartoon, *London Evening Standard*, 5 November 1945; Frank, 'The New Morality', pp. 247–8.
35. Official Report, Fifth Series, Parliamentary Debates, House of Commons, Vol. 416 (1945), 23 November 1945, Col. 763–4.
36. In February 1946 Operation Swallow alone saw 1.5 million people enter the British Zone; see Graham-Dixon, *The Allied Occupation of Germany*, p. 136.
37. Douglas, *Orderly and Humane*, p. 183.
38. Douglas, *Orderly and Humane*, pp. 164–95.
39. Blum, '"My Home, your Castle"', p. 117.
40. Farquharson, *The Western Allies*.
41. Szanajda, *The Allies*, p. 49.
42. The British had also planned to enact extensive land reform but ultimately decided to maintain Nazi land units partly due to the fear of any decline in output; see Carden, Robert W., 'Before Bizonia: Britain's Economic Dilemma in Germany, 1945–46', *Journal of Contemporary History* 14, no. 3 (1979), p. 543, www.jstor.org/stable/260020.

43. Sunday Letter to Phyllis, 25 November 1945, Letters written by Henry Ronald Hughes, 2014-10-27-76, National Army Museum, London.

44. Carden, 'Before Bizonia', p. 543.

45. Malzahn, *Germany 1945–1949*, pp. 185–6; Weber, Anna-Maria, *Zeitgemäßes Kochen* (Tegernsee: 1946), p. 3.

46. Brockway, *German Diary*, p. 78.

47. Germany's Food – The Truth, 29 July 1946, *Pathé News*, newsreel, Issue 1406.06, British Pathé Archive, www.britishpathe.com/.

48. Dickens, *Lübeck Diary*, p. 96.

49. Reel 12, Morris-Metcalf, Harold Frank 'Mick' (Oral History), Sound Recording, Catalogue Number 22077, Imperial War Museum Archive, London.

50. Farquharson, *The Western Allies*, pp. 121–2.

51. Cabinet Minutes, 24 November 1945, CAB 129/5/2 Cabinet: Memoranda (CP and C Series), National Archives, London.

52. Farquharson, *The Western Allies*, p. 244.

53. Brockway, *German Diary*, p. 146.

54. Cabinet Minutes, 3 January 1946, CAB 195/3/85, Cabinet Secretary's Notebooks, National Archives, London.

55. Deighton, Anne, 'Towards a "Western" Strategy: The making of British policy towards Germany 1945–46' in Deighton, Anne (ed.), *Britain and the First Cold War* (Basingstoke; London: Macmillan, 1990), p. 60.

56. Cabinet Minutes, 10 May 1946, CAB 79/48/4, War Cabinet and Cabinet: Chiefs of Staff Committee: Minutes, National Archives, London.

57. Tetlow, Edwin, 'Rations are small, but eyes are bright', *Daily Mail*, 15 February 1946.

58. Reynolds, *Britannia Overruled*, p. 144; Carden, 'Before Bizonia', p. 543.

59. Mitchell, B. R., *British Historical Statistics* (Cambridge: 2011), p. 592.

60. Official Report, Fifth Series, Parliamentary Debates, House of Commons, Vol. 421 (1946), 9 April 1946, Col. 1803–68; Reynolds, *Britannia Overruled*, p. 154.

61. Reynolds, *Britannia Overruled*, p. 148; Farquharson, *The Western Allies*, p. 326; Turner, Ian D., 'British Policy Towards German Industry, 1945–9: Reconstruction, Restriction or Exploitation', in Turner, Ian D. (ed.), *Reconstruction in Post-War Germany: British Occupation Policy and the Western Zones, 1945–55* (Oxford: 1988), p. 79; Meehan, *A Strange Enemy People*, p. 194.

62. Kleßmann, Christoph and Friedemann, Peter, *Streiks und Hungermärsche im Ruhrgebiet 1946-1948* (Frankfurt; New York: 1977), pp. 69-70.

63. Quoted in Reynolds, David, *From World War to Cold War: Churchill, Roosevelt, and the International History of the 1940s* (Oxford: 2006) p. 281.

64. Watt, *Britain Looks to Germany*, p. 55; Marshall, *The Origins of Post-war German Politics*, p. 10.

65. Marshall, *The Origins of Post-war German Politics*, p. 10; Reynolds, *Britannia Overruled*, p. 149.

66. Reynolds, David, 'Great Britain', in Reynolds, David (ed.), *The Origins of the Cold War in Europe: International Perspectives* (New Haven: 1994), p. 80.

67. Quoted in Reynolds, 'Great Britain', p. 83. Also see Marshall, *The Origins of Post-war German Politics*, p. 10.

68. Deighton, Anne, *The Impossible Peace: Britain, the Division of Germany and the Origins of the Cold War* (Oxford: 1993), pp. 111–2.

69. Quoted in Zweiniger-Bargielowska, Ina, *Austerity in Britain: Rationing, Controls, and Consumption, 1939–1955* (Oxford: 2000), p. 216.
70. '4-Day Margin in Our Zone', *Daily Mail*, 3 July 1946.
71. July 21st, 1 July 1946, *Pathé News*, newsreel, Issue 1404.04, British Pathé Archive, www.britishpathe.com/.
72. Official Report, Fifth Series, Parliamentary Debates, House of Commons, Vol. 425 (1946), 18 July 1946, Col. 1386–93; Deveson, Anne, 'She Left London luxury to Pioneer a Farm', obituary (Eleonora Tennant), *Australian Women's Weekly*, 12 February 1964.
73. Duff, *Left, Left, Left*, p. 18.
74. Panton, Selkirk, 'They Blame Us (as usual) For Their Troubles...', *Daily Express*, 28 February 1946.

Chapter Thirteen

1. Sholto Douglas Opening Speech, FO 1039/669, Control Office for Germany and Austria and Foreign Office: Control Commission for Germany (British Element), Economic Divisions: Records, CCG Exhibition London: Vol II, December 1945 – March 1946, National Archives, London.
2. Letter from Campbell, 31 May 1946, FO 946/10 Control Office for Germany and Austria and Foreign Office, German Section: Information Services: Records, 'Germany Under Control' Exhibition, 1946–8, National Archives, London.
3. Street, John, *Mass Media, Politics, and Democracy* (Basingstoke; New York: 2001); Moore, Martin, *The Origins of Modern Spin: Democratic Government and the Media in Britain, 1945–51* (Basingstoke: 2006).
4. Balfour, *Propaganda in War*; McLaine, Ian, *Ministry of Morale: Home Front Morale and the Ministry of Information in World War II* (London: 1979).
5. Crofts, William, *Coercion or Persuasion?: Propaganda in Britain after 1945* (London: 1989), pp. 12–13.
6. In 1948 the PR/ISC would merge with the Information Control Division (ICD) and be renamed the Information Services Division (ISD); see 'Integration of US with UK Information Services', 1948–9, FO 1056/143, Control Office for Germany and Austria and Foreign Office: Control Commission for Germany (British Element), Public Relations and Information Services Division, and U.K. High Commission, Information Services Division: Registered Files (PR, ISC, ISD and other Series), National Archives, London.
7. The PR/ISC had a high proportion of former journalists and editors within its ranks and, in October 1946, Bishop was succeeded by former *Manchester Guardian* journalist Cecil Sprigge; see Wagner, Hans-Ulrich, 'Repatriated Germans and "British Spirit"', *Media History* 21, no. 4 (2015), p. 445, https://doi.org/10.1080/13688804.2015.1011109.
8. Memorandum, November 1945, FO 1056/510, Control Office for Germany and Austria and Foreign Office: Control Commission for Germany (British Element), Public Relations and Information Services Division, and U.K. High Commission, Information Services Division: Registered Files (PR, ISC, ISD and other Series), Issuance of News Policy, National Archives, London.
9. Secretariat CCG to HQ 21st Army Group, memorandum 'Mil Gov Publicity in Allied Press', August 1945, FO 1056/510 Control Office for Germany

and Austria and Foreign Office: Control Commission for Germany (British Element), Public Relations and Information Services Division, and U.K. High Commission, Information Services Division: Registered Files (PR, ISC, ISD and other Series), Issuance of News Policy, National Archives, London.

10. Emphasis in the original; see Secretariat CCG to HQ 21st Army Group, memorandum 'Mil Gov Publicity in Allied Press', August 1945, FO 1056/510 Control Office for Germany and Austria and Foreign Office: Control Commission for Germany (British Element), Public Relations and Information Services Division, and U.K. High Commission, Information Services Division: Registered Files (PR, ISC, ISD and other Series), Issuance of News Policy, National Archives, London; Memorandum on Press Comments on Control Commission/Mil. Gov., 21 September 1945, FO 1056/510 Control Office for Germany and Austria and Foreign Office: Control Commission for Germany (British Element), Public Relations and Information Services Division, and U.K. High Commission, Information Services Division: Registered Files (PR, ISC, ISD and other Series), Issuance of News Policy, National Archives, London.

11. Houghton to Treadwell, 28 July 1945, FO 1056/508 Control Office for Germany and Austria and Foreign Office: Control Commission for Germany (British Element), Public Relations and Information Services Division, and U.K. High Commission, Information Services Division: Registered Files (PR, ISC, ISD and other Series), Releases, Hand-outs, and Policy: Press Conference, 1945, National Archives, London.

12. Letter from Major Twist to Information Section, PR Branch CCG, 20 August 1945, FO 1056/510 Control Office for Germany and Austria and Foreign Office: Control Commission for Germany (British Element), Public Relations and Information Services Division, and U.K. High Commission, Information Services Division: Registered Files (PR, ISC, ISD and other Series), Issuance of News Policy, National Archives, London.

13. Digest of Story Filed by Maurice Pagence, *Daily Herald*, 16 November 1946, FO 1056/510 Control Office for Germany and Austria and Foreign Office: Control Commission for Germany (British Element), Public Relations and Information Services Division, and U.K. High Commission, Information Services Division: Registered Files (PR, ISC, ISD and other Series), Issuance of News Policy, National Archives, London.

14. See FO 946/92 Control Office for Germany and Austria and Foreign Office, German Section: Information Services: Records, Central Office of Information: Films to be made on conditions in Germany, 1947–8, National Archives, London.

15. Williams, Kevin, *Get Me a Murder a Day!: A History of Mass Communication in Britain* (London: 1998), p. 214.

16. Secretariat CCG to HQ 21st Army Group, memorandum 'Mil Gov Publicity in Allied Press', August 1945, FO 1056/510 Control Office for Germany and Austria and Foreign Office: Control Commission for Germany (British Element), Public Relations and Information Services Division, and U.K. High Commission, Information Services Division: Registered Files (PR, ISC, ISD and other Series), Issuance of News Policy, National Archives, London.

17. Press Itineraries, 1949, FO 953/495-512 Visits and tours of editors and journalists to and from the United Kingdom (Germany), National Archives, London.

18. Official Report, Fifth Series, Parliamentary Debates, House of Commons, Vol. 422 (1946), 10 May 1946, Col. 1419.
19. Robrecht, Antje, 'British Press Correspondents in Post World War II Germany', in Bösch, Frank and Geppert, Dominik (eds), *Journalists as Political Actors* (Augsburg: 2008), p. 129.
20. Prittie, Terence, *My Germans: 1933–1983* (London: 1983), p. 101.
21. Robrecht, 'British Press Correspondents', p. 128.
22. Pronay, 'Introduction', p. 21.
23. Letter from Norman Clark Chairman of British Zone Correspondents Association to Sholto Douglas and attached memorandum, 1947, FO 946/47 Control Office for Germany and Austria and Foreign Office, German Section: Information Services: Records, German and Austrian Publicity: British Zone Correspondents' Association, National Archives, London.
24. Meeting, 21 December 1945, FO 1039/669 Control Office for Germany and Austria and Foreign Office: Control Commission for Germany (British Element), Economic Divisions: Records, CCG Exhibition London: Vol II, December 1945 – March 1946, National Archives, London.
25. Reply from Mil. Gov. HQ Staff (Publicity), 22 September 1945, FO 1056/510 Control Office for Germany and Austria and Foreign Office: Control Commission for Germany (British Element), Public Relations and Information Services Division, and U.K. High Commission, Information Services Division: Registered Files (PR, ISC, ISD and other Series), Issuance of News Policy, National Archives, London.
26. Report to Arthur Elton, 12 May 1947, FO 946/92 Control Office for Germany and Austria and Foreign Office, German Section: Information Services: Records, Central Office of Information: Films to be made on conditions in Germany, 1947–8, National Archives, London; Minute Crawford to Sir Oliver Harvey, 23 June 1947, FO 946/92 Control Office for Germany and Austria and Foreign Office, German Section: Information Services: Records, Central Office of Information: Films to be made on conditions in Germany, 1947–8, National Archives, London.
27. Letter Bishop to Mills, 14 December 1945, FO 1039/670 Control Office for Germany and Austria and Foreign Office: Control Commission for Germany (British Element), Economic Divisions: Records, CCG Exhibition London: Vol III, 1945, National Archives, London.
28. Letter from Campbell, 31 May 1946, FO 946/10 Control Office for Germany and Austria and Foreign Office, German Section: Information Services: Records, 'Germany Under Control' Exhibition, 1946–8, National Archives, London.
29. Hynd Opening Speech, FO 1039/669 Control Office for Germany and Austria and Foreign Office: Control Commission for Germany (British Element), Economic Divisions: Records, CCG Exhibition London: Vol II, December 1945 – March 1946, National Archives, London.
30. Letter Catherine Dryden to Mr Edwards, 7 June 1946, FO 1039/669 Control Office for Germany and Austria and Foreign Office: Control Commission for Germany (British Element), Economic Divisions: Records, CCG Exhibition London: Vol II, December 1945 – March 1946, National Archives, London; Richter, *Ivan Hirst*, p. 58.
31. Letter Campbell to Treadwell, 23 June 1946, FO 1039/670 Control Office for Germany and Austria and Foreign Office: Control Commission for Germany

(British Element), Economic Divisions: Records, CCG Exhibition London: Vol III, 1945, National Archives, London.

32. 'Germany – Our Way', Draft – from Director of Public Relations, Control Office for Germany and Austria, FO 946/10 Control Office for Germany and Austria and Foreign Office, German Section: Information Services: Records, 'Germany Under Control' Exhibition, 1946–8, National Archives, London.

33. Script, FO 1039/671 Control Office for Germany and Austria and Foreign Office: Control Commission for Germany (British Element), Economic Divisions: Records, CCG Script for 'Germany under Control' Exhibition in London, National Archives, London.

34. Letter from Campbell and Attachment, 20 February 1946, FO 946/10 Control Office for Germany and Austria and Foreign Office, German Section: Information Services: Records, 'Germany Under Control' Exhibition, 1946–8, National Archives, London; Attached Leaflet, FO 946/10 Control Office for Germany and Austria and Foreign Office, German Section: Information Services: Records, 'Germany Under Control' Exhibition, 1946–8, National Archives, London. Many of these items are now found as part of the Imperial War Museum, London's permanent exhibitions.

35. Minutes, 2 September 1946, FO 946/12 Control Office for Germany and Austria and Foreign Office, German Section: Information Services: Records, Germany Under Control Exhibition – Notes of Meetings, 1946, National Archives, London.

36. Report, 11 June 1946, FO 946/10 Control Office for Germany and Austria and Foreign Office, German Section: Information Services: Records, 'Germany Under Control' Exhibition, 1946–8, National Archives, London; Report, 18 May 1946, FO 946/10 Control Office for Germany and Austria and Foreign Office, German Section: Information Services: Records, 'Germany Under Control' Exhibition, 1946–8, National Archives, London.

37. 'Conditions in "Germany Under Control"', *Western Daily Press*, 4 February 1947.

38. Meeting, 21 June 1946, FO 946/12 Control Office for Germany and Austria and Foreign Office, German Section: Information Services: Records, Germany Under Control Exhibition – Notes of Meetings, 1946, National Archives, London; Letter Croxson to Campbell, 22 June 1946, FO 946/10 Control Office for Germany and Austria and Foreign Office, German Section: Information Services: Records, 'Germany Under Control' Exhibition, 1946–8, National Archives, London; 'BFI Screenonline: Robert Barr 1909-1999', obituary, British Film Institute, accessed 11 May 2018, www.screenonline.org.uk/people/id/901205/index.html; 'BBC: Detective', publicity material, BBC, accessed 11 May 2018, www.bbc.co.uk/mediacentre/proginfo/2013/18/4-extra-detective.

39. Final Report from Campbell to Treadwell, 22 August 1946, FO 946/10 Control Office for Germany and Austria and Foreign Office, German Section: Information Services: Records, 'Germany Under Control' Exhibition, 1946–8, National Archives, London.

40. Letter Campbell to Treadwell, 26 June 1946, FO 946/10 Control Office for Germany and Austria and Foreign Office, German Section: Information Services: Records, 'Germany Under Control' Exhibition, 1946–8, National Archives, London.

41. Letter from Wood, n.d., FO 1039/669 Control Office for Germany and Austria and Foreign Office: Control Commission for Germany (British Element), Economic Divisions: Records, CCG Exhibition London: Vol II, December 1945 – March 1946, National Archives, London; Report from Campbell to Treadwell, 5 July 1946, FO 946/10 Control Office for Germany and Austria and Foreign Office, German Section: Information Services: Records, 'Germany Under Control' Exhibition, 1946–8, National Archives, London; Final Report Campbell to Treadwell, 22 August 1946, FO 946/10 Control Office for Germany and Austria and Foreign Office, German Section: Information Services: Records, 'Germany Under Control' Exhibition, 1946–8, National Archives, London.

42. Report and Letter from Campbell, 23 June 1946, FO 946/10 Control Office for Germany and Austria and Foreign Office, German Section: Information Services: Records, 'Germany Under Control' Exhibition, 1946–8, National Archives, London.

43. Demonstrators Conference, 9 August 1946, FO 946/12 Control Office for Germany and Austria and Foreign Office, German Section: Information Services: Records, Germany Under Control Exhibition – Notes of Meetings, 1946, National Archives, London.

44. Letter Crawford to Elton, 15 December 1947, FO 946/92 Control Office for Germany and Austria and Foreign Office, German Section: Information Services: Records, Central Office of Information: Films to be made on conditions in Germany, 1947–8, National Archives, London; Notes Meeting, 9 January 1948, FO 946/92 Control Office for Germany and Austria and Foreign Office, German Section: Information Services: Records, Central Office of Information: Films to be made on conditions in Germany, 1947–8, National Archives, London.

45. Fox, Jo, 'John Grierson, His "documentary Boys" and the British Ministry of Information, 1939–1942', *Historical Journal of Film, Radio and Television* 25, no. 3 (August 2005), pp. 345–69, https://doi.org/10.1080/01439680500236151.

46. Logan, Philip C., *Humphrey Jennings and British Documentary Film: A Re-Assessment* (Farnham: 2011), p. 283.

47. Logan, *Humphrey Jennings and British Documentary Film*, p. 287.

48. *Yorkshire Post*, 13 March 1946; *Sunday Express*, 17 March 1946.

49. *Daily Worker*, 15 March 1946; *News Chronicle*, 16 March 1946.

50. FO 946/92 Control Office for Germany and Austria and Foreign Office, German Section: Information Services: Records, Central Office of Information: Films to be made on conditions in Germany, 1947–8, National Archives, London; Letter Planning and Policy Section PR Branch to DG PR, 21 March 1946, FO 1056/510 Control Office for Germany and Austria and Foreign Office: Control Commission for Germany (British Element), Public Relations and Information Services Division, and U.K. High Commission, Information Services Division: Registered Files (PR, ISC, ISD and other Series), Issuance of News Policy, National Archives, London.

51. Adamthwaite, Anthony, '"Nation Shall Speak Peace unto Nation": The BBC's Response to Peace and Defence Issues, 1945–58', *Contemporary Record* 7, no. 3 (1993), pp. 557–77, https://doi.org/10.1080/13619469308581267.

52. Letter Douglas to Jenkins, 21 November 1946, FO 946/68 Control Office for Germany and Austria and Foreign Office, German Section: Information

Services: Records, Radio Programme: Spotlight on Germany, National Archives, London; Letter Jenkins to Douglas, 5 December 1946, FO 946/68 Control Office for Germany and Austria and Foreign Office, German Section: Information Services: Records, Radio Programme: Spotlight on Germany, National Archives, London.

53. BBC Transcript of Radio Programme 'World Affairs', 9 January 1947, FO 946/68 Control Office for Germany and Austria and Foreign Office, German Section: Information Services: Records, Radio Programme: Spotlight on Germany, National Archives, London.

54. It would subsequently become a monthly publication.

55. Anthony, Scott, *Public Relations and the Making of Modern Britain: Stephen Tallents and the Birth of a Progressive Media Profession* (Manchester: 2012), pp. 110–2.

56. Letter PR Branch Berlin to HQ PRISC, 16 April 1947, FO 1056/300 Control Office for Germany and Austria and Foreign Office: Control Commission for Germany (British Element), Public Relations and Information Services Division, and U.K. High Commission, Information Services Division: Registered Files (PR, ISC, ISD and other Series), 'British Zone Review' Editorial Board, 1947–1949, National Archives, London.

57. Editorial Meeting Minutes, 27 January 1949 and 16 May 1947, appendix B, FO 1056/300 Control Office for Germany and Austria and Foreign Office: Control Commission for Germany (British Element), Public Relations and Information Services Division, and U.K. High Commission, Information Services Division: Registered Files (PR, ISC, ISD and other Series), 'British Zone Review' Editorial Board, 1947–1949, National Archives, London.

58. Letter J. E. Dowling, 15 January 1948, FO 1056/300 Control Office for Germany and Austria and Foreign Office: Control Commission for Germany (British Element), Public Relations and Information Services Division, and U.K. High Commission, Information Services Division: Registered Files (PR, ISC, ISD and other Series), 'British Zone Review' Editorial Board, 1947–1949, National Archives, London.

59. Letter Head Magazine Section PRISC, 30 April 1948, FO 1056/300 Control Office for Germany and Austria and Foreign Office: Control Commission for Germany (British Element), Public Relations and Information Services Division, and U.K. High Commission, Information Services Division: Registered Files (PR, ISC, ISD and other Series), 'British Zone Review' Editorial Board, 1947–1949, National Archives, London.

60. Editorial Meeting Minutes, 27 January 1949, FO 1056/300 Control Office for Germany and Austria and Foreign Office: Control Commission for Germany (British Element), Public Relations and Information Services Division, and U.K. High Commission, Information Services Division: Registered Files (PR, ISC, ISD and other Series), 'British Zone Review' Editorial Board, 1947–1949, National Archives, London.

61. Letter Moffat (editor), 19 April 1949, FO 1056/128 Control Office for Germany and Austria and Foreign Office: Control Commission for Germany (British Element), Public Relations and Information Services Division, and U.K. High Commission, Information Services Division: Registered Files (PR, ISC, ISD and other Series), 'British Zone Review' Editorial Board: Correspondence, 1948–1949, National Archives, London.

62. Editorial Meeting Minutes, Print Run Allocations, 16 May 1947, FO 1056/300 Control Office for Germany and Austria and Foreign Office: Control Commission for Germany (British Element), Public Relations and Information Services Division, and U.K. High Commission, Information Services Division: Registered Files (PR, ISC, ISD and other Series), 'British Zone Review' Editorial Board, 1947–1949, National Archives, London.

63. Editorial Meeting Minutes, 27 January 1949, appendix A and B, FO 1056/300 Control Office for Germany and Austria and Foreign Office: Control Commission for Germany (British Element), Public Relations and Information Services Division, and U.K. High Commission, Information Services Division: Registered Files (PR, ISC, ISD and other Series), 'British Zone Review' Editorial Board, 1947–1949, National Archives, London.

64. Memorandum Treadwell to Britten, 20 March 1946, FO 1056/510 Control Office for Germany and Austria and Foreign Office: Control Commission for Germany (British Element), Public Relations and Information Services Division, and U.K. High Commission, Information Services Division: Registered Files (PR, ISC, ISD and other Series), Issuance of News Policy, National Archives, London.

65. Blore, Trevor, '£160 Million A Year – To Teach The Germans To Despise Us…', *Daily Mirror*, 8 July 1946.

Chapter Fourteen

1. Letter to his wife, 27 October 1946, Lenanton Papers.
2. Meehan, *A Strange Enemy People*, p. 113.
3. *Manchester Guardian*, 9 August 1946.
4. Meehan, *A Strange Enemy People*, p. 115; 'Conduct of British in Germany', *Times*, 9 August 1946; 'The Outer World – "Zone Will Hit Britain For Years", '"Germany's Soul: Padre Accuses BAOR"', *Daily Mail*, 9 August 1946.
5. 'Corruption in British Zone – Chaplain's Warning', *Manchester Guardian*, 9 August 1946.
6. Official Report, Fifth Series, Parliamentary Debates, House of Commons, Vol. 426 (1946), 29 July 1946, Col. 575.
7. Letter to his wife, 6 April 1946, Lenanton Papers.
8. Letter to his wife, 15 May 1946, Lenanton Papers.
9. Letter R.G. Beerensson to A.C. Robinson, 23 December 1945, FO 936/236 Control Office for Germany and Austria and Foreign Office, German Section: Establishments: Files, Control Commission for Germany: review of basic policy, National Archives, London.
10. Minutes, 2 January 1946, FO 936/236, Control Office for Germany and Austria and Foreign Office, German Section: Establishments: Files, Control Commission for Germany: review of basic policy, National Archives, London.
11. Anonymous letter, 8 February 1946, FO 936/236, Control Office for Germany and Austria and Foreign Office, German Section: Establishments: Files, Control Commission for Germany: review of basic policy, National Archives, London.
12. Letter Brian Robertson to Gilmour Jenkins, 17 July 1946, FO 1030/304, Control Commission for Germany (British Element): Various Private Office Papers and

Administration and Local Government Branch Files, Correspondence DMG/
Permanent Secretary: vol II, National Archives, London.

13. Quoted in Farquharson, 'The British Occupation of Germany', p. 331.

14. Meehan, *A Strange Enemy People*, pp. 57–8; Report, FO 371/55620, Situation in the British Zone: Evolution of Control of Government: Cost of Occupation, Foreign Office: Political Departments: General Correspondence from 1906–1966, National Archives, London.

15. FO 936/236 Control Office for Germany and Austria and Foreign Office, German Section: Establishments: Files, Control Commission for Germany: review of basic policy, National Archives, London.

16. Blum, '"My Home, your Castle"', p. 120.

17. Mary Bouman to her parents, 20 January 1946, Lübbecke, Bouman Papers.

18. Blum, '"My Home, your Castle"', pp. 117–20.

19. Blum, '"My Home, your Castle"', p. 118.

20. Quoted in Blum, '"My Home, your Castle"', p. 119.

21. Quoted in Blum, '"My Home, your Castle"', p. 119.

22. Blum, '"My Home, your Castle"', p. 121.

23. Blum, '"My Home, your Castle"', p. 121.

24. Letter Lane-Norcott to Major Osborne, 17 September 1946, FO 1030/304, Control Commission for Germany (British Element): Various Private Office Papers and Administration and Local Government Branch Files, Correspondence DMG/Permanent Secretary: vol II, National Archives, London; Lane-Norcott, Maurice, Letter to the Editor, *News Chronicle*, 27 September 1946; Lane-Norcott, Maurice, 'Requisitioning', Letter to the Editor, *Times*, 5 October 1946.

25. Letter Gilmour Jenkins to Brian Robertson, 23 October 1946, FO 1030/304, Control Commission for Germany (British Element): Various Private Office Papers and Administration and Local Government Branch Files, Correspondence DMG/Permanent Secretary: vol II, National Archives, London; Lane-Norcott, Maurice, Letter to the Editor, *News Chronicle*, 27 September 1946; Lane-Norcott, Maurice, 'Requisitioning', Letter to the Editor, *Times*, 5 October 1946.

26. Letter, 23 June 1945, Smith Papers.

27. Mary Bouman to her parents, undated letter 'Bummel in Hamburg', Hamburg, Bouman Papers.

28. Letters, 10 and 11 November 1945, Private Papers of J J Allan, Documents.17788, Imperial War Museum Archive, London.

29. Brockway, *German Diary*, pp. 85–7.

30. Letter from Mary Bouman, 25 August 1947, Herford, Bouman Papers.

31. Letter from Mary Bouman, 15 December 1947, Herford, Bouman Papers.

32. Memoir, Private Papers of Mrs N Heather, Documents.12622, Imperial War Museum Archive, London.

33. It was originally known as the Central Pool of Artists.

34. Moore, Roger, *My Word Is My Bond: The Autobiography* (London: 2009), p. 62.

35. Sikov, Ed, *Mr Strangelove: A Biography of Peter Sellers* (New York: 2003), p. 39.

36. *Manchester Guardian*, 30 July 1945 and 31 July 1945; Schleppi, John Ross, 'A History of Professional Association Football in England During the Second World War' (Unpublished PhD dissertation, Ohio State University: 1972), p. 258.

37. Rollin, Jack, *The Army Game: 125 Years of the Army Football Association 1888 to 2013* (Nottingham: 2013), p. 110.
38. Rippon, Anton, *Gas Masks for Goal Posts: Football in Britain During the Second World War* (Stroud: 2005), p. 189.
39. *Daily Mirror,* 19 September 1945; *Times,* 3 September 1945.
40. Rollin, *The Army Game,* p. 102.
41. Rollin, *The Army Game,* p. 109.
42. Rippon, *Gas Masks,* p. 190.
43. Letter, 19 November 1945, Letters written by L/Cpl John William Booth, 2011-01-4-347, National Army Museum, London.
44. Personal Account, Private Papers of G D Pringle, Documents.12385, Imperial War Museum Archive, London.
45. Reel 8, Souper, Robert Reinagle (Oral History).
46. '"Fraternising" on the Football Field', *Manchester Guardian,* 9 January 1946.
47. Brockway, *German Diary,* p. 49.
48. Edna Wearmouth to her father, 17 June 1947, Frankfurt, Wearmouth Papers.
49. Mary Bouman to her parents with enclosed menu, 13 June 1949, Herford, Bouman Papers.
50. 'Menu from NAAFI "Corner House" Club, 5 September 1947', Morris Papers.
51. Edna Wearmouth to her father, 17 June 1947, Frankfurt, Wearmouth Papers.
52. Edna Wearmouth to her father, 16 October 1947, Frankfurt, Wearmouth Papers.
53. Edna Wearmouth to her father, 17 June 1947, Frankfurt, Wearmouth Papers.
54. Edna Wearmouth to her father, 14 April 1947, Herford, Wearmouth Papers.
55. Edna Wearmouth to her father, 2 June 1947, Herford, Wearmouth Papers.
56. Mary Bouman to her parents, 19 May 1947, Herford, Bouman Papers; Mary Bouman to her parents, 12 April 1946, Lübbecke, Bouman Papers.
57. Edna Wearmouth to her father, 18 March 1947, Herford, Wearmouth Papers.
58. Edna Wearmouth to father, 11 May 1947, Herford, Wearmouth Papers.
59. Reel 9, Wayne, Peter (Oral History).
60. Ahrens, Michael, *Die Briten in Hamburg: Besatzerleben 1945-1958* (Hamburg: Dölling und Galitz, 2011), p. 332.
61. Edna Wearmouth to her father, 11 April 1947, Herford, Wearmouth Papers. This is around £2.50 at the time of writing.
62. Reel 9, Dillon, Brian Edevrain (Oral History), Sound Recording, Catalogue Number 23787, Imperial War Museum Archive, London. This is around £3.50 at the time of writing.
63. Letter, 11 November 1945, Allan Papers.
64. Memoir, 'When All The Trees Were Green', Morris Papers.
65. Letter, 24 November 1945, Letters written by L/Cpl John William Booth, 2011-01-4-349, National Army Museum, London.
66. Mary Bouman to her parents, 4 March 1946, Lübbecke, Bouman Papers.
67. Reel 9, Dillon, Brian Edevrain (Oral History).
68. Edna Wearmouth to her father, 27 March 1947, Herford, Wearmouth Papers.
69. Memoir, 'When All The Trees Were Green', Morris Papers.
70. Mannin, Ethel, *German Journey* (London: 1948), p. 87.
71. Ahrens, *Die Briten in Hamburg,* pp. 329–30.
72. Reel 9, Dillon, Brian Edevrain (Oral History).
73. Reel 10, Wayne, Peter (Oral History).

74. Edna Wallace (née Wearmouth), 'Bound for Germany' (unpublished manuscript, undated), Wearmouth Papers; Edna Wearmouth to her father, 29 March 1947, Herford, Wearmouth Papers.
75. Edna Wearmouth to her father, 1 November 1947, Winterberg, Wearmouth Papers.
76. Edna Wearmouth to her father, 19 September 1947, Frankfurt, Wearmouth Papers.
77. Edna Wallace (née Wearmouth), 'Bound for Germany' (unpublished manuscript, undated), Wearmouth Papers.
78. Letter to Joan Hyde from Marjorie, 5 March 1946, Private Papers of Miss J V Hyde, Documents.16534, Imperial War Museum Archive, London.
79. Letter E. G. Ayrton to chancellor of duchy of Lancaster, April 1947, Vol VIII, FO 936/749 Control Office for Germany and Austria and Foreign Office, German Section: Establishments: Files, Miscellaneous complaints: General Public, 1946–51, National Archives, London.
80. Meehan, *A Strange Enemy People*, p. 115.
81. 'Conduct of British in Germany', *Times*, 9 August 1946.
82. Quoted in Meehan, *A Strange Enemy People*, p. 65.
83. Telegram, Prime Minister to Foreign Secretary, 16 November 1946, PREM 8/524, Civilian Administrator or Resident Minister at head of Control Commission in Germany, Prime Minister's Office: Correspondence and Papers, 1945–1951, National Archives, London.

Chapter Fifteen

1. Report, n.d. BT 211/169 Board of Trade: German Division: Files, Alleged Irregular Behaviour of B.I.O.S. Team No. 1972 Investigating the Manufacture of 'Eau-de-Cologne 4711', National Archives, London.
2. FO 936/78, Control Office for Germany and Austria and Foreign Office, German Section: Establishments: Files, Article in New Statesman Alleging Corruption in CCG, 1946–7, National Archives, London.
3. '4711 – Erfrischt und beruhigt die Nerven', Blog, Deutsches Historisches Museum, accessed 12 January 2022, www.dhm.de/blog/2017/06/27/4711-erfrischt-und-beruhigt-die-nerven/.
4. Witness Reports, n.d. BT 211/169 Board of Trade: German Division: Files, Alleged Irregular Behaviour of B.I.O.S. Team No. 1972 Investigating the Manufacture of 'Eau-de-Cologne 4711', National Archives, London.
5. For more see, Longden, *T-Force*.
6. Judt, Burghard and Ciesla, Burghard (eds), *Technology Transfer Out of Germany After 1945* (United Kingdom; Australia: 1996), p. 108.
7. O'Reagan, Douglas M., *Taking Nazi Technology: Allied exploitation of German science after the Second World War* (Baltimore: 2019), pp. 67–9.
8. O'Reagan, *Taking Nazi Technology*, pp. 56–63.
9. O'Reagan, *Taking Nazi Technology*, p. 59.
10. Witness Reports, n.d. BT 211/169 Board of Trade: German Division: Files, Alleged Irregular Behaviour of B.I.O.S. Team No. 1972 Investigating the Manufacture of 'Eau-de-Cologne 4711', National Archives, London.
11. Letter C. S. Low, T-Force, to Miss Chasanovitch, Board of Trade, 17 August

1946, BT 211/169 Board of Trade: German Division: Files, Alleged Irregular Behaviour of B.I.O.S. Team No. 1972 Investigating the Manufacture of 'Eau-de-Cologne 4711', National Archives, London.

12. Meehan, *A Strange Enemy People*, p. 231.

13. Meehan, *A Strange Enemy People*, p. 232; *New York Herald Tribune* (European Edition), 9 November 1946; *New Statesman and Nation*, 9 November 1946.

14. Minutes (Millbank meeting), 22 January 1947, BT 211/169 Board of Trade: German Division: Files, Alleged Irregular Behaviour of B.I.O.S. Team No. 1972 Investigating the Manufacture of 'Eau-de-Cologne 4711', National Archives, London; FO 936/78, Control Office for Germany and Austria and Foreign Office, German Section: Establishments: Files, Article in New Statesman Alleging Corruption in CCG, 1946–7, National Archives, London; Official Report, Fifth Series, Parliamentary Debates, House of Commons, Vol. 430 (1946), 14 November 1946, Col. 238–371.

15. Letter Wood to Jenkins, 7 February 1947, BT 211/169 Board of Trade: German Division: Files, Alleged Irregular Behaviour of B.I.O.S. Team No. 1972 Investigating the Manufacture of 'Eau-de-Cologne 4711', National Archives, London.

16. Letter Jenkins to Wood, 9 May 1947, BT 211/169 Board of Trade: German Division: Files, Alleged Irregular Behaviour of B.I.O.S. Team No. 1972 Investigating the Manufacture of 'Eau-de-Cologne 4711', National Archives, London.

17. Minutes, FO 936/78, Control Office for Germany and Austria and Foreign Office, German Section: Establishments: Files, Article in New Statesman Alleging Corruption in CCG, 1946–7, National Archives, London; Letter Kingsley Martin to John Hynd, 12 November 1946, FO 936/78, Control Office for Germany and Austria and Foreign Office, German Section: Establishments: Files, Article in New Statesman Alleging Corruption in CCG, 1946–7, National Archives, London.

18. *The Third Man*, film, directed by Carol Reed, starring Orson Welles (1949; London: London Films).

19. Roodhouse, Mark, *Black Market Britain, 1939–1955* (Oxford: 2013), p. 243.

20. Roodhouse, *Black Market Britain*, p. 48; Kynaston, *Austerity Britain*, pp. 93–129, 296–325.

21. Tuohy, Ferdinand, 'Racketeering in Germany – Prestige of Occupation Armies is Damaged by Souvenir "Winning"', *Sunderland Daily Echo and Shipping Gazette*, 7 August 1945.

22. 'Berlin – A City of Barter', *Manchester Guardian*, 12 July 1945; 'British Army of the Rhine', *Daily Express*, 13 September 1945; 'Cigarettes: Currency for a Continent', *Daily Mail*, 7 September 1945.

23. Byford-Jones, *Berlin Twilight*, p. 38.

24. Letter from Hazel to Edna Wearmouth, 11 October 1945, Berlin, Wearmouth Papers.

25. Reel 11, Wayne, Peter (Oral History); Reel 9, Dillon, Brian Edevrain (Oral History); Memoir, Private Papers of Lieutenant Colonel R L H Nunn, Documents.11231, Imperial War Museum Archive, London; Meehan, *A Strange Enemy People*, p. 118.

26. Letter from Hazel to Edna Wearmouth, 11 October 1945, Berlin, Wearmouth Papers.

27. Letter to his wife, 17 September 1945, Lenanton Papers.

28. Letter to his wife, 20 November 1945, Lenanton Papers.

29. Salzer, E. Michael, 'Where's the Cat? Germans Ask the Cook', *Daily Mirror*, 25 July 1946.

30. Memoir, 'When All The Trees Were Green', Morris Papers.

31. The public perception of the black market as a moral category, as opposed to an economic or legal one, is discussed in detail in Roodhouse, *Black Market Britain*.

32. Mary Bouman to her parents, 1 June 1948, Herford, Bouman Papers.

33. Edna Wearmouth letter to her father, 28 April 1947, Herford, Wearmouth Papers.

34. Slackman, Michael, 'Berlin Journal: National Dish Comes Wrapped in Foreign Flavoring', *New York Times*, 26 January 2011.

35. Letter from Astor to John Hynd, 18 November 1946, FO 936/743 Control Office for Germany and Austria and Foreign Office, German Section: Establishments: Files, Allegations and Investigations of cases of corruption in CCG, British Zone, 1946–48, National Archives, London; Report for prime minister from John Hynd, 9 December 1946, FO 936/743 Control Office for Germany and Austria and Foreign Office, German Section: Establishments: Files, Allegations and Investigations of cases of corruption in CCG, British Zone, 1946–48, National Archives, London.

36. Meehan, *A Strange Enemy People*, p. 131.

37. 'Yard to Check Zone Control', *Daily Mail*, 13 August 1946; 'The Outer World: Germany: Courts That Try Britons', *Daily Mail*, 14 August 1946; 'Sherlocks For Germany', *Dundee Evening Telegraph*, 21 September 1946; Meehan, *A Strange Enemy People*, p. 116.

38. FO 936/741, Control Office for Germany and Austria and Foreign Office, German Section: Establishments: Files, Operation 'Sparkler' and large-scale blackmarket activities, National Archives, London.

39. 'Trading By Troops in Germany', *Times*, 22 July 1947; Meehan, *A Strange Enemy People*, p. 117.

40. BBB [Bernard Buckham], 'Cigarettes From Home to "Bad Lads" of the Army', *Daily Mirror*, 5 May 1945; Meehan, *A Strange Enemy People*, p. 117.

41. Byford-Jones, *Berlin Twilight*, p. 35.

42. 'Sterling Vouchers in Germany – Stopping Currency Drain', *Manchester Guardian*, 2 August 1946.

43. 'Soldiers' Money Is Called In', *Daily Mirror*, 6 January 1948.

44. Edna Wearmouth to her father, 1 November 1947, Winterberg, Wearmouth Papers.

45. Letter Eve Graham to Prime Minister Attlee, 10 January 1949, FO 936/749 Control Office for Germany and Austria and Foreign Office, German Section: Establishments: Files, Miscellaneous complaints: General Public, 1946–51, National Archives, London.

46. 'Black Market Offences', *Times*, 12 August 1946.

47. 'Offences in British Zone of Germany', *Times*, 24 April 1947; 'Control Officer is Gaoled and Fined £1,000', *Daily Mirror*, 24 March 1947.

48. 'R.A.F. Officer Bartered Food and Cigarettes', *Dundee Evening Telegraph*, 19 July 1949.

49. '"Lord of 3 Manors" Gets Four Years', *Daily Mail*, 27 July 1946.

50. 'Trading By Troops in Germany', *Times*, 22 July 1947; 'Sterling Vouchers in Germany – Stopping Currency Drain', *Manchester Guardian*, 2 August 1946; '£39,500,000 Lost on Continent', *Times*, 15 April 1947; 'Currency Deals in Germany: Heavy Cost to Treasury', *Manchester Guardian*, 23 June 1947; 'Troops Made £20 Million On Smokes', *Daily Express*, 19 February 1947; 'BAOR Ban on the German Mark', *Daily Mail*, 21 May 1946; 'Struggle For Berlin', *Daily Mail*, 6 January 1948; 'Black Marks: Britain Pays', *Daily Mail*, 27 February 1947; 'Black Market Trial For 3 Officers', *Daily Mirror*, 29 December 1945; 'Briton Held in German Gaol – On Charges of Being In Possession of a Control Commission Vehicle and Stealing Seventeen Gallons of Petrol', *Daily Mirror*, 18 January 1947; '"Several Britons to Face Trials In Germany" Shock', *Daily Mirror*, 10 June 1947.

51. 'British Loot Royal Jewels', *Daily Express*, 20 July 1946; 'Treasury Inquiry Opens Today', *Daily Mail*, 8 July 1947; 'RAF Castle Check Opens', *Daily Mail*, 9 July 1947.

52. Meehan, *A Strange Enemy People*, p. 123.

53. Meehan, *A Strange Enemy People*, p. 125.

54. Metropolitan Police Report, 3 April 1947, FO 936/692 Control Office for Germany and Austria and Foreign Office, German Section: Establishments: Files, Investigations Carried Out as a Result of Information given by Mr Pritt MP, 1946–7, National Archives, London.

55. 'Alleged Dealings of British Official', *Times*, 26 March 1947; 'Bought £s with Knives', *Daily Express*, 26 March 1947; 'British Officers Accused of Plot', *Daily Mail*, 25 March 1947; 'Conspiracy: Six For Trial', *Daily Mail*, 22 April 1947; 'Court Told of "Deal" With Customs Official', *Daily Mirror*, 26 March 1947.

56. '7 Britons in "Racket" Trial', *Daily Mail*, 11 June 1947; '2-day Trial Ends in 10/- Fine', *Daily Express*, 13 June 1947; 'Britons Freed', *Daily Mail*, 13 June 1947; *Daily Telegraph*, 13 June 1947; *Daily Graphic*, 13 June 1947; *News Chronicle*, 13 June 1947; 'British Zone Officials Acquitted', *Times*, 14 June 1947.

57. Letter Brian Robertson to Chief Administrative Office et al, Press Economic Sub-commission, 6 May 1947, FO 936/692 Control Office for Germany and Austria and Foreign Office, German Section: Establishments: Files, Investigations Carried Out as a Result of Information given by Mr Pritt MP, 1946–7, National Archives, London.

58. Draft Letter to Brian Robertson, 17 June 1947, FO 936/692 Control Office for Germany and Austria and Foreign Office, German Section: Establishments: Files, Investigations Carried Out as a Result of Information given by Mr Pritt MP, 1946–7, National Archives, London; Letter from Brian Robertson, 20 June 1947, FO 936/692 Control Office for Germany and Austria and Foreign Office, German Section: Establishments: Files, Investigations Carried Out as a Result of Information given by Mr Pritt MP, 1946–7, National Archives, London.

59. Letter from Jenkins to Brian Robertson, n.d., FO 936/692 Control Office for Germany and Austria and Foreign Office, German Section: Establishments: Files, Investigations Carried Out as a Result of Information given by Mr Pritt MP, 1946–7, National Archives, London.

60. 'Illegal Deals In Germany Alleged', *Manchester Guardian*, 17 June 1947; 'Brilliants, Butter in Suitcase', *Daily Express*, 17 June 1947.

61. 'Gifts Retrial Clears Briton', *Daily Mail*, 25 November 1947.

62. 'Drug Traffic in Germany', *Times*, 20 May 1949; 'Trial of Six British Officers', *Times*, 12 November 1945; '"Mean, Nasty" BAOR Wife', *Daily Mail*, 21 May 1947; 'Yard List Dress Deals By Wives', *Daily Mail*, 23 April 1947; 'Yard Men Seek Note Forgers in Germany', *Daily Mail*, 23 June 1945; 'DSO Captain Stole Frau's Wine Set', *Daily Mail*, 13 January 1949; 'RAF Men Alleged To Have Robbed Scared Germans', *Daily Mirror*, 30 August 1946.

63. Peters, *In Germany Now*, pp. 77–8.

64. FO 936/741, Control Office for Germany and Austria and Foreign Office, German Section: Establishments: Files, Operation 'Sparkler' and large-scale blackmarket activities, National Archives, London.

65. 'Gang Spent £250,000 On Bribes', *Daily Mail*, 11 September 1948.

66. Carlin, Wendy, 'Economic Reconstruction in Western Germany, 1945–55: The Displacement of "Vegetative Control"', in Turner, Ian D. (ed.), *Reconstruction in Post-War Germany: British Occupation Policy and the Western Zones, 1945–55* (Oxford: 1988), pp. 37–65.

67. 'Black Zone', *Daily Mirror*, 9 July 1946.

Chapter Sixteen

1. Mary Bouman to her parents, 20 February 1946, Lübbecke, Bouman Papers.

2. Mary Bouman to her parents, 4 March 1946, Lübbecke, Bouman Papers.

3. Mary Bouman to her parents, undated letter 'Bummel in Hamburg', Hamburg, Bouman Papers.

4. Mannin, *German Journey*, pp. 21–2.

5. Gollancz, Victor, *In Darkest Germany* (London: 1947), pp. 95–6.

6. Personal Account, 1985, Private Papers of Miss D E Richardson, Documents.677, Imperial War Museum Archive, London.

7. Meehan, *A Strange Enemy People*, p. 151.

8. Letter, 14 November 1946, Smith Papers.

9. Ramsden, *Don't Mention the War*, p. 240.

10. Memoir, undated, Private Papers of Mrs J Hodges, Documents.8249, Imperial War Museum Archive, London.

11. Brockway, *German Diary*, p. 95.

12. Ramsden, *Don't Mention the War*, pp. 240–41.

13. Meehan, *A Strange Enemy People*, p. 57; Letter to Joan Hyde from Marjorie, 5 March 1946, Hyde Papers.

14. Ahrens, *Die Briten in Hamburg*, pp. 446–7.

15. Mannin, *German Journey*, p. 22.

16. Richter, *Ivan Hirst*, p. 105.

17. Edna Wearmouth to her father, 15 March 1947, France/Germany, Wearmouth Papers.

18. Memoir, 'When All The Trees Were Green', Morris Papers.

19. Cowling, Daniel, '"Gosh… I Think I'm in a Dream!!": Subjective Experiences and Daily Life in the British Zone' in Erlichman, Camilo and Knowles, Christopher (eds), *Transforming Occupation in the Western Zones of Germany: Politics, Everyday Life and Social Interactions, 1945–55* (London: 2018.), pp. 211–30.

20. Edna Wearmouth to her father, 31 July 1947, Frankfurt, Wearmouth Papers.

21. Edna Wearmouth, 'Partnachklamm', photograph album, March 1948, Wearmouth Papers.
22. Edna Wearmouth, 'Hameln', photograph album, May 1947, Wearmouth Papers; Edna Wearmouth, 'Reifenberg am Taunus', photograph album, October 1947, Wearmouth Papers; Edna Wearmouth, 'Garmisch-Partenkirchen', photograph album, March 1948, Wearmouth Papers; Edna Wearmouth, 'Partnachklamm', photograph album, March 1948, Wearmouth Papers.
23. Edna Wearmouth to her father, 28 July 1947, Frankfurt, Wearmouth Papers.
24. Edna Wearmouth to her father, 14 July 1947, Frankfurt, Wearmouth Papers.
25. Mary Bouman to her parents, 27 December 1946, Herford, Bouman Papers.
26. Poem 'Christmas', 24 December 1947, Hamburg, Private Papers of Miss J V Hyde, Documents.16534, Imperial War Museum Archive, London.
27. Malzahn, *Germany 1945–1949*, p. 190.
28. Malzahn, *Germany 1945–1949*, pp. 190–3.
29. Letter to his wife, 25 September 1946, Lenanton Papers.
30. Letters to his wife, 17 and 25 October 1946, Lenanton Papers.
31. Letters to his wife, 27 December 1946, Lenanton Papers.
32. Mary Bouman to her parents, 31 December 1948, Herford, Bouman Papers.
33. Dichter, 'Game Plan for Democracy', p. 144.
34. Gollancz, *In Darkest Germany*, pp. 94–8; Brockway, *German Diary*.
35. This article was reprinted in Gollancz, *In Darkest Germany*, pp. 98–102.
36. Official Report, Fifth Series, Parliamentary Debates, House of Commons, Vol. 426 (1946), 29 July 1946, Col. 559.
37. Official Report, Fifth Series, Parliamentary Debates, House of Commons, Vol. 427 (1946), 17 October 1946, Col. 1154–92.

Chapter Seventeen

1. Ahrens, *Die Briten in Hamburg*, p. 127.
2. Reynolds, *From World War to Cold War*, pp. 277–8; Farquharson, 'The British Occupation of Germany', p. 318.
3. Diefendorf, *In the Wake*, pp. 14–15.
4. Mary Bouman to her parents, 25 April 1946, Lübbecke, Bouman Papers.
5. Diefendorf, *In the Wake*, p. 11.
6. Diefendorf, *In the Wake*, p. 17.
7. Diefendorf, *In the Wake*, pp. 126–7.
8. Diefendorf, *In the Wake*, p. 130.
9. Booklet 'Hamburg', Army Welfare Services, Morris Papers.
10. Ahrens, *Die Briten in Hamburg*, pp. 173–7. These British-only carriages were decommissioned only in 1951.
11. For architectural plans, see 'The Victory Club Hamburg', Antiques catalogue, Antiquariat Michael Kühn, accessed 4 March 2022, www.antiquariat-banzhaf. de/wp-content/uploads/Katalog-19.pdf.
12. Gollancz, *In Darkest Germany*, pp. 98–9.
13. Ahrens, Michael, 'Vier Jahre lang die Herren der Hansestadt', *Welt*, accessed 28 July 2021, www.welt.de/welt_print/vermischtes/hamburg/article4574285/ Vier-Jahre-lang-die-Herren-der-Hansestadt.html.
14. Press Release – Hamburg Project, Appendix A (Secret), 14 June 1946,

FO 1056/520 Control Office for Germany and Austria and Foreign Office: Control Commission for Germany (British Element), Public Relations and Information Services Division, and U.K. High Commission, Information Services Division: Registered Files (PR, ISC, ISD and other Series), Hamburg Project Publicity, National Archives, London.

15. Meehan, *A Strange Enemy People*, p. 140.
16. Meehan, *A Strange Enemy People*, p. 140; Knowles, *Winning the Peace*, pp. 114–8; Official Report, Fifth Series, Parliamentary Debates, House of Commons, Vol. 427 (1946), 17 October 1946, Col. 1154–92.
17. Dunn, Cyril, 'British Wives in Germany – They Say: "We Are Happy but Not Pampered"', *Yorkshire Post*, 13 December 1946.
18. Press Release – Hamburg Project, 14 June 1946, FO 1056/520 Control Office for Germany and Austria and Foreign Office: Control Commission for Germany (British Element), Public Relations and Information Services Division, and U.K. High Commission, Information Services Division: Registered Files (PR, ISC, ISD and other Series), Hamburg Project Publicity, National Archives, London.
19. Public Safety Branch – Daily Situation Report, 1800 Hour 27 June 1946, FO 1056/520 Control Office for Germany and Austria and Foreign Office: Control Commission for Germany (British Element), Public Relations and Information Services Division, and U.K. High Commission, Information Services Division: Registered Files (PR, ISC, ISD and other Series), Hamburg Project Publicity, National Archives, London.
20. PR Branch CCG to Chief PR/ISC, Press Reports on Hamburg Demonstration (with press cuttings), 28 June 1946, FO 1056/520 Control Office for Germany and Austria and Foreign Office: Control Commission for Germany (British Element), Public Relations and Information Services Division, and U.K. High Commission, Information Services Division: Registered Files (PR, ISC, ISD and other Series), Hamburg Project Publicity, National Archives, London.
21. Petersen, Rudolf, 'Hamburgs Interessen und die CDU', 1946 election programme, Konrad Adenauer Stiftung, accessed 1 February 2022, www.kas.de/en/web/geschichte-der-cdu/wahlprogramme-des-cdu-landesverbands-hamburg.
22. Watt, *Britain Looks to Germany*, p. 74.
23. Quoted in Knowles, *Winning the Peace*, p. 67.
24. Quoted in Balfour and Mair, *Four Power Control*, p. 186.
25. Quoted in Knowles, *Winning the Peace*, p. 70.
26. Quoted in Knowles, *Winning the Peace*, p. 76.
27. Balfour and Mair, *Four Power Control*, pp. 186–8.
28. *Hamburger Nachrichten-Blatt*, 16 May 1945; *Hamburger Allgemeine Zeitung*, 25 June 1946.
29. Public Safety Branch – Daily Situation Report, 1800 Hour 27 June 1946, FO 1056/520 Control Office for Germany and Austria and Foreign Office: Control Commission for Germany (British Element), Public Relations and Information Services Division, and U.K. High Commission, Information Services Division: Registered Files (PR, ISC, ISD and other Series), Hamburg Project Publicity, National Archives, London.
30. PR Branch CCG to Chief PR/ISC, Press Reports on Hamburg Demonstration (with press cuttings), 28 June 1946, FO 1056/520 Control Office for Germany and Austria and Foreign Office: Control Commission for Germany (British

Element), Public Relations and Information Services Division, and U.K. High Commission, Information Services Division: Registered Files (PR, ISC, ISD and other Series), Hamburg Project Publicity, National Archives, London.

31. Beveridge, *An Urgent Message*, p. 2.
32. Beveridge, *An Urgent Message*, p. 18.
33. Brockway, *German Diary*, p. viii.
34. Meehan, *A Strange Enemy People*, pp. 144–5.
35. Official Report, Fifth Series, Parliamentary Debates, House of Commons, Vol. 427 (1946), 17 October 1946, Col. 1154–92.
36. Meehan, *A Strange Enemy People*, p. 145.
37. Quoted in Marshall, Barbara, 'German attitudes to British Military Government 1945–1947', *Journal of Contemporary History* 15, no. 4 (1980), p. 661.
38. Kleßmann and Friedmann, *Streiks und Hungermärsche*.
39. Diary entry, 4 October 1946, Ostermann Papers.
40. Knowles, *Winning the Peace*, pp. 107–22.
41. Quoted in Knowles, *Winning the Peace*, p. 120.

Chapter Eighteen

1. Paterson, Sarah, 'The Children of *Operation Union*: Setting up the initial infrastructure for British Families in Germany, 1946–1949' in, Fäßler, Peter E., Neuwöhner, Andreas and Staffel, Florian (eds), *Briten in Westfalen 1945-2017 Besatzer, Verbündete, Freunde?* (Paderborn: 2019), p. 197.
2. B.A.O.R. Wife, 'Soldiers' Wives', letter to the editor, *Daily Telegraph*, 13 November 1945; Acworth, C. B., 'Wives in Germany', letter to the editor, *Daily Telegraph*, 16 November 1945.
3. Carruthers, *The Good Occupation*, p. 269; '18s-a-week Maids for BAOR Wives', *Daily Mail*, 22 January 1946.
4. Reynolds, *From World War to Cold War*, p. 276. This sentiment was already growing strong in America; see Carruthers, *The Good Occupation*, pp. 263–98.
5. 'Troops in Germany Ask for Company', *Yorkshire Post*, 22 May 1945.
6. Illingworth, Joe, 'Soldiers' Wives in Germany – Problems They May Help to Solve', *Yorkshire Post*, 24 August 1946.
7. Russell, G. L. and Gower, Victoria Leveson, 'B.A.O.R. Families', letter to the editor, *Times*, 13 September 1946.
8. B.A.O.R. Husband, 'Soldiers' Wives in Germany – Not Suitable For Them Yet', letter to the editor, *Daily Telegraph*, 24 November 1945.
9. Meehan, *A Strange Enemy People*, p. 133.
10. Meehan, *A Strange Enemy People*, p. 135.
11. Adler, Karen H., 'Selling France to the French: The French Zone of Occupation in Western Germany, 1945 – c.1955', *Contemporary European History* 21, no. 4 (2012), pp. 577–8.
12. Meehan, *A Strange Enemy People*, p. 135; '"Show a Good Example to the Germans", Attlee Tells Wives of BAOR Men', *Daily Mirror*, 18 August 1946.
13. 'B.A.O.R. Wives Land at Cuxhaven', *Manchester Guardian*, 2 September 1946.
14. 'BAOR's "Ugliest" Escorts Wives', photograph, *Daily Mail*, 17 August 1946.
15. 'The First of the British Wives to Join Their Husbands in Berlin', photograph, *Picture Post*, 31 August 1946.

16. 'Picture Gallery – Off to Berlin Soon', photograph, *Daily Mail*, 20 July 1946; 'Picture Gallery – 87 BAOR Wives Say "Farewell Britain" – and on to Germany', photograph, *Daily Mail*, 16 August 1946.

17. See, for instance, 'BAOR Wives Off to Germany', *Yorkshire Post*, 14 August 1946, a report focusing on the trip of Betty Fourness of Burley, Leeds.

18. 'B.A.O.R. Families in Germany – General McCreery's Welcome – A British Example', *Times*, 2 September 1946.

19. 'Brickbats etc', *Daily Mail*, 10 September 1946; 'B.A.O.R. Wives Land at Cuxhaven', *Manchester Guardian*, 2 September 1946.

20. 'B.A.O.R. Families' Reunion – Early Impressions of Germany', *Times*, 3 September 1946.

21. Defence: Wives of Servicemen Stationed in Germany Leave to Join Husbands, 5 September 1946, *Gaumont-British News*, newsreel, Ref BGU410130015, ITN Source Newsreels, www.itnsource.com/en; Germany: Army Wives and Children Reunited With Husbands, 12 September 1946, *Gaumont-British News*, newsreel, Ref BGU410130030, ITN Source Newsreels, www.itnsource.com/en; BAOR Families Are Off, 5 September 1949, *British Movietone News*, newsreel, Issue 47419, British Movietone News Digital Archive, www.movietone.com; BAOR Families Settle Down, 12 September 1949, *British Movietone News*, newsreel, Issue 47419, British Movietone News Digital Archive, www.movietone.com.

22. Crookston, Elizabeth, 'Soldiers' Wives', letter to the editor, *Daily Telegraph*, 26 August 1946.

23. Quoted in 'Mr. Attlee's Message to B.A.O.R. Wives', *Times*, 16 August 1946.

24. Quoted in 'British Wives in Germany', *Times*, 19 August 1946.

25. Where BAOR Wives Will Live, 5 August 1946, *Pathé News*, newsreel, Issue 1406.15, British Pathé Archive, www.britishpathe.com/.

26. Peacocke, Marguerite, 'When the Joneses Go To Germany – BAOR Wives Will Find Life in Germany a Mixture of Undreamed-of Luxury and Make-do-or-go-without', *Daily Mirror*, 15 July 1946.

27. Buckley, F. H. and Smith, W. W., *The Origins of the British Families Education Service* (Rheindahlen: 1976), p. 3.

28. Buckley and Smith, *The Origins of the British Families Education Service*, pp. 6–8.

29. Buckley and Smith, *The Origins of the British Families Education Service*, p. 12.

30. Buckley and Smith, *The Origins of the British Families Education Service*, pp. 12–3.

31. Buckley and Smith, *The Origins of the British Families Education Service*, p. 13.

32. 'BAOR Wives: First Go Out in June', *Daily Mail*, 21 January 1946; '18s-a-week Maids for BAOR Wives', *Daily Mail*, 22 January 1946; 'All mod. con. For BAOR', *Daily Mail*, 25 January 1946.

33. 'What B.A.O.R. Wives Will Find in Germany', *Aberdeen Press and Journal*, 16 July 1946.

34. 'Wives in BAOR "spoiled darlings"', *Daily Mail*, 16 August 1946.

35. Letter from Mary Bouman, 25 August 1947, Herford, Bouman Papers.

36. Mary Bouman to her parents, 6 August 1947, Herford, Bouman Papers.

37. '"Stay Out of Germany" Call to Wives', *Daily Mirror*, 2 August 1946; 'Treatment of B.A.O.R. Wives – British Girls Complain', *Manchester Guardian*, 5 September 1946.

38. 'Biggest BAOR Family Leave Small Home Here for a 14-room House', *Daily Mirror*, 3 September 1946.
39. Captain D. E. H., 'Viewpoint', letter to the editor, *Daily Mirror*, 5 May 1947.
40. 'Wives in BAOR "spoiled darlings"', *Daily Mail*, 16 August 1946.
41. 'Brickbats etc', *Daily Mail*, 10 September 1946
42. Letter J. N. Walton to the prime minister, 17 January 1947, Vol III, FO 936/749 Control Office for Germany and Austria and Foreign Office, German Section: Establishments: Files, Miscellaneous complaints: General Public, 1946–51, National Archives, London.
43. S., 'The Herrenvolk', letter to the editor, *Manchester Guardian*, 16 January 1947.
44. Letter Ernest E. Laws to the prime minister, 1 February 1947, Vol. V, FO 936/749 Control Office for Germany and Austria and Foreign Office, German Section: Establishments: Files, Miscellaneous complaints: General Public, 1946–51, National Archives, London.
45. Atholl, Katharine, Allen of Hurtwood, Marjory, Barlow, Anna, Cadbury, Elizabeth M., Colville, Cynthia, Craven, C. M., Eardley-Wilmot, Amabel, Fry, Margery, Gainsborough, Alice, Isaacs, Susan, Jebb, Geraldine, Pethick-Lawrence, Emmeline, Snowden, Ethel, Thornbike, Sybil, Waddell, Helen, Wedgewood, Florence, Wootton, Barbara and Wrench, Hylda, 'British Wives in Germany', letter to the editor, *Times*, 10 October 1946.
46. Churchill, Clementine S., 'British Wives in Germany', letter to the editor, *Times*, 11 October 1946.
47. B.A.O.R Wife, 'British Wives in Germany', letter to the editor, *Times*, 17 October 1946.
48. Elford, Ruth, 'British Wives in Germany', letter to the editor, *Times*, 15 October 1946.
49. Illingworth, Joe, 'Soldiers' Wives in Germany – Problems They May Help to Solve', *Yorkshire Post*, 24 August 1946.
50. Dunn, Cyril, 'British Wives in Germany – They Say: "We Are Happy but Not Pampered"', *Yorkshire Post*, 13 December 1946.
51. 'The Outer World – All Is Not Easy For BAOR Wife', *Daily Mail*, 20 August 1946; also see 'Few Homes, No Furniture for BAOR Wives', *Daily Mail*, 20 July 1946.
52. 'B.A.O.R. Wives in Tears', *Nottingham Evening Post*, 31 August 1946.
53. 'Army Cuts BAOR Wives Lists: Too Few Houses', *Daily Mirror*, 20 December 1946.

Chapter Nineteen

1. Diary Entry, 9 February 1947, Klaus Behr Tagebücher 1938-1956, Diary of a POW at Springhill Camp 185, Translation, Chipping Campden History Society Archives, www.chippingcampdenhistory.org.uk.
2. Reynolds, *Britannia Overruled*, p. 137.
3. Quoted in Robertson, Alex J., *The Bleak Midwinter: 1947* (Manchester: 1987), p. 103.
4. Watt, *Britain Looks to Germany*, p. 53.
5. There were also growing calls for decolonization from within the Labour Party

itself, further piling the pressure on Attlee. See Reynolds, *Britannia Overruled*, p. 152.

6. Reynolds, *Britannia Overruled*, pp. 155–6.
7. For an overview see, Black, Ian, *Enemies and Neighbours: Arabs and Jews in Palestine and Israel, 1917–2017* (London: 2017).
8. Knowles, *Winning the Peace*, pp. 139–40.
9. Quoted in Reynolds, *Britannia Overruled*, p. 157.
10. Reynolds, *Britannia Overruled*, p. 157.
11. Reynolds, *Britannia Overruled*, pp. 148–9.
12. Quoted in Kynaston, *Austerity Britain*, p. 196.
13. Robertson, *The Bleak Midwinter*, p. 10.
14. Robertson, *The Bleak Midwinter*, p. 11
15. Robertson, *The Bleak Midwinter*, p. 13.
16. Memoir, Heather Papers.
17. Memoir, 'When All The Trees Were Green', Morris Papers.
18. Memoir of service with Control Commission Germany, 1947–51, Edward Pye Rich papers, BL Mss Eur Photo Eur 389, British Library, London.
19. Bark, Dennis L. and Gress, David R., *A History of West Germany*, vol. 1, *From Shadow to Substance, 1945–1963* (Oxford: 1989), p. 130.
20. Bark and Gress, *A History of West Germany*, p. 131.
21. Reynolds, *Britannia Overruled*, p. 158.
22. Buchanan, Tom, *Europe's Troubled Peace: 1945 to the Present*, 2nd ed. (Malden, Mass.; Oxford: 2012), p. 38.
23. Meehan, *A Strange Enemy People*, pp. 59–60.
24. Watt, *Britain Looks to Germany*, pp. 76–7.; Adams, Bianka J., *From Crusade to Hazard: The Denazification of Bremen Germany* (Lanham, Md.; Plymouth: 2009), p. 48.
25. Memoir of service with Control Commission Germany, 1947–51, Edward Pye Rich papers, BL Mss Eur Photo Eur 389, British Library, London.
26. *British Zone Review*, vol. 1, no. 34, 4 January 1947, quoted in Knowles, *Winning the Peace*, p. 119.
27. Watt, *Britain Looks to Germany*, pp. 77–8.
28. Herbert, *A History of 20th-Century Germany*, p. 467.
29. Jürgensen, Kurt, 'The Concept and Practice of "Re-education" in Germany, 1945–50', in Pronay, Nicholas and Wilson, Nicholas (eds), *The Political Re-education of Germany and her Allies after World War II* (London; Sydney: 1985), p. 90.
30. Watt, *Britain Looks to Germany*, p. 81.
31. Meehan, *A Strange Enemy People*, pp. 179–80.
32. Bark and Gress, *A History of West Germany*, p. 156.
33. Bölsche, Jochen, 'Obituary: John Seymour Chaloner (1924-2007)', *Der Spiegel International*, accessed 17 March 2023, www.spiegel.de/international/spiegel/obituary-john-seymour-chaloner-1924-2007-a-468130.html.
34. Knowles, *Winning the Peace*, pp. 145–9.
35. Quoted in Knowles, *Winning the Peace*, p. 154.
36. Quoted in Knowles, *Winning the Peace*, p. 157.
37. Knowles, *Winning the Peace*, p. 147.
38. Edna Wearmouth to her father, 17 June 1947, Frankfurt, Wearmouth Papers.
39. Edna Wearmouth to her father, 7 July 1947, Frankfurt, Wearmouth Papers.

40. Quoted in Deighton, *The Impossible Peace*, p. 112.
41. Deighton, 'Towards a "Western" Strategy', p. 58.
42. Watt, *Britain Looks to Germany*, pp. 83, 89; Farquharson, 'The British Occupation of Germany', p. 337.
43. Letter E. S. Biddough to Lord Pakenham, 21 July 1947, Vol XI, FO 936/749 Control Office for Germany and Austria and Foreign Office, German Section: Establishments: Files, Miscellaneous complaints: General Public, 1946–51, National Archives, London.
44. Bullock, *The Life and Times of Ernest Bevin*, vol. 3, p. 352.
45. Reynolds, *Britannia Overruled*, pp. 158–9.
46. Knowles, *Winning the Peace*, pp. 139–40.
47. Schwarz, Hans-Peter, 'The Division of Germany, 1945-1949', in Leffler, Melvyn P. and Westad, Odd Arne (eds) *The Cambridge History of the Cold War*, vol. 1, *Origins* (Cambridge: 2009), p. 143.
48. Reynolds, 'Great Britain', p. 84.
49. Reynolds, 'Great Britain', p. 87.

Chapter Twenty

1. Owen, Frank, 'Good Morning – Let's Get Our Heads Out Of The Sand In Germany', *Daily Mail*, 11 October 1946.
2. 'The Cuckoo in the Nest', Cartoon, *Daily Mail*, 6 August 1947. The bespectacled bird appears to be a caricature of Lord Pakenham.
3. 'Get Out Of Germany', *Daily Mail*, 26 July 1947.
4. Deighton, Anne, 'Britain and the Cold War, 1945–1955', in Leffler, Melvyn P. and Westad, Odd Arne (eds) *The Cambridge History of the Cold War*, vol. 1, *Origins* (Cambridge: 2009), p. 123; Reynolds, *From World War to Cold War*, p. 285.
5. Deighton, *The Impossible Peace*, p. 226; Reynolds, *From World War to Cold War*, p. 277.
6. Deighton, 'The "Frozen Front"', p. 462.
7. 'Zone Officials Resigning – Control System Thwarts Initiative', *Daily Telegraph*, 28 July 1947.
8. 'Frustration', editorial, *Daily Telegraph*, 4 August 1947.
9. Blount, B. K., 'The British in Germany', letter to the editor, *Times*, 22 August 1947; Carter, Tracy, 'The British in Germany', letter to the editor, *Times*, 30 August 1947.
10. Connell, Brian, 'The Palsied Hand in the Velvet Glove', *Daily Mail*, 11 August 1947.
11. 'Germany', editorial, *Daily Mail*, 13 August 1947.
12. Deighton, 'The "Frozen Front"', p. 462.
13. 'C-in-C Offers Files to Yard', *Daily Mail*, 21 August 1947.
14. 'Disgrace to Britain', editorial, *Daily Mail*, 21 August 1947.
15. Minutes E. Underwood to J. Mark and Pakenham, 22 August 1947, FO 946/62 Control Office for Germany and Austria and Foreign Office, German Section: Information Services: Records, Press Campaign 'Get Out of Germany', 1947, National Archives, London.
16. Letter Pakenham to Rt. Hon. Viscount Rothermere, 22 August 1947, FO

946/62 Control Office for Germany and Austria and Foreign Office, German Section: Information Services: Records, Press Campaign 'Get Out of Germany', 1947, National Archives, London; Letter from Pakenham to Frank Owen, 25 August 1947, FO 946/62 Control Office for Germany and Austria and Foreign Office, German Section: Information Services: Records, Press Campaign 'Get Out of Germany', 1947, National Archives, London.

17. Letter from Frank Owen to Pakenham, 26 August 1947, FO 946/62 Control Office for Germany and Austria and Foreign Office, German Section: Information Services: Records, Press Campaign 'Get Out of Germany', 1947, National Archives, London.

18. Potter, John Deane, 'Germany: A Report on the British Zone by John Deane Potter, who recently returned from Hamburg after an 11-weeks investigation into life under British control', *Daily Express*, 4 September 1947.

19. Letter from Mary Bouman, 11 September 1947, Herford, Bouman Papers.

20. Letter from Mary Bouman, 1 January 1948, Herford, Bouman Papers.

21. Draft Letter to Arthur Christiansen, n.d., appendix A, FO 946/62 Control Office for Germany and Austria and Foreign Office, German Section: Information Services: Records, Press Campaign 'Get Out of Germany', 1947, National Archives, London.

22. Letter FO German Section to (Acting) Chief PR/ISC, Berlin, 13 September 1947, Appendix C, FO 946/62 Control Office for Germany and Austria and Foreign Office, German Section: Information Services: Records, Press Campaign 'Get Out of Germany', 1947, National Archives, London; Telegram Brownjohn to Dean, 13 September 1947, FO 946/62 Control Office for Germany and Austria and Foreign Office, German Section: Information Services: Records, Press Campaign 'Get Out of Germany', 1947, National Archives, London.

23. DUS to Jenkins, 17 September 1947, FO 946/62 Control Office for Germany and Austria and Foreign Office, German Section: Information Services: Records, Press Campaign 'Get Out of Germany', 1947, National Archives, London.

24. Telegram Brownjohn to Dean, 13 September 1947, FO 946/62 Control Office for Germany and Austria and Foreign Office, German Section: Information Services: Records, Press Campaign 'Get Out of Germany', 1947, National Archives, London; Message from commander-in-chief, appendix B, FO 946/62 Control Office for Germany and Austria and Foreign Office, German Section: Information Services: Records, Press Campaign 'Get Out of Germany', 1947, National Archives, London; Telegram Dean to Brownjohn, 29 September 1947, FO 946/62 Control Office for Germany and Austria and Foreign Office, German Section: Information Services: Records, Press Campaign 'Get Out of Germany', 1947, National Archives, London; Letter from Jenkins to Ernest Bevin, 3 October 1947, FO 946/62 Control Office for Germany and Austria and Foreign Office, German Section: Information Services: Records, Press Campaign 'Get Out of Germany', 1947, National Archives, London; Letter from Bevin to Douglas, 6 October 1947, FO 946/62 Control Office for Germany and Austria and Foreign Office, German Section: Information Services: Records, Press Campaign 'Get Out of Germany', 1947, National Archives, London.

25. There were also attempts to refute the allegations entirely; see 'Behaviour of

Troops in Germany – Mr. Shinwell's Praise', *Times*, 17 January 1948; 'Shinwell Finds No Excesses', *Manchester Guardian*, 17 January 1948.

26. Telegram Westropp to Dean, 1 October 1947, FO 946/62 Control Office for Germany and Austria and Foreign Office, German Section: Information Services: Records, Press Campaign 'Get Out of Germany', 1947, National Archives, London.

27. 'Control Commission Staff Defended', *Times*, 20 October 1947.

28. '£80,000,000 On Misfits', *Daily Graphic*, 30 August 1947; North, Rex, *Sunday Pictorial*, 15 October 1947. For more, see assorted cuttings: FO 946/62 Control Office for Germany and Austria and Foreign Office, German Section: Information Services: Records, Press Campaign 'Get Out of Germany', 1947, National Archives, London.

29. Hemmingway, W., 'Live Letters', letter to the editor, *Daily Mirror*, 6 November 1947; Dixon, E. P., 'Live Letters', letter to the editor, *Daily Mirror*, 5 September 1947.

30. Minutes, FO 946/62 Control Office for Germany and Austria and Foreign Office, German Section: Information Services: Records, Press Campaign 'Get Out of Germany', 1947, National Archives, London; Douglas-Smith, Aubrey, 'British Policy in Germany', letter to the editor, *Times*, 1 October 1947.

31. Panton, Selkirk, 'Anger Over Morality Memo', *Daily Express*, 1 October 1947.

32. Draft Letter r.e. 'Press Attacks on Control Commission for Germany', Croxson, n.d., FO 946/62 Control Office for Germany and Austria and Foreign Office, German Section: Information Services: Records, Press Campaign 'Get Out of Germany', 1947, National Archives, London.

33. Letter Croxson to Underwood and attached cuttings: 'morals memo angers zone staff' (carried by nearly every paper today), 1 October 1947, FO 946/62 Control Office for Germany and Austria and Foreign Office, German Section: Information Services: Records, Press Campaign 'Get Out of Germany', 1947, National Archives, London.

34. 'Control Commission', editorial, *Manchester Guardian*, 5 June 1948.

35. Farquharson, 'The British Occupation of Germany 1945–6', p. 327; Adler, 'Selling France to the French', p. 578.

36. Memoir of service with Control Commission Germany, 1947–51, Edward Pye Rich papers, BL Mss Eur Photo Eur 389, British Library, London.

37. Bloxham, 'British War Crimes Trial Policy', pp. 91–2.

Chapter Twenty-One

1. Letter Elton to Crawford, 19 January 1948, FO 946/91 Control Office for Germany and Austria and Foreign Office, German Section: Information Services: Records, Central Office of Information: Film of German Education, 1947–8, National Archives, London.

2. INF 6/990 Crown Film Unit Productions, A School in Cologne 1948, 1947–50, National Archives, London.

3. Raymond, Jack, 'Ruhr Strikes Laid to War on U.S. Aid', *New York Times*, 10 January 1948.

4. Letter Elton to Crawford, 19 January 1948, FO 946/91 Control Office for Germany and Austria and Foreign Office, German Section: Information

Services: Records, Central Office of Information: Film of German Education, 1947–8, National Archives, London.

5. Croxson to Underwood, Publicity To Off-set Recent Newspaper Articles Against Control Commission Personnel, 30 September 1947, FO 946/62 Control Office for Germany and Austria and Foreign Office, German Section: Information Services: Records, Press Campaign 'Get Out of Germany', 1947, National Archives, London.

6. Letter PR/ISC to CAO, FO 1056/176, 14 February 1948, Control Office for Germany and Austria and Foreign Office: Control Commission for Germany (British Element), Public Relations and Information Services Division, and U.K. High Commission, Information Services Division: Registered Files (PR, ISC, ISD and other Series), Publicity General Vol. 1, November 1947 – August 1948, National Archives, London.

7. Shaw, 'The British Popular Press and the Early Cold War', p. 80; Smith, Lyn, 'Covert British Propaganda: The Information Research Department: 1947–77', *Millennium – Journal of International Studies* 9, no. 1 (1980), pp. 67–83; Lashmar, Paul and Oliver, James, *Britain's Secret Propaganda War: The Foreign Office and the Cold War, 1948–77* (Stroud: 1998), p. xvi; Fletcher, R. J. 'British Propaganda since World War II – a Case Study', *Media, Culture & Society* 4, no. 2 (1982), pp. 97–109; Shaw, Tony, 'The Information Research Department of the British Foreign Office and the Korean War, 1950–53', *Journal of Contemporary History* 34, no. 2 (1999), pp. 263–81.

8. Letter Crawford to Birley, 19 August 1947, FO 946/92 Control Office for Germany and Austria and Foreign Office, German Section: Information Services: Records, Central Office of Information: Films to be made on conditions in Germany, 1947–8, National Archives, London; Letter Crawford to Elton, 20 September 1947, FO 946/92 Control Office for Germany and Austria and Foreign Office, German Section: Information Services: Records, Central Office of Information: Films to be made on conditions in Germany, 1947–8, National Archives, London; Termination of film on coal industry, FO 946/92 Control Office for Germany and Austria and Foreign Office, German Section: Information Services: Records, Central Office of Information: Films to be made on conditions in Germany, 1947–8, National Archives, London; Letter from Norman Clark Chairman of British Zone Correspondents Association to Sholto Douglas and attached memorandum, 1947, FO 946/47 Control Office for Germany and Austria and Foreign Office, German Section: Information Services: Records, German and Austrian Publicity: British Zone Correspondents' Association, National Archives, London.

9. Minutes, FO 946/92 Control Office for Germany and Austria and Foreign Office, German Section: Information Services: Records, Central Office of Information: Films to be made on conditions in Germany, 1947–8, National Archives, London; Letter Crawford to Triton, 7 August 1947, FO 946/92 Control Office for Germany and Austria and Foreign Office, German Section: Information Services: Records, Central Office of Information: Films to be made on conditions in Germany, 1947–8, National Archives, London.

10. INF 6/401 Crown Film Unit Productions, Trained To Serve, National Archives, London.

11. INF 6/395 Crown Film Unit Productions, Kreis Resident Officer – Germany

(problems in post-war German districts) 1947, 1947–51, National Archives, London.

12. 'New Educational Films', *Monthly Film Bulletin*, 1 January 1948.

13. Oppen, Beate Ruhm von, *Documents on Germany under Occupation, 1945–1954* (London: 1955), pp. 210–11.

14. Oppen, von *Documents on Germany under Occupation*, pp. 211–17.

15. Cassidy, Velma Hastings, *Germany, 1947–1949: The Story in Documents* (Washington, DC: US Dept. of State, 1950), pp. 21–32.

16. Pathé Pictorial Looks At Berlin, 24 November 1947, *Pathé News*, newsreel, Issue 1355.21, British Pathé Archive, www.britishpathe.com/.

17. Barkley, William, 'William Barkley's Notebook – Watch Out, They'll Cheat Us Yet!', *Daily Express*, 11 November 1947.

18. Reynolds, 'Great Britain', p. 85.

19. Official Report, Fifth Series, Parliamentary Debates, House of Commons, Vol. 445 (1947), 18 December 1947, Col. 1874–87.

20. Deighton, *The Impossible Peace*, p. 223.

21. Reynolds, *Britannia Overruled*, p. 165; Shaw, 'The British Popular Press and the Early Cold War', pp. 80, 82; Bullock, *The Life and Times of Ernest Bevin*, vol. 3, pp. 552–6; Hennessy, Peter, *Never Again: Britain 1945–1951* (London: 2006), p. 252.

22. 'In Brief – De-Nazification of British Zone of Germany is Now Considered Complete', *Daily Mirror*, 6 January 1948; Bloxham, 'British War Crimes Trial Policy', pp. 105–6; Bloxham, Donald, 'Punishing German Soldiers during the Cold War: The Case of Erich von Manstein', *Patterns of Prejudice* 33, no. 4 (1999), pp. 24–45, https://doi.org/10.1080/003132299128810687; Dale Jones, 'British Policy Towards German Crimes'.

23. Cowling, Daniel, 'Anglo–German Relations After 1945', *Journal of Contemporary History* 54, no. 1 (2019), https://doi.org/10.1177/0022009417697808.

24. Boehling, Rebecca, 'Transitional Justice? Denazification in the US Zone of Occupied Germany', in Erlichman, Camilo and Knowles, Christopher (eds), *Transforming Occupation in the Western Zones of Germany: Politics, Everyday Life and Social Interactions, 1945–55* (London: 2018.), pp. 63–80.

25. Bloxham, 'British War Crimes Trial Policy', pp. 91–2.

26. Herbert, *A History of 20th-Century Germany*, p. 460.

27. A good overview of British denazification efforts is Turner, Ian D., 'Denazification in the British Zone', in Turner, Ian D. (ed.), *Reconstruction in Post-War Germany: British Occupation Policy and the Western Zones, 1945–55* (Oxford: 1988), pp. 239–67.

28. Bark and Gress, *A History of West Germany*, p. 86.

29. Szanajda, *The Allies*, pp. 81–3.

30. Szanajda, *The Allies*, p. 83.

31. 'London Deal on Germany', *Soviet News*, 16 June 1948.

32. Official Report, Fifth Series, Parliamentary Debates, House of Commons, Vol. 452 (1948), 30 June 1948, Col. 2221–9.

33. Gollancz, Victor, 'Our Attitude to Germany', letter to the editor, *Manchester Guardian*, 27 July 1948.

Chapter Twenty-Two

1. 'Hooded Man Put In Cell', *Daily Express*, 10 April 1948.
2. Cobain, Ian, *Cruel Britannia: A Secret History of Torture* (London: 2012), p. 49.
3. Kurt Robert HERRMANN, aliases Robert Edward Alexander von BUTTLAR BRANDENFELS [*sic*], Karl JENSSON, Karl HILGER, Robert HELLMAN, Karl HJERRING, HJERRBERG: German, KV 2/4098-4100, The Security Service: Personal (PF Series) Files, World War II, Subjects of Security Service Enquiry, National Archives, London.
4. Cobain, *Cruel Britannia*, pp. 49–50.
5. Jeffery, Keith, *MI6: The History of the Secret Intelligence Service, 1909–1949* (London: 2010), p. 668.
6. Aldrich, Richard J., *The Hidden Hand: Britain, America and Cold War Secret Intelligence* (London: 2001), p. 181.
7. Aldrich, *The Hidden Hand*, p. 181.
8. West, Nigel, *The Friends: Britain's Post-War Secret Intelligence Operations* (London: 1988), p. 21.
9. Jeffery, *MI6*, p. 665.
10. Aldrich, *The Hidden Hand*, p. 182.
11. Aldrich, *The Hidden Hand*, p. 183.
12. Aldrich, *The Hidden Hand*, p. 200.
13. Aldrich, *The Hidden Hand*, p. 183.
14. West, *The Friends*, p. 24; Aldrich, *The Hidden Hand*, p. 188.
15. Aldrich, *The Hidden Hand*, p. 190.
16. Jeffery, *MI6*, p. 654.
17. Tyas, Stephen, *SS-Major Horst Kopkow: From the Gestapo to British Intelligence* (Stroud; Charleston, SC: 2017), p. 224.
18. Tyas, *SS-Major Horst Kopkow*, pp. 225–6.
19. Tyas, *SS-Major Horst Kopkow*, pp. 226–8.
20. Aldrich, *The Hidden Hand*, p. 184; Dorril, Stephen, *MI6: Fifty Years of Special Operations* (London: 2000), pp. 200–1.
21. *The SS in Britain*, TV documentary film, directed by Julian Hendry (2001; Leeds: Yorkshire Television).
22. Aldrich, *The Hidden Hand*, p. 195.
23. Quoted in Jeffery, *MI6*, p. 668.
24. Aldrich, *The Hidden Hand*, p. 196.
25. Aldrich, *The Hidden Hand*, p. 188.
26. Reel 3, James, George Philip Henry (Oral History).
27. West, *The Friends*, p. 27.
28. West, *The Friends*, p. 23.
29. West, *The Friends*, p. 23, fn. 2.
30. West, *The Friends*, p. 27.
31. FO 1093/549, Defector from Berlin: Lieutenant Colonel Gregory Tokaev (codename EXCISE); reports and information, Foreign Office: Permanent Under-Secretary's Department: Registered and Unregistered Papers: Cold War Issues, including Espionage and Defectors, National Archives, London.
32. Quoted in Aldrich, *The Hidden Hand*, p. 192.
33. Cobain, *Cruel Britannia*, p. 5.

34. Fry, Helen, *The London Cage: The Secret History of Britain's World War II Interrogation Centre* (New Haven: 2017); Cobain, *Cruel Britannia*, pp. 1–37.

35. Cobain, *Cruel Britannia*, pp. 23–5.

36. Cobain, *Cruel Britannia*, pp. 16, 25.

37. Cobain, *Cruel Britannia*, p. 46.

38. Cobain, *Cruel Britannia*, p. 67.

39. Cobain, Ian, 'Britain's Secret Torture Centre', *The Guardian*, 17 December 2005.

40. Hayward Report, FO 1030/272, Control Commission for Germany (British Element): Various Private Office Papers and Administration and Local Government Branch Files, Assistant Inspector General, Public Safety, report on Bad Nenndorf Detailed Interrogation Centre, National Archives, London.

41. Cobain, *Cruel Britannia*, p. 53.

42. Quoted in Cobain, *Cruel Britannia*, p. 48.

43. Cobain, *Cruel Britannia*, p. 38.

44. Cobain, *Cruel Britannia*, p. 39.

45. Hayward Report, FO 1030/272, Control Commission for Germany (British Element): Various Private Office Papers and Administration and Local Government Branch Files, Assistant Inspector General, Public Safety, report on Bad Nenndorf Detailed Interrogation Centre, National Archives, London.

46. Cobain, *Cruel Britannia*, pp. 40–1

47. Quoted in Cobain, *Cruel Britannia*, p. 43.

48. *Quick*, 3 March 1952.

49. Official Report, Fifth Series, Parliamentary Debates, House of Commons, Vol. 435 (1947), 24 March 1947, Col. 1018.

50. Cobain, *Cruel Britannia*, pp. 60–2.

51. Hayward Report, FO 1030/272, Control Commission for Germany (British Element): Various Private Office Papers and Administration and Local Government Branch Files, Assistant Inspector General, Public Safety, report on Bad Nenndorf Detailed Interrogation Centre, National Archives, London.

52. Quoted in Cobain, *Cruel Britannia*, p. 62.

53. Cobain, *Cruel Britannia*, p. 62.

54. Memorandum on court martial of several members of staff at Bad Nenndorf Detailed Interrogation Centre in British Zone, 1948, PREM 8/794, Prime Minister's Office: Correspondence and Papers, 1945–1951, Germany (miscellaneous), National Archives, London.

55. Official Report, Fifth Series, Parliamentary Debates, House of Commons, Vol. 445 (1947), 17 December 1947, Col. 337. It was a comment that perturbed the higher-ups in MI5, not least because they weren't actually responsible for the camp. Guy Liddell wrote in his diary that this kind of misinformation was 'extremely harmful to our work, since it built us up in the minds of the public as a kind of Gestapo'; see Diary Entry, 18 December 1947, KV 4/469, Diary of Guy Liddell, Deputy Director General of the Security Service, May to December 1947, National Archives, London.

56. *Daily Express*, 18 December 1947.

57. Cobain, *Cruel Britannia*, pp. 67–8.

58. Wighton, Charles, 'M.I.5 Methods told to Court', *Daily Express*, 11 March 1948.

59. Quoted in 'Lieut. Langham Acquitted', *Manchester Guardian*, 1 April 1948.

60. Cobain, *Cruel Britannia*, p. 69.

61. 'Lieut R. O. Langham Acquitted', *Times*, 1 April 1948.

62. FO 371/70829, Foreign Office: Political Departments: General Correspondence from 1906–1966: No 10 Disposal Interrogation Centre, Bad Nenndorf. Trial and acquittal of Lt Col R W G Stephens, OBE, in connection with alleged brutalities, National Archives, London.

63. Memorandum on court martial of several members of staff at Bad Nenndorf Detailed Interrogation Centre in British Zone, 1948, PREM 8/794, Prime Minister's Office: Correspondence and Papers, 1945–1951, Germany (miscellaneous), National Archives, London. We learn from Guy Liddell's diaries that Stephens had actually received off-the-record legal advice from senior figures in MI5; see Diary Entries, 28 June, 1 July, 19 July, 26 July, 2 October, 1 December 1947, KV 4/469, Diary of Guy Liddell, Deputy Director General of the Security Service, May to December 1947, National Archives, London; Diary Entry, 6 July 1948, KV 4/470, Diary of Guy Liddell, Deputy Director General of the Security Service, January to December 1948, National Archives, London.

64. Cobain, *Cruel Britannia*, p. 74; Letters from Hartley Shawcross, PREM 8/794, Prime Minister's Office: Correspondence and Papers, 1945–1951, Germany (miscellaneous), National Archives, London.

65. Report: Bad Nenndorf Trials, PREM 8/794, Prime Minister's Office: Correspondence and Papers, 1945–1951, Germany (miscellaneous), National Archives, London.

66. Cobain, *Cruel Britannia*, p. 70.

67. Cobain, *Cruel Britannia*, p. 72.

68. Diary Entry, 19 July 1948, KV 4/470, Diary of Guy Liddell, Deputy Director General of the Security Service, January to December 1948, National Archives, London.

69. Diary Entries, 26 July, 19 October 1948, KV 4/470, Diary of Guy Liddell, Deputy Director General of the Security Service, January to December 1948, National Archives, London.

70. Report: Bad Nenndorf Trials, PREM 8/794, Prime Minister's Office: Correspondence and Papers, 1945–1951, Germany (miscellaneous), National Archives, London.

71. Meehan, *Strange Enemy People*, p. 84; 'Bad Nenndorf', *Die Zeit*, 15 April 1948.

72. FO 371/70830, Foreign Office: Political Departments: General Correspondence from 1906–1966: No. 10 Disposal Interrogation Centre, Bad Nenndorf. Trial and acquittal of Lt Col R W G Stephens, OBE, in connection with alleged brutalities, 1948, National Archives, London.

73. Letter from 'German internal Department, FO' (draft penned by Marsden-Smedley) to The Chancery, British Embassy, Brussels, 26 October 1948, FO 371/70830, Foreign Office: Political Departments: General Correspondence from 1906–1966: No. 10 Disposal Interrogation Centre, Bad Nenndorf. Trial and acquittal of Lt Col R W G Stephens, OBE, in connection with alleged brutalities, 1948, National Archives, London.

74. Letter Knapton to Marsden-Smedley, 14 October 1948, FO 371/70830, Foreign Office: Political Departments: General Correspondence from 1906–1966: No. 10 Disposal Interrogation Centre, Bad Nenndorf. Trial and acquittal of Lt Col R W G Stephens, OBE, in connection with alleged brutalities, 1948, National Archives, London.

75. Letter from 'German internal Department, FO' (draft penned by Marsden-Smedley) to The Chancery, British Embassy, Brussels, 26 October 1948, FO 371/70830, Foreign Office: Political Departments: General Correspondence from 1906–1966: No. 10 Disposal Interrogation Centre, Bad Nenndorf. Trial and acquittal of Lt Col R W G Stephens, OBE, in connection with alleged brutalities, 1948, National Archives, London.

76. Letter Knapton to Marsden-Smedley 23 September 1948, FO 371/70830, Foreign Office: Political Departments: General Correspondence from 1906–1966: No. 10 Disposal Interrogation Centre, Bad Nenndorf. Trial and acquittal of Lt Col R W G Stephens, OBE, in connection with alleged brutalities, 1948, National Archives, London.

Chapter Twenty-Three

1. Reel 1, Coan, Pip (Oral History), Sound Recording, Catalogue Number 19006, Imperial War Museum Archive, London.

2. Shlaim, Avi, 'Britain, the Berlin Blockade and the Cold War', *International Affairs* 60, no. 1 (1983), p. 3, https://doi.org/10.2307/2618926.

3. Shlaim, 'Britain, the Berlin Blockade and the Cold War', p. 3; *Foreign Relations of the United States*, 1948, vol. II, Germany and Austria, ed. Slany, William and Sampson, Charles S. (Washington: United States Government Printing Office, 1973), p. 159.

4. Mary Bouman to her parents, 24 March 1948, Herford, Bouman Papers.

5. Turner, Barry, *The Berlin Airlift: The Relief Operation that Defined the Cold War* (London: 2017), p. 106.

6. *News Chronicle*, 6 April 1948.

7. *Foreign Relations of the United States*, 1948, Western Europe, vol. III, ed. Stauffer, David H., Goodwin, Ralph R., Kranz, Marvin W., Smyth, Howard McGaw, Aandahl, Frederick and Sampson, Charles S. (Washington: United States Government Printing Office, 1974), The Ambassador in the United Kingdom (Douglas) to the Under Secretary of State (Lovett), 17 April 1948, Document 73.

8. Shlaim, 'Britain, the Berlin Blockade and the Cold War', p. 4.

9. Mary Bouman to her parents, 10 May 1948, Herford, Bouman Papers.

10. Jähner, Harald, *Aftermath: Life in the Fallout of the Third Reich* (London: 2021), pp. 421–2.

11. Szanajda, *The Allies*, p. 88; Lee, *Victory in Europe*, pp. 32–3.

12. Jähner, *Aftermath*, p. 424.

13. Shlaim, 'Britain, the Berlin Blockade and the Cold War', p. 5.

14. As far as the British were concerned, there had been little appetite for a unified German state ever since the summer of 1946 when Bevin's commitment to the 'Western option' paved the way towards semi-permanent division of the country between East and West. In particular, the prospect of a new Germany under the influence of the Soviet Union was regarded as a worst-case scenario.

15. Shlaim, 'Britain, the Berlin Blockade and the Cold War', pp. 6–10.

16. Official Report, Fifth Series, Parliamentary Debates, House of Commons, Vol. 452 (1948), 30 June 1948, Col. 2229–34.

17. Shlaim, 'Britain, the Berlin Blockade and the Cold War', pp. 8–10.

18. It is striking quite how little interest the British press paid to the potential

moral implications of Britain hosting a foreign power's nuclear arsenal. As it happens, these particular B-29s were not armed with atomic weapons – although this fact was intentionally concealed from the world.

19. Mary Bouman to her parents, 19 July 1948, Herford, Bouman Papers.

20. FO 1030/220 Control Commission for Germany (British Element): Various Private Office Papers and Administration and Local Government Branch Files: Berlin airlift: final report, 1949, National Archives, London.

21. Turner, *The Berlin Airlift*, p. 130; Reel 4, Daw, Francis George (Oral History), Sound Recording, Catalogue Number 15538, Imperial War Museum Archive, London.

22. FO 1030/220 Control Commission for Germany (British Element): Various Private Office Papers and Administration and Local Government Branch Files: Berlin airlift: final report, 1949, National Archives, London.

23. Reel 3, Cherry, Robert 'Bob' (Oral History), Sound Recording, Catalogue Number 26729, Imperial War Museum Archive, London.

24. Reel 1, Coan, Pip (Oral History).

25. FO 1030/220 Control Commission for Germany (British Element): Various Private Office Papers and Administration and Local Government Branch Files: Berlin airlift: final report, 1949, National Archives, London.

26. Reel 3, Cherry, Robert 'Bob' (Oral History).

27. Unmarked letter, Private Papers of Miss P Braithwaite, Documents.13545, Imperial War Museum Archive, London.

28. FO 936/623 Control Office for Germany and Austria and Foreign Office, German Section: Establishments: Files: Movement of CCG families from Berlin: 'Operation Pickle', National Archives, London; FO 936/622 Control Office for Germany and Austria and Foreign Office, German Section: Establishments: Files: Movement of CCG families from Germany: 'Operation Chivalrous', National Archives, London.

29. Letter Sharp to Antrobus, 13 August 1948, FO 936/622 Control Office for Germany and Austria and Foreign Office, German Section: Establishments: Files: Movement of CCG families from Germany: 'Operation Chivalrous', National Archives, London.

30. Report, Antrobus to Sharp, 17 August 1948, FO 936/622 Control Office for Germany and Austria and Foreign Office, German Section: Establishments: Files: Movement of CCG families from Germany: 'Operation Chivalrous', National Archives, London.

31. INF 6/555 Crown Film Unit Productions, Berlin Airlift (June 1948), 1949, National Archives, London.

32. The idea that the Berlin Airlift radically changed British perceptions of Germany is a much-repeated cliché, with little grounding in fact. See Watt, *Britain Looks to Germany*; Lee, *Victory in Europe*, p. 37; Cowling, Daniel, 'Britain and the Occupation of Germany, 1945–49' (Unpublished PhD dissertation, The University of Cambridge: 2018).

Chapter Twenty-Four

1. Pocock, Tom, 'Don't Let's Be Beastly To The British!', *Daily Mail*, 12 April 1949.

2. Carlin, 'Economic Reconstruction', p. 55.

3. Knapp, Manfred, Wolfgang F. Stolper and Michael Hudson, 'Reconstruction and West-Integration: The Impact of the Marshall Plan on Germany', *Zeitschrift für die Gesamte Staatswissenschaft / Journal of Institutional and Theoretical Economics* 137, no. 3 (1981), pp. 415–33, www.jstor.org/stable/40750368.

4. For a detailed assessment of the dismantling programme and its impact upon the German economy, see Kramer, Alan, *Die britische Demontagepolitik am Beispiel Hamburgs 1945-1950* (Hamburg: 1991), which argues that dismantling had a very limited impact upon economic recovery.

5. 'German Says: Stop Dismantling, or You'll Have To Rebuild', *Daily Mirror*, 30 November 1946; 'Setting Limits to Dismantling in Anglo-US Zone', *Manchester Guardian*, 15 September 1947; Wiesen, Jonathan S., *West German Industry and the Challenge of the Nazi Past, 1945–1955* (Chapel Hill, NC: 2001), p. 65.

6. 'Dismantling', editorial, *Manchester Guardian*, 27 October 1947.

7. Gollancz, Victor and Stokes, Richard, 'Dismantling in Germany', letter to the editor, *Manchester Guardian*, 18 November 1947.

8. Kramer, Alan, *The West German Economy, 1945–1955* (Oxford: 1991), pp. 117–21.

9. Herbert, *A History of 20th-Century Germany*, p. 463.

10. Bark and Gress, *A History of West Germany*, p. 259.

11. 'Demonstrations At Kiel', editorial, *Times*, 9 December 1948; 'Ruhr Men On The Carpet – Riot Act To Be Read', *Daily Mail*, 9 June 1949; 'Dismantling and Disgruntling', *Daily Telegraph*, 9 June 1949. For a detailed overview of the German response to dismantling, see Jarausch, Konrad H., *After Hitler: Recivilizing Germans, 1945–1995* (New York: 2006), pp. 37–97.

12. 'Stares Stop the Crowbar Squad', *Daily Mirror*, 14 June 1949.

13. '"We'll Stamp Out German Resistance," Britain Warns', *Daily Mirror*, 13 June 1949; 'Works Shut If Dismantling Opposed, We Warn Germans', *Daily Mirror*, 15 September 1949.

14. 'Ruhr Workers Defy British', *Daily Express*, 4 January 1949.

15. 'Demonstrations At Kiel', editorial, *Times*, 9 December 1948.

16. 'Dismantling', editorial, *Manchester Guardian*, 11 June 1949; 'Dismantling', editorial, *Manchester Guardian*, 19 August 1949.

17. de la Mahotière, Stuart R., 'Dismantling in the Ruhr', letter to the editor, *Times*, 15 June 1949.

18. Gollancz, Victor, 'Dismantling in the Ruhr', letter to the editor, *Times*, 16 June 1949; Stokes, Richard, 'Dismantling in the Ruhr', letter to the editor, *Times*, 18 June 1949.

19. Connell, Brian, 'Meatless Sunday For The Guenthers', *Daily Mail*, 31 January 1949.

20. 'Made In Germany', editorial, *Daily Mail*, 24 January 1949.

21. 'The League of Diamond Men Starts a Battle', *Daily Mirror*, 10 February 1949; 'The Drain', editorial, *Daily Mirror*, 11 February 1949.

22. 'Germany As Trade Rival', *Manchester Guardian*, 10 February 1949.

23. 'No Threat in Germany Speed-up', *Daily Mail*, 3 March 1949.

24. Restoration of German Cities, 25 July 1949, *British Movietone News*, newsreel, Issue 52269, British Movietone News Digital Archive, www.movietone.com; Money Changes Reform German Economy, 25 July 1949, *Pathé News*,

newsreel, Issue 1419.09, British Pathé Archive, www.britishpathe.com/; Europe's Biggest Poultry Farm Re-Opens, 23 June 1949, *Pathé News*, newsreel, Issue 1415.21, British Pathé Archive, www.britishpathe.com/.

25. 'Made In Germany' – Out To Capture World Market, 16 June 1949, *Pathé News*, newsreel, Issue 1415.14, British Pathé Archive, www.britishpathe.com/.

26. Walker, David, 'This Way For Steak and Eggs', *Daily Mirror*, 1 March 1949.

27. 'Opinion: Roughing it – the German Way', editorial, *Daily Mirror*, 18 June 1949.

28. Arthur, Bill, 'For a Good Square Meal... I'll Go Back to Germany', *Daily Mirror*, 3 June 1949.

29. Official Report, Fifth Series, Parliamentary Debates, House of Commons, Vol. 468 (1949), 21 October 1949, Col. 968–80.

30. 'Misplaced Sympathy', editorial, *Hull Daily Mail*, 20 December 1949.

Chapter Twenty-five

1. Lawson, Colin, 'The Dictatorial Dismissal that made Dr Adenauer Forever Suspicious', *Times*, 1 December 1980.

2. Letter from Barraclough to Adenauer, 6 October 1945, FO 1013/701, Control Office for Germany and Austria and Foreign Office: Control Commission for Germany (British Element), North Rhine-Westphalia Region: Records: German officials: Dr Adenauer, National Archives, London.

3. Ferguson Memorandum, 10 July 1945, FO 1013/701, Control Office for Germany and Austria and Foreign Office: Control Commission for Germany (British Element), North Rhine-Westphalia Region: Records: German officials: Dr Adenauer, National Archives, London. Underlining in the original. Ferguson's report was influenced, in part, by Adenauer's outspoken remarks on the future of Germany, which had appeared in the British press a week earlier. Adenauer warned that a Nazi revival was imminent save action from the Allies; see *Scottish Daily Express*, 2 July 1945.

4. Lawson, Colin, 'The Dictatorial Dismissal that made Dr Adenauer Forever Suspicious', *Times*, 1 December 1980.

5. Letter from Barraclough to Adenauer, 6 October 1945, FO 1013/701, Control Office for Germany and Austria and Foreign Office: Control Commission for Germany (British Element), North Rhine-Westphalia Region: Records: German officials: Dr Adenauer, National Archives, London.

6. Letter from Barraclough to Hamilton, 10 October 1945, FO 1013/701, Control Office for Germany and Austria and Foreign Office: Control Commission for Germany (British Element), North Rhine-Westphalia Region: Records: German officials: Dr Adenauer, National Archives, London.

7. Letters from Hamilton to Barraclough, 12 and 15 October 1945, FO 1013/701, Control Office for Germany and Austria and Foreign Office: Control Commission for Germany (British Element), North Rhine-Westphalia Region: Records: German officials: Dr Adenauer, National Archives, London.

8. Lawson, Colin, 'The Dictatorial Dismissal that made Dr Adenauer Forever Suspicious', *Times*, 1 December 1980.

9. Herbert, *A History of 20th-Century Germany*, p. 470.

10. Herbert, *A History of 20th-Century Germany*, p. 471.

11. Herbert, *A History of 20th-Century Germany*, p. 473.

12. Herbert, *A History of 20th-Century Germany*, p. 472.

13. Bark and Gress, *A History of West Germany*, pp. 116–7.

14. Herbert, *A History of 20th-Century Germany*, p. 473.

15. Bark and Gress, *A History of West Germany*, pp. 107–9.

16. Bark and Gress, *A History of West Germany*, pp. 237–8.

17. 'What I Hope From My Vote', *Picture Post*, 20 August 1949.

18. Connell, Brian, 'Germany Takes Her Biggest Step Along the Road Back', *Daily Mail*, 11 August 1949.

19. The costs of maintaining the occupation were estimated to be 36 per cent of the federal budget in 1949; see Schwarz, Hans-Peter, *Konrad Adenauer: A German Politician and Statesman in a Period of War, Revolution and Reconstruction*, vol. 1 (Providence; Oxford: 1995), p. 476.

20. 'Anti-Semitism in Germany – Jewish Allegations', *Manchester Guardian*, 25 July 1949. Also see 'Anti-Semitism in West Germany: British Jews Visit Minister', *Manchester Guardian*, 30 September 1949; 'Anti-Semitism in Germany: MP For Trial? Speech in Defence of Hitler', *Manchester Guardian*, 14 December 1949; 'German Deputy Suspended – Anti-Semitic Speech', *Manchester Guardian*, 15 December 1949; 'Return of Nazism in Germany', *Manchester Guardian*, 22 November 1949.

21. 'Restoring the Reich – Party's Programme: New Deal For Ex-Nazis', *Manchester Guardian*, 6 August 1949.

22. 'Above Criticism?', editorial, *Manchester Guardian*, 22 July 1949.

23. 'Seeds of Trouble: Scepticism as to the New German State', *Manchester Guardian*, 9 August 1949.

24. 'Attempts to Revive German Nationalism – Conference of Right-wing Politicians and Officers', *Manchester Guardian*, 23 June 1949; 'Did We Raise a Ghost In Germany?', *Picture Post*, 17 September 1949.

25. 'Pro-Nazi Press Revival – British Fears', *Manchester Guardian*, 27 August 1949. Also see: 3 Nations Sit In Europe's First Parliament, 18 August 1949, *Pathé News*, newsreel, Issue 1421.17, British Pathé Archive, www.britishpathe.com/.

26. 'Curb Nazis, Germans Told', *Daily Mirror*, 31 August 1949.

27. 'Nazis', editorial, *Daily Mirror*, 1 September 1949.

28. Gollancz, Victor, 'Dismantling in Germany', letter to the editor, *Times*, 17 August 1949.

29. In the following days, commentators from both sides of the wartime debate contributed, including Blumenfeld, Erik, 'Nationalism in Germany', letter to the editor, *Times*, 19 August 1949; de la Mahotière, Stuart R., 'Nationalism in Germany', letter to the editor, *Times*, 19 August 1949; Pickthorn, Kenneth, 'Dismantling in Germany', letter to the editor, *Times*, 20 August 1949; Murray, Gilbert, 'Germany and Europe', letter to the editor, *Times*, 22 August 1949; Corbishley, T. 'Germany and Europe', letter to the editor, *Times*, 22 August 1949; Law, E. A., 'Germany and Europe', letter to the editor, *Times*, 22 August 1949; Collins, Rev. John, 'Dismantling in Germany', letter to the editor, *Manchester Guardian*, 26 August 1949.

30. Vansittart, Robert, 'Dismantling in Germany', letter to the editor, *Manchester Guardian*, 1 September 1949. This inspired a reply from his long-term adversary; see Gollancz, Victor, 'Dismantling in Germany', letter to the editor, *Manchester Guardian*, 3 September 1949. In turn, Vansittart snapped

back, claiming that Gollancz and his ally Rev. John Collins were mistaken in thinking Christ would have been on their side; see Vansittart, Robert, 'Dismantling in Germany', letter to the editor, *Manchester Guardian*, 8 September.

31. For a detailed overview of the Federal Republic's party system and the 1949 election campaign, see Nicholls, Anthony J., *The Bonn Republic: West Germany 1945–1990* (London: 1997), pp. 34–49, 70–72.

32. Lee, *Victory in Europe*, pp. 44–50. For a comprehensive overview of Adenauer's relationship with the West, see Granieri, Ronald J., *The Ambivalent Alliance: Konrad Adenauer, The CDU/CSU, and the West, 1949–1966* (New York; Oxford: 2003); Müller, Christoph Hendrik, *West Germans Against the West: Anti-Americanism in Media and Public Opinion in the Federal Republic of Germany 1949–1968* (Basingstoke: 2010).

33. 'Thoughts On The New Germany', editorial, *Daily Telegraph*, 30 August 1949.

34. 'Federal Germany', editorial, *Daily Telegraph*, 13 September 1949.

35. 'To The Right', editorial, *Manchester Guardian*, 16 August 1949.

36. 'The German Outlook', *Manchester Guardian*, 25 August 1949.

37. 'Bridgehead At Bonn', editorial, *Daily Mail*, 7 September 1949.

38. Connell, Brian, 'Give My Germany A Chance', interview with Konrad Adenauer, *Daily Mail*, 16 September 1949.

39. Ames, Kenneth, 'Berlin Express', *Daily Mail*, 12 September 1949.

40. Newte, Horace, 'No Time To Haul Down the British Flag', letter to the editor, *Daily Mail*, 14 October 1949.

41. Wighton, Charles, 'It's All As Well To Know The Kind Of Man They Want', *Daily Express*, 18 August 1949.

42. Memoir of service with Control Commission Germany, 1947–51, Edward Pye Rich papers, BL Mss Eur Photo Eur 389, British Library, London.

43. Bark and Gress, *A History of West Germany*, p. 233.

44. 'Lest We Forget', editorial, *Daily Mail*, 2 September 1949.

45. Connor, William, 'These Germans… William Connor Flew to the Ruhr to Write the Story Behind… The Picture That Shocked Britain', *Daily Mirror*, 7 September 1949; 'Briton Beaten Up By German Oil Workers', *Daily Mirror*, 1 September 1949; 'Works Shut If Dismantling Opposed, We Warn Germans', *Daily Mirror*, 15 September 1949.

46. Further examples include Cooper, Duff, 'Now On To Act 2 – Will It Be Peace On Earth?', *Daily Mail*, 31 December 1949; 'An End To Post-War Germany', *Picture Post*, 26 November 1949.

47. Delmer, Sefton, 'Can Germany Harm Us?', *Daily Express*, 12 September 1949.

Chapter Twenty-Six

1. *It's Not Cricket*, film, directed by Alfred Roome and Roy Rich, starring Basil Radford and Naunton Wayne (1949; London: Gainsborough Pictures).

2. In the immediate post-war period, many British commentators and writers observed a general sense of national deterioration and decline stalking the country; see Judt, Tony, *Postwar: A History of Europe since 1945* (London: 2005), p. 205.

3. The crises of 1947 had dented British self-confidence and wartime enthusiasm;

see Morgan, Kenneth O., *Britain Since 1945: The People's Peace* (Oxford: 2001), pp. 68–9.
4. Letter from Mary Bouman, 2 October 1949, Herford, Bouman Papers.
5. Memoir, 'When All The Trees Were Green', Morris Papers.
6. Letter, 5 December 1946, Smith Papers.
7. Quoted in Knowles, *Winning the Peace*, p. 107.
8. Letter to 'Ma', 8 January 1946, Letters written by Henry Ronald Hughes, 2014-10-27-78, National Army Museum, London.
9. Invitation to mother to attend his 'bowler hat' (i.e. demobilization) celebration at Selsdon Park Hotel on 23 February 1946, undated, Letters written by Henry Ronald Hughes, 2014-10-27, National Army Museum, London.
10. Letter, 25 February 1946, Letters written by L/Cpl John William Booth, 2011-01-4-393, National Army Museum, London.
11. Letter, 10 April 1946, Letters written by L/Cpl John William Booth, 2011-01-4-423, National Army Museum, London. The letter itself had a hand-drawn red crayon border.
12. Robertson, Brian, Lord Robertson of Oakridge, 'A Miracle?: Potsdam 1945 – Western Germany 1965', *International Affairs* 41, no. 3 (1965), pp. 401–10, https://doi.org/10.2307/2609802. This assessment has been repeated much more recently; see Schwarz, 'The Division of Germany', p. 152.
13. Reinisch, *The Perils of Peace*, p. 7; Annan, Noel, *Changing Enemies: The Defeat and Regeneration of Germany* (London: 1995), p. 147.
14. Cabinet Office (Great Britain), *The Report of the Iraq Inquiry*, vol. VI (London: HMSO, 2016), pp. 383–4.
15. Cabinet Office, *The Report of the Iraq Inquiry*, vol. VI, p. 439.
16. Cabinet Office, *The Report of the Iraq Inquiry*, vol. X, p. 24.

Bibliography

Primary Sources

British Library, London

Memoir of service with Control Commission Germany, 1947–51, Edward Pye Rich papers, BL Mss Eur Photo Eur 389.

Chipping Campden History Society Archives

Diary Entry, 9 February 1947, Klaus Behr Tagebücher 1938-1956, Diary of a POW at Springhill Camp 185, Translation, Chipping Campden History Society Archives.

Churchill Archives Centre, Cambridge

VNST II/1/10, Correspondence: January 1941 – November 1941, Correspondence with publishers and The Sunday Times about Vansittart's book 'Black Record'.
VNST II/1/23, Correspondence about the 'Never Again' Association.

Harry S. Truman Library, Independence, Mo.

Papers of Harry S. Truman Pertaining to Family, Business, and Personal Affairs.

Imperial War Museum Archive, London

Private Papers

Documents.677. Private Papers of Miss D E Richardson.
Documents.1159. Private Papers of Miss K M Morris.
Documents.2379. Private Papers of Miss D E Smith.
Documents.5413. Private Papers of Miss E Wearmouth.
Documents.8249. Private Papers of Mrs J Hodges.
Documents.9550. Private Papers of Miss J McFarlane.
Documents.11120. Private Papers of Sir Gerald Lenanton.

Documents.11231. Private Papers of Lieutenant Colonel R L H Nunn.
Documents.12385. Private Papers of G D Pringle.
Documents.12622. Private Papers of Mrs N Heather.
Documents.13545. Private Papers of Miss P Braithwaite.
Documents.14502. Private Papers of N A Skinner.
Documents.15377. Private Papers of Miss M K Ostermann.
Documents.16534. Private Papers of Miss J V Hyde.
Documents.16779. Private Papers of Miss M Bouman.
Documents.17788. Private Papers of J J Allan.
Documents.19794. Private Papers of J E Rhys.

Sound Recording

Catalogue Number 3790. Johnson, Peter William (Oral History).
Catalogue Number 9093. Sassoon, Agnes (Oral History).
Catalogue Number 14837. James, George Philip Henry (Oral History).
Catalogue Number 15437. Williams, William Richard (Oral History).
Catalogue Number 15538. Daw, Francis George (Oral History).
Catalogue Number 19006. Coan, Pip (Oral History).
Catalogue Number 21030. Chester, Charles (Oral History).
Catalogue Number 22077. Morris-Metcalf, Harold Frank 'Mick' (Oral History).
Catalogue Number 23787. Dillon, Brian Edevrain (Oral History).
Catalogue Number 26729. Cherry, Robert 'Bob' (Oral History).
Catalogue Number 27774. Suster, Ilya (Oral History).
Catalogue Number 29540. Cole, Norman (Oral History).
Catalogue Number 30638. Wayne, Peter (Oral History).
Catalogue Number 33336. Souper, Robert Reinagle (Oral History).

Mass-Observation Archive, University of Sussex, Brighton

File report 1543, 'Germany After the War', December 1942.
File report 1624, 'Private Opinion About the German People', March 1943.
File report 2565, 'Attitudes to the German People', February 1948.

National Archives, London

BT 211/169, Board of Trade: German Division: Files, Alleged Irregular Behaviour of
    B.I.O.S. Team No. 1972 Investigating the Manufacture of 'Eau-de-Cologne 4711'.
CAB 128/12/34, Cabinet: Minutes (CM and CC Series).
CAB 128/13/28, Cabinet: Minutes (CM and CC Series).
CAB 129/5/2, Cabinet: Memoranda (CP and C Series).
CAB 129/10/18, Cabinet: Memoranda (CP and C Series).
CAB 129/25/2, Cabinet: Memoranda (CP and C Series).
CAB 195/3/85, Cabinet Secretary's Notebooks.
CAB 79/31/11, War Cabinet and Cabinet: Chiefs of Staff Committee: Minutes.
CAB 79/33/16, War Cabinet and Cabinet: Chiefs of Staff Committee: Minutes.
CAB 79/48/4, War Cabinet and Cabinet: Chiefs of Staff Committee: Minutes.

FO 1013/701, Control Office for Germany and Austria and Foreign Office: Control Commission for Germany (British Element), North Rhine-Westphalia Region: Records: German officials: Dr Adenauer.

FO 1013/725, Control Office for Germany and Austria and Foreign Office: Control Commission for Germany (British Element), North Rhine-Westphalia Region: Records, Military Government on administrative, local and regional government: democratisation and decentralisation.

FO 1030/174, Control Commission for Germany (British Element): Various Private Office Papers and Administration and Local Government Branch Files, Marriages with Ex-enemy Nationals.

FO 1030/220, Control Commission for Germany (British Element): Various Private Office Papers and Administration and Local Government Branch Files: Berlin airlift: final report, 1949.

FO 1030/272, Control Commission for Germany (British Element): Various Private Office Papers and Administration and Local Government Branch Files, Assistant Inspector General, Public Safety, report on Bad Nenndorf Detailed Interrogation Centre.

FO 1030/304, Control Commission for Germany (British Element): Various Private Office Papers and Administration and Local Government Branch Files, Correspondence DMG/Permanent Secretary: vol II, National Archives, London.

FO 1032/697, Economic and Industrial Planning Staff and Control Office for Germany and Austria and Successor: Control Commission for Germany (British Element), Military Sections and Headquarters Secretariat: VD control in British Zone, National Archives, London.

FO 1039/669, Control Office for Germany and Austria and Foreign Office: Control Commission for Germany (British Element), Economic Divisions: Records, CCG Exhibition London: Vol II, December 1945 – March 1946.

FO 1039/670, Control Office for Germany and Austria and Foreign Office: Control Commission for Germany (British Element), Economic Divisions: Records, CCG Exhibition London: Vol III, 1945.

FO 1056/128, Control Office for Germany and Austria and Foreign Office: Control Commission for Germany (British Element), Public Relations and Information Services Division, and U.K. High Commission, Information Services Division: Registered Files (PR, ISC, ISD and other Series), 'British Zone Review' Editorial Board: Correspondence, 1948–1949.

FO 1056/143, Control Office for Germany and Austria and Foreign Office: Control Commission for Germany (British Element), Public Relations and Information Services Division, and U.K. High Commission, Information Services Division: Registered Files (PR, ISC, ISD and other Series).

FO 1056/176, 14 February 1948, Control Office for Germany and Austria and Foreign Office: Control Commission for Germany (British Element), Public Relations and Information Services Division, and U.K. High Commission, Information Services Division: Registered Files (PR, ISC, ISD and other Series), Publicity General Vol. 1, November 1947 – August 1948, National Archives, London.

FO 1056/300, Control Office for Germany and Austria and Foreign Office: Control Commission for Germany (British Element), Public Relations and Information Services Division, and U.K. High Commission, Information Services Division: Registered Files (PR, ISC, ISD and other Series), 'British Zone Review' Editorial Board, 1947–1949.

FO 1056/508, Control Office for Germany and Austria and Foreign Office: Control Commission for Germany (British Element), Public Relations and Information Services Division, and U.K. High Commission, Information Services Division: Registered Files (PR, ISC, ISD and other Series), Releases, Hand-outs, and Policy: Press Conference, 1945.

FO 1056/510, Control Office for Germany and Austria and Foreign Office: Control Commission for Germany (British Element), Public Relations and Information Services Division, and U.K. High Commission, Information Services Division: Registered Files (PR, ISC, ISD and other Series), Issuance of News Policy, National Archives, London.

FO 1056/520, Control Office for Germany and Austria and Foreign Office: Control Commission for Germany (British Element), Public Relations and Information Services Division, and U.K. High Commission, Information Services Division: Registered Files (PR, ISC, ISD and other Series), Hamburg Project Publicity.

FO 1093/549, Defector from Berlin: Lieutenant Colonel Gregory Tokaev (codename EXCISE); reports and information, Foreign Office: Permanent Under-Secretary's Department: Registered and Unregistered Papers: Cold War Issues, including Espionage and Defectors.

FO 371/46730, Allied Control Commission: Policy in Occupied Germany: Post-Defeat Military Government Planning for Germany: Situation in Occupied Germany, Foreign Office: Political Departments: General Correspondence from 1906–1966.

FO 371/64240, Long-term staffing policy of the Control Commission for Germany.

FO 371/70829, Foreign Office: Political Departments: General Correspondence from 1906–1966: No. 10 Disposal Interrogation Centre, Bad Nenndorf. Trial and acquittal of Lt Col R W G Stephens, OBE, in connection with alleged brutalities.

FO 371/70830, Foreign Office: Political Departments: General Correspondence from 1906–1966: No. 10 Disposal Interrogation Centre, Bad Nenndorf. Trial and acquittal of Lt Col R W G Stephens, OBE, in connection with alleged brutalities, 1948.

FO 936/236, Control Office for Germany and Austria and Foreign Office, German Section: Establishments: Files, Control Commission for Germany: review of basic policy.

FO 936/622, Control Office for Germany and Austria and Foreign Office, German Section: Establishments: Files: Movement of CCG families from Germany: 'Operation Chivalrous'.

FO 936/623, Control Office for Germany and Austria and Foreign Office, German Section: Establishments: Files: Movement of CCG families from Berlin: 'Operation Pickle'.

FO 936/692, Control Office for Germany and Austria and Foreign Office, German Section: Establishments: Files, Investigations Carried Out as a Result of Information given by Mr Pritt MP, 1946–7.

FO 936/741, Control Office for Germany and Austria and Foreign Office, German Section: Establishments: Files, Operation 'Sparkler' and large-scale blackmarket activities.

FO 936/743, Control Office for Germany and Austria and Foreign Office, German Section: Establishments: Files, Allegations and Investigations of cases of corruption in CCG, British Zone, 1946–8.

FO 936/749, Control Office for Germany and Austria and Foreign Office, German Section: Establishments: Files, Miscellaneous complaints: General Public, 1946–51.

FO 936/78, Control Office for Germany and Austria and Foreign Office, German

Section: Establishments: Files, Article in New Statesman Alleging Corruption in CCG, 1946–7.

FO 946/10, Control Office for Germany and Austria and Foreign Office, German Section: Information Services: Records, 'Germany Under Control' Exhibition, 1946–8.

FO 946/12, Control Office for Germany and Austria and Foreign Office, German Section: Information Services: Records, Germany Under Control Exhibition – Notes of Meetings, 1946.

FO 946/47, Control Office for Germany and Austria and Foreign Office, German Section: Information Services: Records, German and Austrian Publicity: British Zone Correspondents' Association.

FO 946/62, Control Office for Germany and Austria and Foreign Office, German Section: Information Services: Records, Press Campaign 'Get Out of Germany', 1947.

FO 946/68, Control Office for Germany and Austria and Foreign Office, German Section: Information Services: Records, Radio Programme: Spotlight on Germany.

FO 946/91, Control Office for Germany and Austria and Foreign Office, German Section: Information Services: Records, Central Office of Information: Film of German Education, 1947–8.

FO 946/92, Control Office for Germany and Austria and Foreign Office, German Section: Information Services: Records, Central Office of Information: Films to be made on conditions in Germany, 1947–8.

FO 953/495-512, Visits and tours of editors and journalists to and from the United Kingdom (Germany).

INF 6/395, Crown Film Unit Productions, Kreis Resident Officer – Germany (problems in post-war German districts) 1947, 1947–51.

INF 6/401, Crown Film Unit Productions, Trained To Serve.

INF 6/555, Crown Film Unit Productions, Berlin Airlift (June 1948), 1949.

INF 6/990, Crown Film Unit Productions, A School in Cologne 1948, 1947–50.

KV 2/4098-4100, The Security Service: Personal (PF Series) Files, World War II, Subjects of Security Service Enquiry.

KV 4/466, Diary of Guy Liddell, Deputy Director General of the Security Service, June to November 1945.

KV 4/469, Diary of Guy Liddell, Deputy Director General of the Security Service, May to December 1947.

KV 4/470, Diary of Guy Liddell, Deputy Director General of the Security Service, January to December 1948.

PREM 4/100/10, Treatment of Major War Criminals, Prime Minister's Office: Confidential Correspondence and Papers.

PREM 8/391, Command Paper (CM) (46) 94th Conclusions, 4 November 1946, Prime Minister's Office: Correspondence and Papers, 1945–1951, Trial of German Industrialists before an International Military Tribunal, National Archives, London.

PREM 8/524, Civilian Administrator or Resident Minister at head of Control Commission in Germany, Prime Minister's Office: Correspondence and Papers, 1945–1951.

PREM 8/794, Prime Minister's Office: Correspondence and Papers, 1945–1951, Germany (miscellaneous).

National Army Museum, London

2011-01-4. Letters written by L/Cpl John William Booth, 5th Royal Tank Regiment.
2014-10-27. Letters written by Henry Ronald Hughes.

Parliamentary Debates

Official Report, Fifth Series, Parliamentary Debates, House of Commons. Vol. 351 (1939). 1 September 1939. Col. 125–39.

Official Report, Fifth Series, Parliamentary Debates, House of Commons. Vol. 414 (1945). 26 October 1945. Col. 2351–454.

Official Report, Fifth Series, Parliamentary Debates, House of Commons. Vol. 416 (1945). 23 November 1945. Col. 763–4.

Official Report, Fifth Series, Parliamentary Debates, House of Commons. Vol. 421 (1946). 9 April 1946. Col. 1803–68.

Official Report, Fifth Series, Parliamentary Debates, House of Commons. Vol. 422 (1946). 10 May 1946. Col. 1419.

Official Report, Fifth Series, Parliamentary Debates, House of Commons. Vol. 425 (1946). 18 July 1946. Col. 1386–93.

Official Report, Fifth Series, Parliamentary Debates, House of Commons. Vol. 426 (1946). 29 July 1946. Col. 559.

Official Report, Fifth Series, Parliamentary Debates, House of Commons. Vol. 426 (1946). 29 July 1946. Col. 575.

Official Report, Fifth Series, Parliamentary Debates, House of Commons. Vol. 427 (1946). 17 October 1946. Col. 1154–92.

Official Report, Fifth Series, Parliamentary Debates, House of Commons. Vol. 430 (1946). 14 November 1946. Col. 238–371.

Official Report, Fifth Series, Parliamentary Debates, House of Commons. Vol. 435 (1947). 24 March 1947. Col. 1018.

Official Report, Fifth Series, Parliamentary Debates, House of Commons. Vol. 445 (1947). 17 December 1947. Col. 337.

Official Report, Fifth Series, Parliamentary Debates, House of Commons. Vol. 445 (1947). 18 December 1947. Col. 1874–87.

Official Report, Fifth Series, Parliamentary Debates, House of Commons. Vol. 452 (1948). 30 June 1948. Col. 2221–9.

Official Report, Fifth Series, Parliamentary Debates, House of Commons. Vol. 452 (1948). 30 June 1948. Col. 2229–34.

Official Report, Fifth Series, Parliamentary Debates, House of Commons. Vol. 468 (1949). 21 October 1949. Col. 968–80.

Official Report, Fifth Series, Parliamentary Debates, House of Commons. Vol. 470 (1949). 5 December 1945. Col. 1524.

Official Report, Fifth Series, Parliamentary Debates, House of Commons. Vol. 485 (1951). 14 March 1951. Col. 174W.

Official Report, Fifth Series, Parliamentary Debates, House of Lords. Vol. 126 (1943). 10 March 1943. Col. 535–82.

Official Report, Fifth Series, Parliamentary Debates, House of Lords. Vol. 136 (1945). 1 May 1945. Col. 61–97.

Published Primary

Anonyma, *Eine Frau in Berlin: Tagebuchaufzeichnungen vom 20. April bis 22. Juni 1945*, 1st ed. published 1953, Frankfurt am Main: Eichborn, 2003.

Astley, Joan Bright, *The Inner Circle: A View of War at the Top*, London: Hutchinson, 1971.

Beveridge, William, *An Urgent Message from Germany*, London: Pilot Press, 1946.

Brailsford, Henry Noel, *Our Settlement with Germany*, Harmondsworth: Penguin, 1944.

Braunthal, Julius, *Need Germany Survive?*, London: Gollancz, 1943.

Brinton, Henry, *Vengeance Is Dear*, London: Pendragon Press, 1946.

Brockway, Fenner, *German Diary*, London: Gollancz, 1946.

Brown, Douglas, *Commonsense versus Vansittartism*, London: Independent Labour Party, 1943.

Butler, Rohan, *The Roots of National Socialism*, London: Faber & Faber, 1941.

Byford-Jones, Wilfred, *Berlin Twilight*, London; New York: Hutchinson, 1947.

Cabinet Office (Great Britain), *The Report of the Iraq Inquiry*, vols VI, X, London: HMSO, 2016.

Carr, Edward Hallett, *Conditions of Peace*, London: Macmillan, 1942.

Cassidy, Velma Hastings, *Germany, 1947–1949: The Story in Documents*, Washington, D.C.: US Dept. of State, 1950.

Cole, G. D. H., *Europe, Russia, and the Future*, London: Gollancz, 1941.

Coole, W. W. and Potter, M. F. [Władysław Wszebór Kulski] (eds), *Thus Spake Germany*, 2nd ed., London: Routledge, 1941.

Dickens, Arthur Geoffrey, *Lübeck Diary*, London: Gollancz, 1947.

Diplomaticus [Konni Zilliacus], *Can the Tories Win the Peace? And How They Lost the Last One*, London: Gollancz, 1945.

Einzig, Paul, *Can We Win the Peace?*, London: Macmillan, 1942.

Eisler, Robert and Hart, Robert George, *Winning the Peace: A Comprehensive Policy*, London: Frederick Muller, 1948.

E., Neuwöhner, Andreas and Staffel, Florian (eds), *Briten in Westfalen 1945–2017 Besatzer, Verbündete, Freunde?*, Paderborn: 2019' – cited on p. 422 (ch 18 n 1)

The Foreign Office, *Instructions for British Servicemen in Germany, 1944*, Oxford: The Bodleian Library, 2007.

Foreign Relations of the United States, 1948, Germany and Austria, vol. II, ed. Slany, William and Sampson, Charles S., Washington: United States Government Printing Office, 1973.

Foreign Relations of the United States, 1948, Western Europe, vol. III, ed. Stauffer, David H., Goodwin, Ralph R., Kranz, Marvin W., Smyth, Howard McGaw, Aandahl, Frederick and Sampson, Charles S., Washington: United States Government Printing Office, 1974.

Foreign Relations of the United States, Diplomatic Papers, Conferences at Malta and Yalta, 1945, ed. Barron, Bryton, Washington: United States Government Printing Office, 1955, Document 290.

Foreign Relations of the United States, Diplomatic Papers, The Conference of Berlin (The Potsdam Conference), 1945, vol. II, ed. Dougall, Richardson, Washington: United States Government Printing Office, 1960.

Fraenkel, Heinrich, *Vansittart's Gift for Goebbels: A German Exile's Answer to Black Record*, London: Fabian Society, 1941.

Fraenkel, Heinrich and Acland, Richard, *The Winning of the Peace*, London: Gollancz,

1942.

Geyer, Curt, FitzGerald, Edward and Loeb, Walter, *Gollancz in German Wonderland*, London: Hutchinson, 1942.

Goebbels, Joseph, *The Goebbels Diary*, trans. Lochner, L. P., New York: Doubleday, 1948.

Gollancz, Victor, *Shall Our Children Live or Die?: A Reply to Lord Vansittart on the German Problem*, London: Gollancz, 1942.

Gollancz, Victor, *Europe and Germany: Today and Tomorrow*, London: Gollancz, 1945.

Gollancz, Victor, *Our Threatened Values*, London: Gollancz, 1946.

Gollancz, Victor, *In Darkest Germany*, London: Gollancz, 1947.

Gordon Walker, Patrick, *The Lid Lifts*, London: Gollancz, 1945.

Keynes, John Maynard, *The Economic Consequences of the Peace*, London: Macmillan, 1919.

Lach, Donald F., 'What *They* Would Do about Germany', *The Journal of Modern History* 17, no. 3 (1945), pp. 227–43, www.jstor.org/stable/1898987.

Laski, Harold J., *The Germans – Are They Human? A Reply to Sir Robert Vansittart*, London: Gollancz, 1941.

McCallum, Ronald Buchanan, *Public Opinion and the Last Peace*, Oxford: Oxford University Press, 1944.

Mannin, Ethel, *German Journey*, London: Jarrolds, 1948.

Minshall, Thomas H., *On Disarming Germany*, London; New York: Hutchinson, 1945.

Moore, Roger, *My Word Is My Bond: The Autobiography*, London: Michael O'Mara, 2009.

Morgan, J. H., *Assize of Arms: Being the Story of the Disarmament of Germany and Her Rearmament (1919–1939) in Two Volumes*, vol. 1, London: Methuen, 1945.

Mosley, Leonard O., *Report From Germany*, London: Gollancz, 1945.

Oppen, Beate Ruhm von, *Documents on Germany under Occupation, 1945–1954*, London: Oxford University Press, 1955.

Peters, William, *In Germany Now: The Diary of a Soldier – A Diary of Impressions in Germany, August–December, 1945*, London: Progress Publishing, 1946.

Pierrepoint, Albert, *Executioner: Pierrepoint*, London: Coronet, 1974.

Pollitt, Harry, *How to Win the Peace*, London: The Communist Party, 1944.

Reckitt, B. N., *Diary of Military Government in Germany 1945*, Ilfracombe: 1989.

Robertson, Brian, Lord Robertson of Oakridge, 'A Miracle?: Potsdam 1945 – Western Germany 1965', *International Affairs* 41, no. 3 (1965), pp. 401–10, https://doi.org/10.2307/2609802.

Saran, M., Eichler, W., Heidorn, W. and Specht, M. (eds), *Re-making Germany*, London: International Publishing Company, 1945.

Spender, Stephen, *European Witness*, London: Hamilton, 1946.

Taylor, A. J. P., *The Course of German History: A Survey of the Development of Germany Since 1815*, London: Hamish Hamilton, 1946.

Taylor, Frederick, *Exorcising Hitler: The Occupation and Denazification of Germany*, London; New York; Berlin: Bloomsbury, 2011.

Tell, Rolf, *The Eternal Ger-Maniac: Hitler and His Spiritual Ancestors*, London: Allen & Unwin, 1942.

Vansittart, Robert, *The Singing Caravan: A Sufi Tale*, Newtown: Gregynog Press, 1932.

Vansittart, Robert, *Black Record: Germans Past and Present*, 1st ed., London: Hamish Hamilton, 1941.

Vansittart, Robert, *Black Record: Germans Past and Present*, 15th ed., London: Hamish Hamilton, 1941.

Vansittart, Robert, *The Roots of the Trouble*, London: Hutchinson, 1941.

Vansittart, Robert, *Lessons of My Life*, London: Hutchinson, 1943.

Vansittart, Robert, *Bones of Contention*, London: Hutchinson, 1945.

Vansittart, Robert, *The German Octopus – 'Win the Peace' Pamphlet No.2*, London: Hutchinson, 1945.

Vansittart, Robert, 'The Problem of Germany: A Discussion', *International Affairs* 21, no. 3 (1945), pp. 313–23.

Vansittart, Robert, *Events and Shadows: A Policy for the Remnants of a Century*, London; New York: Hutchinson, 1947.

Vansittart, Robert, *The Mist Procession*, London: Hutchinson, 1958.

Weber, Anna-Maria, *Zeitgemäßes Kochen*, Tegernsee: Helmut Kinon, 1946.

Weymouth, Anthony [Dr Ivo Geikie-Cobb] (ed.), *Germany: Disease and Treatment – Based on the Memoranda of the Post-War Policy Group*, London; New York: Hutchinson, 1945.

Yasamee, H. J. and Great Britain Foreign and Commonwealth Office, *Documents on British Policy Overseas*, vol. 1, *Conference at Potsdam, July–August 1945*, London: HMSO, 1984.

Websites

'BFI Screenonline: Robert Barr 1909-1999', obituary, British Film Institute. Accessed 11 May 2018, www.screenonline.org.uk/people/id/901205/index.html.

Ahrens, Michael. 'Vier Jahre lang die Herren der Hansestadt'. *Welt*. Accessed 28 July 2021. www.welt.de/welt_print/vermischtes/hamburg/article4574285/Vier-Jahre-lang-die-Herren-der-Hansestadt.html.

Antiquariat Michael Kühn. 'The Victory Club Hamburg'. Antiques catalogue. Accessed 4 March 2022. www.antiquariat-banzhaf.de/wp-content/uploads/Katalog-19.pdf.

BBC. 'BBC: Detective'. Publicity material. Accessed 11 May 2018. www.bbc.co.uk/mediacentre/proginfo/2013/18/4-extra-detective.

BBC. 'Richard Dimbleby describes Belsen'. Archive broadcast. Accessed 27 April 2023. www.bbc.co.uk/archive/richard-dimbleby-describes-belsen/zvw7cqt.

Bölsche, Jochen. 'Obituary: John Seymour Chaloner (1924-2007)'. *Der Spiegel International*. Accessed 17 March 2023. www.spiegel.de/international/spiegel/obituary-john-seymour-chaloner-1924-2007-a-468130.html.

Cambridge Central Library. 'Gwydir Street VE Day Party'. Cambridgeshire Collection. Accessed 14 April 2021. https://capturingcambridge.org/petersfield/gwydir-street/gwydir-street-ve-day-party/.

Deutsche Bahn. 'DB Station&Service AG: 100 Jahre Hamburger Hauptbahnhof'. Commemorative booklet. Accessed 1 September 2021. www.bahnhof.de/site/shared/de/dateianhaenge/publikationen__broschueren/ub__personenbahnhoefe/100__jahre__hamburg__hbf.pdf.

Deutsches Historisches Museum. '4711 – Erfrischt und beruhigt die Nerven'. Blog. Accessed 12 January 2022. www.dhm.de/blog/2017/06/27/4711-erfrischt-und-beruhigt-die-nerven/.

Gedenkstättenportal zu Orten der Erinnerung in Europa. 'Wolfenbüttel Prison Memorial'. Accessed 19 March 2023. www.memorialmuseums.org/eng/staettens/view/44/Wolfenbüttel'-Prison-Memorial.

KZ-Gedenkstätte Neuengamme. 'Porta Westfalica-Barkhausen'. History. Accessed

1 July 2021. www.kz-gedenkstaette-neuengamme.de/en/history/satellite-camps/satellite-camps/porta-westfalica-barkhausen/

The National Archives. 'Currency converter: 1270–2017'. Historic currency conversion. Accessed 25 March 2022. www.nationalarchives.gov.uk/currency-converter/#currency-result.

Petersen, Rudolf. 'Hamburgs Interessen und die CDU'. 1946 election programme. Konrad Adenauer Stiftung. Accessed 1 February 2022. www.kas.de/en/web/geschichte-der-cdu/wahlprogramme-des-cdu-landesverbands-hamburg.

Robbins, Ron Cynewulf. 'Finest Hour 112: Sixty Years On: The Atlantic Charter 1941-2001'. International Churchill Society. Accessed 13 July 2021. https://winstonchurchill.org/publications/finest-hour/finest-hour-112/sixty-years-on-the-atlantic-charter-1941-2001-1/.

Salzgitter AG Corporate Archives. 'Zur Geschichte des Produktionsstandortes Salzgitter'. The history of the Salzgitter-Konzerns. Accessed 1 January 2022. https://geschichte.salzgitter-ag.com/de/einzelne-geschaeftsbereiche-und-standorte/geschaeftsbereich-flachstahl/salzgitter/ungewisse-zukunft.html.

W & G Foyle Limited. 'About Foyles'. Accessed 21 April 2020. https://web.archive.org/web/20200422183518/https://www.foyles.co.uk/about-foyles.

Westminster Abbey. 'Westminster Abbey and VE Day'. Accessed 4 August 2021. www.westminster-abbey.org/about-the-abbey/history/ve-day-75.

Westminster Abbey. 'Westminster Abbey. A short thanksgiving for victory'. Accessed 4 August 2021. www.westminster-abbey.org/media/4109/ve-day-1945.pdf.

Newsreels

British Movietone
British Pathé
Gaumont-British News

Discography

Coward, Noël. 'Don't Let's Be Beastly to the Germans'. Song. His Master's Voice, 1943.

Films

Hendry, Julian, dir. *The SS in Britain*. TV documentary film. Leeds: Yorkshire Television, 2001.

Jennings, Humphrey, dir. *A Defeated People*. Film. London: Crown Film Unit, 1946.

Jennings, Humphrey, dir. *A School in Cologne*. Film. London: Crown Film Unit, 1948.

Jennings, Humphrey, dir. *K.R.O. – Germany 1947*. Film. London: Crown Film Unit, 1948.

Jennings, Humphrey, dir. *Trained to Serve*. Film. London: Crown Film Unit, 1948.

Reed, Carol, dir. *The Third Man*. Film. Starring Orson Welles. London: London Films, 1949.

Roome, Alfred and Roy Rich, dir. *It's Not Cricket*. Film. Starring Basil Radford and Naunton Wayne. London: Gainsborough Pictures, 1949.

Singer, Andre, dir. *Night Will Fall*. Documentary film. London: British Film Institute, 2014.

Wilder, Billy, dir. *A Foreign Affair*. Film. Starring Marlene Dietrich. Hollywood, CA: Paramount Pictures, 1948.

Newspapers and Periodicals

Aberdeen Press and Journal
Australian Women's Weekly
Bath Chronicle and Weekly Gazette
Belfast News-Letter
Birmingham Daily Gazette
Birmingham Mail
Birmingham Post
British Zone Review
Daily Express
Daily Graphic
Daily Herald
Daily Mail
Daily Mirror
Daily Telegraph
The Dundee Courier
Dundee Evening Telegraph
The Economist
Hamburger Allgemeine Zeitung
Hamburger Nachrichten-Blatt
Hull Daily Mail
The Independent
Lancashire Evening Post
The Listener
Liverpool Daily Post
Liverpool Echo
London Evening Standard
The London Gazette
The Manchester Guardian (after 1951, simply *The Guardian*).
The Monthly Film Bulletin
New Statesman and Nation
New York Herald Tribune
The New York Times
News Chronicle
Official Gazette of the Control Council for Germany
People
Picture Post
Quick
The Scotsman
Scottish Daily Express
Soviet News

Standard-Sentinel
Sunday Express
Sunday Pictorial
The Sunday Post
The Sunday Times
Sunderland Daily Echo and Shipping Gazette
Time
The Times
The War Illustrated
Western Daily Press
Whitstable Times and Herne Bay Herald
The Yorkshire Post
Die Zeit

Secondary Sources

Monographs and Edited Collections

Adams, Bianka J., *From Crusade to Hazard: The Denazification of Bremen Germany*, Lanham, Md.; Plymouth: Scarecrow Press, 2009.

Ahrens, Michael, *Die Briten in Hamburg: Besatzerleben 1945-1958*, Hamburg: Dölling und Galitz, 2011.

Aldgate, Anthony and Richards, Jeffrey, *Britain Can Take It: The British Cinema in the Second World War*, Oxford: Blackwell, 1986.

Aldrich, Richard J., *The Hidden Hand: Britain, America and Cold War Secret Intelligence*, London: John Murray, 2001.

Annan, Noel, *Changing Enemies: The Defeat and Regeneration of Germany*, London: HarperCollins, 1995.

Anthony, Scott, *Public Relations and the Making of Modern Britain: Stephen Tallents and the Birth of a Progressive Media Profession*, Manchester: Manchester University Press, 2012.

Bacchetta, Paola and Power, Margaret, *Right-wing Women: From Conservatives to Extremists Around the World*, London; New York: Routledge, 2003.

Balfour, Michael, *Propaganda in War: Organisations, Policies and Publics in Britain and Germany*, London: Routledge & Kegan Paul, 1979.

Balfour, Michael and Mair, John, *Four Power Control in Germany and Austria 1945–1946*, Oxford: Oxford University Press, 1956.

Bark, Dennis L. and Gress, David R., *A History of West Germany*, vol. 1, *From Shadow to Substance, 1945–1963*, Oxford: Basil Blackwell, 1989.

Beattie, Andrew H., *Allied Internment Camps in Occupied Germany: Extrajudicial Detention in the Name of Denazification, 1945–1950*, Cambridge: Cambridge University Press, 2020.

Bedessem, Edward N., *The U.S. Army Campaigns of World War II: Central Europe*, Washington: U.S. Army Center of Military History, 1996.

Beevor, Antony, *The Second World War*, London: Weidenfeld & Nicolson, 2012.

Bessel, Richard, *Germany 1945: From War to Peace*, London: Simon & Schuster, 2009.

Bew, John, *Citizen Clem: A Biography of Attlee*, London: riverrun, 2017.

Biddiscombe, Perry, *Werwolf! The History of the National Socialist Guerrilla Movement, 1944–1946*, Toronto: University of Toronto Press, 1998.

Biddiscombe, Perry, *The Last Nazis: SS Werewolf Guerrilla Resistance in Europe 1944–1947*, Stroud: Tempus, 2000.

Black, Ian, *Enemies and Neighbours: Arabs and Jews in Palestine and Israel, 1917–2017*, London: Allen Lane, 2017.

Black, Monica, *A Demon-Haunted Land: Witches, Wonder Doctors, and the Ghosts of the Past in Post-WWII Germany*, New York: Metropolitan Books, 2020.

Bloxham, Donald, *Genocide on Trial: War Crimes Trials and the Formation of Holocaust History and Memory*, Oxford: Oxford University Press, 2001.

Bösch, Frank and Geppert, Dominik (eds), *Journalists as Political Actors*, Augsburg: Wissner, 2008.

Bosworth, Richard J. B. and Maiolo, Joseph (eds), *The Cambridge History of the Second World War*, vol. 2, *Politics and Ideology*, Cambridge: Cambridge University Press, 2015.

Buchanan, Tom, *Europe's Troubled Peace: 1945 to the Present*, 2nd ed., Malden, Mass.; Oxford: Wiley-Blackwell, 2012.

Buckley, F. H. and Smith, W. W., *The Origins of the British Families Education Service*, Rheindahlen: British Families Education Service, North-West Europe, 1976.

Bullock, Alan, *The Life and Times of Ernest Bevin*, vol. 3, *Ernest Bevin: Foreign Secretary 1945–1951*, New York; London: W. W. Norton, 1983.

Cairncross, Alec, *Years of Recovery: British Economic Policy 1945–51*, London; New York: Methuen, 1985.

Cairncross, Alec, *The Price of War: British Policy on German Reparations 1941–49*, Oxford: Basil Blackwell, 1986.

Calder, Angus, *The Myth of the Blitz*, London: Jonathan Cape, 1991.

Carruthers, Susan L., *The Good Occupation: American Soldiers and the Hazards of Peace*, Cambridge, Mass.: Harvard University Press, 2016.

Chandler, Andrew, *The Church and Humanity: The Life and Work of George Bell, 1883–1958*, Farnham; Burlington, Vt: Ashgate, 2012.

Chaney, Sandra, *Nature of the Miracle Years: Conservation in West Germany, 1945–1975*, New York; London: Berghahn, 2008.

Chrystal, Paul, *British Army of the Rhine: The BAOR, 1945–1993*, Barnsley: Pen & Sword Military, 2018.

Cobain, Ian, *Cruel Britannia: A Secret History of Torture*, London: Portobello, 2012.

Connor, Ian, *Refugees and Expellees in Post-War Germany*, Manchester: Manchester University Press, 2014.

Crofts, William, *Coercion or Persuasion?: Propaganda in Britain after 1945*, London: Routledge, 1989.

Cull, Nicholas John, Holbrook, David and Welch, David (eds), *Propaganda and Mass Persuasion: A Historical Encyclopedia, 1500 to the Present*, Santa Barbara: ABC-CLIO, 2003.

Day, Barry, *The Letters of Noël Coward*, London: Bloomsbury, 2014.

Deighton, Anne (ed.), *Britain and the First Cold War*, Basingstoke; London: Macmillan, 1990.

Deighton, Anne, *The Impossible Peace: Britain, the Division of Germany and the Origins of the Cold War*, Oxford: Clarendon, 1993.

Diefendorf, Jeffry M., *In the Wake of the War: The Reconstruction of German Cities After World War II*, New York; Oxford: Oxford University Press, 1993.

Dilks, David (ed.), *Alexander Cadogan / The Diaries of Sir Alexander Cadogan, O.M., 1938–1945*, London: Cassell, 1971.

Dobbs, Michael, *Six Months in 1945: From World War to Cold War*, London: Hutchinson, 2012.

Donnison, Frank, *Civil Affairs and Military Government, North-West Europe 1944–1946*, London: HMSO, 1961.

Donnison, Frank, *Civil Affairs and Military Government, Central Organization and Planning*, London: HMSO, 1966.

Dorril, Stephen, *MI6: Fifty Years of Special Operations*, London: Fourth Estate, 2000.

Douglas, R. M., *Orderly and Humane: The Expulsion of the Germans after the Second World War*, New Haven, Conn.: Yale University Press, 2012.

Duff, Peggy, *Left, Left, Left: A Personal Account of Six Protest Campaigns, 1945–65*, London: Allison and Busby, 1971.

Edwards, Ruth Dudley, *Victor Gollancz: A Biography*, London: Gollancz, 1987.

Erlichman, Camilo and Knowles, Christopher (eds), *Transforming Occupation in the Western Zones of Germany: Politics, Everyday Life and Social Interactions, 1945–55*, London: Bloomsbury Academic, 2018.

Eubank, Keith, *Summit at Teheran*, New York: Morrow, 1985.

Evans, Richard J., *The Hitler Conspiracies*, New York: Oxford University Press, 2020.

Farquharson, J. E., *The Western Allies and the Politics of Food: Agrarian Management in Postwar Germany*, Leamington Spa: Berg, 1985.

Fäßler, Peter E., Neuwöhner, Andreas and Staffel, Florian (eds), *Briten in Westfalen 1945-2017 Besatzer, Verbündete, Freunde?*, Paderborn: 2019.

Feis, Herbert, *Between War and Peace: The Potsdam Conference*, Princeton, NJ: Princeton University Press, 1960.

Foschepoth, Josef and Steininger, Rolf (eds), *Britische Deutschland- und Besatzungspolitik*, Paderborn: Ferdinand Schöningh, 1985.

Frank, Matthew, *Expelling the Germans: British Opinion and Post-1945 Population Transfer in Context*, Oxford: Oxford University Press, 2007.

Fritz, Stephen G., *Endkampf: Soldiers, Civilians, and the Death of the Third Reich*, Lexington: The University Press of Kentucky, 2004.

Fry, Helen, *The London Cage: The Secret History of Britain's World War II Interrogation Centre*, New Haven: Yale University Press, 2017.

Graham-Dixon, Francis, *The Allied Occupation of Germany: The Refugee Crisis, Denazification and the Path to Reconstruction*, London; New York: I.B. Tauris, 2013.

Granieri, Ronald J., *The Ambivalent Alliance: Konrad Adenauer, the CDU/CSU, and the West, 1949–1966*, New York; Oxford: Berghahn, 2003.

Griffiths, Richard, *Fellow Travellers of the Right: British Enthusiasts for Nazi Germany 1933–1939*, Oxford: Oxford University Press, 1983.

Hennessy, Peter, *Never Again: Britain 1945–1951*, London: Penguin, 2006.

Herbert, Ulrich, *A History of 20th-Century Germany*, trans. Fowkes, Ben, Oxford: Oxford University Press, 2019.

Holmila, Antero, *Reporting the Holocaust in the British, Swedish and Finnish Press, 1945–50*, Basingstoke; New York: Palgrave Macmillan, 2011.

Howson, Peter, *Britain and the German Churches 1945–1950: The Role of the Religious Affairs Branch in the British Zone*, Woodbridge: Boydell & Brewer, 2021.

Jähner, Harald, *Aftermath: Life in the Fallout of the Third Reich*, London: Virgin Digital, 2021.

Jarausch, Konrad H., *After Hitler: Recivilizing Germans, 1945–1995*, New York: Oxford University Press, 2006.

Jeffery, Keith, *MI6: The History of the Secret Intelligence Service, 1909–1949*, London: Bloomsbury, 2010.

Johnson, B. S. (ed.), *All Bull: The National Servicemen*, London: Allison and Busby, 1973.

Jordan, Ulrike (ed.), *Conditions of Surrender: Britons and Germans Witness the End of the War*, London; New York: I. B. Tauris, 1997.

Judt, Burghard and Ciesla, Burghard (eds), *Technology Transfer Out of Germany After 1945*, United Kingdom; Australia; Harwood Academic, 1996.

Judt, Tony, *Postwar: A History of Europe since 1945*, London: Penguin, 2005.

Kershaw, Ian, *The End: Germany, 1944–45*, London: Allen Lane, 2011.

Kleßmann, Christoph and Friedemann, Peter, *Streiks und Hungermärsche im Ruhrgebiet 1946-1948*, Frankfurt; New York: Campus, 1977.

Knowles, Christopher, *Winning the Peace: The British in Occupied Germany, 1945–1948*, London; New York: Bloomsbury Academic, 2017.

Kramer, Alan, *Die britische Demontagepolitik am Beispiel Hamburgs 1945-1950*, Hamburg: Verein für Hamburgische Geschichte, 1991.

Kramer, Alan, *The West German Economy, 1945–1955*, Oxford: Berg, 1991.

Kushner, Tony, *The Holocaust and the Liberal Imagination: A Social and Cultural History*, Oxford: Blackwell, 1994.

Kynaston, David, *Austerity Britain, 1945–51*, London: Bloomsbury, 2007.

Lashmar, Paul and Oliver, James, *Britain's Secret Propaganda War: The Foreign Office and the Cold War, 1948–77*, Stroud: Sutton, 1998.

Lawson, Tom, *The Church of England and the Holocaust: Christianity, Memory and Nazism*, Cambridge: Cambridge University Press, 2013.

Lee, Sabine, *Victory in Europe: Britain and Germany since 1945*, Harlow: Longman, 2001.

Lee, Sabine, *Children Born of War in the Twentieth Century*, Manchester: Manchester University Press, 2017.

Leffler, Melvyn P. and Westad, Odd Arne (eds) *The Cambridge History of the Cold War*, vol. 1, *Origins*, Cambridge: Cambridge University Press, 2009.

Logan, Philip C., *Humphrey Jennings and British Documentary Film: A Re-Assessment*, Farnham: Ashgate, 2011.

Longden, Sean, *To the Victor the Spoils: Soldiers' Lives from D-Day to VE-Day*, London: Robinson, 2007.

Longden, Sean, *T-Force: The Race for Nazi War Secrets, 1945*, London: Constable, 2009.

Longerich, Peter, *Heinrich Himmler: A Life*, Oxford: Oxford University Press, 2012.

Lupa, Markus, *The British and Their Works: The Volkswagenwerk and the occupying power 1945-1949*, Wolfsburg: Volkswagen AG, 2005.

Lupa, Markus, *Changing Lanes under British Command: The Transformation of Volkswagen from a Factory into a Commercial Enterprise, 1945–1949*, Volkswagen Aktiengesellschaft: Wolfsburg: Volkswagen AG, 2011.

MacDonogh, Giles, *After the Reich: From the Fall of Vienna to the Berlin Airlift*, London: John Murray, 2008.

McLaine, Ian, *Ministry of Morale: Home Front Morale and the Ministry of Information in World War II*, London: Allen & Unwin, 1979.

Madsen, Chris, *The Royal Navy and German Naval Disarmament, 1942-1947*, London: F. Cass, 1998.

Malzahn, Manfred, *Germany 1945–1949: A Sourcebook*, London: Routledge, 2003.

Margolian, Howard, *Unauthorized Entry: The Truth About Nazi War Criminals in Canada, 1946–1956*, Toronto; Buffalo; London: University of Toronto Press, 2000.

Marshall, Barbara, *The Origins of Post-War German Politics*, London: Croom Helm, 1988.

Mazower, Mark, *Dark Continent: Europe's Twentieth Century*, London: Penguin, 1999.

Mee, Jr, Charles L., *Meeting at Potsdam*, London: Deutsch, 1975.

Meehan, Patricia, *A Strange Enemy People: Germans under the British, 1945–1950*, London: Peter Owen, 2001.

Mitchell, B. R., *British Historical Statistics*, Cambridge: Cambridge University Press, 2011.

Moore, Martin, *The Origins of Modern Spin: Democratic Government and the Media in Britain, 1945–51*, Basingstoke: Palgrave Macmillan, 2006.

Moran, Charles, *Churchill at War, 1940–1945*, New York: Carroll and Graf, 2002.

Morgan, Kenneth O., *Britain Since 1945: The People's Peace*, Oxford: Oxford University Press, 2001.

Morley, Sheridan, *A Talent to Amuse: A Life of Noël Coward*, London: Dean Street Press, 2016.

Müller, Christoph Hendrik, *West Germans Against the West: Anti-Americanism in Media and Public Opinion in the Federal Republic of Germany 1949–1968*, Basingstoke: Palgrave Macmillan, 2010.

Naimark, Norman, *The Russians in Germany: A History of the Soviet Zone of Occupation, 1945–1949*, Cambridge, Mass.; London: Harvard University Press, 1995.

Naimark, Norman, *Fires of Hatred: Ethnic Cleansing in Twentieth-Century Europe*, Cambridge, Mass.; London: Harvard University Press, 2002.

Neiberg, Michael S., *The Treaty of Versailles: A Concise History*, Oxford: Oxford University Press, 2017.

Nicholas, Siân, *The Echo of War: Home Front Propaganda and the Wartime BBC, 1939–45*, Manchester: Manchester University Press, 1996.

Nicholls, Anthony J., *The Bonn Republic: West Germany 1945–1990*, London: Longman, 1997.

O'Reagan, Douglas M., *Taking Nazi Technology: Allied exploitation of German science after the Second World War*, Baltimore: Johns Hopkins University Press, 2019.

Olick, Jeffrey K., *In the House of the Hangman: The Agonies of German Defeat, 1943–1949*, Chicago: Chicago University Press, 2005.

Overy, Richard, *The Bombing War: Europe 1939–1945*, London: Penguin, 2014.

Panayi, Panikos, *Enemy in Our Midst: Germans in Britain During the First World War*, Oxford: Berg, 1991.

Panayi, Panikos, *German Immigrants in Britain during the 19th Century*, Oxford: Berg, 1995.

Panayi, Panikos, *Prisoners of Britain: German Civilian and Combatant Internees During the First World War*, Manchester: Manchester University Press, 2012.

Parrissien, Steven, *The Life of the Automobile: A New History of the Motor Car*, London: 2013.

Phillips, David, *Educating the Germans: People and policy in the British zone of Germany, 1945–1949*, London: Bloomsbury Academic, 2018.

Pick, Daniel, *The Pursuit of the Nazi Mind: Hitler, Hess, and the Analysts*, Oxford: Oxford University Press, 2012.

Prittie, Terence, *My Germans: 1933–1983*, London: O. Wolff, 1983.

Pronay, Nicholas and Wilson, Nicholas (eds), *The Political Re-education of Germany and her Allies after World War II*, London; Sydney: Croom Helm, 1985.

Ramsden, John, *Don't Mention the War: The British and Germans since 1890*, London: Little Brown, 2006.

Reichel, Peter, *Vergangenheitsbewältigung in Deutschland: Die Auseinandersetzung mit der NS-Diktatur in Politik und Justiz: Die Auseinandersetzung mit der NS-Diktatur von 1945 bis heute*, Munich: Beck, 2001.

Reilly, Joanne, *Belsen in History and Memory*, London: Frank Cass, 1997.

Reinisch, Jessica, *The Perils of Peace: The Public Health Crisis in Occupied Germany*, Oxford: Oxford University Press, 2013.

Reynolds, David, *Britannia Overruled: British Policy and World Power in the Twentieth Century*, London: Longman, 1991.

Reynolds, David (ed.), *The Origins of the Cold War in Europe: International Perspectives*, New Haven: Yale University Press, 1994.

Reynolds, David, *From World War to Cold War: Churchill, Roosevelt, and the International History of the 1940s*, Oxford: Oxford University Press, 2006.

Richter, Ralf, *Ivan Hirst: British Officer and Manager of Volkswagen's Postwar Recovery*, Wolfsburg: Volkswagen AG, 2013.

Rippon, Anton, *Gas Masks for Goal Posts: Football in Britain During the Second World War*, Stroud: Sutton, 2005.

Robertson, Alex J., *The Bleak Midwinter: 1947*, Manchester: Manchester University Press, 1987.

Rollin, Jack, *The Army Game: 125 Years of the Army Football Association 1888 to 2013*, Nottingham: Tony Brown, 2013.

Roodhouse, Mark, *Black Market Britain, 1939–1955*, Oxford: Oxford University Press, 2013.

Rose, Norman, *Vansittart: Study of a Diplomat*, London: Heinemann, 1978.

Rose, Norman, 'Vansittart, Robert Gilbert, Baron Vansittart (1881–1957)', *Oxford Dictionary of National Biography* (Oxford: 2004).

Ryan, Louise and Webster, Wendy (eds), *Gendering Migration: Masculinity, Femininity and Ethnicity in Post-War Britain*, Aldershot: Ashgate, 2008.

Sands, Philippe (ed.), *From Nuremberg to The Hague: The Future of International Criminal Justice*, Cambridge: Cambridge University Press, 2003.

Schwarz, Hans-Peter, *Konrad Adenauer: A German Politician and Statesman in a Period of War, Revolution and Reconstruction*, vol. 1, Providence; Oxford: Berghahn, 1995.

Shephard, Ben, *The Long Road Home: The Aftermath of the Second World War*, London: Bodley Head, 2010.

Short, K. R. M. and Dolezel, Stephan (eds), *Hitler's Fall: The Newsreel Witness*, London: Croon Helm, 1988.

Sikov, Ed, *Mr Strangelove: A Biography of Peter Sellers*, New York: Hyperion, 2003.

Simms, Brendan, *Britain's Europe: A Thousand Years of Conflict and Cooperation*, London: Allen Lane, 2016.

Später, Jörg, *Vansittart: Britische Debatten über Deutsche und Nazis 1902-1945*, Göttingen: Wallstein, 2003.

Stibbe, Matthew, *German Anglophobia and the Great War, 1914–1918*, Cambridge: Cambridge University Press, 2006.

Street, John, *Mass Media, Politics, and Democracy*, Basingstoke; New York: Palgrave, 2001.

Szanajda, Andrew, *The Allies and the German Problem, 1941–1949: From Cooperation to Alternative Settlement*, Basingstoke: Palgrave Macmillan, 2015.

Treber, Leonie, *Mythos Trümmerfrauen: Von der Trümmerbeseitigung in der Kriegs- und Nachkriegszeit und der Entstehung eines deutschen Erinnerungsortes*, Essen: Klartext, 2014.

Turner, Barry, *The Berlin Airlift: The Relief Operation that Defined the Cold War*, London: Icon, 2017.

Turner, Ian D. (ed.), *Reconstruction in Post-War Germany: British Occupation Policy and the Western Zones, 1945–55*, Oxford: Bloomsbury Academic, 1988.

Tusa, Ann and Tusa, John, *The Nuremberg Trial*, New York: Skyhorse, 2010.

Tyas, Stephen, *SS-Major Horst Kopkow: From the Gestapo to British Intelligence*, Stroud; Charleston, SC: Fonthill, 2017.

Van Hook, James C., *Rebuilding Germany: The Creation of the Social Market Economy, 1945–1957*, Cambridge: Cambridge University Press, 2004.

Watt, Donald Cameron, *Britain Looks to Germany: British Opinion and Policy towards Germany since 1945*, London: O. Wolff, 1965.

Weber-Newth, Inge and Steinert, Johannes-Dieter, *German Migrants in Post-War Britain: An Enemy Embrace*, Oxford; New York: Routledge, 2006.

Weight, Richard, *Patriots: National Identity in Britain, 1940–2000*, London: Macmillan, 2002.

West, Nigel, *The Friends: Britain's Post-War Secret Intelligence Operations*, London: Weidenfeld and Nicolson, 1988.

Wiesen, Jonathan S., *West German Industry and the Challenge of the Nazi Past, 1945–1955*, Chapel Hill, NC: University of North Carolina Press, 2001.

Williams, Kevin, *Get Me a Murder a Day!: A History of Mass Communication in Britain*, London: Arnold, 1998.

Williamson, David G., *The British in Interwar Germany: The Reluctant Occupiers, 1919–30*, London: Bloomsbury Academic, 2017.

Winterberg, Sonya, *Wir sind die Wolfskinder: Verlassen in Ostpreußen*, Munich: Piper, 2014.

Zweiniger-Bargielowska, Ina, *Austerity in Britain: Rationing, Controls, and Consumption, 1939–1955*, Oxford: Oxford University Press, 2000.

Journal Articles and Unpublished Theses

Adamthwaite, Anthony, '"Nation Shall Speak Peace unto Nation": The BBC's Response to Peace and Defence Issues, 1945–58', *Contemporary Record* 7, no. 3 (1993), pp. 557–77, https://doi.org/10.1080/13619469308581267.

Adler, Karen H., 'Selling France to the French: The French Zone of Occupation in Western Germany, 1945 – c.1955', *Contemporary European History* 21, no. 4 (2012), pp. 575–95.

Aster, Sidney, 'Appeasement: Before and After Revisionism', *Diplomacy and Statecraft* 19, no. 3 (2008), pp. 443–80.

Balfour, Michael, 'Another Look at "Unconditional Surrender"', *International Affairs* 46, no. 4 (1970), pp. 719–36, https://doi.org/10.2307/2614534.

Baylis, John, 'British Wartime Thinking about a Post-War European Security Group', *Review of International Studies* 9, no. 4 (1983), pp. 265–81.

Bloxham, Donald, 'Punishing German Soldiers During the Cold War: The Case of Erich von Manstein', *Patterns of Prejudice* 33, no. 4 (1999), pp. 24–45, https://doi.org/10.1080/003132299128810687.

Bloxham, Donald, 'British War Crimes Trial Policy in Germany, 1945–1957: Implementation and Collapse', *The Journal of British Studies* 42, no. 1 (2003), pp. 91–118, https://doi:10.1086/342687.

Born, Lester K., 'The Ministerial Collecting Center near Kassel, Germany', *The American Archivist* 13, no. 3 (1950), pp. 237–58, www.jstor.org/stable/40288828.

Burridge, Trevor, 'Great Britain and the Dismemberment of Germany at the End of the Second World War', *The International History Review* 3, no. 4 (1981), pp. 565–79.

Carden, Robert W., 'Before Bizonia: Britain's Economic Dilemma in Germany, 1945–46', *Journal of Contemporary History* 14, no. 3 (1979), pp. 535–55, www.jstor.org/stable/260020.

Cowling, Daniel, 'Britain and the Occupation of Germany, 1945–49', Unpublished PhD dissertation, The University of Cambridge (2018).

Cowling, Daniel, 'Anglo–German Relations After 1945', *Journal of Contemporary History* 54, no. 1 (2019), https://doi.org/10.1177/0022009417697808.

Dack, Mikkel, 'Crimes Committed by Soviet Soldiers Against German Civilians, 1944–1945: A Historiographical Analysis', *Journal of Military and Strategic Studies* 10, no. 4 (2008), http://jmss.org/jmss/index.php/jmss/article/view/75.

Dack, Mikkel, 'Questioning the Past: The Fragebogen and Everyday Denazification in Occupied Germany', Unpublished PhD dissertation, University of Calgary (2016).

Dale Jones, Priscilla, 'British Policy Towards German Crimes Against German Jews, 1939–1945', *The Leo Baeck Institute Yearbook* 36, no. 1 (1991), pp. 339–66, https://doi.org/10.1093/leobaeck/36.1.33.

Deighton, Anne, 'The "Frozen Front": The Labour Government, the Division of Germany and the Origins of the Cold War, 1945–7', *International Affairs* 63, no. 3 (1987), pp. 449–65, https://doi.org/10.2307/2619245.

Farquharson, J. E., '"Emotional but Influential": Victor Gollancz, Richard Stokes and the British Zone of Germany, 1945–9', *Journal of Contemporary History* 22, no. 3 (1987), pp. 501–19, https://doi.org/10.1177/002200948702200308.

Farquharson, J. E., 'Land Reform in the British Zone, 1945–1947', *German History* 6, no. 1 (1988), pp. 35–56.

Farquharson, J. E., 'The British Occupation of Germany 1945–6: A Badly Managed Disaster Area?' *German History* 11, no. 3 (1993), pp. 316–38.

Farquharson, J. E., 'Anglo-American Policy on German Reparations from Yalta to Potsdam', *The English Historical Review* 112, no. 448 (1997), pp. 904–26.

Fletcher, R. J. 'British Propaganda since World War II – a Case Study', *Media, Culture & Society* 4, no. 2 (1982), pp. 97–109.

Fox, Jo, 'John Grierson, His "documentary Boys" and the British Ministry of Information, 1939–1942', *Historical Journal of Film, Radio and Television* 25, no. 3 (August 2005), pp. 345–69, https://doi.org/10.1080/01439680500236151.

Frank, Matthew, 'The New Morality – Victor Gollancz, "Save Europe Now" and the German Refugee Crisis, 1945–46', *Twentieth Century British History* 17, no. 2 (2006), pp. 230–56.

Euros, Glesni, 'The post-war British "re-education" policy for German universities and its application at the universities of Göttingen and Cologne (1945–1947)', *Research in Comparative and International Education* 11, no. 3 (2016), pp. 247–66.

Goldman, Aaron, 'Germans and Nazis: The Controversy over "Vansittartism" in Britain during the Second World War', *Journal of Contemporary History* 14, no. 1 (1979), pp. 155–91.

Haggith, Toby, 'The 1945 Documentary German Concentration Camps Factual Survey and the 70th Anniversary of the Liberation of the Camps', *The Holocaust in History and Memory* 7 (2014), pp. 181–97.

Hodenberg, Christina von, 'Of German Fräuleins, Nazi Werewolves, and Iraqi Insurgents: The American Fascination with Hitler's Last Foray', *Central European History* 41, no. 1 (2008), pp. 71–92, www.jstor.org/stable/20457312.

Jones, Jill, 'Eradicating Nazism from the British Zone of Germany: Early policy and practice', *German History* 8, no. 2 (1990), pp. 145–62.

Kleinau, Elke and Schmid, Rafaela, '"Occupation Children" in Germany after World War II — Problems and Coping Strategies', *Children & Society* 33 (2019), pp. 239–52, https: doi.org/10.1111/chso.12323.

Knapp, Manfred, Wolfgang F. Stolper, and Michael Hudson, 'Reconstruction and West-Integration: The Impact of the Marshall Plan on Germany', *Zeitschrift für die Gesamte Staatswissenschaft / Journal of Institutional and Theoretical Economics* 137, no. 3 (1981), pp. 415–33, www.jstor.org/stable/40750368.

Marshall, Barbara, 'German attitudes to British Military Government 1945–1947', *Journal of Contemporary History* 15, no. 4 (1980), pp. 655–84.

Marrus, Michael R., 'The Holocaust at Nuremberg', *Yad Vashem Studies* 26 (1998), pp. 4–45.

'Musketeer', 'The 21st Army Group in North-West Europe – IV', *Royal United Services Institution Journal* 103, no. 610 (1958), pp. 230–42, https://doi.org/10.1080/03071845809433549.

Schleppi, John Ross, 'A History of Professional Association Football in England During the Second World War', Unpublished PhD dissertation, Ohio State University (1972).

Sharman, Claire Louise, 'War Crimes Trials between Occupation and Integration: The Prosecution of Nazi War Criminals in the British Zone of Germany', Unpublished PhD dissertation, University of Southampton (2007).

Shaw, Tony, 'The British Popular Press and the Early Cold War', *History* 83, no. 269 (1998), pp. 66–85, https://doi.org/10.1111/1468-229X.00063.

Shaw, Tony, 'The Information Research Department of the British Foreign Office and the Korean War, 1950-53', *Journal of Contemporary History* 34, no. 2 (1999), pp. 263–81.

Shlaim, Avi, 'Britain, the Berlin Blockade and the Cold War', *International Affairs* 60, no. 1 (1983), pp. 1–14, https://doi.org/10.2307/2618926.

Smith, Barbara, 'The Rules of Engagement: German Women and British Occupiers, 1945-1949', Unpublished PhD dissertation, Wilfrid Laurier University (2009).

Smith, Lyn, 'Covert British Propaganda: The Information Research Department: 1947–77', *Millennium – Journal of International Studies* 9, no. 1 (1980), pp. 67–83.

Stark, John Robert, 'The Overlooked Majority: German Women in the Four Zones of Occupied Germany, 1945–1949, a Comparative Study', Unpublished PhD dissertation, Ohio State University (2003).

Tombs, Isabelle, 'The Victory of Socialist "Vansittartism": Labour and the German Question, 1941–5', *Twentieth Century British History* 7, no. 3 (1996), pp. 287–309, https://doi.org/10.1093/tcbh/7.3.287.

Wagner, Hans-Ulrich, 'Repatriated Germans and "British Spirit"', *Media History* 21, no. 4 (2015), pp. 443–58, https://doi.org/10.1080/13688804.2015.1011109.

Image Credits

Index